Harry A. Blackmun

Harry A. Blackmun

The Outsider Justice

Tinsley E. Yarbrough

OXFORD
UNIVERSITY PRESS

2008

OXFORD
UNIVERSITY PRESS

Oxford University Press, Inc., publishes works that further
Oxford University's objective of excellence
in research, scholarship, and education.

Oxford   New York
Auckland   Cape Town   Dar es Salaam   Hong Kong   Karachi
Kuala Lumpur   Madrid   Melbourne   Mexico City   Nairobi
New Delhi   Shanghai   Taipei   Toronto

With offices in
Argentina   Austria   Brazil   Chile   Czech Republic   France   Greece
Guatemala   Hungary   Italy   Japan   Poland   Portugal   Singapore
South Korea   Switzerland   Thailand   Turkey   Ukraine   Vietnam

Published by Oxford University Press, Inc.
198 Madison Avenue, New York, New York 10016

www.oup.com

Oxford is a registered trademark of Oxford University Press

Library of Congress Cataloging-in-Publication Data
Yarbrough, Tinsley E., 1941–
Harry A. Blackmun : the outsider justice / Tinsley E. Yarbrough.
     p.   cm.
Includes bibliographical references.
ISBN 978-0-19-514123-8
1. Blackmun, Harry A. (Harry Andrew), 1908–1999.
2. Judges—United States—Biography.
3. United States. Supreme Court—Biography. I. Title.
KF8745.B555Y37 2007
347.73'2634—dc22
[B]   2007011750

9 8 7 6 5 4 3 2 1

Printed in the United States of America
on acid-free paper

To Mary Alice

Preface

Asked late in life to describe his feelings on first taking a seat on the Supreme Court, one of the nation's most powerful and influential institutions, Justice Harry Andrew Blackmun gave a surprising response. "I don't know how it affects other people," he confessed, "but I think there is a feeling of [being] almost desperate...wondering whether one is qualified to be there. After all, this is the end of the line. I well remember going into the robing room and the then-justices were lined up, and there were Hugo L. Black and William O. Douglas and William J. Brennan, Jr. and John Harlan, and...I asked myself, 'What am I doing here?' "[1]

Examining the record he compiled during nearly a quarter century on the high bench, many of Justice Blackmun's critics wondered the same thing. In many ways, his life was the typical American success story. Raised in the humble Dayton's Bluff section on the east side of St. Paul, Minnesota, the future justice compiled an outstanding high school record. Despite working many hours at a host of jobs to supplement a tuition scholarship, he graduated summa cum laude from Harvard College in 1929 and completed his law studies at Harvard in 1932, at the height of the Depression. After clerking eighteen months for John B. Sanborn, a distinguished judge of the U.S. Court of Appeals for the Eighth Circuit, Blackmun took a position with a leading Minneapolis firm, becoming a junior partner in 1939 and general partner in 1943. An undergraduate mathematics major who originally considered a career in medicine rather than law, he served in 1950–59 as resident counsel at Rochester, Minnesota's famed Mayo Clinic. In 1959, Judge Sanborn took senior status on the Eighth Circuit, but only after getting some assurance from the Eisenhower administration that his former clerk would be his replacement. In 1970, after eleven years on the appeals bench, Blackmun was elevated by Richard Nixon to the Supreme Court, where he would serve for twenty-four years. As the author of *Roe v. Wade* (1973), which Blackmun often said would be etched on his tombstone, the justice became one of the most familiar and controversial members of the Burger and Rehnquist Courts, basking in the adulation of pro-choice admirers, a target of outrage among critics, who compared *Roe* to the infamous *Dred Scott* decision denying citizenship to African Americans, and excoriated Blackmun for condoning "baby killers."

Without his association with that spectacularly controversial ruling and its progeny, however, Justice Blackmun arguably would have achieved little prominence as a justice. Even with the *Roe* connection, one might seriously question whether he is a worthy choice for a judicial biography, at least by the usual standards used to select such subjects. The copious case summaries that he personally dictated to secretaries prior to hearing oral argument in cases clearly reflected a firm grasp of doctrinal issues confronting the Court, as did his detailed accounts for his clerks of the justices' conference discussions of argued cases. But Blackmun left the drafting of his opinions and their doctrinal content largely to his clerks, and though he meticulously edited their efforts, he seemed more alert to grammatical and spelling errors the opinions might contain than to the substantive arguments they embraced.

In fact, and no doubt to his clerks' tremendous relief, Justice Blackmun was most likely to assume the initiative in drafting opinions for narrow tax and related cases that his clerks, and those in other chambers, considered the "dogs" of the Court's docket, but that the former tax and estate lawyer still found fascinating. It is thus hardly surprising that in a recent survey of lawyers, judges, and prelaw students, only the students ranked Blackmun among the "great" justices—and they were doubtless influenced more by his association with *Roe* than by familiarity with his entire record.[2]

Of course, some justices—most notably, perhaps, Blackmun's senior colleague William J. Brennan Jr.—achieve reputations as outstanding jurists not on the basis of a distinctive constitutional philosophy, but as a result of their skill at marshaling majorities. For Brennan, "five" (as in 5–4 majority) was the most important word in the legal lexicon. To obtain that vote, he not only regularly called on his consummate people skills to negotiate the result he desired, but was also entirely willing to manipulate constitutional doctrine towardthat end. Blackmun, who spent much of each day cloistered in the Court's library, had neither the personality nor the talent for such maneuvering.

As a jurisprudential giant or gifted Court tactician, then, Justice Blackmun hardly qualifies for biographical treatment. The very feelings of self-doubt and inadequacy that plagued his ascent to the Court, however, make him a fascinating subject for exploration. No justice has been more closely associated with empathy for society's "outsiders" or "little people," those denizens of that "other world out there," to whom Blackmun so sympathetically referred in his judicial opinions. His colleagues could focus, if they wished, on legal doctrine; he would keep his eye firmly on the human dimension of cases and the Court's impact on real people. Blackmun's feelings on that score have been attributed to a variety of factors, including a growing awareness of social injustices to which he was regularly exposed as a justice, his defensiveness about *Roe* and the rulings it spawned, and his growing estrangement from his boyhood friend Warren Burger and the chief justice's conservative stance on social issues facing the Court. But Blackmun's concern for "little people" also arguably reflected in considerable part his own self-image as an outsider. During the extensive oral history that he conducted with the justice, former clerk Harold Koh asked Blackmun how he had developed an affinity for "the little people" and "the outsiders," about whom the justice not only wrote in his opinions, but had even referred to during his Senate confirmation testimony. "Well," Blackmun replied, "I suppose growing up as I did there on the east side of St. Paul the people I knew were people of not great influence politically or by wealth or otherwise. They lived on the other side of town. And naturally I probably had empathy for them."[3]

The justice might well have added that he considered himself one of society's outsiders. Blackmun grew up in a household plagued with financial instability. His father, a constant disappointment to his only son, drifted from position to position and was frequently unemployed. At times, young Harry watched as his doting mother, whom he adored, cried uncontrollably, terrified at what the future might bring to the family. The opportunity to attend Harvard was obviously of incalculable value to Blackmun's chances for a rewarding professional career. But his letters to his parents from Cambridge suggest the difficulty he had feeling a real part of that "other world," an elite enclave dominated, especially in those days, by students drawn largely from families of wealth and influence. Indeed, his Harvard experience may have done more to intensify than assuage his childhood insecurities. When Harold Koh asked Blackmun about his reputation for hard work and extraordinarily long hours, the veteran justice replied, "Oh, I don't know, maybe I was very frightened or scared if I didn't get in a lot of time, I'd fall on my face or something."[4]

Humble roots, of course, by no means inevitably lead to permanent feelings of inferiority and self-doubt. Warren Burger came from a much poorer background than Justice Blackmun did, yet seemed, on the surface at least, inordinately self-assured and confident of his abilities. So, too, were Hugo L. Black, William O. Douglas, and any number of other justices from similar backgrounds. But Blackmun's feelings of inadequacy manifested themselves in various ways not only in childhood and early adult life, but throughout his career. Nominated to the Court only after Clement Haynsworth and G. Harrold Carswell—President Nixon's first two choices to fill the seat vacated by Justice Abe Fortas—had gone down to defeat in the Senate, Blackmun regularly referred to himself as "Old Number Three." From the first, he questioned "Why am I here?" He agonized more than most justices over his decisions, not infrequently revealing his doubts in his opinions. During his first term, he often recalled, Justice Hugo L. Black had gently chided the newest justice about the tentative, indecisive cast of a draft Blackmun opinion, pointing out that the legitimacy of the Court's decisions depended to a substantial degree on the justices' willingness to take a firm stance—whatever their inner doubts—on the issues before them. But Blackmun was never able to honor his elderly colleague's admonition. When circulating opinions to other chambers, he was typically self-deprecating, referring to his drafts as "feeble" efforts.

Humility is a much-admired quality, and Blackmun is rightly remembered as a humble, kind, warm, affectionate justice. But his humility also appeared to reflect what one respected scholarly critic has privately termed an "unbelievable inferiority complex." When such frustrations came bubbling to the surface, the justice could be quick-tempered, petty, and filled with barely concealed self-pity.

In her funeral eulogy to her father, the justice's eldest daughter, Nancy, a clinical psychologist, depicted him as, in some ways, a sad, lonely man and alluded to the enduring impact of childhood scars on his personality. But the connection between the justice's complicated self-image and his strong sympathy for society's worthy less-fortunate also makes Blackmun one of the modern Court's most provocative justices. His plaintive cry of "Poor Joshua!" for a hapless child woefully neglected by a social services bureaucracy, left permanently and hopelessly brain-damaged by a brutish father, then denied federal judicial relief by a Supreme Court majority, comes closest perhaps to capturing Justice Blackmun's genuine and profound concern for society's underdogs. In his deepest inner being, however, the justice may also have been crying out, throughout his life, for "Poor Harry!"[5]

Blackmun's authorship of *Roe v. Wade* also makes him a compelling subject for study. *Roe*'s rationale has been subjected to more sustained and scathing scholarly and popular criticism than any other Supreme Court opinion, even by those supportive of the Court's recognition of a constitutional abortion right. In his thoroughgoing account in *Roe* of the history of abortion laws, to cite but one concern of critics, Blackmun established that restrictive abortion legislation dated only from the Civil War. But "the fact that early-stage abortion had been a serious crime for 'only' a century," as one critic put it, "scarcely made it a constitutional right. There was simply no logical connection between the history that Blackmun so painstakingly assembled and his conclusion that abortion was a constitutional right."[6]

Whatever its shortcomings as constitutional law, however, *Roe* remains the most controversial ruling of the Burger and Rehnquist Court periods. And though Justice Blackmun was one member of a 7–2 majority, he is the single justice admirers and critics alike associate most closely with *Roe* and its progeny. Because of *Roe* he received more mail than any other justice, enough to fill an entire room. At the Court and when he traveled, he required special security precautions. A bullet fired into his apartment in 1985 may have been a random shot; the government's investigation was inconclusive. But there is no mistaking the vile hate mail and death threats he was forced to endure. As the pivotal figure in the most contentious litigation the Court has confronted since *Brown v. Board of Education*, Blackmun clearly warrants close study.

Finally, of course, Justice Blackmun's career raises intriguing questions regarding the degree to which he changed as a justice over his years on the high bench. The conventional wisdom is that the justice underwent a major transformation; indeed, that initially was to have been the central theme of this book. Originally, the thesis runs, Blackmun and Burger were the "Minnesota Twins," with the chief justice the dominant partner in that alliance. Gradually, however, Blackmun's vigorous defense of, and defensiveness about, *Roe v. Wade*, his mounting resentment of his reputation as Burger's "Hip Pocket Harry" and the chief justice's domineering personality, and his growing ties to Justices Brennan and Marshall made Blackmun increasingly receptive to most civil liberties claims.

Blackmun's voting record certainly lends some credence to such thinking. Early in his career, he, like Chief Justice Burger, rarely assumed a pro–civil liberties stance. Later, he was most closely allied with Court liberals. In his last two terms (1992 and 1993), for example, he agreed most regularly with John Paul Stevens and David H. Souter, the two most liberal Rehnquist Court justices of those terms.

Like all justices, Justice Blackmun clearly did change over time. Even so, there is considerable evidence to support his assertion that he did not change nearly so much as the Court and the issues changed. He would remain relatively conservative on criminal justice issues throughout his career. Indeed, he did not reject capital punishment until his final term on the Court, and then only because he was finally convinced that government efforts to eliminate arbitrary executions were doomed to failure, not because he considered the death penalty itself fundamentally at odds with the standards of a modern, civilized society—the central objection of Justices Brennan and Marshall to capital punishment. From the beginning, moreover, Blackmun arguably embraced, in *Roe* and other cases, the deep empathy for outsiders that would ultimately form the core of his record and arguably flowed from his own feelings of inadequacy and self-doubt, with early apparent deviations from that central theme of his career explainable by the circumstances of particular early cases, rather than as a reflection of a marked change in his later jurisprudence.

This book examines Justice Blackmun's life, career, and judicial record. Its focus, however, is on those elements that make him most fascinating as a jurist: the roots of his "outsider" self-image and its reflection in his conduct and demeanor as a justice, his empathy for society's "little people," his central role in the abortion debate, and elements of continuity and change in his judicial record. Blackmun will never rank among the Court's jurisprudential giants. But perhaps no justice better personified the controversy swirling within and about the Court during the Burger and Rehnquist eras. Arguably, moreover, the justice's close identity with society's outsiders throughout his career worked to produce a judicial record that was remarkably consistent over time. As Blackmun contended, the Court and the issues, not the justice, changed most during his years on the high bench.

Responsibility for what follows is, of course, entirely mine. But completion of this book was possible only with the cooperation of many persons and institutions. I am grateful to the Earhart Foundation and to the East Carolina University Research/Creative Activities Committee for generous financial support of my research. A number of Justice Blackmun's clerks, as well as his longtime secretary Wanda Martinson, generously shared their memories of the justice in recorded interviews. The voluminous Harry A. Blackmun Papers in the Manuscript Division of the Library of Congress were indispensable. Connie L. Cartledge, curator of the Blackmun Papers, and her staff did a magnificent job organizing this superb collection for researchers. Other collections in the Manuscript Division, including the papers of Justices Hugo L. Black, William O. Douglas, William J. Brennan Jr., and Thurgood Marshall, were immensely helpful, as were the Lewis F. Powell Jr., Papers at Washington and Lee University and John N. Jacob, archivist of the Powell Papers. Cynthia Manning Smith and Sheila Ellis provided their usual excellent clerical assistance. My Oxford University Press editor, James Cook, carefully reviewed the manuscript, offering useful suggestions throughout. Finally, I am grateful for the support and patience of my wonderful family—Sarah, Cole, Christine, Todd, Ben, Jonah, and especially Mary Alice, to whom this book is lovingly dedicated.

Contents

Harry A. Blackmun

Chapter 1

Dayton's Bluff to Harvard

Births are traumatic as well as joyful events, even under the best of circumstances. Harry Blackmun's arrival may have been a particularly angst-ridden time for his mother. As her baby's delivery date approached, Theo Blackmun was alone in the cold-water flat she and her husband rented on LaSalle Street in Minneapolis, while Corwin Blackmun, a fruit buyer, was out West purchasing produce for Twin Cities Wholesalers. "I think mother just decided," the justice later said, "that she wasn't going to have me alone in Minneapolis," so she returned to her family's home in Nashville, Illinois. There, on November 12, 1908, in the same room of the house in which she had been born, she gave birth to a future justice of the Supreme Court.[1]

Ancestors

Justice Blackmun's parents had deep Midwestern roots. According to a genealogical survey presented to the justice in 1994, the American ancestry of Corwin Manning Blackmun extended back to Captain Miles Standish, who was among the first group of Pilgrims who landed at Plymouth,

Massachusetts, in 1620. In 1864, the justice's paternal grandfather, Andrew Perkins Blackmun, a Union Army veteran, married Eliza Jane Cooley, who apparently was of French Huguenot descent, in Mooers, New York. After the war, they homesteaded near Hancock, a small town in central Minnesota, where the justice's father was born in 1881. Their farm flourished for a time, and they had a large family. But when they lost four of their nine children in the diphtheria epidemic of 1892, they lost hope, abandoning the farm and moving sixty miles east to the Twin Cities, where Andrew found work primarily as a carpenter. "He was a great guy," Blackmun later said. "I well remember him."[2]

Blackmun's maternal grandfather, Theodore Louis Reuter, was born in Germany, immigrated to the United States in his teens, and served in the 117th Illinois infantry during the Civil War. Naturalized as a citizen in 1866, he lived until 1925. His wife, Mary, was the daughter of John Huegely, a native of Germany who reportedly came to the United States to escape military conscription. Eventually, he made his way to Illinois, where he found work as a flour mill hand, then established his own prosperous mill in Nashville, Illinois. As his children grew up and married, Blackmun's great-grandfather Huegely built houses for them on Mill Street in Nashville. The justice's mother, Theo Huegely Reuter, was born in one of those houses in 1884. Years later, Blackmun would fondly recall Great-grandfather Huegely: "To me, he was Vater, we called him Vater. And every Sunday we kids had to go down, pay our respects to him and get a shiny nickel from Vater."[3]

John Huegely did not die until 1914, at age ninety-five. But in 1890, he had turned over mill operations to his sons and son-in-law, Justice Blackmun's Grandfather Reuter. The justice's mother thus grew up in comfortable, prosperous surroundings. But a number of family tragedies left a permanent scar on her spirits. In 1913, her brother Philip was found dead in the warehouse of a St. Louis manufacturing concern he and his brother-in-law W. R. Jones, the husband of Theo's sister Annette, owned. A newspaper account of Philip's death delicately avoided mentioning that he had committed suicide. But it did note that he "died suddenly" and that his brother-in-law found the body after Philip had been missing for a day. Philip and Jones were facing embezzlement charges at the time. Jones later went to prison, and Annette, Harry's favorite aunt, divorced him. Their son, Harry's favorite cousin, died in the 1918 influenza epidemic.[4]

Late in life, Justice Blackmun recounted the devastating effect the death of another of her brothers had on his mother. Theo Blackmun studied music in college and played piano. But her brother Harry, a pianist of considerable promise, had studied in Berlin with Teresa Carreno, a pianist and opera conductor who had emigrated from Venezuela. Harry and Carreno were scheduled to take a concert tour of Australia in 1907, when Theo's brother contracted pneumonia, dying within three days. "This is a loss," the justice said, that "my mother never got over....I'm named after him, his name is Harry. And my inability to do very much at the piano, I think, was always a great disappointment for my mother. Because he evidently was very good, he composed and played just as well."[5]

Dayton's Bluff

Theo Reuter and Corwin Blackmun were both Methodists. They first met while attending tiny Central Wesleyan College in Warrenton, Missouri. They were married in Nashville on January 18, 1908, and their oldest child, Harry, arrived ten months later. In 1911, after the family had moved from Minneapolis to St. Paul's Dayton's Bluff neighborhood, their second son, Corwin Manning Jr., was born, but lived only three days, further aggravating Theo's persistent melancholy. The justice's sister Theo, nicknamed Betty, was born in 1917.[6]

Corwin Blackmun had studied philosophy in college and hoped to become a lawyer, acquiring a number of law books in pursuit of his goal. But he would never realize that dream, drifting instead from one business venture and job to another. Initially a produce buyer, he was briefly proprietor of a wholesale fruit and vegetable business, which soon failed, then was representative for the Twin Cities Building and Loan Association and later a district manager for the Mutual Life Insurance Company. He did serve honorably with the Minnesota National Guard for many years. When guard units were federalized in 1941, on the eve of World War II, he went to Riverside, California, with his regiment, the 216th. His guard dress sword would hang in Justice Blackmun's chambers for many years. As a family provider, however, the father was clearly a disappointment to his son. "I don't mean to speak ill of him at all, but he never was a person who was able to make money. He either wasn't interested in it or, in part it was because he was pretty stubborn and never would compromise on things, and he often alienated people."[7]

Corwin Blackmun's financial failures placed a strain on the family, especially on his wife's already fragile spirits. But Theo Blackmun doted on her only son. Carefully preserved in the justice's papers is his mother's record of "Some of Harry's [Childhood] Sayings." On one occasion, he complained to Theo, "I got such a cold and there are so many tears in my nose." He had the "bumps" rather than the "mumps." The department store Santa Claus had "such nice white feathers on his face, but Grandpa's are black." When his mother quietly scolded a restless Harry in church one Sunday, he promptly responded, "Mother, you told me we must not talk in church." But some of his sayings may have hit too close to home. "Mother," he once asked, "if Jesus was dead only three days, why isn't Uncle Phil alive now?" Another time, he exclaimed, "Oh, pshaw! Everybody's getting automobiles and babies but us."[8]

His mother's bouts with depression and his father's failings as family provider also combined, however, to leave an indelible mark on Harry's confidence and sense of self-esteem. Beginning in 1919, he found a kind of self-defining, self-revealing refuge in diary entries, a practice he, unlike most youth, would continue for nearly two decades. Soon, his entries became daily rituals, detailing the often trivial and mundane developments in his life, but also enabling him to vent his frustrations and disappointments, as well as the occasional triumph, in ways that the shy, insecure boy was not yet prepared to reveal to the rest of the world.

Whatever his family circumstances or insecurities, Justice Blackmun would later have pleasant memories of growing up in Dayton's Bluff. "It was distinctly lower middle class, I would say, occupied mostly by working people—they were good, solid people, but nearly all in modest circumstances. It was a good place to grow up actually." He became particularly close friends with three neighborhood playmates. John Francis Briggs would go on to realize his childhood ambition, becoming a cardiologist despite the concerns of his Irish mother that he should not "waste all that time becoming a physician [and] just go out and get a job." Another playmate, Robert Damkroger, became a successful insurance executive. "And the third," as Blackmun later put it, "was none other than Warren

Earl Burger," whom the justice first met when their mothers packed them off to Sunday School at "about age five or six."[9]

Born in St. Paul in 1907 and raised in a Swiss German Protestant family, Warren Burger was the fourth of seven children. His father was a railroad cargo inspector and traveling salesman, but his mother was the family's anchor. "[Burger's] mother," Blackmun remembered, "in my estimation was a saint; she brought up a large family on little or nothing. We didn't have much, but the Burgers had less than we did." Blackmun worked during high school and while at Harvard. But Burger joined the workforce at age eleven, delivering the *St. Paul Dispatch* to 265 customers, once even covering his route on skis and towing a toboggan when an April storm dumped hip-deep snow on St. Paul.[10]

Blackmun and his friends had typical childhoods focused largely on sports, especially softball and later tennis. He also acquired an extensive stamp collection, noting in a 1921 diary entry, "I counted my stamps. I have 872." Even at that time, however, the diminutive Harry's feelings for the tall, muscular Warren Burger were complex. "Warren was always a little stronger than the rest of us, much to my annoyance.... He liked to dominate things and, in a nice way,... make himself known. But he was a good pal, a good companion in every way. No question about this."[11]

Blackmun and Burger attended Van Buren Elementary School, first built in 1882, but their paths parted in high school. St. Paul had recently established school districts, and Burger enrolled at Johnson High School, to which Dayton's Bluff students were assigned. But John Briggs, two years Blackmun's senior, attended Mechanic Arts High School in downtown St. Paul. Originally a trade school, Mechanic Arts had become a full-time high school with an excellent faculty. Blackmun, as he later put it, "wrangled" a way to circumvent the new district system and join his friend Briggs at Mechanic Arts.[12]

Harry excelled in high school. In his junior year, he won an oratorical contest on the topic of the U.S. Constitution. Fittingly, given the flexible approach to constitutional meaning with which he would be closely associated on the Supreme Court, he began his essay with the resounding exclamation, "It lives! The Constitution of the United States, our Constitution, still lives!" During his senior year, he was manager of Mechanic Arts' champion swim team, class president, and president of the student council. He would graduate fourth in a class of 450 students and later said that he benefited not only from his school's academic excellence but also from its diverse student body, which included a large number of African Americans from St. Paul's Rondo Street neighborhood. Two of them became his "pretty close friends. We discussed their problems and I discussed mine. None of us had any money, it was common in that respect, had to work outside a little bit."[13]

In his autobiographical first theme as a Harvard freshman, Blackmun would exude satisfaction about his high school experience. "The breach" between grammar school and Mechanic Arts, he observed at one point, had "seemed wide but it was conquered with little difficulty and I found myself in a world of new things." In truth, of course, he had suffered the usual frustrations of adolescence. On his birthday in 1924 he wrote in his diary, "Sweet 16 and never been kissed! What a world!" His diary entries for that period also suggest, however, that the melancholy increasingly afflicting his mother had also begun to affect her son. On September 8, 1924, the first day of his senior year, he wrote, "School started today. It is the same old dump & dull as ever." In a November 21 entry that year, he asked, "What is the matter with me. I seem to have absolutely no courage, either physically or mentally. I must overcome it." Of graduation night at Mechanic Arts, he wrote, "All in all it was a fearful night and I can't talk any more about it."[14]

Harvard Square

Whatever the honor of being admitted to one of the nation's finest colleges, Blackmun's transition from St. Paul to Cambridge, Massachusetts, also may have done more to exacerbate than allay his feelings of insecurity and self-doubt. He was easily admitted to the University of Minnesota. But the Harvard Club of Minnesota awarded tuition scholarships to outstanding high school students, and two of Harry's English teachers, Miss Deem and Miss Copley, suggested that he apply for one and put him in contact with the Harvard Club's membership committee, which was composed of two Minneapolis lawyers and two from St. Paul. Blackmun approached the prospect of attending Harvard with mixed emotions. "Tuition was fine, but I knew I had to eat and do some other things," he later said. At one point, he went to the office of Edward B. Young, one of the scholarship committee members, a very short man, Blackmun noticed, whose feet did not touch the floor as he sat in his swivel chair talking to Harry. Blackmun would come to consider Young "the kindest fellow I think I ever saw." But when the lawyer asked, "So you want to go to Harvard?" Harry defensively shot back, "Who said that? I don't know anything about Harvard. I was just told to come and see you."[15]

Theo Blackmun's brother Bert Reuter lived in Buffalo, Wyoming. The previous summer, a friend had arranged a job for Harry at the HF Bar dude ranch, situated in a beautiful valley bordering the Bighorn National Forest, about thirty-five miles from Reuter's home. Blackmun ran the ranch store in the morning and rode horseback with guests the rest of the time. "I show some photographs to my current law clerks all the time," he reported years later. "They're amazed to see me on a horse [wearing] chaps and all the rest."[16]

While working at the HF Bar the summer following graduation from Mechanic Arts, Blackmun received a telegram from the Minnesota Harvard Club, informing him that he had been awarded a scholarship and asking for a response within four days. The stipend totaled $350, including a $100 loan he would be expected to repay. "My dream of the past year is realized," he exclaimed in a diary entry dated July 24, 1925. "I am so shaky I can hardly write." The next day, he wrote that "several of the dudes seemed quite elated over my winning the scholarship....I had quite a talk with [one] this evening. She said that it was wonderful that there was a place where those who were really deserving could get such a thing as a scholarship. On the other hand that it was very discouraging when one's own boys, after one had spent practically thousands of dollars to send them east to expensive prep schools,...flunk[ed] out." Given his family's precarious financial situation, however, Harry "didn't know what to do." During the summer, a ranch guest, the wife of a descendant of President Garfield, had become interested in his future. She insisted that he take the scholarship. "She kept, almost nagging me for a while. I think she influenced me in my decision." To a well-connected matron, Blackmun's decision must have seemed obvious. But Harry left the ranch for home early, anxious to determine whether attending Harvard would be at all financially feasible. One day, while his father was shaving, his son asked him, "Aren't you pleased that the scholarship has come along?" Corwin Blackmun replied, "Yes, I'm pleased but that doesn't answer everything." He was, the justice knew, "worried about how to get me through, what his obligations of support were and so forth. But I finally determined more or less on my own that I'd go."[17]

For young Harry, however, nothing, it seemed, was easy. Given his class standing at Mechanic Arts, he was entitled to be admitted to Harvard without examination. When E. B. Young of the Harvard Club visited Cambridge that June, he was informed that Blackmun had been admitted. But on September 15, five days before Harry's planned departure east, he visited Young's office, distraught that he had received no formal notification of admission or dormitory assignment. Young wrote Henry Pennypacker, chairman of Harvard's admissions committee, that same day. "If there is any doubt about his being admitted or an omission in [his application] papers...kindly telegraph me at my expense in order that the omission may be corrected before he leaves or so that he may save himself the expense of a useless trip."[18]

As it turned out, Harvard had not received notice of Blackmun's scholarship, and the financially strapped applicant had instructed admission officials not to cash his $9 admission fee check until notified of the scholarship. Finally, on September 18, two days before Harry's planned departure, the admissions committee notified Young that the scholarship notice had been received and Blackmun admitted to the freshman class.[19]

The reaction of Mechanic Arts principal Dietrich Lange to Blackmun's admission did nothing to bolster Harry's confidence. Lange, a native of Germany whom the justice later described as "an old German Prussian...with flaming white hair and a distinct accent," was principal from 1916 until 1940, the year before his death. An active conservationist and the author of juvenile historical fiction on Native Americans and wildlife as well as other nature books, Lange was a memorable figure with whom Blackmun would form a close friendship after high school. He may also have had some hand in nurturing Blackmun's life-long interest in the outdoors and concern for the plight of the American Indian, as well as the justice's childhood curiosity about historic battles between the Sioux and Chippewa. But Lange could also be brutally frank. When Harry proudly informed him that he would attend Harvard, the principal reminded his student that the previous year's recipient of a Harvard Club scholarship had not done well. "If you [also] flunk out," warned Lange, "we'll never get another student into Harvard." Blackmun was stricken. "I thought, in later years, what a thing to tell me. It just added to the burden of going east in a new culture and all the rest. But he was so desperate about it."[20]

On September 20, Blackmun boarded a train for the trip, his first east of Chicago. A young person's first long trip far from home is almost always difficult, and Harry, for whom every silver lining seemingly had a dark cloud, was no exception, as his first letter home from Cambridge, written on September 24, made painfully clear. During an uneventful trip to Chicago, he "nearly froze." In Chicago, he had lunch and a long visit with relatives until time to board his connecting train to Boston. "That," he wrote, "came almost too soon and I got on." At Boston station, he took the subway to Harvard Square, where he received "the glorious news that there were no rooms left in the freshman dorms." Given his late admission, he had no chance to participate in the initial drawing for rooms. Another drawing was to be held soon, but "400 kids [would be] after 75 rooms so there [was] not much chance" for him. A housing officer advised Harry "that the only thing to do was to go out and shag up a room for myself....It sure made me feel blue. All the houses around here were just plain holes and the rent they wanted!"[21]

After meeting Norman and Trevor Grimm, brothers from Los Angeles, Harry and his two companions began their search. "We hunted and hunted around darn near every block." They liked an apartment at 65 Winthrop Street in Cambridge, but the rent was high, so Harry wired his parents for advice. That night, a woman at one house loaned them blankets and offered to let them spend the night with Hosea, her elderly and very gregarious housekeeper, who kept them awake talking for hours. "We finally tried to go to sleep at eleven. Try is right. We slept about two hours and froze all the time." The next morning, after Harry had received a telegram from his parents approving the expense, the trio rented the Winthrop Street apartment, a two-room flat with a small bedroom, large study, and two cots in the study.[22]

Soon, the three would find dormitory rooms, Blackmun in Persis Smith Hall and the Grimm brothers in Gore Hall. By that point, though,

Blackmun thought that he had received "a rather rotten reception" at Harvard. By contrast, "young Cutler," son of William Cutler, one of the prosperous lawyers on the Minnesota Harvard Club's membership committee, was "set up nicely." (Cutler's parents had accompanied their son to Cambridge on the same train Harry had taken east.) His expenses to that point, he added, had also left him "flat, so could you send me some more [money] right away."[23]

Blackmun attempted to end his September 24 letter on a positive note, but was only partially successful in that effort. "You folks have sure been nice and I hope this year will not overburden you. I sure do not want to do that. If I can have a little more money now I will feel much better.... Gosh I hope everything will go on all right from now on. It sure seems mixed up now. Love to you all. I hope that the next time I write things will look brighter and I will feel not so balled up."[24]

As Blackmun moved to Harvard, his parents left the modest house they had occupied at 747 East Fourth Street, moving into a larger home at 1808 Stanford Avenue. Corwin Blackmun could ill afford the new house, but Harry tried to be enthusiastic about the change. He also wrote cheerful letters to his sister Betty, his "Little Honey Bunch," ever interested in the child's activities and even solicitous about the Raggedy Ann doll he had given her several years earlier. "Tonight is Tuesday," he wrote Betty about a month after arriving at Harvard, "and I am in an awful rush for business is very good, study business not monkey business I mean." He had recently attended a high Episcopal service in Boston with one of his roommates. "Hot dog, you should have seen me." His friend "had to go," he explained, although "he likes church like I do coconut." After that experience, he decided that he was "pretty well satisfied with Methodism."[25]

But word from home during Blackmun's first term at Harvard was hardly cause for optimism. "Dad," he anxiously wrote on October 10, "have you gotten any news of a job yet[?] Will you be able to make the next payment on the house? I sure hope that things are going all right." His frustration with Harvard and Cambridge hardly abated either. Soon he confessed to "a touch of homesickness," but added, "I don't care. Everybody gets them sometimes. Only June seems a long way off." Even as a Supreme Court justice, he would never feel entirely comfortable in Harvard Square. As a freshman, he felt almost excruciatingly isolated, even though he forged a number of enduring friendships. "Harvard College," he wrote his parents dejectedly on one occasion, "is run just like any other big place only more so. If you want to do something, you have to know the ropes and have a real big drag. Those are my first impressions and it gets me. The world is the same all over, isn't it[?]" Defiantly, he added, "But then we will show them, sometime, that drag is not everything that counts." Several days later, though, his bravado had largely disappeared. "Things are not what they might be out here. I just can't seem to get in with the kids but I suppose that that will come later."[26]

In one of his many freshman themes, Harry almost took the opportunity to air his frustrations about Harvard more openly. Following the obligatory autobiography, he submitted papers on a number of mundane topics, including handball, the value of libraries, life on a western dude ranch, and the importance of the lowly clerk to modern businesses. But he found the topic of his second assignment, "My Reception at Harvard and my Suggestions as to How it May be Improved," entirely to his liking. "Am I going to tell them something!" he exclaimed in his next letter home. "They told us to say what we think and we are."[27]

Whether discouraged in his plans by his parents or by his own considerable inhibitions, Harry's frustrations are barely discernible in the theme he actually submitted. Indeed, the final product seemed the very antithesis of the impressions of Harvard he had shared with his family. When he first decided to attend Harvard, he wrote, he "was warned against the formalities of the Easterners, told of the odd habits and customs prevelent [sic] in Boston and the surrounding territory, and, finally, informed as to what my own reaction would be when I would arrive in Cambridge. As a result of this well-meant advice,...I expected to find a faculty, cold, unapproachable, and a student body as unimpressive. Such were my thoughts as I set forth a few weeks ago."[28]

Once in Boston, however, "these pictures vanished." In his letters home, Blackmun's descriptions of Boston and Cambridge had hardly been flattering. "Boston...is a funny town," he wrote at one point. "The extremely elite residential section is nothing, not half as nice as our block at home. Everything is apartments and more of them. They do have [a] swift subway system here..., but then they ought to have one." In his theme, however, Harry praised his new home as "a modern city not at all like the ancient

Dayton's Bluff to Harvard

13

one I had expected." His description of the Harvard populace was equally positive. "I walked through the college yard and entered University Hall. I was received with civility and as much politeness and attention as one might expect in such a place. I visited the Philip Brooks House [Harvard's venerable student-led public service organization] and there found some of the most congenial men on the campus. My 'impressions' had vanished and in their place others were being formed, planted by the seeds of my own personal experience." Nor did he have any "real suggestions for improving the reception" given new students. "The rooming accommodations might well be better. However, these conditions are probably unavoidable and might be present anywhere. There is much talk about the campus that a so-called 'pull or drag' is necessary to accomplish anything in Harvard. If this is true, it must be remedied." But that was as close as he got to criticizing his new home, and even those concerns, he concluded, were "only the first impressions of a lowly freshman, a child who 'is to be seen and not heard.' As time passes these impressions will probably change and day by day I shall learn to love the school with the watchword of 'veritas' and be glad to say that I am one of the multitude within its gates." So much for the "rotten reception" he had complained about to his parents.[29]

As the term progressed, Harry's meager finances continued to be a problem, his spirits improved only in part by gifts his parents, at times responding to not so subtle hints from their son, sent him. "A bathrobe would not come in unhandy," he wrote at one point, "but I guess I can do without one." A bathrobe soon arrived from home. Perhaps in an effort to impress on his parents the high cost of even the bare necessities, he regularly sent them detailed accountings of his expenses. As one demonstration of his frugality, he wrote them that he was saving nearly a dime a week by washing his own socks. "I would do my own handkerchiefs too," he added, "only I tore one when I tried [washing] it." Whether for pay or free admission to games, Harry, even then a devoted sports fan, also began ushering at Harvard's football games. He was alarmed not only at his school's poor gridiron record, but by what he considered the Prohibition-era fans' excessive drinking. "That kind of stuff is quite prevalent around here," he wrote his parents. "It makes me disgusted."[30]

Initially, at least, Blackmun also found the rigors of Harvard academics daunting—much more challenging than high school. Following a conference with Professor Joseph Warren of the law school, he decided to enroll his first term in English, a mathematics class in analytic geometry and one in introductory calculus, history, and French. "That French course," he soon reported, "is going to be a beezer. The prof has to use an acousticon because he is so deaf....Everyone says that he is one of the hardest profs in Harvard. That always seems to be my luck." Harry was also obliged to take an examination testing his reading comprehension of Latin or German. He opted for the Latin exam. "When I found out about Latin, I took a great gasp and headed for the library and grabbed a volume of Cicero and Virgil for the Latin exam would come off the next day. I tried to revive my long lost memories of Miss Prendergast [his Mechanic Arts Latin teacher] and dug in." Afterward, he was hardly optimistic about the results. "Smoley Hoke! It was a real one. I can only hope for the results as it was a pippin. Gosh it was hard."[31]

As he probably anticipated, Blackmun failed his Latin exam, then, in the fashion of students everywhere, attempted to console his parents, and himself, by emphasizing that he had "only found one fellow who passed it. Everyone else has flunked." He could try to pass the German examination next year, but he was clearly disappointed. "It sure made me feel blue and discouraged. Yet everyone here is in the same boat. Things are not at all easy." He received a C+ on his first English theme, his instructor declaring his paragraphing and punctuation "poor" but the paper not "without interest." When one of his professors returned a set of themes one day in late October, he announced that he would read and discuss one in class. "Well, of course, the old bum had to pick out mine. And he sure did pick it OUT. Gosh, he literally tore it up and threw it in my face....I sat there and swallowed it all." On Halloween, he wrote home that he would resist the temptation "to go dump a few garbage cans just for the fun of it," adding, "A lot of kids will step out tonight but not me—too much studying."[32]

A week later, he urged his parents not to "tell anyone that I do not like it here, because I do like the place....Do not think that I am discouraged either." Even so, he appeared thoroughly dejected. "Here I have been at Harvard six weeks now and what have I got? I have not done a darn thing but grind and have not gotten any results. I have made no acquaintances to speak of and have not exactly gotten any spirit into me. It may be my fault but I cannot understand it."[33]

Physical ailments were an additional aggravation. Blackmun would be plagued with, and intrigued by, medical problems, real and perhaps imagined, throughout his life. He even wrote a detailed high school essay on his appendectomy and got permission to witness the procedure when Betty went under the knife. In diary entries, he regularly recalled the anniversary of his surgery. In fact, he was able to recall its precise date—March 8, 1923—in a get-well note to Justice Sandra Day O'Connor when she underwent an appendectomy in 1988. Long a sufferer from eyestrain, he was pictured wearing glasses in his high school senior photograph. Colds and back pain were other chronic maladies.[34]

In his first term at Harvard, Harry complained of eyestrain but was most distressed by intense back pain. Following a particularly vigorous bout on the handball court, he saw a school doctor, who thought he might need to wear a back brace and suggested that he see a specialist in Boston. Alarmed at the expense that might entail, Blackmun instead began visiting an osteopath. "Imagination you say," he wrote his perhaps skeptical parents. "Maybe, maybe not." In late November, he reported that his back was "a lot better," although he added, "It hurts at times of course, but he said that would wear off soon." In the same letter, Harry detailed a recent struggle with a cold. "I was just plain miserable. On top of it all, the work just kept right up. I doctored myself all up and it is now breaking up. [But] my old head and eyes did sure hurt for a few days."[35]

In time, Blackmun's spirits would also improve. From the beginning, an easterner cousin and her husband, Florence and Irvin Finke, were solicitous, taking Harry on automobile tours of the area and inviting him to meals at their home. Initially, he seemed only mildly impressed with his dormitory suite mates. "The Armenian," he wrote of one, "we do not see much of." Robert Ethan Merry, who ultimately became an Episcopal canon, was "more or less one of these saintly kind," while the other two were "kind of wild." They were, he concluded, "on the whole...not a bad bunch and I think that we will get along all right." But he doubted that he "would want one of them for a room-mate next year." Of course, he conceded, "that is a long way off. I have to see first whether I can get through this year." Soon, though, his attitude about his suite mates had mellowed considerably. "This bunch of room-mates," he wrote his parents in early November, "are a merry crowd. One is a dumbbell, another is one of these humerous [sic] guys, the third is a saint, and the fourth is an atheist....The first and third kind of look to me for more or less paternal advice and I get along all right with the other two....We have a lot of fun....We set one of the alarm clocks at three the other morning. Was he mad[!]"[36]

At Thanksgiving, Bob Merry took pity on Harry, inviting him to spend the holiday with his family in Duxbury, Massachusetts, south of Boston. That visit included not only a good turkey dinner (Merry's father was a butcher) but a drive on Cape Cod and Blackmun's "first real view" of the Atlantic Ocean. "It was cold as deuces," he wrote his sister, "but oh, that ocean was beautiful." They also took in several historic sites, passing by a house that once belonged to John Alden and getting a quick glance at Plymouth Rock. Only many years later would the justice be amused to learn that he was descended from Miles Standish.[37]

Given the Blackmun family financial situation, a trip home to Minnesota, even for Christmas, was out of the question. Late on Christmas night, Harry wrote "Dearest Dad and Mother and Betty" a twelve-page letter. In it, he confessed that the day had "been full of a sort of homesick loneliness" and that he had "come to realize what home has meant to me and what great pals you three have been to me and what all you have done for me, and, well, everything." Recalling the "great times" and "fun" he had enjoyed with his family, he sneered, "It makes one pretty disgusted to hear fellows talking of disliking to go home and being tied down after being so free here. But what is the use of talking of all this drearyness [sic]. There is enough of it in the world without talking of it here and on Christmas."[38]

He assured his family, moreover, that he had "not been moping around; in fact,...just the opposite." Thereupon, he launched into a detailed account of his holiday activities. The dormitories were virtually deserted, but on Tuesday before Christmas on Friday, Harry—like his mother and sister, an inveterate moviegoer—went with a Florida friend to a Leon Errol comedy ("paying one ten for gallery seats[!]"), which he pronounced "surely a scream and a good night's entertainment." Afterward, he, his friend, and a law student "argued till three o'clock as to whether the world was getting better or worse." They had drawn no conclusion, "but the law man said that he was talking to a pair of darn good optimists." Alone in his "palatial abode" that night, he slept until one o'clock the next afternoon. After devoting most of Wednesday and Christmas Eve to his studies, he opened gifts from friends, including a tie from Warren Burger. Then, at about eight o'clock that evening, the Finkes came by and took Harry and the "Brothers Grimm," as Blackmun often called them, "down town to the Beacon Hill, or elite, section of the city." Harry was impressed. "It seemed as though all Boston was there. The streets were crowded. Every window in every house had its row of candles. And every few blocks was a group of people singing carols. It was a truly beautiful sight and one typically Bostonian." Later, the Grimms returned to Harry's dorm, where they ate cookies and read a German reader.[39]

On Christmas morning, he slept until eleven o'clock. "That sounds so terrible, but I considered myself only an hour late as it was but ten in St. Paul." After opening gifts from family, he and the Grimms went to the Finkes for dinner. "I never ate so much in my life....Florence did surely have a wonderful dinner....Man!!!...It was a mighty nice day that the Finkes gave us. I don't know how we shall ever thank them." That night the three went to the Philips Brooks House for refreshments and cider. "There were quite a few Japs there," he reported. "They have quite a way to go home."

Finally, observing that his letter was "getting to be a book and [was], as Warren Burger has been claiming of all of [my letters], terribly incoherent," he closed. Early in the letter, he had lamented that a morning snow unfortunately "was the wet kind...and [had] made the day itself rather miserable, yet [also] helps a lot for the season." But he also assured his family, "I guess I am straight with the world now, and can go on," then attempted to end his letter on what, for Blackmun, was a cheerful note. "It has been a fine Christmas on all sides, and one that chases the gloom away."[40]

Soon, it became clear that Harry would be an academic success at Harvard. His early grades and November midterm marks were clearly acceptable for a Harvard freshman in those quaint days before rampant grade inflation, but a disappointment to Harry. When he made a 67 on his first history theme, he "nearly caved in and asked the fellow if the system was based on a hundred [points]," but was told that he had written a good paper and assigned one of the higher grades in the class. At Harvard, he soon learned, 50 was a passing grade. Overall, his midterm grades were average, and Harry defensive. "Personally I am not ashamed," he wrote Betty. "Maybe that is not the way to talk, but I feel that I put all I had in me to the work. When one sees fellows with straight D's and E's [F's] it makes him feel better. A Harvard A is a scarce thing if I do say it myself. I think Miss Prout [a Mechanic Arts teacher] realizes that and it is just as well for her to know....Monday, we have another important History exam. It is a chance to redeem myself. I hope that I will. I feel that I can raise that C plus. But one can never tell. Of course there are fellows that have all A's. Fine chance of my getting them, though."[41]

Mechanic Arts principal Dietrich Lange wrote to congratulate his former student on his "very good" November grades, but characteristically also urged Harry to "keep it up, so that the Harvard Club will be glad to pick another Mechanic Arts student next year." E. B. Young of the Harvard Club was more diplomatic and encouraging. Terming Blackmun's November performance "very satisfactory," Young predicted, "If you do your best work your marks will be even higher because the preparation given in a public school [such as Mechanic Arts] is usually not quite as distinctly fitted to prepare for an Eastern college as it might be made. If your future marks are as good as the present we shall certainly feel that we have made no mistake in choosing you this year to represent Minnesota Club."[42]

Lange and Young must have been very pleased with Harry's end-of-term marks, which the Mechanic Arts' student newspaper pronounced "brilliant." Drawing on a letter Blackmun had written, probably to Lange, *The Cogwell* boasted that the school's alumnus had "display[ed] his customary ability, for which he was so well known at Mechanic Arts." He made an A, his highest mark, in mathematics, earning 181 of a possible 190 honor points, and ranking fifth out of 860 students. With a B, he ranked seventh out of 800 students in English. He also received Bs in history and in two French courses. "These," the paper stressed, perhaps prompted by Harry, "are very excellent averages considering that at Harvard A and B are regarded as honor roll mention." Blackmun had written "that the subjects were not so difficult in themselves, but that the volume of work made the courses heavy. He also suggested that the social advantages are more favorable in the East, but that the college seems to lack the friendly atmosphere which pervades at Mechanics." Recalling "with pride [Harry's] admirable qualities and brilliant ability," the paper "wishe[d] him all the success in the world."[43]

In an early letter to his mother after arriving in Cambridge, Harry informed his parents that he had not yet sought a job, adding, "Do you think I should?" But in the spring, his confidence bolstered by his first-term grades and perhaps yielding to pressure from home, he took on the first, his favorite, of a series of campus jobs he would hold during his years at Harvard. One afternoon, Bob Merry informed him that he had just been hired to drive the launch for the coach of the varsity rowing crew and thought that a driver was also needed for the freshman coach. Blackmun rushed down to Weld Boat House, got the job, and kept it until his last year of law school. Early each weekday, he would go down to the boathouse, get his launch into shape, and between classes take the freshman coach out on the Charles River with the rowing crew until dark. "It was a great job," he recalled years later, "because it got me out of doors for one thing, and it paid three dollars a day…fifteen bucks a week, which was a fair amount of money. I could eat on that." Each winter, when the launches were dry-docked, Harry spent three or four weeks scraping barnacles off their hulls. As an employee of the Harvard Athletic Association, he also cleaned handball courts, which "consisted largely," he later explained, "of getting [out] spit [players left in] the corners…a dirty job." Later, as a mathematics major, he corrected papers for a professor and tutored students, including two African American students. "There were a lot of Jewish kids around [but] not many African-Americans….They were having a terrible struggle, but we got them through, and they passed their courses….It taught me a lot of what was troubling to other people."[44]

Asked years later about Harvard's rigid social structure and the distinction there between "rich kids and scholarship kids," Blackmun readily acknowledged the sense of isolation he initially experienced in Cambridge. Wealthy students came to Harvard with their "social circles [of prep school classmates] already made," while "those of us who came out alone were pretty much alone and of course had a much lower social status than the effete easterners." But, he added, not entirely convincingly, "We got over that after a while."[45]

As noted earlier, Blackmun would never be entirely comfortable at Harvard, even as a justice. Over his years in Cambridge, however, he steadily expanded his social calendar and contacts. Serving as driver of the freshman rather than varsity crew launch gave him the opportunity to become acquainted with a variety of students, including Jimmy Roosevelt, son of the future president. He also joined the Lambda Chi Alpha social fraternity, regularly attended college dances, and continued to serve as a head usher at football games.[46]

From his first year in Cambridge through law school, Blackmun also sang baritone with the famous Harvard Glee Club. He got in, he modestly said, "with the lowest possible [audition] grade," but would always have particularly fond memories of that association. "It was...great, for me, a great musical experience.... The Harvard Glee Club at that time was...almost an unofficial choir for the Boston Symphony. And I remember the thrill of sitting in behind the Boston Symphony for rehearsals." In 1929, Harry's senior year as an undergraduate, the glee club's spring tour included a White House performance for President Herbert Hoover, who had taken office the previous month.[47]

Harry's musical mother was no doubt pleased with Harry's glee club activities. His parents would not have approved, though, of another aspect of his Harvard lifestyle. During his childhood, Harry's parents had not been unduly strict with him in matters religious. "Mother was fairly strict in the sense that she didn't sew on Sundays, she didn't play cards on Sunday even though she liked to play cards. But as far as the kids were concerned, we could go out and play all day Sunday. We weren't restricted to the house to read the Bible or anything like that." Both parents were active in the Methodist Church. But during his Harvard years, their son, like many college students, was, as he later put it, "distinctly inactive."[48]

Blackmun had hoped to remain in Cambridge over the summer after his freshman year but was not, of course, one of Harvard's "rich kids." Thus, he was obliged to return to St. Paul and get a job. Turned down by a bank and the United Lead Company, a manufacturer of pipe, he eventually got work delivering milk. The milk company was beginning to convert to Model-T Fords, but Harry enjoyed making his early morning rounds in a horse-drawn wagon. "Those old horses were great, because they knew the route.... They'd go along and stop, and I knew that house was where I was supposed to go."[49]

That summer he also arranged store window displays for the Ry-Krisp Company, which was based in Minneapolis. A company official was impressed with "the nice windows" he trimmed but had no work for him in the Boston area the next school year, and his hopes to trim windows the following summer were dashed when the company became a subsidiary of Ralston Purina in St. Louis, with all advertising to be handled by the home office. But Blackmun continued, of course, working with the rowing crew each school year and also landed a variety of summer jobs in Minneapolis, continuing milk deliveries for regular drivers who went on vacation and at one point becoming a counselor at Camp St. Croix, operated by the YMCA. In a further effort to supplement his income, Harry had his name placed on a list of blood donors at the Massachusetts General Hospital.[50]

Despite constant financial concerns, Blackmun compiled an impressive undergraduate record—regularly making the dean's list, earning a Phi Beta Kappa key, albeit, he was always quick to note, in his senior rather than junior year—and winning additional scholarships. At commencement ceremonies on June 20, 1929, honoring the largest Harvard graduating class in its history, he graduated summa cum laude, the event marred only slightly for the Minnesota Republican by his school's choice of New York Governor Franklin D. Roosevelt, whose son Jimmy was also graduating that day, as commencement speaker. "I viewed him with some suspicion," Blackmun later said, "because he was out of New York, he was an easterner, and I was a Midwesterner, and they didn't pay much attention to anybody west of the Hudson River in those days....He had that seeming arrogance with the cigarette and the long cigarette holder and his distinct speech. You can recognize it anywhere. But he was an impressive guy, there's no question about it."[51]

Blackmun's parents attended his graduation. Asked years later whether they were happy with his decision to attend Harvard, he was typically ambivalent. "I suppose they were. I was never criticized for it. My father never said a great deal. Mother talked a good bit about it and fortunately the grades were pretty good that were coming in. They went out for graduation, and I think they went proudly."[52]

An undergraduate concentration in mathematics, in which even his first grades were excellent, seemed a natural choice for the meticulous, methodical Blackmun, although years later he confessed that he had recently run across his senior mathematics thesis and found it baffling. Selecting a course of advanced study had been more difficult. Corwin

Blackmun, who had aspired to study law himself, urged his son to become a lawyer. "I was just a kid," the justice would later say, a note of desperation in his words, "and he kept grinding at me." As noted earlier, however, Harry had also become fascinated in childhood with his medical condition, as well as that of those around him, and as a boy he often talked about becoming a physician. The decision of his childhood friend John Briggs to study medicine further whetted his interest, as did the example of, among others, the Blackmun family doctor and the ophthalmologist to whom Harry's parents were referred when he began suffering from eyestrain. In the summer before his senior year at Harvard, he even wrote the University of Minnesota medical school, seeking information regarding admissions requirements and the course of instruction. He particularly "wish[ed] to be sure as to exactly what courses are necessary for admission to the Medical School." Whatever his interest in studying law, on the other hand, he never visited a Harvard law class during his undergraduate years. "No. I could see the law school students walking around the yard, some of the other places, with those green bags, holding huge books that seemed to be rather baffling." As the deadline approached for making a decision, he "drifted along for a while,...torn between medicine and the law." Ultimately, he chose law, in part perhaps because of doubts that he "could do very well in basic sciences," even though he excelled in mathematics. As with much of his life, though, he would agonize over his choice. "I jokingly say," he remarked years later, "that I didn't take up law until my senior year in law school."[53]

At least he was not bothered that his undergraduate concentration in mathematics was not a major closely associated with law study. In a speech to Blackmun's freshman class, Harvard's venerable president A. Lawrence Lowell had advised the students to major in whatever "good subject" they chose, adding, "I went on to law school but I majored in mathematics." If "that was good enough for...Lowell," Blackmun thought, "it was good enough for me."[54]

For a time in his senior year, probably overwhelmed by the thought of further financial drain and undoubtedly strained by his efforts to juggle classes and work, Harry had considered teaching for a year before beginning law school. Warren Burger attempted to discourage his friend from that course. While Blackmun was excelling at Mechanic Arts, Burger, despite only average grades, had become a leader at St. Paul's Johnson High School, writing for the student newspaper and winning election in 1924 as the school's first student council president. Shown wearing a fedora in a photograph accompanying a newspaper article announcing his election as council president, Burger looked years older than his age, a marked contrast to the slight, frail-looking, bespectacled, somewhat sad-faced youth with delicate features pictured in Blackmun's senior photograph.[55]

After high school, the two friends' lives had led them in somewhat different directions. Given his family's impoverished circumstances, Burger had been obliged to turn down a scholarship offer from Princeton. For most young persons in his situation, the prospects for a law career of any sort might have seemed dim indeed. But Warren Burger never lacked for confidence. While Blackmun made plans to attend Harvard, Burger found summer work pouring concrete for the construction of St. Paul's Robert Street Bridge. At the end of the summer, he got a job with the Mutual Life Insurance Company's St. Paul office, advancing from office boy to senior bookkeeper during his six years with the company. While working at Mutual and selling insurance policies in his "spare time," as he later put it, Burger also took extension courses through the University of Minnesota, then enrolled in night classes at the St. Paul College of Law in 1927. The school, located at that time in an old Victorian mansion, was no Harvard. But Burger graduated magna cum laude in 1931 and joined an established St. Paul firm.[56]

Burger had learned from Blackmun's mother of his friend's plans to delay beginning law school. "I trust," he wrote sometime later, "that you have [now] decided to stay by the guns for the last lap for I have seen so many instances here where [those with] high ambitions and good intentions have been tempted from the path of struggling student days to bigger and better remuneration. Most of them left school for a year or two and most of them will never crack a law book again." Burger had no doubt, he wrote, that Harry would return to school but found it "difficult to see just what could be gained to compensate for the year lost." Perhaps playing to whatever martyr tendencies he had already detected in his friend, the future chief justice acknowledged that Blackmun had "given [up] much" for what he had gained, "family, home, friends, and no end of comfort for the damnable struggle to stay near the top and keep working to make those old ends meet." But he was confident that Harry's sacrifices would one day be well rewarded. "Believe me, old man, I have no end of admiration for you, for your courage and for your determination and fighting spirit that has carried you to the top....I am sure and know that the day is not far when you will come to a place as high in life as you are now in the esteem of your friends."[57]

Whatever his motivation, Harry did begin law school that fall. During his first year, he lived in a graduate dormitory. But when the new Lowell House opened as an undergraduate dorm the following year, Harvard officials decided that a student representative from each of the graduate and professional schools should live in the house with the undergraduate residents. Blackmun became the law school's student representative. "Of course," he later said, "my friends...at law school thought I was crazy because I was down there in an undergraduate atmosphere and couldn't engage in bull sessions far into the night up around the law school. But it was a happy time, I enjoyed living there." His decision to live apart from the law students, he might have added, perhaps also reflected his continued ambivalence about his chosen profession.[58]

Blackmun had his first class, in torts, with Calvert Magruder, who later served twenty years as a judge on the U.S. Court of Appeals for the First Circuit. Most of his professors were, or would become, prominent figures in American law and politics. James M. Landis, for example, would be chairman of the Securities and Exchange Commission (1935–37) in the Roosevelt administration. Not surprisingly, Harry was not happy with all his courses or professors. He took constitutional law with Thomas Reed Powell, one of Harvard's most distinguished faculty members. Harry found Powell "as dogmatic as anybody could be." In later years, he could remember little about Powell's course, except that "it was not my favorite class." His favorite was a course on property with Barton Leach, who had served as Justice Oliver Wendell Holmes's legal secretary and was beginning a long career at Harvard. When Leach had difficulty reading his seating chart one day, dubbing his student Harry "Blackhorse," Blackmun's classmates immediately gave him a new nickname. "I endured that for a while," the justice recalled years later.[59]

Leach, of course, would not be the only person to mispronounce or misspell Blackmun's name over the years. Harry took a course on public utilities with future justice Felix Frankfurter. The students, Blackmun later said, considered Frankfurter unduly "positive in his position, almost arrogant." He also had a reputation for "playing favorites among students. He'd get about ten or twenty and put them up in the front row and his Socratic dialogue was always with those particular students and not with the rest of the common people or those of us who sat in the back rows." Frankfurter always called Harry " 'Blackmur,' M-U-R." Nor would the professor soon get it right. While clerking for Judge John Sanborn of the Eighth Circuit following law school, Blackmun, as he put it, "was presumptuous enough to write [Frankfurter] now and then about cases" then before Judge Sanborn. Frankfurter always responded, but one letter was to "My dear Blackmur"; an earlier one had the correct spelling, but only via a typeover changing the "r" to an "n." Not surprisingly, the supremely self-assured Frankfurter was also somewhat condescending toward his former student. When Harry wrote him about one case he was researching for Judge Sanborn, Frankfurter responded, "I am not at all surprised that it is fascinating to run down the evolution of the *Abilene* case doctrine."[60]

Not surprisingly, Blackmun found law school decidedly more challenging than his undergraduate years had been. "I sensed immediately when I got up there," he later said, "a different kind of atmosphere from that which had prevailed at Harvard College. I think it was due to a couple of things. One was the fact that the students came from all over.... [The law students] came from every conceivable college and were sharp. The second distinction I noticed,... right away, was that it was all business at that time. We were now in a professional school and studying the basic art of a profession and it was competitive. It was not the old college days anymore." Almost from the first day, he found that "this was business from here on,... and we better be good and let the devil take the hindmost.... I felt it anyway."[61]

Blackmun clearly took his law courses seriously, characteristically amassing extremely detailed notes on the cases to be covered in his classes. But he seemed equally determined to maintain an active social life and sports calendar. After the Lowell House squash team won a tournament, members of the team presented him, their captain and manager, with a squash racket. The racket would later hang in the justice's chambers.[62]

Harry's rigorous law courses, sports activities, and continuing work obligations—he once estimated holding ten jobs over his years at Harvard—took their toll. He was unable to match his superlative undergraduate grade average and did not make law review. He did take part in a winning moot court competition, but he was not one of the two members of his group selected to make oral arguments in the final round. "The rest of us," he reported in response to a question late in life, "wrote the brief and formed the cheering section."[63]

Through most of law school it was perhaps even more imperative that Harry work than during his undergraduate years. In his first year of law study, the nation had fallen into the grips of the Great Depression. Initially, Blackmun was unconcerned. "I can well remember," he later said, "Black Friday in October 1929, walking up to Harvard Square, going somewhere,...and the newsboys were hawking their papers, [shouting] 'Stock Market Crash,' and I said smugly to myself, 'I don't have any money, I'm broke, it just can't hurt me at all,' and congratulated myself on how lucky I was." Soon, of course, "[I realized] how wrong I was because it affected all of us." In those days, law students rarely found summer jobs clerking for law firms, and Blackmun was no exception. Instead, he was obliged to return to Minnesota each summer, delivering milk and finding other ways to finance his next year of law study. In his senior year, he convinced his parents that he should drop his jobs, and his grades improved. But overall, in seventeen law school courses, he made only two As, both in property classes; he earned three of his four Bs in his third year; and he received eight Cs and three Ds in the remaining courses.[64]

Perhaps hoping to avoid returning, perhaps permanently, to Minnesota after law school, Harry made the rounds of Boston law offices and, "to [his] amazement," even got a tentative offer from one lawyer. But when his father became ill, he gave up that quest, reluctantly returning to St. Paul to begin his career. He would always remain ambivalent about the path he had chosen. Reflecting later in life on his years as counsel at the Mayo Clinic as "the happiest decade of my life," he observed, "If I had it to do over again, I'd probably go to medical school."[65]

Chapter 2

Minnesota Lawyer

On returning home from Harvard, Harry Blackmun made the rounds of law offices, but without success. The previous February, Robert Driscoll of Minneapolis's Junell, Oakley, Driscoll and Fletcher, in which Harry would eventually become a partner, had written him that his firm's plans to take on additional associates had not yet "crystalliz[ed]" and that Driscoll could not offer "any assurance" that an opening would become available after Harry finished law school. Blackmun, suggested Driscoll, should not "pass up any other opportunities in reliance on…an opening [here]."[1]

For a time, those prospects for "other opportunities" seemed dim indeed. But then fate stepped in. John Benjamin Sanborn had recently been appointed to a seat on the U.S. Court of Appeals for the Eighth Circuit, and Sanborn needed a law clerk. When Blackmun approached Bergmann Richards of the Minnesota Harvard Club about working in his office, Richards introduced Harry to the judge at a state bar association meeting, then wrote Sanborn a strong supporting letter. Given recent cuts in the federal judiciary's budget, the judge initially was doubtful that he would have the necessary funds to hire a clerk. But Blackmun had come to his chambers for an interview and, Sanborn wrote Richards, "made a very good impression on me." The judge may also have recalled serving as a judge when Harry won the high school oratorical contest for his essay on the U.S. Constitution.[2]

In July, Harry began working in Judge Sanborn's St. Paul chambers on the assumption that his position would ultimately be funded. On August 1, Ethel Larson, the judge's secretary, informed him that funds were available, albeit at $2,200 rather than $2,400 as a result of the budget cuts. Harry was hardly disappointed. "How much that looks to me now!" he wrote his diary. The *Nashville Journal* in his mother's hometown was duly impressed, but not surprised. After all, the paper noted, prompted perhaps by Harry's Grandmother Reuter or his mother, "During the past year he was one of a group of eight to win the Ames Competition, an historic three-year [moot court] elimination at Harvard law school based on the preparation of briefs and the presentation of arguments of moot cases."[3]

Clerking for Judge Sanborn

John Sanborn was born in St. Paul in 1883. His father was a Civil War general and lawyer; his cousin Walter Henry Sanborn had preceded him on the Eighth Circuit. Judge Sanborn's career had been remarkably wide-ranging: private practice in St. Paul, service in the Minnesota House of Representatives, a stint as the state's comptroller of insurance, member of the Minnesota Tax Commission, World War I service as an Army private, and several years (1922–25) as a Minnesota state judge before his appointment by President Coolidge as a U.S. district judge in 1925. In 1932, President Hoover elevated him to the Eighth Circuit bench.

For years, the Eighth Circuit was the largest and most populous of the federal circuits, stretching a thousand miles from Canada to Louisiana and a thousand miles from the Mississippi River to Utah. With the creation of the Tenth Circuit in 1929, however, its size had been reduced considerably. When Harry Blackmun began clerking for Judge Sanborn, the circuit's jurisdiction covered Minnesota, both Dakotas, Nebraska, Iowa, Missouri, and Arkansas. Sitting in three-judge panels or, on relatively rare occasions, en banc, its judges primarily heard appeals from federal district courts. Ironically, although Judge Sanborn would become one of the Eighth

Circuit's most distinguished jurists, he would never be senior in terms of service among his colleagues, and thus never the circuit's chief judge.[4]

Blackmun started his clerkship for Judge Sanborn with typical anxiety. His diary entry for his first official day on the job read in part, "The judge was dry as usual and said little other than that we would try things this way for a while.... Gosh, I do hope things will work out now. The Judge is very distant, however." Over six weeks later, he was not yet comfortable in the position. "Spent the whole day up in the dirty library and did not even see the Judge. I have not seen him since Friday. He will think I have given up the job." The next day, however, he reported with apparent relief that he "had a chat or two with the Judge today." And when Sanborn, an inveterate hunter, returned from a hunting trip in early November, presenting Harry and the judge's secretary with two ducks each, Blackmun decided that Sanborn was "a good fellow," adding in an entry the next day, "He has been good to me." Some months later, when Sanborn told him that he was still in a quandary about a pending patent case, Harry assumed that "spoke ill" for the memorandum he had prepared in the case. "But [the judge] hastened to correct that impression. He is a great guy."[5]

Soon after starting with Judge Sanborn, Harry also learned, somewhat to his surprise, that he had passed the Minnesota bar examination on his first attempt. In a move hardly characteristic of the angst-ridden youth or the later justice, he had taken the bar exam with little preparation. "I arrived in Minnesota on a Saturday and took the bar on a Monday," he later recalled. "I had to rationalize a little because over the weekend I looked at the books and found out what the rule against perpetuities was and the statutes of limitations, but otherwise I didn't prepare for it, but convinced myself that I probably would flunk and if I did there wasn't any harm done and I should not excoriate myself for it but fortunately I got by." On September 13, 1932, he was presented to the Minnesota Supreme Court for formal admission to the bar.[6]

Judge Sanborn, like Harry, was new at his job and somewhat uncertain about how to use his clerk. "Initially, he wrote his own opinions on yellow legal pads. I can see him there grinding them out. He didn't know how to use me, and I didn't know how to act." But Harry wrote a number of bench memos summarizing cases for the judge before oral argument, and eventually he began drafting some opinions himself. "We worked pretty well together," he later recalled. At that time, clerks usually did not travel with judges when they held court in other cities. Instead, Blackmun simply "tried to help [Sanborn] get prepared" for those trips. Whether in St. Paul or on a rare trip to St. Louis for a term of court, Harry and clerks for other judges often attended court sessions, too. "Usually," he remembered, "we sat on the side where a jury normally would be....It was a lot of fun."[7]

While clerking, Harry also managed to attend the trial of Chicago mobster Roger Touhy and codefendants charged with kidnapping William Hamm, a wealthy St. Paul brewer. Blackmun was present in a packed courtroom when the trial judge read the jury's verdict acquitting all the defendants. "Such is the jury system," he later wrote in his diary. "I am more and more convinced it is NG [no good], but what is better?" The case was the first prosecution the federal government had lost there in years. "It was bungled from start to finish, I think," Harry complained. "Oh hell."[8]

Blackmun's frustration with the not guilty verdict in the Touhy case was mild, however, compared to his disappointment with the outcome of the previous year's presidential election. Early in that campaign season, he and his mother had attended a speech "for the Republican cause" by the sister of Charles Curtis, President Hoover's vice president. "I enjoy those things," he wrote in his diary. "I get enthused for politics." The next day, Judge Sanborn shared some of his political history with his clerk and suggested that he contact a prominent GOP operative were he interested in becoming active in the campaign.[9]

As election day approached, Harry became increasingly impatient with the process, declaring in one diary entry, "I will be glad when this fool campaign is over with." The campaign also brought out more than his political biases. Of one speaker, he wrote, "He is a little Jew, but presented a fairly interesting talk."[10]

Harry would remain a very enthusiastic supporter of Herbert Hoover's reelection, however. On November 4, the president stopped in St. Paul for his last major speech before going home to vote. Tickets to the event were scarce, but Harry, with the assistance of Warren Burger and Judge Sanborn, managed to get excellent seats only five rows behind the press table. When the president entered, "the crowd went wild." Blackmun considered Hoover "a great man...and one who will be appreciated more and more

[as] the years pass, regardless of his victory or defeat next Tuesday. And what a contrast to Roosevelt!!" But that evening, the president, already aware of near certain defeat, "looked very bad, utterly exhausted. He stammered several times in his speech." Even so, the Blackmun family "went home late, but happy to have heard this great American President" and confident that "Hoover gained much by [his] speech." Harry was clearly impressed. "Gosh, things like that fill a fellow with the desire to do."[11]

Blackmun realized the election's significance and found it difficult to keep his mind on his work at court. "People," he wrote in his diary, "are hungry for leadership and a solution to their difficulties." But unfortunately for Hoover, and Harry, voters saw the incumbent president more as cause than solution to the nation's problems. The day before the election, Harry had become pessimistic about the outcome. "I argued this noon," he wrote to his diary, "and became quite heated about it. Hoover will not win, I fear, and this is the kind of gratitude a country which he has served fully since 1915 gives a man!!!"[12]

On November 8, Harry cast his vote for president, marking his ballot "emphatically for Hoover and Curtis." But early returns favored Roosevelt, especially in New York. "And Hoover needs New York State. Oh Hell." Minnesota and Michigan voted Democrat for the very first time; in fact, no state west of the Mississippi River went into the GOP column. "It sickens me…a very great man has been defeated." Blackmun wrote, "[I do] not give much of a care about the defeat of the Republican organizations, but I do care a lot about Herbert Hoover…a man who has served his country unceasingly for 17 years."[13]

Blackmun would vote for FDR at least once, he later conceded. But he would not soon forgive the new president for Hoover's defeat. When Roosevelt closed the banks his first day in office, Harry sarcastically hooted (to his diary), "Hooray, hooray," adding, "This is a great period of history to be living through. What an Inauguration Day." A radio set had been installed for the occasion in Judge Sanborn's chambers. "We listened in to the festivities most of the morning, heard the [inaugural] address, and listened Hoover out and Roosevelt in. Let's hope something moves now. I wonder." But his resentment of the political revolution the Depression had brought on would not soon abate. When a labor riot erupted in Minneapolis in 1935, he gloated, "Even the liberal regime has its troubles."

During the 1938 slump in the Roosevelt recovery effort, he took some pleasure in a parody of the Twenty-third Psalm circulating in Republican circles at the time. It began, "Mr. Roosevelt is my shepherd, I am in want," and concluded,

> Surely unemployment and poverty will follow me
> all the days of my life
> And I will dwell in a mortgaged house forever.[14]

Whatever the progress of FDR's New Deal, financial strains in Blackmun's family had hardly ceased with his graduation from law school. Harry's parents had provided him with financial assistance while he was at Harvard. But when Corwin Blackmun asked his son for money on the morning of September 27, 1933, Harry's obviously deep resentments of his father, if not his family, came bubbling to the surface in a revealing diary entry he wrote that same afternoon.

> This morning first thing Dad asked me for $300.00. I knew it was coming eventually. Perhaps I am very selfish and all that, but I am a little disturbed at the way the family has been hinting of late about how much money they borrowed to put me thru school. They really did not send me so much. I realize too that things are rough now and that Dad is in bad shape, but I also know that I shall never get this amount back ever. Dad is no producer and during these last years of inactivity he has done nothing to improve, to better himself. It has been spent in sleep and complaining and one never gets anywhere on that basis. I will hand it over, but it wrecks my own plans, puts me into a jam on my insurance and in paying off of my own notes, and absolutely upsets any plans that I may ever have had of getting married. I am tied down now to support the family. [Sister] Betty I want to go thru school, but——. Never can I remember a time when Dad was ever a step ahead of the world; he was always worrying and stewing about when he should get the instant batch of bills paid off. Well, so it goes. I am writing this this afternoon more to get it off my mind than anything else. It

sounds bad, but I am quite disturbed. Buying that house was a messy mistake, and maintaining and operating that car the way it is operated is an unnecessary expense.[15]

Justice Blackmun was hardly the first prominent figure to consider his father a failure. But few have left such feelings so exposed for public review. Nor was Harry's disappointment with his father limited to his shortcomings as a family provider. Apparently, during a 1931 trip to Idaho, Corwin Blackmun had been sentenced to six months and a $300 fine for violation of the National Prohibition Act. After he had served a substantial portion of his sentence and assisted in preventing a jail break, President Hoover, on Christmas Eve 1931, commuted his sentence to time served and remitted the fine. By that point, Prohibition violations were rampant— almost a badge of honor. But his son, not to mention his devout wife, no doubt viewed his offense with disdain.[16]

For Harry and his mother, however, a Prohibition conviction could not have been nearly so disturbing as another revelation that came to light in early 1933. In his diary, Blackmun termed February 20 of that year "one of the toughest days I have ever lived." During a conference that day with his father's physician, who mistook Harry for his patient's brother, not his son, the doctor revealed that Corwin Blackmun was suffering from a venereal disease. Harry, characteristically, summarized the conversation for his diary in clinical detail. "[Dr. Hammes] declared that it was syphilis, centered in the spinal fluid; that it has three possible locations, the brain, the spine, the blood; that Dad admitted having a chancre back in 1918; that his Wasserman spinal was continually positive, [though] considerably improved between 1926 and 1927; that his blood Wasserman of the latter date was questionable; that if the trouble lay in his teeth, he would get well."[17]

Harry was frantic. "It was like a blow between the eyes....I was like a whipped dog. They had told Dad he would go blind. His eyes are now bothering him, six years later. I am worried about contact with Betty and Mums. And where in hell would Dad ever pick such a thing up?" Seemingly dubious of the doctor's findings, Corwin Blackmun resented having to pay anything for the diagnosis and had even threatened a malpractice suit. But he was "glad to have it settled," Harry told his diary, when he learned that night that his son had paid the doctor $50. The medical fee, of course, was the least of Harry's worries. "Dad is not well, and I wonder. Good lord, what that may develop into!! The old world is full of trouble. I asked Dad what their diagnosis had been [originally] and was told that they had said it was a mere spinal infection. Hammes said Dad knew. Does he disbelieve them or has he kept it from me....Why have not I been told of this. I shall quiz Mother when Dad is away this week." Harry had spent that evening with friends. "[But] my mind was too far afield for talking intelligently. This whole thing bids fair to break and tumble dreams of years."[18]

By the next day, Blackmun had resolved to "investigate syphilis myself, a bit, perhaps see Dr. Hammes again, and then draw my conclusions. Just the same, the world is troublous." Apparently, his father's condition proved less serious than initially feared. At least, there were no more diary entries on the subject.[19]

Concerns about his father and his duties as clerk did not deter Harry from an active social life. In late July before his clerkship began, Blackmun, Warren Burger, and several other friends made what, for Harry, was his first camping trip to northern Minnesota—"expeditioning," as Burger put it. The following summer included a canoe trip into Canada. "My beard needs shaving, for it has developed greatly," he boasted to his diary during that excursion. "I am quite proud of it and have far exceeded the others." After an outing with Dietrich Lange, his high school principal, which he pronounced "one of the finest days I have spent in me life," he exclaimed, "what a relief from law[!]" At every opportunity, moreover, he was on the tennis, handball, or badminton court.[20]

Harry also regularly escorted his mother and dates to motion pictures, plays, symphony concerts, and similar events. He and his mother remained avid moviegoers. He even compiled a list of "Good Photoplays I Have Seen," beginning with *Birth of a Nation* and continuing with the list until 1950. His diary entries also rated the films he saw. He liked *Gold Diggers of 1933* but did "not place it on a par with '42d Street.'" After seeing a Marlene Dietrich film, he declared to his diary that "'La Dietrich' is all beauty and can do everything." Concerts did not escape his judgment either. "We all had dinner at the Forum in Minneapolis, to give Mother a treat....Then to the Symphony to hear an all-Strauss program. I found it great, for it was light." A Minneapolis Symphony program that included selections by Wagner, Schubert, and Berlioz he pronounced "perfect."[21]

Blackmun and Warren Burger had resumed their friendship on Harry's return from Cambridge. "My eyes went bad today," Blackmun reported in one July 1933 diary entry, "but the evening worked out for Warren dropped in and we sat on the porch chewing the fat for most of the evening. The evening star was beautiful. I do like the summertime." That September, Burger told Harry that his engagement to Elvera Stromberg of St. Paul would be announced in October and that they were to be married in November. "It made quite an effect upon me, for that is the beginning of things and the breakup," he wrote in his diary. "She is a peach of a girl, too, and I wish I had one like her. I phoned [Elvera] and extended my felicitations, which I think she appreciated." Soon Burger asked his friend to be best man at the November nuptials, a small affair at the home of the bride's parents. "I followed Warren about ten paces and [we] were up to the front of the room in no time.... The Lutheran ceremony itself was very impressive.... As usual, when someone close to me is married, it 'got' me a little. It is a solemn and awful ceremony, for large are the promises made. And how worthwhile it seems to have kept one's self clean and pure and to have someone who loves you as dearly as you do her. There are a few things in life worthwhile, after all." Later Harry watched as the couple climbed into Warren's old Model-T, freshly retrieved from a repair shop, for a short drive to an area inn for their wedding night, followed by a trip to Chicago for the World's Fair and then to Washington. Burger's law firm had given him $50 and a month off, Blackmun noted, "so they may even wander South." As they drove off, Harry thought, "My friend's gone down with a strange woman, and I'm left alone."[22]

Blackmun clerked with Judge Sanborn for seventeen months. His diary entries suggest that he may not have given the position the total dedication modern judges almost invariably expect of their law clerks. After one late-night outing, he promised himself that he would go to bed early the next night. "[I] even nodded at work again with the Judge just across the table from me!! Not so good." "I should have worked with the Judge this afternoon," he wrote one "beautiful Saturday,...but I left early and walked home instead, taking the usual hour. I am getting a hankering to learn chess." After the judge and his secretary left town for a term of court in St. Louis, he wrote, "Alone at the fort....Accordingly, I spent most of the day at the Touhy trial." The judge's secretary was also skeptical about Harry's commitment. "Miss Larson and I had a bit of a set-to," one diary entry read. "She...informed me that I had things pretty soft around here. No words flew particularly, but I believe she was upset."[23]

At times, Blackmun seemed overwhelmed by the duties of a judge and doubtful of his success as a clerk. "Gosh," he wrote in April 1933, "there is so much for one to know [in order to be] a judge. I feel so damn incompetent and illiterate." But he hardly limited his loathing to himself and his family. After he attended a bar association dinner, he revealed to his diary, "I was disgusted with the mess, as I have been at every bar dinner I have attended. What a world we are living in, a world of morons, crooks, and selfishness." When memorial services honoring Civil War veterans did not go off smoothly, he wrote, "Bungling, and moronic is mankind. How convinced I am of that."[24]

Whatever Miss Larson's misgivings about Blackmun, Judge Sanborn seemed more than satisfied with his clerk. When Harry turned in his proposed opinion for a property dispute case, the judge, he proudly recorded in his diary, "accepted it flatly as far as the law was concerned and made some change in language only because, he said, he just would not so express himself. I feel quite proud and good about it. He said it was a good analysis." Following a practice Blackmun would emulate as a justice, Sanborn, immediately after he and his colleagues discussed and voted on a case in conference, shared the outcome with Harry. "Ninety-five percent of the cases," Blackmun later said, "it was the way his vote was, initially, so it didn't surprise me."[25]

Sanborn also took a personal interest in Harry. "He was particularly nice to me," Blackmun later said. "I don't know whether it was because he was childless or what. He had a place on the St. Croix river, a very nice home actually. He and Mrs. Sanborn would let me go weekends up there by myself and just get out in the woods, it is a lovely place. He liked the out of doors, he was a great canoeist and got me interested in canoeing."[26]

Judge Sanborn probably would have been happy for Blackmun to continue clerking into 1934. But whether out of concern about his seemingly permanent obligations to his parents or simply a desire to get on with his life, Harry decided to leave his clerkship at the end of 1933.

Toward that end, he began making contact with local firms. He also had an opportunity to go to Washington and work in the Roosevelt administration. One of Blackmun's friends at Harvard Law School, although two years' Harry's senior, was Charles E. Wyzanski Jr., who eventually would become one of the most distinguished federal trial judges, serving from 1941 until his death in 1986 on the federal district court in Boston. In 1933, Wyzanski became solicitor in the U.S. Department of Labor. He wanted Blackmun to join him there, and while acknowledging that "a certain number of political ramifications" meant that he could not "definitely guarantee" his friend a position, he was "rather sure that if you wanted to come I could put you through on the basis of your record." When Blackmun ultimately turned the offer down, Wyzanski conceded that he was "not sure that, looking at it impartially, you decided unwisely. From my experience I should say that work for a Judge is infinitely better training than work in an administrative branch of the government."[27]

In 1934, Wyzanski again tried to lure Blackmun to Washington and the Department of Labor. On this occasion, the future justice conceded that he was "tempt[ed]...exceedingly" by the offer "to plunge into the center of activity at Washington, lend my own meager aid in the creation of constructive legislation, and to take a chance on the future developing itself," not to mention the opportunity of working with Wyzanski "and so many others whom [sic] I know are very great attractions, indeed." But once more, he declined. Since January 1934 he had been doing tax work with a Minneapolis firm that he considered "the best...in this part of the country." He thus questioned whether "a year or two" in Washington would advance his career. "Will it, in fact, afford me any professionally meaningful thing other than a very pleasant period of work and the satisfaction that comes from participating in such work?" Perhaps hopeful, however unrealistically, that the Republicans would regain control of Washington in the 1936 elections, he was also doubtful that he should give up whatever career progress he had made in Minneapolis "unless I were fairly certain that in a year or two I would not be searching for a job." He had promised to talk with Judge Sanborn, "who is an invaluable adviser to me," before making a final decision. But "resolving the matter purely from a selfish angle," he ultimately "hesitate[d] to lose what little progress I have made here" for an exciting but more uncertain future in Washington.[28]

The Dorsey Firm

The firm Blackmun joined when his clerkship with Judge Sanborn ended was Junell, Driscoll, Fletcher, Dorsey and Barker, the Minneapolis firm he had approached unsuccessfully while finishing law school. Through much of its modern history, James Dorsey would be the lead partner in the firm's title, and it would simply be known as the Dorsey firm. Harry had first become acquainted with several of the firm's lawyers through their involvement in proceedings involving Wilbur B. Foshay, a prominent but failed area developer whose enterprises had gone into receivership. Judge Sanborn had been in charge of several of the Foshay receiverships, and when elevated to the Eighth Circuit, he was permitted to continue presiding in those cases. "The result," Blackmun later said, "was that regularly people from the Dorsey office would come to St. Paul and his chambers to get orders signed or to have short hearings....I got to know them fairly well, rather welcomed them." That Judge Sanborn was handling the receiverships could not have hurt either. Eventually, Blackmun was asked if he were interested in joining the firm.[29]

At that time, the firm had only fifteen to twenty lawyers. But it was the largest and most prominent in Minneapolis. When called for an initial interview, Blackmun met with John Junell, "the head guy." Junell was a graduate of the University of Michigan Law School, and Harry had been advised to praise the school and Michigan's upper peninsula, from which Junell hailed. He did, and the two "got along very well. He turned me over to a couple of his partners at that time, and they were nice enough to ask me to come." On September 12, 1933, Harry voted against repeal of Prohibition in a referendum the state had called to test voter feelings on the issue. Then he had a meeting with Jim Dorsey, whom he "saw...to be a regular 1898 crew type of a man...very pleasant." Dorsey introduced Blackmun to others in the office, and negotiations began. Harry was also talking with members of other firms, and he found the high-handed bargaining tactics of one firm in particular offensive. "That damn outfit," he wrote in his diary. "But he knows the Junell offer brews. I will get a job yet." On December 28, two days before his clerkship was scheduled to end, he had another meeting with Dorsey and "the great JJ." After "the usual fight talk," Harry was offered a position starting at a salary higher than he had expected. "It nearly floored me. They are putting me at the same place I would have been had I been there from the time I started with the Judge....I observe that nearly everyone there is a law review man of one school or another. And little I coming in!"[30]

Blackmun told John Junell that he would talk over the offer with Judge Sanborn and "let him know." But he had already made up his mind. "I shall take it,...though it is a bad time to leave the Judge out in the cold." When he and Sanborn spoke the next morning, the judge was enthusiastic, telling his clerk "to go to it, that it was the opportunity I have been waiting for, and that it should not be passed up." Sanborn did suggest that Harry try the position out for thirty days and then return to his chambers if he did not like it. "Meanwhile he would hire no one for that time. What a prince of men he is! He says little but does much. I feel I have made a friend there, and I know he has." The day before his initial interview with the Dorsey firm, he and Warren Burger had lunch. Now he told his friend about the offer "and found him jubilant about it."[31]

The next day, Harry worked "like the devil" to finish a memorandum for Judge Sanborn, completing the task at 6:15 that evening. When Miss Larson "took her leave," she "threatened weeping so she said. She has been a good scout to me." He and Sanborn then talked for a time and left the chambers together. The future appeared bright indeed. But Blackmun seemingly could never fully relish a moment. On the way home that evening, he bought roses "for Ma." But at home he found a letter from a girl he had been dating, informing him that she planned to announce her engagement to someone else in February. His diary entry for that day concluded, "Mother broke down tonight to weep about Dad's discouragement and next year's dread. What a day—Dad down and out, no money, leaving of a good job, and the loss of a girl I had learned almost to love. And yet in a way it has been a good year."[32]

When Blackmun began his first day of law practice on January 2, 1934, the Dorsey firm occupied the thirteenth floor of the First National Soo Line Building, home of Minneapolis's First National Bank, which had been the firm's first major client, and the Minneapolis, St. Paul and Sault Sainte Marie, or Soo Line, railway. Jim Dorsey's name would not advance to first among partners until 1943. But Blackmun would later remember Dorsey as "always a dominant figure in the firm. He was an old litigator, a business-getter and was the map of Ireland on his face and had a tender concern for the young lawyers....If he ever had to let one of them go because he wasn't cutting the mustard it nearly broke his heart."[33]

At that time, the firm had only two or three young associates, "cubs," Justice Blackmun called them. Initially, Blackmun sat at a double desk with another cub facing him. When one of them was conferring with a client, the other cub was obliged to leave the room. One of the associates, he soon learned, was to be assigned to a partner who specialized in tax law. "We all groaned, none of us wanted to get into that....None of us [volunteered]. We waited for the ax to fall." Much to the relief of other cubs, the ax fell on Blackmun, even though he had never had a course in tax law. Perhaps because of his mathematics background, however, he soon learned that he had a real affinity for his new specialty. "It was the best thing that ever happened to me," he later said.[34]

That did not mean, of course, that he was invariably happy with assignments sent his way, or that the partners were always pleased with his work. "Dorsey spoiled the day," one February 1936 diary entry read, "by having me make detailed computations of corporation rates. Gosh, that gripes me, when there is so much to be done and so many others in the office who know that stuff offhand that could do it in much less time." The next month, another diary entry: "Dorsey griped me no end today when he sent me chasing for a certain Congressional record when the lawyers of the office are not half so busy as we in [the] tax department. But I should be glad he does that, perhaps. I growled to [Leland] Scott [head of the department] and thereby probably put meself in place. [Another partner] also griped me when he squandered much of my time on his personal tax matters." "The old buzzard," he complained about Dorsey on another occasion; "he makes me satisfy him with respect to every damn statement I make." When a partner critiqued a brief Harry had drafted, dismissing it as "too ABC," Blackmun was indignant. "Hell, I regard that as a compliment, not a criticism. If every brief could have that said about it, I would be satisfied." But another time he defensively wrote in his diary, "I got in a bit of a jam by not having the Anderson Holding Company mess up to date. Evidently, [a client] called [a partner] to ask what the hell was being done. I got going right away, nothing prejudicial having happened anyway." On yet another occasion, a partner "hinted that [Blackmun] might have been saying too much to [a] revenue agent…who is now checking the partners' returns."[35]

Whatever the tribulations of a Dorsey firm cub, Blackmun's advancement there was apparently never in doubt. When state businessmen asked the firm to prepare tax legislation favorable to their interests for submission to the Minnesota legislature, Hugh Barber, the firm member principally responsible for drafting legislation for legislators and client groups, quickly enlisted Blackmun in the effort. "I had a date arranged…for tonight," he recorded in his diary one Friday evening, "but when I was in the midst of my preparatory bath, Hugh Barber called and drafted me for a tough weekend of labor." The bill was to be ready the following Tuesday morning. Harry worked until 11:30 Saturday night and midnight on Sunday. "A beautiful Sunday and St. Patrick's Day," he complained, "but I was little aware of it.…What labor. This drawing of bills has its possibilities, but it is thankless work."[36]

Minnesota legislators must have liked his work. The next Friday, Barber informed Blackmun that the firm was to draft an omnibus tax bill for a subcommittee of the state house of representatives. During a meeting with legislators to determine what sorts of provisions they wanted, the future justice "found most of them woefully ignorant of the laws they are trying to amend, arrogant, narrowminded, and politicians to the last degree. It is such legislators that almost makes one desire a dictator." He and Barber also conferred with a group of Twin Cities department store heads about the kind of sales tax they would find easiest to administer. "Again arrogance to some degree. Why are humans made that way?" With Blackmun concentrating on amendments to the state income tax, and Barber on sales tax provisions, the pair worked all night, went home for a shave and a clean shirt, then presented their drafts to the subcommittee. Several legislators "wondered how in hell some of the provisions went into the bill, and said that the subcommittee had never authorized them." Barber "took hell" but was too weary to argue, instead accepting revisions that subcommittee members insisted on including in the legislation. At three o'clock that afternoon, Blackmun "hit the hay" after leaving instructions that his parents awaken him for dinner. "Evidently the folks could not arouse me, for I came to at seven AM Wednesday morning." Soon, a grateful Barber telephoned, asking that the young associate join him for a round of golf at the Minneapolis Golf Club. "We were the only ones on the course," Blackmun informed his diary. "I started calling him Hugh and found him a good egg. Caddies and poor golf, but it did us good."[37]

The same year that Blackmun helped to draft the tax legislation, he also had a hand in one of the first cases argued before the U.S. Supreme Court in its magnificent new "Marble Palace" across the street from the Capitol. In *Douglas v. Willcuts* (1935), the firm represented a recently divorced husband, arguing that alimony paid to his former wife should be regarded as income on which she would be obliged to pay taxes. Speaking through Chief Justice Charles Evans Hughes, the Court unanimously rejected that interpretation of federal law. According to the report of the case, Leland Scott argued the case for the husband, and Clark Fletcher, another partner, joined Scott on the brief submitted in the case. "Well," Justice Blackmun explained years later, "Mr. Fletcher hadn't anything to do with the case but they had to put somebody on the brief. I'd written the brief but I wasn't admitted to the Supreme Court Bar so they couldn't put my name on it."[38]

In 1943, Blackmun was involved in *Dobson v. Commissioner of Internal Revenue*, another complicated dispute between a firm client and the IRS over computation of federal income taxes. The firm won for their client in the federal Tax Court, but the Court of Appeals for the Eighth Circuit reversed. Even though the partners considered the case a "flat loser," they petitioned the Supreme Court for review. "I thought for a while that maybe they'd send me down to argue it because they had nothing to lose if it was a loser." Instead, William L. Prosser, a University of Minnesota law professor who was then in the firm and would soon become the preeminent national authority on tort law, was assigned to argue the case before the justices. Prosser, Blackmun later said, "didn't know anything about taxes. He knew just about as much as I did when I went into the tax department" nearly a decade earlier. Leland Scott and Blackmun attempted to prepare their colleague, "tried to tell him what this case was all about. [But] the office generally said, ... don't be concerned if you lose it because it's a loser. Well, it turned out that he won it, nine–zip, to his utter amazement. ... Of course, Bill Prosser, being Bill, would never let the rest of us forget about it." After World War II, when Blackmun was teaching as an adjunct at Minnesota, he and Prosser had the same students in back-to-back classes. "And pretty soon I discovered that Bill was insulting me from the beginning of the hour to the end of the hour, as to my character generally, as to my inability to teach classes and the like. So I returned the favor. We had a lot of fun."[39]

Miss Clark

When Blackmun became a junior partner in 1939, his professional future seemed secure. His father's financial situation was still a constant source of strain. In June 1935 Corwin Blackmun was laid off from his most recent job. His employer attributed it to the general state of the economy, but Harry suspected that his father had simply "been saying too much. He has a terrifically inflexible code of ethics, which is all very fine and wholesome in its place, but it does not protect jobs when one is desperately in need of them. That such things exist does not speak well for our system of existence, but they do exist. What will be done I do not know. I am thankful that I have my work. If it goes, we are thru."[40]

But Harry did now have a good job with excellent prospects for a secure future. Only a few days before his father's most recent disturbing revelation, in fact, he had bought his first car, a new Ford coupe complete with rumble seat. The transaction had hardly gone smoothly. The first vehicle delivered to Blackmun "was a wreck, with gashes in the finish on both doors, green instead of yellow wheels and two cuts in the upholstery. We would not accept it, and I am more than ever disgusted." Even when the car he wanted finally arrived in good shape, he remained irritated with one Peterson, who had accepted Harry's money to broker the deal, then ended up owing money to his client. That fall, Peterson died. "That is the end of that hope of getting anything [from Peterson]," Harry rather uncharitably recorded in his diary. "I must absorb the loss and shut up."[41]

Whatever his frustrations, Blackmun was thrilled with his purchase. Pronouncing it "as sweet a running little boat as can be," he quickly decided that it was "just as I want it, with rumble and all," adding, "We rode tonight." Duly recorded in his diary were the new vehicle's license plate number (B512680) and even its engine number (1933829).[42]

Now, it seemed, Blackmun lacked but one trapping of the successful professional: a wife and children. During his clerkship with Judge Sanborn and early years with the Dorsey firm, Harry dated regularly, his diary entries dotted with references to that aspect of his social life—and his at times blunt assessments of the women in his life. Hardly a romantic, he declared one November 1932 date "very sweet, very much like every other woman, and with a bit of foul-breath tonight." Another, Mary Townsend, he termed "one beautiful brunette." Yet another woman alerted Harry to rumors "that I have been wandering around with a little Catholic girl. Not so good, such rumors. I must stop that." "That moon wanes," he decided after one date, "though she is a good kid." One date told him that she was breaking up with her boyfriend, but Blackmun was skeptical. "I am sure she will return to Joe. And then it will be as strong as ever. He is not good enough for her. Home late, with no monkey business whatever." He seemed impressed with another girl he described as "of the masculine, efficient type, owns a PBK [key], and drives her own Ford." Yet another he termed "not a pretty girl" and "a Swede," but conceded that she had "poise and brains, I think." A woman named Ginger he found "pretty and attractive, but wonder[ed] how deep she really is." He seemed particularly attracted to Gretchen Kollner, a singer in local productions, but frustrated as well. "Damn, that wench tipples me," he confessed following one of her performances, "more than anyone I have ever known." After a date with Gretchen, he still found her "hellishly attractive to me, but a plain damn fool in search of a good time and money. She runs me a merry chase, and I should not bother with her—but I do." In less than a year, however, he had decided, following dinner with several others at Gretchen's home, that "the old spark is gone and I am no longer comfortable with her. I found Ruthy Newman much more attractive."[43]

A lengthy hospital stay in October 1935 provided Harry with other date prospects and much feminine attention. Still enjoying ill health, he telephoned his physician friend John Briggs after a sleepless night aggravated by a sore throat, draining tonsils, and a swollen neck. Briggs ordered him to St. Johns Hospital for treatment of strep throat combined with, Blackmun informed his diary, "possible mastoidal complications. Ho hum." There "followed nine days of throat irrigating, tough swallowing, themalities, thantis lozenges, some tough sleeps, but some good ones, too.

I walked in my sleep on two successive nights due to dope they had given me." Briggs "termed the mess a retrophyingeal abcess, streptococcus throat with a 33% fatality record." The patient not only lived, but clearly relished the attention of Judge Sanborn, Warren Burger, other friends, and especially his nurses. The nurses "would always congregate in my room when they had a moment off," he told his diary, "and it was fun. I must take some of them out." By that point he had been adjunct teaching at the St. Paul College of Law. Burger and Martin Hurley, another friend, covered his classes. When Blackmun received a stipend from the law school, he sent his friends checks to cover their teaching for him. "Hurley returned his check to me," Harry noted in his diary, "Warren did not. But that is all right too."[44]

Blackmun apparently never dated any of his nurses. But during this same period he and a New York woman, identified only as "Sherry" in numerous diary entries, had begun to fall deeply in love. Asked during his oral history interviews whether he had ever "seriously date[d]" anyone other than Mrs. Blackmun, he not only conceded that he had, but said that he remained in contact with "one, in particular," adding, "She was a nice person. She died recently." The justice's longtime Supreme Court secretary Wanda Martinson remembered that he was "saddened and sentimental" when he learned of her death. She may well have been the "Sherry" of his diary.[45]

Harry apparently met Sherry while he was at Harvard. When he returned to Minnesota, they continued to correspond. His diary entry for September 23, 1932, read in part, "I got one of the sweetest letters from Sherry I have ever received. She is a peach of a kid. And yet, our friendship was a most curious one. I feel she learned to care for me a little bit, anyway. But hell, out here there is little left." A year later, their correspondence continued. "Wrote Sherry a long letter and perhaps said more than was good for me."[46]

In July 1935, shortly after purchasing his new Ford, Harry and his sister, Betty, made a road trip. Betty had not been feeling well when they set out. Harry was alarmed, but soon reported to his diary that she "was feeling better, which pleased me, for the curse had hit her, as she says." At Boston, they attended the dog races at Suffolk Downs. "What an experience that was. I lost a couple of bucks....Any way, I know the parimutual system now." In New York, they met college friends at an apartment. "We had much bull throwing. The usual remarks about my [ample] butt crept in, so I felt at home." Later, he telephoned Sherry and made a date for lunch. "How good it was to see her. Smoother than ever, smoking too much, but very much the same old gal." At dinner that evening, Harry learned that Sherry was planning to be married in the fall to a man she had known for years, "that she was not in love with him, that she felt something had to be done....I said what I thought. We drove out the Island afterward under a very swell moon, near Fort Teton and watched the water until we were told to move. Then hamburgers and milk and home after four. It was a long way [back to his friend's apartment in] Brooklyn but I had much to think about."[47]

A month later, Sherry went out to Minnesota for a visit with her anxious suitor. "Lord, how I hope I can make her time pleasant. It seems to me so far just to come to see me. I am terribly complimented, but somewhat worried"—particularly, he might have added, about his parents, with whom he still lived. Harry gave Sherry his room and slept on the parlor floor. "The folks were very hospitable and I only hope the hell they stay that way. I doubt myself if they are able to do so. Frankly, I know they do not like the arrangement of her coming here just to see me but therein is where they are very narrow." That evening, he and Sherry drove to the Radisson Inn, "had a snifter and a whale of a good talk....I felt closer to her than I have ever been." That night, she told Harry, was to have been her wedding night. "So she did have a reason for coming." She had also brought with her a name for his new car, "Mignon." "I like it," Harry wrote in his diary, "and it shall stay." One evening they went to a lodge, where they encountered another couple, with whom they shared a room for the night. "People around wondered, perhaps, but let them wonder." He and Sherry talked until very late. "I like her a lot and am learning to know her when she has that snooty external appearance off." The next day, he talked "more freely and intimately with Sherry than ever before....I hope to hell she is having a good time."[48]

For Harry, the remainder of Sherry's visit was a mixture of bliss and tension. When she asked him what he disliked in her, he naïvely responded, telling her that she was "brutally frank [and] smoked too much." His own candor, he quickly decided, "was a mistake and I will never hear the end of it." But one night they drove along the old dirt road to Hastings. "I told Sherry I loved her and had her response. Life is good." The next evening, they went "out to our usual road where things were very sweet. I do think she has fallen a bit but I want it perfect." The day before her departure was nearly perfect, an afternoon of canoeing with Betty and a night of dinner and dancing. "She looked great in her white evening gown, and the world was good. She gave me a sentiment-full HS ring which I shall wear on my watch chain....It was raining [hard] afterward, but the rain seemed good in Mignon. Back to our old spot again. I gave her a pencil and my fraternity pin and guard. She is the first one ever to wear it save Betty....She tells me she loves me. She was wondrously sweet to me."[49]

The atmosphere at home, however, had become increasingly tense during Sherry's visit. After Harry recorded one tender evening in his diary, he added, "The folks will not approve." The reason for his parents' attitude was unclear. Perhaps Sherry was too worldly or too "eastern" for them; perhaps they feared the effect a marriage would have on Harry's role as a family provider. In any event, when the couple returned home after Sherry's last evening with him, "the folks were positively frigid and made me madder at them than I have ever been in my life. Courtesy and civility are the least one can expect. They were neither. The girl went away broken up because of it. And little old Betty was crushed. I know she and Sherry were much attracted to one another." At the airport the next day, Harry gave her an orchid, "the first I have ever given a girl," and she told him that she had worn his pin the previous night. "Sweet kid. It was so damn hard to see her go....Damn, but I love her. I shall never forget that plane going over the West Saint Paul bluffs."[50]

Following her visit, Harry and Sherry continued to correspond and telephone. When the press of his law practice reduced the quantity and quality of his letters, she telephoned him from New York while he was in conference with a client. "She appeared very piqued, observed that she had never known of such indifference, etc., etc. I was not in a position to talk and it was somewhat disconcerting....The little devil." In March 1936 he indicated in his diary that he had managed to write her a "meager note" after attempting "for a long while to get something said in a definite way," then added, "I am concerned about things there and must make up my mind soon." Later that month he wrote a long letter to her, then told his diary, "I do not know how she will take it." But that September he saw her during a trip east for a Harvard class reunion. "Sherry and I were close tonight. I know, and I know definitely that I love her. I am pretty sure, too, of her love for me." A week later, he pronounced that trip "the best vacation I have ever had."[51]

As the responsibilities of his law practice grew, and whatever psychic needs his diary had long served perhaps diminished, the detailed entries that he had so meticulously compiled much of his life since 1919 gradually subsided and then ended altogether. His diary thus contains no account of the ultimate fate of his relationship with Sherry.

At least part of the answer, however, lay with the events of one fateful day in 1937. Whatever his skill, Blackmun had remained a vigorous competitor in squash and tennis matches, his exploits regularly recorded in the articles and photographs of area publications. One Sunday morning he and a friend were playing tennis on a local court. "That was August one, nineteen hundred and [thirty]-seven and it was a blistering hot, Sunday morning," the justice recalled years later. "I had a regular Sunday morning tennis date with a friend of mine whose tennis was about the same as mine.... We got three sets under our belt and down the court,... in the far end there were two young women playing tennis and I suggested let's go down and see if they'll play a set of doubles, we can ease off that way. So we went down and they said sure. And Dottie was one of them. She walked to the other side of the net and I just followed her...over there because I thought her legs were rather pretty and after we had that set, why, we went and took a swim. Both of us were pretty hot and very offensive, I suppose, at that point."[52]

Dottie, or "Miss Clark," as the justice affectionately referred to her, was Dorothy Eugenia Clark, a native of Cloquet, near Duluth. Her parents "didn't have any money," and after high school she had taken a secretarial course at Macalester College, then became secretary to a prominent St. Paul businessman. Not long after she and Harry met, he took her to a Dorsey firm party on Lake Minnetonka, where one of the partners had a summer house. When Blackmun introduced Dottie to Jim Dorsey, "he looked her over from top to toe and his greeting was, 'How do you do Miss Clark? When are you and Harry going to get married?' Which, of course, translated means that he approved. So it was." By all accounts, Dottie was—and would always be—as vivacious, optimistic, and spontaneous as Blackmun was reserved, repressed, and methodical. She also enjoyed sports; at least one tennis doubles match that they lost to another couple was recorded in a local paper. Harry was clearly smitten. But they dated for four years, two after he had made junior partner, before the cautious future justice finally considered himself sufficiently secure to propose marriage. "If Dottie were here," he later said, "she would make a joke and say that I proposed to her in bed.…What that means is that she was ill at the time and I went over to see her and thought she was in a helpless condition and so I, while she was stretched out in bed I asked the fatal question."[53]

Harry and Dottie were married on June 21, 1941. By that point, as the nation moved closer to total involvement in world war, Corwin Blackmun's unit had been dispatched to Riverside, California, and Theo Blackmun had joined her husband there. In April, Harry wrote Frank Sloss, a San Francisco attorney and friend, informing Sloss that because of his parents' situation, and for "various other [unstated] reasons," he and Dottie were considering being married in Los Angeles. Blackmun was interested in California's marriage laws, specifically "whether we can be married out there without too much legal ado." Sloss responded on April 30, listing two requirements that could be inconvenient. One was the three-day waiting period for securing a marriage license. The other, adopted by the state in 1939, was the requirement that a syphilis test be administered no more than thirty days before issuance of a license. On May 12, Harry wrote Sloss again, thanking him for the information but indicating that "inasmuch as my father anticipates being ordered into the Mohave Desert for firing [exercises] around June 21st, we have concluded not to come to California to be married."[54]

Instead, he and Dottie were married in a small ceremony at his parents' St. Paul home. Blackmun had been Warren Burger's best man at Burger's marriage several years earlier, but he chose John Briggs to assume that role in his marriage. Perhaps to his relief, given the stress his parents, especially his father, had so often caused him over the years, neither his father nor, apparently, his mother was present for the ceremony, although Theo Blackmun did visit St. Paul for over a month later that summer.[55]

The Dorsey firm had generously given Harry a month off. Following their wedding night at the Kahler Hotel in Rochester (the groom had

requested "a comfortable double room for myself and Mrs. Blackmun"),
they traveled in the car Sherry had dubbed Mignon south to New Orleans
and then over to Miami and the Broadmoor by the Sea on Miami Beach,
"a hotel way out in the hinterland at that time; of course, it's all built
up now, but we rather liked it because it was so far out and quiet, and
we enjoyed the ocean." On their return, they became the first occupants
of a new apartment at 2445 Third Avenue, South, near the Minneapolis Institute of Art. They were in their apartment the next December
when news of the Pearl Harbor attack came over the radio. Facing the
probability of military service, Blackmun later recalled, "Dottie and
I decided we had a little time coming and [went] back to Miami Beach....
I can remember staying there at the same hotel with...soldiers patrolling
the beaches, because there were rumors of German submarines off the
coast."[56]

"Those were tough times," he later said, "and some of my young
friends, young lawyers were lost in the war." Blackmun, however, managed
to avoid service in World War II, although he had been a member of the
Minnesota National Guard in 1927–30, while a student at Harvard. When
first called up by his draft board, he was classified 4-F, probably because
of his weak eyes and chronic back pain. When called up again in the fall
of 1942, he wrote the board a letter. Noting his previous draft classification in effect exempting him from the draft for medical reasons, and that
he was "a practicing attorney having many cases in my hands in various
stages of preparation," he "respectfully request[ed] that [he] be given a
pre-induction physical examination." In "fairness to my clients," he added,
"it is desirable that I have as much notice of my induction as possible, so
that the transfer of these matters to other attorneys may be effected upon
adequate notice to all concerned. I wish also to avoid the situation where,
having transferred all of my pending work to other attorneys, I might find
myself disqualified from service by reason of the physical examination at
the time of induction."[57]

Blackmun was not drafted, but in 1944 his Harvard professor Barton
Leach contacted him about joining the legal section of the Army Air
Corps's Operations Analysis Division, which Leach had helped to organ-
ize and headed. The division included a number of nationally prominent lawyers, among them John Marshall Harlan, with whom Blackmun

would briefly serve on the Supreme Court. Blackmun was at least sufficiently intrigued to write David Raudenbush, a Minnesota friend then serving with the Army Air Corps in Florida. "Operations Analysis covers practically the entire waterfront of AAF operations and activities," Raudenbush replied. Without knowing what particular job Leach had in mind for his friend, he added, "It would be impossible for me to make any comments which would be helpful to you in making up your mind." Blackmun had apparently inquired whether the position would be "worthwhile" and "satisfying." "There is no question but that this work I am engaged in is 'worthwhile' in the sense that it has to be done by somebody. By the same token it is 'satisfying' if…one bears in mind that this is the army in the midst of a war for which it was not initially prepared. A perfectionist…would be disappointed in much that he saw and heard. A realist would find plenty to admire." Blackmun decided to stay with his firm, and the war was soon over.[58]

While her husband was facing possible military conscription, Dottie Blackmun had become pregnant with the first of their three daughters. Apparently, Harry Blackmun was truly methodical in every aspect of his life. Their first daughter, Nancy Clark, was born on July 8, 1943, followed by Sally Ann on July 7, 1947, and Susan Manning, or Susie, on July 1, 1949. Soon, the young family had outgrown their small apartment. "[When] the babies arrived at their respective times," as Harry later put it, "it got a little bit crowded. When Susie arrived, we knew we had to do something." In August following Susie's birth, construction began on a $40,000 home in Golden Valley, a Minneapolis suburb.[59]

In March 1945, Dottie's mother suffered a severe stroke. Harry opposed both his wife's frequent train trips to care for her ailing mother and her determination to bring her mother back to Minnesota to live. With Dottie absent, Harry began working late at the office and having dinner downtown. Although then only a toddler, their daughter Nancy, who was to become a psychologist, sensed the tension the episode created between her parents and in their home. Years later, in a collection of reminiscences drawn from people born during World War II that she coedited, Nancy wrote, "In the disagreement between my parents and in the strained period that followed, the loving heart of their romantic relationship collapsed permanently and could not be recovered."[60]

To all outward appearances, however, the Blackmuns appeared to have a perfect marriage. Harry's professional career also continued to thrive. Made a senior partner at the Dorsey firm in 1943, he had become his office's most respected tax and estates specialist, frequently lecturing on income tax regulations and related matters before a variety of groups. He had become active in the local bar as well, serving as chairman of the junior bar section of the Hennepin County (Minneapolis) Bar Association in 1939, the year he became a junior partner. He also served as president of the Harvard Club of Minnesota. Not surprisingly, most senior members of the firm still regarded him as one of the practice's "younger men" and treated him according. In 1947, Charles F. Noonan and his wife invited the "so-called 'younger men' " and their wives for a card party and ice cream social on the lawn of their home. "If you can come no response to this invitation is necessary," Noonan warned. "I have, during my social career, been deeply saddened by witty and poetic responses to similar invitations and, hence, this friendly but firm admonition. If you can come, simply keep your peace and arrive on time. If you cannot, please advise us not later than noon of November 1 as we do not want Mr. Gill, the undertaker from whom we are borrowing the chairs, to lug over more than are actually needed." In Twin Cities legal circles by that point, Blackmun had clearly arrived. Dottie quickly became a familiar figure in the social life of the area as well. One 1947 issue of the *St. Paul Pioneer Press* pictured her with others involved in planning for St. Paul's annual winter carnival. The same year, the couple became members of Minneapolis's Hennepin Avenue Methodist Church.[61]

Harry had also continued to do adjunct teaching at St. Paul College, subsequently renamed the William Mitchell College of Law, and later at the University of Minnesota's law school. Many of his diary entries indicated that he enjoyed those assignments, at least in the early days. In 1945, Minnesota law dean Everett Fraser even attempted to persuade the future justice to become a full-time member of the faculty. Harry readily conceded that he had always found the prospect of teaching law appealing, but ultimately declined the offer. "In justice to my family," he wrote Fraser, "I cannot make a change which would produce less than $10,000 per year." The dean had offered him $8,000.[62]

Mayo Clinic

In 1950, Blackmun did make a significant career change, one combining the law with his enduring interest in medicine. The Mayo Clinic in Rochester, Minnesota, ninety miles south of the Twin Cities, had enjoyed a reputation as one of the nation's premier medical centers since the early years of the twentieth century. English-born William Worrall Mayo had begun the general practice of medicine in Rochester in 1864, later forming a partnership with his two surgeon sons, William James and Charles Horace. Soon, other physicians joined the practice; by 1914, when the Mayos opened the first building formally designated the Mayo Clinic, they were treating thirty thousand patients a year and offering complete care for practically any condition. By 1964, the number of patients had grown to 220,000. In the beginning, the Mayos formed a close working relationship with St. Mary's Hospital in Rochester; later, Methodist Hospital was constructed in Rochester primarily to serve the patients of the clinic when the Mayos chose not to establish their own hospital.[63]

Mayo's legal interests were represented for years by a firm in Winona, Minnesota. But in 1949, Harry J. Harwick, its administrative head, decided that the clinic needed a larger firm. One day, Blackmun recalled years later, a member of the clinic staff came to the Dorsey firm with a minor tax problem. Leland Scott was home ill that day, and Blackmun handled that first contact with the clinic, a minor gift tax issue for Donald C. Balfour, one of the clinic's leading surgeons. "I've always felt it was rather a…test case.…Out of that grew more and more things for Mayos, many of which landed on my desk or, particularly, on Mr. Scott's." One of Mayo's neurosurgeons liked Blackmun's work in preparing his will, and soon five other neurosurgeons had him draft their wills as well. By 1949, the future justice was devoting about 60 percent of his time to Mayo matters, going to Rochester each month for several days of full appointments with clinic staff.[64]

A. J. Lobb had acted as resident counsel at Mayo's for a number of years. As Lobb neared retirement, Blackmun seemed a natural choice to be his replacement. When Harry Harwick visited Minneapolis to discuss the matter, Blackmun replied that he would need to talk with Judge Sanborn and Jim Dorsey, but was told that the clinic had already contacted both men. Harwick generously gave Blackmun eight months to make a decision. "I fussed and stewed about it," he later said. "It was a difficult decision because the sun was rising after the great Depression. The firm looked ahead to...prosperous years and all the cubs I worked with were [still] there....Of course, they stayed on and retired eventually—they're all multimillionaires. I know they are." At one point, Harry and Dottie spent a weekend at Chicago's Palmer House hotel, talking "for hours about...the pros and cons" of Harwick's proposition. They were building their dream house in Golden Valley; a move to Rochester would mean construction of another home. "I wouldn't get away with not having [Dottie] have her house. It also meant a reduction in income, immediately, as well as in the long run."[65]

Ever loyal, Dottie left the decision entirely up to her husband. During discussion about Blackmun's becoming a law professor at the University of Minnesota, Dean Everett Fraser had asked what Blackmun really wanted to do with his life. Ultimately, that became the basis for his decision to go to Rochester. "I wasn't entirely sure I wanted to be engaged solely in client care. It would have been a satisfying occupation all right, but in a way I thought I wanted to do some other things. [Dean Fraser] influenced me in that respect, as did Mr. Harwick, who said...the job is yours, you can make of it what you want. And that was pretty appealing."[66]

In January 1950, Blackmun wrote Harwick, "Assuming you are still willing, I have decided that I am interested in coming to Rochester." Characteristically, however, he emphasized that the decision had not been "easy," adding, "From my own selfish viewpoint, I trust that I am not making a grave mistake in forsaking the basic practice of my profession." He also asked that he be allowed to delay his starting date until October 1.[67]

In a separate letter, he broached what he termed a "difficult and somewhat embarrassing personal problem." The Blackmuns' Golden Valley dream house was then under construction. They hoped to move from their cramped apartment to that house in March and live there until a similar home could be constructed in Rochester. Without outside assistance, he would be unable to cover the mortgages on both houses until the Minneapolis home sold. Slade Schuster, another member of the Mayo administrative staff, "and I believe you also," Blackmun wrote Harwick, had earlier suggested that Mayo would be able to assist him in meeting "this financial obstacle," and Blackmun hoped that offer still stood. "I do not wish to come to Rochester troubled with financial worries." Were they to stay in Minneapolis, he had no doubt that he could handle the complete financing of the home there, but he did "not look forward to the thought of carrying two obligations." His move to Rochester would be "necessarily contingent," he concluded, "upon solving this problem."[68]

Harwick's response was prompt and enthusiastic. Mayo, he assured Blackmun, would be "glad" both to finance the new house in Rochester while the Minneapolis home was being sold and also to loan the clinic's new resident counsel "whatever you need over and above your own funds to complete the construction and furnishing of the home. You can write your own ticket." All staff members, Harwick added, had greeted with "enthusiasm…the fact that you might come to the clinic. You will come here with an entree, an acquaintanceship and prestige that should make things very easy for you."[69]

With their financial concerns resolved, the Blackmuns made plans for the move to Rochester, including purchase of a home site in the bucolically named Sunny Slopes development. But not without some complaining on Blackmun's part. Inquiring about one housing lot, he pointedly wrote, "Don't hit me too hard, for I am already rather prejudiced about the substantial cost of things in Rochester. We have recently completed a new home here in Minneapolis on a lot which is better than any I have found in Rochester and which cost about 50 percent of what the going rates seem to be in your city. Give me your absolute rock bottom price." When a brief item about his move appeared in a Minneapolis newspaper, he immediately wrote Harwick that he had nothing to do with the leak. "I am greatly embarrassed and distressed…for I dislike anything of this kind which is not forthcoming through authorised channels." He may also have been worried about the huge number of Rochester concerns that contacted him with various propositions. One of his colleagues in the Dorsey firm humorously wrote a Rochester banker that his friend had been inundated with letters from "insurance salesmen, food purveyors,…popcorn stand men,…and literally thousands of others, including…several bootblacks."[70]

Blackmun began work at Mayo in October 1950. In December the Dorsey firm hosted a dinner in his honor. He was "pleased to accept" the invitation, albeit with "some trepidation…based…on past experience at these firm gatherings." But "worn down a little…by the Mayo Clinic

'and its affiliated institutions' and their somewhat startling problems," he
hoped that he would not be "asked to perform in any way...prefer[ring
instead] to relax and enjoy the situation." His former Dorsey colleague
David Bronson had asked Blackmun to suggest a "suitable gift" for the
occasion. "I could ask that you supply the prospective new house here in
Rochester," he jokingly replied, "but because in a very real sense the firm
has already given us the Minneapolis one, I must respect the bounds of
decency and forego that small request. My personal needs are few. Miss
Clark knows about our joint ones and if you wish, might make some
suggestions. Even a doorbell would be most welcome and sufficient."[71]

The affair, held on December 1, apparently went off without a hitch.
At one point, the guests sang nineteen verses of doggerel summarizing
Blackmun's life and career after Harvard. Entitled "The Short, Sad Story
of a Lawyer or Working for Jim Dorsey," the last verse read,

> Nineteen Hundred and Fifty-one
> Went to Mayo's, the son-of-a-gun
> Went to Mayo's, the son-of-a-gun
> Working for Jim Dorsey.[72]

Blackmun's impact on the Mayo organization was not long in coming.
In January 1951, the by-laws of the Mayo Association were changed for
the first time in thirty-one years. The size of the association's board
was enlarged; lowering of the retirement age from seventy to sixty-five
(consistent with the clinic's policy for staff) obliged five long-time board
members to step down; a term of office (four years) was established for
the first time; and three prominent businessmen were added as "public"
members of the board, leaving Harry Harwick the only board member
carried over from the previous arrangement. When Harwick reached age
sixty-five in 1952, he retired. In 1953, Blackmun became a board member
and the group's secretary treasurer.[73]

Blackmun's duties as resident counsel were extensive. Once, he
prepared a lengthy memorandum regarding the implications of U.S.
citizenship and state medical licensing requirements for a number of clinic
staff members. Interestingly, given his later concern as a justice about
legal distinctions between citizens and aliens, he observed in concluding

the memorandum, "From a purely legal, as distinguished from a policy, point of view, the lack of United States citizenship in and of itself does not concern me. When it operates to prevent the licensing of an individual, it does concern me." He was also involved, of course, in clinic reactions to the complaints of patients, including one convinced that he had "lost my manhood" as a result of prostate surgery. Blackmun was equally alert to possible copyright violations involving clinic literature, among them distribution of a Mayo-recommended diet by Pan American World Airways.[74]

On occasion, Blackmun was obliged to recommend what response, if any, the clinic should make to potentially negative publicity. In 1955, the *Houston Chronicle*, in a story headlined "In Agony, Penniless Man Pleads for Death," profiled the plight of Alton Glenn, a thirty-year-old man with extremely brittle bones, who had suffered a hundred fractures during his life, the first at birth, and had become addicted to Demerol as a result of injections to relieve his chronic and intense pain. As an addict, his mother said, he was ineligible for admission to a charity hospital. In a briefer article the next day, headlined "Mayo Clinic Won't Take Houstonian," the *Chronicle* reported that a Robert E. Pye of Minneapolis had posted the money needed to fly Glenn to Rochester, but quoted Pye as saying that he had "exhausted efforts to get him in" at Mayo.[75]

When George W. Waldron, a Houston doctor formerly of Rochester, contacted the clinic about the *Chronicle* articles, Blackmun conducted an investigation. Robert Pye, it turned out, previously had been secretary of the Minnesota Bankers Association but was then executive secretary of the Minnesota 10,000 Lakes Association, a branch of the Minneapolis Chamber of Commerce. While in Texas promoting Minnesota tourism, Pye had visited the *Chronicle*'s office, where a reporter covering the Glenn story asked whether Pye might get Glenn admitted to Mayo and suggested that he cover Glenn's transportation expenses to Rochester. Pye had telephoned R. A. Bezoier, vice president of Rochester's First National Bank, asking that Bezoier contact Mayo on Glenn's behalf. Bezoier pointedly suggested that Pye contact the clinic directly or have Glenn's physician do so. The banker also told Pye that the clinic, as Blackmun later put it in a memorandum about the incident, "would not welcome any publicity on these charity cases." Pye made no attempt to contact the clinic. After the *Chronicle* stories appeared, an angry Bezoier told him that "his activity [had] resulted in great injustice to the Clinic and that if he was on a good will tour in Texas, he was certainly producing exactly the opposite result." Bezoier also exacted a promise from Pye that he would contact Blackmun. "I let Pye have the works to a degree," Blackmun later wrote, "and he sounded contrite over the phone. I frankly pointed out, as did Bezoier, that…the Clinic was embarrassed and wronged, and that Bezoier was upset, disturbed, and irritated and also embarrassed. He groaned over the phone, and was particularly distressed about Bezoier's status."[76]

In a cover letter to the memorandum that reflected the sort of skepticism about the press Blackmun would at times display as a justice, he indicated that he was maintaining a permanent "file of incidents of what I regard as press irresponsibility." At the same time, he recommended that "we take no positive action in this matter," including no "attempt to make any complaint to the newspaper at this time." Dr. Howard K. Gray of the clinic staff had expressed a desire to write a letter of acknowledgment to Dr. Waldron, the Houston physician who had alerted Gray to the newspaper stories. "I hope," Blackmun cautioned Gray, that "he does not make an issue of it with the newspaper." Later he wrote Waldron directly. "We feel strongly, of course, that nothing should be done in an attempt to correct or rectify this unfortunate publicity. Such an attempt usually compounds the situation and we are content to let the matter rest as it is." Waldron readily complied, agreeing with Blackmun that "nothing should be done," and adding, "It is a pity that the ethics of newspaper reporting have never gained the high caliber which we try to maintain in your profession or mine. Though I left Rochester more than twenty years ago I am just as proud of the Clinic's reputation as I was then and any attempt, whether willful or negligent, to mar that reputation disturbs me greatly." When Glenn was admitted to a federal hospital in Texas, Waldron notified Dr. Gray and took another potshot at the press, declaring, "The shame of the whole affair is that damage done by reckless reporting can never be corrected."[77]

About the time the controversy over Alton Glenn arose, Blackmun and the clinic's Committee on Medical Relations and the Administrative Committee also took note of an article that appeared in a New Orleans newspaper. Funds had recently been raised there to send a local teenager to Mayo's for treatment of a serious heart condition. When his physician told reporters that the patient had been sent to Rochester because adequate local facilities were not available for diagnosis of his condition, the New Orleans medical establishment protested, asserting that the surgery contemplated for the boy had been successfully performed for the past five years at the city's Charity Hospital and Ochsner Clinic. Blackmun circulated the clipping to clinic staff with the recommendation that no action be taken, but he also noted that Ochsner's public relations director, the source of the article, was a son-in-law of Dr. Alton Ochsner, that clinic's head. Typed in at the bottom of the clipping Blackmun circulated were the words "Sour grapes."[78]

The author of that bit of editorializing was no doubt Dr. James Eckman, director of publications at Mayo and one of Blackmun's close friends at the clinic. The witty Eckman seemed a perfect counterpoint to the generally reserved Blackmun. When the New Orleans story appeared, Eckman wrote his friend, "I suspected that sooner or later that Ochsner clan…would get out the Bowie knife and cut us up, but this time they slashed us real proper-like. The newspaper doubtless was delighted to serve up such a mess of paprika; but…the story could not have been written at all if some Ochsner 'spokesman' had not been willing to talk." On another occasion, Eckman composed a gag letterhead for the firm of "Eckmun, Jackmun, Hachmun & Blackmun," with a description of each partner's area of "specialty," including this one for his friend:

So he done you wrong, my dear?
Lend a wounded shell-pink ear
to H. Blackmun.[79]

As Mayo's resident counsel, Blackmun regularly gave talks to civic and bar groups, sharing his detailed knowledge of tax and estates law. He and Dottie also became heavily involved in Rochester's social and civic life. Under pressure from Mayo, he later said, he joined the Rotary Club, that citadel of American middle-class values, even becoming president of the Rochester club in 1955. His strikingly handsome bride appeared in fashion shows, served on the consumer advisory board of a local department store, organized and became president of the women's auxiliary of Rochester's Methodist Hospital, was a hostess for local balls, and was active in their Methodist congregation, the local Red Cross, and a host of other organizations. In 1957, a local radio station presented her with its good citizenship award; in 1959, she was included in the first edition of *Who's Who of American Women*. Their family home at 38 Skyline Drive, which she had designed, was featured in a family magazine. Dottie also saw to it that their three daughters had childhoods typical of financially comfortable, socially connected families. Nancy studied dance and regularly appeared in local ballet performances; Sally became an accomplished violinist, performing in All-State Orchestra and at the Interlochen music camp in Michigan. In 1956, little Susie was one of the winners in an Easter hat contest.[80]

In preparing for his oral history years later, Blackmun asked his wife what the family had done as a group during those years. "Dottie said we did absolutely nothing which was a criticism of me that I was all work and no play. But we did a number of things. We took trips together, and I remember taking all of us to Florida one time in a station wagon we had. We had a great time....One vivid recollection I have was Susie's encounter with a pelican....I took the two older girls to Chicago [sightseeing].... Nancy went with us to my 25th reunion at Harvard. She was the only one [old enough to attend]. I tried to teach them a little bit about the out of doors. But Dottie is quite right, I didn't spend as much time with them as I should." He may also have felt some guilt that he was not as attentive to his mother during those years as he might have been. Corwin Blackmun had died in 1947 following a brief illness. But Blackmun's mother continued to live in St. Paul. Her son telephoned her every week and tried to visit her once a month. But, he later said, she "was disappointed that we were that far away, especially when the children came along and she wasn't able to spend as much time with them as she would have liked, but she was a great lady."[81]

Blackmun served as Mayo resident counsel until 1959. Professionally, he considered those years the "happiest" of his life. "Rochester," he later said, was "a special place. The schools are good, the level of intelligence and ability in the citizens...is really very high. There weren't any slums there at the time." His daughters later said that they, too, had enjoyed growing up there, but had a caveat for their father. " 'Daddy,' " he would remember their saying, " 'it isn't the real world.' And it wasn't." Soon, however, Blackmun was to make another career change, one taking him closer to that "real world."[82]

Chapter 3

Circuit Judge

As a Minneapolis lawyer and Mayo Clinic's resident counsel, Harry Blackmun avoided the partisan political activities so often prominent in the backgrounds of federal judges. He had remained a Republican, of course, but only nominally so. Moreover, his legal specialties in tax and estate law were generally far removed from the political arena; his law partners and Mayo colleagues might well have frowned on his active involvement in party politics; and he was simply poorly suited by personality and temperament for such activities.

Not so his boyhood friend. Warren Burger had also achieved considerable professional success in the St. Paul firm of Faricy, Burger, Moore, and Costello. But he had become deeply immersed in Republican politics as well. Early on, Burger hitched his aspirations to Harold Stassen, the GOP wunderkind, for a time, of Minnesota politics. Elected governor at age thirty-one, Stassen would go on to make many bids for the presidency between 1948 and 1992, although never winning his party's nomination, much less election. Burger headed Stassen's 1948 campaign and was a delegate pledged to Stassen at the 1952 national convention. There, he and Herbert Brownell, manager of New York governor Thomas E. Dewey's failed 1948 campaign against Harry Truman, became allies.

Brownell switched to the Eisenhower camp at the convention, while Burger, at Brownell's request, led a credentials committee fight against the seating of delegates pledged to Ike's principal opponent, conservative senator Robert A. Taft of Ohio. Following Eisenhower's election, Burger joined the new administration, becoming head of the Civil Division at the Department of Justice. On learning of the appointment, Blackmun wrote his friend, "I think you know how Dottie and I feel about the whole thing. We and your many friends in this area will miss you and, in that sense, regret your temporary departure from St. Paul. On the other hand, we know the nature of the task before you, and we are both proud of you and the challenge it presents." Burger's response was prompt: "In both of us there is something deep which makes service a thing which neither of us can avoid. You have elected one form which gave you more positive expression than [law] practice. Temporarily now I elect another." When Burger wrote his friend to express some uncharacteristic doubt about his qualifications, Blackmun offered encouragement: "You are indeed in the big league now, but your capabilities and capacities are equal to the rest. I am willing to bank on Dayton's Bluff and the St. Paul College of Law any time so far as you are concerned."[1]

Blackmun and Burger corresponded regularly and had many personal contacts during and after Burger's work in the Eisenhower administration. Much of their correspondence, and no doubt their conversations, centered on Burger's work, the changing political climate in Washington, and the Supreme Court. While Burger was preparing for argument of a case in the Second Circuit Court of Appeals, Blackmun recalled his "only experience with that court,...back in the Learned Hand days. He was extremely rough with Clark Fletcher and, in my opinion, unreasonably so. As a consequence, I do not share the worshipful attitude that most graduates of Harvard have for that judge. We were happy to see the Supreme Court tip him over [in that case]." Burger was present for the opening of the Supreme Court's 1953 term with its new chief justice, Earl Warren. "I must say," he conceded later, "that the new Chief handled the business of admissions [to the Supreme Court bar] with the routine, but rather tricky verbiage that goes with it, as though he'd been doing it for a hundred years." Ninety-five percent of the people he had talked to, Blackmun responded, "regard [Warren's selection] as wholly a political appointment....I suppose the only course is the usual one, namely, let's wait and see what happens."[2]

In an eight-page ("Look what a Dictaphone does to some people!") "Dear John, Harry and Bob" letter to his Dayton's Bluff friends Blackmun, John Briggs, and Robert Domkroger the night of his first annual White House Judiciary Dinner, Burger reminisced about old times. Twenty years ago that night, he reminded them, he and his wife, Vera, were at the Wardman Park Hotel in Washington on their wedding trip. Before leaving St. Paul, Burger had given Harry two crisp $20 bills, to be forwarded, "in the event of a distress signal,...by special delivery airmail to whatever point I was then stranded." In Washington, Burger "had completely run out of funds....For better or worse, we had to stay at the Wardman Park until Blackmun's letter arrived with my two $20 bills on which we were to make our way from Washington back to St. Paul in my 1929 Ford!"[3]

Some of Burger's letter was undoubtedly intended to impress his friends with the new heights to which their Dayton's Bluff playmate had risen. "I sat ten places to the left of the President...there was no dearth of fine wines...brandy and cigars after dinner." But he devoted much of his attention to the failure of Democrats to recognize the communist and Soviet threats to national security and the refusal of the new regime to fall into the same trap. "The contrast," declared Burger, "between men who so incredibly and tragically misjudged the Communist threat to this country and the men who were now dealing with it effectively for the first time in 20 years was something that could not go unnoticed."[4]

Nor was Burger's national security zeal confined to rhetoric. Perhaps his most controversial action as a Justice Department official involved the case of John P. Peters, a Yale professor dismissed from his position as a consultant to the U.S. Public Health Service in 1953 on loyalty-security grounds. Convinced that Peters's constitutional rights had been violated, Eisenhower's solicitor general Simon Sobeloff refused to defend the government in the Supreme Court. Agreeing to take Sobeloff's place, Burger cited the separation of powers doctrine, arguing that courts had no authority over the hiring and firing of government officials. Albeit on narrow, procedural grounds, the Supreme Court ruled against the administration. Afterward, Burger sent Blackmun a copy of "the argument I could have made [during oral argument in *Peters*] had the Court not wanted to make speeches!"[5]

In his oral history years later, Justice Blackmun would praise President Truman, whom he so closely resembled in stature. He also recalled with apparent alarm the Red-baiting tactics of Wisconsin senator Joseph McCarthy during the Eisenhower years. "I remember how difficult it was, and it got worse. Here he was from a neighboring state. I remember a lot of conversations that we had in the Mayo Section of Administration as to what this was doing, how far it would go, how dangerous it was, if he was dangerous at all. It was a depressing period, especially to have him come out of Wisconsin where one would expect the opposite kind of thing." In the 1950s, however, Blackmun may well have shared some of Burger's sentiments, but was simply too apolitical or prudent to embrace them openly, and certainly not in the extreme language to which his friend resorted.[6]

In other areas, Blackmun often served as a voice of restraint to his at times tempestuous friend. When a three-judge Eighth Circuit panel reversed the trial court decision in a civil case he had won before joining the Eisenhower administration, Burger was enraged. The case, he vehemently wrote Blackmun, had turned almost entirely on factual issues, which in turn depended on the credibility of a witness who, the trial court had concluded, was lying. Federal appeals courts had authority to overturn the factual findings of trial judges only if they were "clearly erroneous," yet the Eighth Circuit had reversed without making that determination and despite "overwhelming evidence" that the opposition's principal witness was a liar.[7]

Burger had shared the Eighth Circuit's ruling with "one of the leading Supreme Court practitioners in the country." His reaction, Burger wrote, "includes the words 'shocking' and 'inexplicable,' and in substance that the only admissable [sic] and permissible explanation is the senility of the members of the court, all of them being over 80." Because the case turned on factual issues, Burger doubted that the Supreme Court would grant a petition for a writ of certiorari granting review in the case. "Thus," he asserted, "the petition may be cast in such terms as will close forever—or at least until 3 funerals—my practice before that Court. We must virtually make an attack on the integrity of the court, unless we elect to make an issue of the senility point. That's clearly a difficult choice but will be implicit, in the eyes of some, in our request extraordinary for remand and review [of the case] by another court."[8]

In his response, Blackmun was sympathetic. "I know how very much of yourself you had put into that litigation and how strongly you must feel about obtaining justice for your client." At the same time, he doubted that "much can be gained by the approach on the grounds of senility or the other point which you [imply]." Blackmun was also more confident than Burger, he wrote, that the Supreme Court might accept the case. "If there was substantial evidence to support the [trial judge's] results…, why in the name of justice should the Supreme Court allow such a situation to stand[?]"[9]

Burger immediately sought to assuage any anxiety he might have caused his friend, writing Blackmun, "Lest you be concerned that I will get myself disbarred in the 8th [Circuit] be assured I was letting off a little steam—our petition for rehearing en banc [by the entire circuit bench] & for cert. will be sharp but sedate & reasonably conventional. However with the paucity of grants of cert. we must make a case that there has been a flagrant deviation from the proper scope of review & in effect a retrial de novo [of the factual issues] without the full case being before the Court. As you know, the 8th is the only circuit in the U.S. system which uses the archaic 'narrative record' approach" to reviewing trial court decisions.[10]

Judge Burger

By mid-1954, Burger had become restless, expressing an interest, among other possibilities, in a position on a court of appeals. Blackmun was encouraging. "I have…foremost in my mind," he wrote his friend in August, "the Court of Appeals business, and, frankly, I am glad you are tempted by it. Your appointment to that Bench would be a tremendous thing both for it and, I think, for you, for I am sure you would find some great personal satisfaction in what you could do and in the dispensation of real justice." But Blackmun conceded that he was "tempted also to think, as we used to once in a while, of the firm of Burger and Blackmun and wonder just where that would take us. In other words, I guess I need a good long visit with you."[11]

In 1955, President Eisenhower nominated Burger to a seat on the U.S. Court of Appeals for the District of Columbia. When Senate confirmation was delayed, largely as a result of charges raised by former government employees the nominee had fired for incompetence, Blackmun wrote supporting letters to, among others, influential Georgia Democratic senator Richard Russell, whom he had met while Russell was being treated at Mayo, as well as to Minnesota senator Hubert H. Humphrey, for whom Blackmun had rung doorbells during Humphrey's campaign for mayor of Minneapolis. In a letter to Wisconsin senator Alexander Wiley, he wrote, "I have known Warren Burger since childhood and have been impressed with his legal ability, his idealism and his devotion to his State and his Nation." Blackmun undoubtedly also praised his friend when Senate majority leader Lyndon B. Johnson was a Mayo patient, although it is unlikely he had the same opportunity when the president was a patient. At that point at least, Burger admired Johnson. "Hope you fellows get Lyndon Johnson patched up as well as the President," Burger wrote Blackmun at the time. "They are both badly needed in these times. . . . The President has often, privately where there is no political motivation, expressed his great admiration for Johnson's leadership in the Senate. Personally I wish we had something like it on our side of the aisle!"[12]

The Senate took no action on Burger's nomination in 1955. In January 1956, his name was again submitted to the Senate. On March 27, the nominee wrote Blackmun that the Senate had "virtually surrendered" and that he was "trying to defer the swearing in until you arrive. . . . You can then represent [Scout] Troop 18, Van Buren [School], Dayton's Bluff and Minnesota!" The next day, the Senate confirmed Burger's nomination. When he took the oath of office at the U.S. courthouse in Washington on April 13, Blackmun and other Minnesota friends were in the audience of five hundred. The new judge termed himself a "moderate liberal," a Washington newspaper reported. He and his family were living, the paper added, on a six-acre estate, Happy Hill, in Arlington County, Virginia. "I can't tell you how much it meant to me to have you on hand last Friday—again as my Best Man in a sense," he wrote Blackmun. "The latch string hangs low at the Burger Guest House awaiting the B's and their tribe as well. The House will easily handle all the Blackmun women and Blackmun too! And if they object we can put you in the Stable!"

Blackmun continued to have regular contact following Burger's appointment to the D.C. Circuit. They and their families vacationed together in Florida, and the two saw each other on their occasional trips to Minnesota and Washington. They also exchanged views about the quality of federal judicial appointments in general, as well as about particular prospective nominees. Aware, of course, that Judge Sanborn, a Minnesotan, was on the Eighth Circuit, and perhaps already entertaining some interest, however vague, in a seat on the federal bench himself, Blackmun complained to Burger about the insistence of some that the circuit courts be geographically balanced. "While I realize the political implications of this kind of thing and the political necessities on occasion, it does not make complete good sense, in my mind, to say that the Eighth Circuit has to have a judge from each state within it." When a district judgeship in Arkansas was not filled, and the Eighth Circuit's chief judge assigned Ronald Davies of North Dakota to the controversial Little Rock school desegregation case, Blackmun was also critical. "I personally suspect that any Arkansas man who might have been appointed," he wrote Burger after Davies ordered the integration of Little Rock's Central High School, "would have reached exactly the same conclusions Judge Davies reached, but at least they would have been made by a Southerner and one of [Arkansas governor Orval] Faubus's 'arguments' about a northern judge dispensing southern justice would have been avoided." When Justice Stanley Reed retired from the Supreme Court in 1957 and Burger wrote Blackmun that he was among those being considered, according to Washington newspapers, for the vacancy, Mayo's resident counsel responded promptly, asking "what, if anything, I can do out here to advance your candidacy," and adding, "There is nothing that I could be more enthusiastic about." But on that occasion, the nod went to Eighth Circuit judge Charles Evans Whitaker, whose Supreme Court tenure would be brief and tragic.[13]

For his part, Burger kept Blackmun abreast of his work on the D.C. Circuit and temporary assignments elsewhere, including one memorable experience sitting with Learned Hand, long since a senior judge, on a Second Circuit panel. "The old chief," he reported, "is...keen as tacks. He complained at lunch today that he thinks he's slipping a bit. After 5–6 martinis he says he can begin to feel the liquor and that's a bad sign." But Burger also expressed growing frustration with David Bazelon and other D.C. appeals judges whom he characterized as "suppressed and frustrated politicians at heart [willing to] use the judiciary as the vehicle for reforms which burn in their breasts." Throughout his adult life, Burger had been a "pusher-forward." Now he found himself "a 'holder-backer' most of the time just to maintain what seems to me reasonable balance and thoughtful progress in the law. Being a holder-backer is far less fun." There were days, he wrote Blackmun in 1957, "when I'd like to apply for a spot as your assistant or go to practice again. Then I see that this leaves the field to the Judge...Bazelons and I try to go back to my post."[14]

Much of Burger's correspondence with Blackmun, however, was lighthearted and humorous. During a trip to Austria, he ordered a dry wine at a Salzburg restaurant. Seemingly perplexed, the waiter asked, "ein dry wine," and Burger impatiently repeated, "Dry Wine." Thereupon, the waiter brought to the table "drei white wine—all [three] bottles uncorked and ready for use. What could I do? It isn't decent to waste good wine.... We spent about 2 hours or more over dinner, then with the aid of my ladies,... we got home in due course, utterly relaxed."[15]

Judge Blackmun

Soon, of course, Blackmun would also win appointment to the federal bench. By 1958, Judge Sanborn had decided to retire or, more precisely, assume the status of a senior judge, enabling President Eisenhower to make a new nomination to the Eighth Circuit. To the extent possible, however, Sanborn was also determined to assure that his former clerk would be his successor.

At Judge Sanborn's invitation, he and Blackmun had dinner at the Minneapolis Club on November 7. There, the judge told his younger friend of his plans to retire and his concern about the advancing age of the Eighth Circuit judges. He also said that he would like Blackmun to succeed him on the court.[16]

Characteristically, Blackmun wrote the judge the next day, listing his misgivings about "the one matter we talked about at some length" the previous evening. "I appreciate your comments more than I can tell you, but I strongly feel my lack of experience and of qualifications. In addition, there are, of course, the more practical problems of my family's attitude, my responsibilities here and the prevailing political atmosphere.

At this early moment, I do not know what to say other than to mention again, as I have so many times in the past twenty-six years, how grateful I am for your personal interest and confidence. Your friendship has been one of the main and dominant factors in my life, and your judicial work and attitude have always been examples of which I know few parallels."[17]

But the judge was not to be dissuaded. "Don't question your qualifications," he asserted in a November 10 letter. "You have everything that is needed to make an outstanding circuit judge." The morning after their dinner, Sanborn informed Blackmun, the judge had written Warren Burger, "asking him to find out if he could whether the Court of Appeals could trade a 75 year old Sanborn for a 50 year old Blackmun." The judge urged Blackmun to talk with Burger, who "perhaps…can arrange a meeting with the Attorney General." Politics, he added, "ought not to have too much influence [in the matter] and anyway they can't do much until there is a vacancy which depends on me."[18]

On getting Sanborn's message, as well as a letter and roses from Blackmun, Burger wrote his friend that he was "overjoyed by [the] note from JB which is a step toward which I have been working for a long time." Blackmun, he added, referring to his boyhood playmate's many gestures of friendship over the years, was "a gem among friends—indeed the rarest jewel of all." The other "principals," Burger thought, would be "at least receptive [to his appointment]. The problem will be to get Blackmun in the right mood!" In a separate, handwritten note, Burger congratulated his friend on his approaching fiftieth birthday and praised him for developing a career that had "turned, as I thought it was bound to, out of the market place and into what probably is the only place where real values reside in the long run. My bankers would like me to get more money to pay off my notes, but most of the time I couldn't care less and we share that attitude toward life I think."[19]

Later that month, Blackmun visited Washington and spoke with Burger about the Sanborn seat. During their meeting, Burger was not entirely enthusiastic in urging Blackmun to accept an appointment. He had enjoyed his work in the Justice Department, he reported, more than his seat on the bench. "It is sitting with men who are themselves arch-advocates that disturb[s] me," he wrote Blackmun after their conversation. "I have laid aside my sword—or beaten it into a letter opener—but my 'friends' have not." Burger had a "100% conviction," however, that Blackmun was "ideally equipped to be an appellate judge—a better one, I assure you, than I." Were he enjoying the bench as much as the Justice Department, he declared, "I would be a better advocate for *urging* you on."[20]

When Blackmun shared the news with his mother, she naturally was pleased. "I think you have earned such a position of trust and I feel in my head that it is going to come thr[ough]. God bless you, son. Dad would be so proud of you but not more than I am." Not surprisingly, given her own fragile personality, Theo Blackmun saw another advantage in an appointment to the bench. "If you can be relieved of some of the tension [apparently created by his work at Mayo Clinic]," she wrote, "that makes it worthwhile too."[21]

Although Judge Sanborn's wishes would carry great weight, he was not the only figure of significance in the selection of his successor. Minnesota Democratic congressman Eugene McCarthy had defeated Republican senator Edward J. Thye in the state's November senatorial election, and Minnesota's "Happy Warrior," Hubert Humphrey, the state's senior senator, was also a Democrat. Humphrey and McCarthy could at least delay confirmation. Minnesota Republicans, moreover, were hardly united behind a single prospective nominee. In February, Judge Sanborn and Warren Burger discussed the vacancy with Deputy Attorney General Lawrence Walsh. The judge "made it plain" to Walsh, as Sanborn put it in a letter to Blackmun, that he would not retire unless he was "sure that my retirement would not weaken the Court." Both the judge and Burger, he added, "told [Walsh] that we regarded you as the best qualified person to succeed me." But the deputy attorney general had also contacted Senator Thye and Minnesota Republican congressman Walter Judd; although both had given "favorable responses" when asked about Blackmun, Thye also mentioned another possibility whom Sanborn did not "even know and would not consider acceptable." Perhaps Thye was obligated politically to the person whose name he had raised, "but no political debts," Sanborn declared, were "going to be paid off at my expense, if I can help it." The judge was "not at all sure" that he would retire "if I am to be succeeded by a person other than yourself," but Sanborn conceded that he "was hardly in a position to say take it or leave it."[22]

Clearly, from the beginning the administration considered Blackmun a leading candidate for Sanborn's seat. On February 26, 1959, according to his chronology of events, Blackmun received a telephone call from Walsh, asking whether he would accept the appointment were it offered and explaining that the administration wanted to avoid the embarrassment of having Blackmun decline a nomination. Blackmun agreed that he would accept but, characteristically, asked Walsh "whether he would tell me how to educate three kids on the salary." For over a decade, the American Bar Association's Committee on Federal Judiciary had been reviewing and rating prospective federal judges. In March, Roy Willy, a South Dakota lawyer, contacted members of the Minnesota bar as part of the ABA's review process. Morris B. Mitchell, a prominent Minneapolis attorney, was among those interviewed. "Of course," Mitchell assured Warren Burger, "I gave Harry the highest recommendation possible, as I feel that he is a man of the highest character and ability. Although no one has told me, I think I know the job for which he is being considered, and if there is anything which I can do to help him get it I certainly would be glad to do it."[23]

As time passed, Sanborn and Burger, among others, became concerned that Blackmun's nomination might never make it to the Senate Judiciary Committee. Twenty-six judicial vacancies were unfilled, and they feared that Mississippi Democrat James O. Eastland, the committee chair, might hold up all nominations as the Eisenhower administration approached an end. Lawrence Walsh had told them some months earlier, moreover, that he thought the Senate would soon stop confirming the administration's nominees altogether.[24]

In late April, however, Burger wrote Blackmun that Walsh had told him during lunch that day that "he was now waiting on a 'final' letter from JB [Sanborn] and that *your* name would then go up!" Burger had explained to Walsh that he thought Sanborn was waiting "on *him* but [was] reluctant to call [Walsh] for fear of [Walsh's] thinking he is pressing him unduly." Burger had written Sanborn a note that day "suggesting *he* consider calling [Walsh] to clear the air. I think JB wants to know *what* name is going up *before* he acts...and I would too!"[25]

Two days later, on April 30, Sanborn wrote Blackmun, informing him that Walsh and Burger had "things...lined up as well as they can be."

On Thursday, May 7, the judge was to submit his letter to the president, with his retirement effective June 30. Walsh, he added, had suggested that date, assuring Sanborn that it would "not prejudice your chances in any way, and will enable me to carry out my commitments before handing in my dinner pail." The judge conceded that "the best plans sometimes miscarry," but added, "I certainly hope ours won't."[26]

While Sanborn and Burger, among others, had been promoting his nomination with the administration, Blackmun had driven to Salt Lake City alone, which had given him "a chance to think some things through and which was enjoyable anyway." Dottie joined him there by plane for a drive through Utah, Arizona, and New Mexico. He had "thoroughly enjoyed Utah and never realized before what a beautiful state it was."[27]

When Blackmun returned to his office in early May, he found Judge Sanborn's April 30 letter on his desk. He was clearly touched. "I say again that I deeply appreciate your confidence, and I think I understand what all of this kind of business must mean to you personally. Whatever happens, I cannot imagine you 'handing in your dinner pail.' It is very hard for me to make any appropriate comment, for you have always known what your example and ability and your personal friendship have meant to me."[28]

By mid-May, Roy Willy had contacted Blackmun on behalf of the ABA's review committee. At Willy's request, Blackmun furnished him with a biographical sketch. "The sketch," he noted in a cover letter, "does not include any reference to specialization, bar admissions or political inclinations, and I believe you mentioned the latter in your telephone call to me." Referring to his political leanings, he wrote, "I am a Republican by inclination, but I must confess that I have not been engaged publicly in political activity and have held no political office or office in any political organization." In the letter, he also itemized his legal specialties—tax work as a lawyer in Minneapolis, and probate, wills, trusts, estate planning, and death taxes, as Mayo's lawyer—areas of expertise, he might have added, that were hardly likely to spark debate, except that some might find them irrelevant to the most important work of federal courts.[29]

On May 18, the White House announced Judge Sanborn's retirement effective June 30, and Minnesota papers soon began running articles speculating that Blackmun was the "top choice" for the Sanborn seat. "Such excitement!" Theo Blackmun exclaimed to her son. "All my friends calling and saying they are pulling for you." Traditionally, the FBI conducts a security investigation of all prospective nominees. On the day Sanborn's retirement was announced, an FBI agent telephoned Blackmun to begin that process, ordered, he said, as "top priority." Probably in response to a query from Blackmun, Warren Burger conceded, "I don't know what is going on now but that's inevitable. It's like a pregnancy—you can start it but it's hard to control after that." Whatever happened, he added, "it is a good try for the Republic. I'm still not sure how good for Blackmun but we shall see." Burger had seen Lawrence Walsh at a dinner the previous evening. "He was non-committal except [to say] that it was now in the laps of the 'gods.' What is covered by that, I don't know."[30]

The first Minneapolis newspaper article about the Sanborn vacancy, an item in the *Morning Tribune*, mentioned several possible nominees in addition to Blackmun, including two Minnesota federal district judges and former U.S. attorney George MacKinnon, who would later serve on the D.C. court of appeals. Blackmun, according to the article, was "said to have" Sanborn's support, as well as that of his "friend" Warren Burger, who had recently been "named to the board of the Mayo Association" and was a "close friend of Attorney General William Rogers, whose task it will be to name the new judge." The article also noted that Blackmun had not sought the position and that he was "believed to be a Republican even though he is unknown to party" leaders.[31]

Blackmun was "distresse[d]" by the article's reference to Judge Sanborn and Warren Burger "as factors" influencing his chances for the nomination. "I hope," he wrote Burger, "it is not too embarrassing for you." Soon Burger provided his friend with a lengthy list of unresponsive responses Blackmun might give to reporters' likely questions. Faced with those replies, he was confident, "the Reporter will give up and go off for a triple Martini but he has a good story anyway!" "You and I are thinking very much alike," Blackmun soon wrote his friend; "the answers you proposed are precisely those which I had in mind in the event of need."[32]

Blackmun was also perturbed when various district bar associations in the state adopted resolutions to the attorney general endorsing his nomination. On discovering, "somewhat to my horror," one such resolution, he promptly wrote Burger. "The boys, I am sure, were well-intentioned, but I hope the [Justice Department] does not regard this as instigated by me. This kind of business, it seems to me, is appropriate only after a man has been appointed but not yet confirmed." Blackmun probably welcomed, however, supporting letters that state judges wrote the president and Minnesota's senators in his behalf.[33]

In June, before leaving on another European family vacation, Burger spoke again with Deputy Attorney General Walsh, then wrote Judge Sanborn. The delay at that point, Burger surmised from his conversation with Walsh, was a result of Minnesota pressure on the administration to "do something for" George MacKinnon. "They have, [Walsh] says, no intention of appointing him but they are—as usual waiting for the dust to settle. It's incredible to me that experience has not taught them dust rarely settles in these matters." Burger suggested that Sanborn telephone Walsh and point out the risks of further delay. "He should also be told—as I have already intimated to him—...if anything goes wrong and they are *not* going to nominate HB. They should give him several days or a week's notice of that fact so he can 'rehabilitate' himself and mend his fences at the Clinic." Burger concluded with characteristic exasperation: "I can stand people who make mistakes but Heaven help us from those who can't make up their minds!"[34]

Judge Sanborn forwarded Blackmun a copy of Burger's letter. The judge questioned the wisdom of his contacting Walsh but agreed to do so if Blackmun wished. Sanborn feared that "Minnesota may lose the judgeship or that the matter may be delayed so long that no judicial confirmation can be obtained." Blackmun apparently responded that Sanborn should do nothing and professed to be unconcerned about the continued delays in the process. But he wrote Burger on July 9 that he was concerned about Sanborn's "disappointed and almost rebellious mood" regarding the administration's handling of the matter, and also about his own need for a reasonable time to prepare for his departure from Mayo. "I cannot leave this institution on a moment's notice if the appointment should come this way and I find myself free to accept. The arrangement for my successorship cannot be completed overnight." Otherwise, he assured Burger, he was "actually very patient and...content, come what may," although he thought "that whatever the decision in Washington delay is dangerous and can accomplish little."[35]

Burger regretted Judge Sanborn's decision not to press Lawrence Walsh. "[Sanborn's retirement] was specifically predicated on a prompt replacement which would avoid a potential hassle and he can certainly *ask* what is going on," he wrote Blackmun. "We should have told [Attorney General Rogers and Walsh] the retirement letter could not be delivered *until* they were ready (as [Walsh] said once they were) to send a name to the WH."[36]

Several days later, the *St. Paul Pioneer Press* ran an item from its Washington bureau indicating that supporters of former Republican congressman Joseph P. O'Hara were urging his appointment to the vacancy. According to the paper, the administration was attempting to avoid political appointments, while "leading political figures" were seeking to block nonpolitical appointments proposed by Attorney General Rogers. "One report here," the article added, "is that this is what happened to the administration's idea of naming Harry Blackmun…to Judge Sanborn's seat." In a letter to the judge, Blackmun noted both the article and Burger's "rather disgruntled letter," from which Blackmun had gathered that his friend "proposes to do some stirring up if nothing has happened by the time of his return [from Europe] about August 9." For his part, Judge Sanborn expressed dismay over the O'Hara story. "If it turns out that I have done nothing except furnish the politicians with some patronage, I shall be thoroughly humiliated. Perhaps Warren can do something when he gets back. I'm sorry he left Washington when he did." Blackmun sought to appear calm. "Washington will move if and when it chooses to do so and not any sooner….Maybe they will come up with an unexpected and wonderful appointment after all," he wrote Sanborn.[37]

Apparently, Burger did "stir up" things on his August 9 return from Europe. "Shocked," as he put it in a later letter to Judge Sanborn, that no nomination had gone to the Senate, Burger complained to administration officials that the continued delay "came close to a breach of faith with [Sanborn]." Finally, on August 18, President Eisenhower acted, sending Blackmun's name to the Senate. Burger was one of the first to offer his congratulations, by telephone and a note. "I am delighted! So are we all!" When Blackmun received a letter attacking his nomination, Burger promptly replied, "That 'crank' letter is controlled by Res Ipsa Loquitur [the thing speaks for itself]." Blackmun, in turn, was grateful for the role Burger and

Judge Sanborn had played in securing his nomination. "I cannot express to you," he wrote Burger, "my gratitude for your sympathetic understanding through these last months and the many things, many of them, I am sure, embarrassing to you, which you did. You and John B. are certainly way out on a limb and almost personally responsible for what I may do, say or decide in the future. As always, you demonstrate your friendship with unbelievable actions, and it is overwhelming to me. I can say no more, but I am sure that you understand the depth of my feeling about all of this."[38]

There remained, of course, the Senate confirmation process. Initially, Burger was optimistic, sending his friend a *New York Times* article suggesting that the Senate was preparing to end its logjam on nineteen federal judgeship nominations, with the following note attached: "I don't want to create false hopes of speedy action, but my check up indicates you might well get a hearing in 2 weeks and ride through with those who have been delayed 6–8 months in [the Judiciary] Committee. My guess is they will all go through when the 'thaw' comes." On September 1, however, Burger complained to Judge Sanborn that Senator Humphrey—either "to show who is boss" or for other reasons—had not given the Judiciary Committee "the traditional 'go' sign [from a senator of the circuit] essential to set up a hearing." He recommended that Minnesota congressmen, state bar officials, and all the district judges in Minnesota be recruited to urge Humphrey and Senator McCarthy to clear the way for an early hearing.[39]

Soon Humphrey and McCarthy were getting the message. Prominent citizens sent letters supporting confirmation. All the past presidents of the Minnesota bar, save one who did not know Blackmun, sent them a telegram praising the nominee's "ability,…integrity and…human understanding." Morris Mitchell sent a copy of the telegram to Bernard G. Segal, the Philadelphia lawyer who was then head of the ABA's Committee on Federal Judiciary, and also alerted Segal that he had suggested to the editor of the *Minneapolis Star Tribune* that the paper contact Segal regarding the outstanding rating the ABA committee had given Blackmun. The next day, the paper ran an editorial, "The Delay on Blackmun," suggesting that Minnesota might lose the appointment entirely. Noting that the ABA had accorded the nominee its highest recommendation of "exceptionally well qualified"—a rating given only eight of around 275 rated by the organization in the previous three years—the *Star* could not understand why the judiciary committee had "not even called hearings on Blackmun's nomination." Holding Senators Humphrey and McCarthy partly responsible for the delay, the paper questioned their assertions that they "had no prior official word before Blackmun's nomination" was announced and thus wanted "to find out more about [him]" before calling for hearings. "Since there is no known objection to Blackmun, and he is highly regarded by the state and national bar associations," the paper asserted, "we think the Minnesota senators ought to have informed themselves about him and asked the Democratically-controlled senate judiciary committee for hearings." Senator McCarthy had said that there probably would not be time for a hearing in any event, given the "rush" to adjourn Congress. The paper was not impressed. A Texas judicial nominee favored by Senate majority leader Lyndon Johnson had been given a hearing the day after his nomination reached the chamber. "This particular delay will cost Minnesota an important appointment," the *Star* concluded, "and—what is more important—the nation the services of an outstanding judge unless there is a sudden burst of activity on behalf of Blackmun by Minnesota's senators and the senate judiciary committee." A recess appointment for the nominee while the Congress was adjourned was not likely, especially because it would lapse if not confirmed in the next Senate session. Instead, the paper predicted, "the likelihood…is for a new nomination to be sent up in January— and it might even be from one of the other states in this eighth [circuit]."[40]

Such lobbying had the desired effect. Minnesota newspapers continued to predict that Blackmun would not be confirmed before Congress's September adjournment. According to a later Associated Press account, however, Humphrey and McCarthy finally went to Judiciary Committee chairman James O. Eastland, asking that he schedule a hearing on the nomination. On September 14, the last day of the session, Eastland hastily convened a subcommittee hearing, before which Humphrey and McCarthy presented and profusely praised the nominee, who had been summoned to Washington from Rochester. At about noon that day, the full committee approved the nomination and sent it to the Senate floor, where, at about 2:30 a.m. the following morning, Blackmun was unanimously confirmed.[41]

Blackmun's mother and his sister, Betty, now Mrs. Peter Gilchrist, were then living in White Bear Lake, Minnesota. "I am so very, very proud of you," Betty wrote her brother, "and can't help thinking how [their father] C.B. would be bursting his buttons over the whole thing. On the other hand, had he been around, I am certain he would have called out the Guard and marched on [Senator] Humphrey, thereby lousing up the whole deal." An emotional Theo Blackmun wrote her son that her heart "was filled with love for you and pride in your accomplishments. I wish Dad were here to share it all with me."[42]

Others close to the new judge were equally pleased. Judge Sanborn even speculated that "the delay in sending in your name did you more good than harm, since the publicity and the efforts of your friends certainly gave you a send-off and a reputation that you would not otherwise have had initially." Responding to a letter from Blackmun thanking him for his support, the ABA's Bernard Segal praised Morris Mitchell and more than a dozen other Minnesotans who had taken part in "the all-out-effort to blast your nomination loose and to have the Senate act on it." For his part, Senator Humphrey attempted to mend relations with the Blackmun family. "Your Dad and I had a good talk about you," he wrote the Blackmuns' youngest daughter, Susie, "and I hope that now you think a little better of your Senator." He also asked that Susie "give my best wishes to your Mother and Dad."[43]

Blackmun had always attempted to remain philosophical about his chances. "Maybe all this is for the best," he wrote one supporter who had complained about the lengthy delay in the process, "for...I am very happy and content here at the Mayo Clinic. In fact, my wife and I have been joking to the effect that every time I move our income goes down and it is about time we stopped moving. Perhaps I am too much of an idealist. Most of my former partners in Minneapolis questioned my sanity in coming to Rochester nine years ago, and I am sure they would question my sanity again about this judicial matter." But he had undoubtedly found the initial inaction of Humphrey and McCarthy annoying. Writing Sanborn at one point about "many details [of the process] which I yearn to tell you about," he wryly noted that "the final detail, of course, is the fact that Senator McCarthy refuses to move 'at this time,' wishes to make his own investigation, and says he has no personal animus so far as I am concerned." When a friend sent Blackmun a letter from Humphrey describing the new judge as "a fine and good man," Blackmun replied, with at least a hint of sarcasm, that he found that sentence "so striking that it almost impresses me," adding, "Perhaps you will not mind if I hold it here for a little while, for there are some individuals around here who could stand looking at it."[44]

Blackmun was also annoyed by an item in the *Minneapolis Sunday Tribune* shortly after his confirmation. A column by John C. McDonald, a *Tribune* staff writer, noted that Blackmun "was a 'nonpartisan' appointee if ever there was one" and that Minnesota Republican leaders "never had heard of him." McDonald also quoted Democrat Gerald W. Heaney, whom President Lyndon Johnson would appoint to the Eighth Circuit in 1966. "Heaney...says the new judge is 'as much independent as Republican,' since, according to Heaney, he supported Democrat Hubert Humphrey the first time he ran for mayor of Minneapolis, and later he contributed to Humphrey's campaign to unseat Republican Sen. Joe Ball."[45]

Years later, Blackmun would say that he had "punched door bells for him" when Humphrey "first ran for public office, for Mayor of Minneapolis." But he was irritated at the erroneous assertion that he had supported Humphrey's defeat of Senator Ball and concerned at the effect such a story would have on his relations with Minnesota Republicans. "This, I understand," he wrote Warren Burger, "was most disturbing to George MacKinnon....Where this kind of information came from I do not know, and the allegation that I contributed to the campaign against Joe Ball is completely false." The reaction of Blackmun's volatile friend was predictable. Calling McDonald a "bastard," but then replacing that epithet with the milder "buzzard," Burger recommended that Blackmun write a reporter a "short, curt letter categorically denying" support of Humphrey in the mayoral or Senate races. "You are still a lawyer and not a sitting judge," added Burger, "and you are free to punch hard if you wish." Although Blackmun could not deny supporting Humphrey's race for mayor, he did write McDonald a letter. Referring to Heaney's statement that he had contributed to Humphrey's Senate campaign against Senator Ball, he declared, "This statement is completely untrue, and it has caused me embarrassment." Ultimately and characteristically, however, he decided against mailing the letter.[46]

As his installation drew closer, Blackmun focused largely on what most judges might have considered a minor matter: where his chambers were to be located. "You had better have that man Collier in some way work out acceptable chambers for me here in Rochester or the senator from Arkansas can have his judgeship," he somewhat petulantly wrote Burger in early October. He immediately added, "I do not mean that literally of course." But he was clearly adamant. There was no room in the Rochester post office building for his chambers. "If Rochester is out of the question, the situation really becomes complicated. I will not move to Winona, and [leaving Rochester] would involve a return to the Twin Cities. My girls are upset about this, and I suppose it means that I would commute at least until Nancy is through high school. That is not so good. We like this town and would prefer to stay here." Ultimately, the Olmstead County Board of Commissioners expressed an interest in renting Blackmun space in Rochester's new county courthouse, thus resolving the issue.[47]

Blackmun was also obliged to make decisions about a site, time, and other arrangements regarding his installation ceremony. As in most matters, Warren Burger was eager to offer advice. When ex-Senator Thye became perturbed, in Burger's words, that Senator Humphrey was saying "privately as well as in the press that the HAB appointment was his idea (H.H.'s) as a bipartisan move to keep the judiciary clean and pure," Thye had expressed the hope that he would be invited to the swearing-in unless it was a purely private affair. Burger used Thye's request as the opportunity to offer Blackmun various suggestions. If the ceremony were not "*purely private* without pictures,…Ed [Thye], as one of the key indispensables in the process, should be invited, even if only as an 'old friend.'" Because St. Louis was the seat of the Eighth Circuit, Burger also thought a "St. Louis swearing in while perhaps inconvenient for your mother and the girls would solve all problems." He saw no need, however, for Blackmun "to be concerned with [inviting Humphrey or Senator McCarthy] who, had they not had fires put under them, would have blocked what Ed Thye was a large factor in making possible."[48]

Blackmun obligingly offered to telephone Senator Thye. He also decided, however, to take the oath in Judge Sanborn's St. Paul chambers or one of the courtrooms there rather than in St. Louis. Although he assumed that the ceremony would "be very quiet, short and simple," he wrote Burger, he "suspect[ed] that this is like getting married and starting with a front room ceremony but ending up with visiting the cathedral." Following discussion with Burger, he had purchased a judicial robe. "I hope it wears well," he declared, in an indirect reference to the further financial sacrifice his latest career change would entail, "for I plan to wear it at all times during the day to cover up anticipated threadbare places in my suits. I have told Miss Clark that there will be no new ones from now on."[49]

On November 4, at 10 a.m., Judge Sanborn administered the oath of office to Blackmun in the same room where he had taken his oath as Sanborn's clerk years before. While professing that "there is nothing I would like better than to have you present when I take the oath," Blackmun had discouraged Burger from going to the time and expense of attending the ceremony. Burger was not present, but assured his friend in a note that "few things would be more pleasant than to see the fulfillment of what J.B. and I, among many others, have long wanted." Blackmun's comment about the tendency of such events to mushroom in size proved prophetic. More than 125 persons crammed into Judge Sanborn's chambers with Dottie and their daughters to hear him swear to "administer justice without respect to person…do equal right to the poor and to the rich, and…faithfully and impartially discharge and perform all the duties incumbent upon me…agreeably to the Constitution and laws of the United States." The next day Theo Blackmun wrote her son, thanking him "for never having been a disappointment to your Dad and me."[50]

Riding Circuit

By and large, Harry Blackmun enjoyed his years on the Eighth Circuit and most of his colleagues. Characteristically, however, his adjustment to his new assignment was at times frustrating for him. He went on the court harboring some resentment for its old chief judge, Archibald K. Gardner. Although then in his nineties, Gardner had continued as the circuit's chief judge, denying Judge Sanborn the opportunity to hold the court's center seat. But after losing two cases before Gardner while in the Justice Department, Warren Burger had pushed for legislation forbidding court of appeals and district judges to serve as chief judge after age seventy. In 1960, therefore, Gardner was obliged to step down. Initially at least, Blackmun was not happy with Gardner's successor either. Judge Sanborn had assured him that he would like the new chief judge, Harvey Johnsen. But Blackmun had been "deeply disappointed," finding Johnsen "very cold and hard to get to know, utterly unlike Judge Sanborn." At the first court session Blackmun attended in St. Louis, Johnsen invited him to have breakfast with him at the Mayfair Hotel, where all the judges stayed during sessions in the Missouri city. Blackmun arrived three minutes late for their meal together. "You're late," Johnsen muttered. "No smile on his face, 'you're late.' Well, from then on we were at cross-purposes for a while.... I don't think he had any humor in him at all, but he was a good judge."[51]

Blackmun also found that his colleagues were decidedly set in their ways. After breakfast each morning at the Mayfair, the judges marched, in order of seniority, to the federal courthouse, invariably following the same route. One day while the group was stopped by a red light, Blackmun "knew we had to cross the street to the right, and I made the helpful suggestion, 'Why don't we go on the green light across the street?' Everybody turned around and glared at me.... We go down on this side of the street and keep your mouth shut. Don't give us these foolish ideas. I learned a lot on that first march."[52]

Individually, some of the judges were somewhat eccentric as well. Joe Woodrough, a Texan transplanted to Omaha, wore white socks and campaigned unsuccessfully to have the other judges follow his lead as a symbol of the circuit. Years later, however, Blackmun had fond memories of most of his fellow judges. Charles Vogel of North Dakota, for example, was a "very lovable guy"; Martin Van Oosterhout of Iowa "a large man with one of the most lovable dispositions that one could have"; and Marion Matthes of St. Louis "a fine judge,... a good person."[53]

At that point, Eighth Circuit judges were each allotted one clerk. In preparing for oral argument of a case before a three-judge panel or the full court, Blackmun typically had his clerk prepare a bench memorandum, a practice he would continue on the Supreme Court. With respect to his judicial opinions, he later said, "I started off trying to write all of my own, and then when I had confidence in particular clerks, I would ask them to do the first draft, and they did it very well." That, too, was to be his practice on the Supreme Court.[54]

Blackmun would write 217 opinions as a court of appeals judge. Much of his caseload involved judicial constructions of federal statutes and administrative regulations. In 1969, for example, he spoke for a unanimous panel in adding another chapter to the protracted antitrust and related litigation stimulated by the breakup of the Standard Oil trust years earlier.

When he did confront the sorts of constitutional issues that he would later face as a justice, moreover, his judgment was hardly unfettered. First, of course, as a lower court judge he was obliged to follow Supreme Court precedent, whatever his personal preferences. When assigned to draft opinions for circuit panels, he also had to take into account the leanings of colleagues, particularly those most likely to dissent. Nevertheless, Blackmun's votes and opinions on the circuit bench did provide signals to the positions he would assume as a justice. Arguably, they also provide additional support for the thesis that he was largely consistent in his jurisprudence throughout his career.

Privacy Claims

On the court of appeals, Blackmun heard almost no suits over the sorts of privacy issues with which he would become so closely associated on the Supreme Court, and none involving abortion. His stance in one case, however, foreshadowed his ultimate support on the high bench for homosexual privacy claims. In *Marion v. Gardner* (1966), he spoke for a unanimous panel in overturning the denial of social security disability benefits to a homosexual with a history of "deviance directed toward young boys" who had been committed to a mental institution. But he studiously avoided a direct confrontation with the issue of whether homosexuality in itself was a legitimate basis for government interference with individual liberty. Instead, he rejected any suggestion "that homosexuality in itself is a disability within the meaning of the [federal law]," adding, "History and common knowledge teach us otherwise and disclose that many persons with homosexual tendencies have been economically productive and, indeed, have achieved marked success in many fields." The court was simply declaring that the "unfortunate young man" whose status was at issue in the case was within the reach of the law, especially given his commitment to a mental institution.[55]

Blackmun's Mayo friend Dr. Howard Rome had been hopeful that the judge would go further. When Blackmun shared a draft of his opinion with Rome, the physician applauded the ruling as "the first of a necessary series of small steps that ultimately will lead to a Brown v. Board of Education for…another civil right which will have to be furnished more adequate protection in the future than we have given it in the past…the much needed redress of our arbitrary and punitive discrimination against the deviant." Blackmun, wrote Rome, had "chosen to climb the decision tree by a different," more cautious, "node to node" route than Rome would have chosen. But Rome was "confident that you and I will live to see the time when we do more than segregate the goats from the sheep."[56]

Blackmun realized, he soon replied, that he had "disappointed" Rome "in not plowing a deeper furrow here and, perhaps, in not providing a new and judicial approach to deviance." In his defense, he conceded that he had tried, "perhaps too much so," to keep the opinion and its result simple so that he could not be accused "of burying the result in a welter of medical and psychiatric terminology"—a charge that later would be raised against his opinion in *Roe v. Wade*. He was also concerned, he added, that one member of the panel might dissent, and he was "mildly hopeful that what you call the node-to-node approach will bring him along. I would like to have the opinion unanimous for I feel the slight advance it makes will then be all the more secure. I am almost positive a dissent will be forthcoming if I do not take his approach." Blackmun's strategy worked. Judge Roy L. Stephenson, who "previously felt it would be necessary…to write a dissent," concluded that Blackmun's proposed opinion "covered all the matters that caused me difficulty. I was particularly afraid that we might be opening the door [presumably regarding the recognition of homosexual rights], but I am satisfied that the opinion does not do so." Although Dr. Rome would have preferred that Blackmun open that door, he thought his friend had at least "shifted the anchor and we are as a consequence a little farther up stream." Blackmun's letter to Rome at least hinted, moreover, that he had already begun to form attitudes that, years later, would lead him to favor the extension of privacy rights to homosexual sodomy.[57]

Racial Cases

His circuit record would provide little indication of his likely approach to privacy issues on the Supreme Court, but Blackmun did confront on the appeals bench many of the sorts of constitutional issues he would later encounter as a justice. Although fully supportive of the high Court's school desegregation rulings, he appeared more sympathetic with southern judges and school officials than at least one of his colleagues. In a number of cases, he and Donald Lay, a 1966 Lyndon Johnson appointee to replace Harvey Johnsen on the circuit, debated a lower court dictum in *Briggs v. Elliott*, the South Carolina counterpart to *Brown v. Board of Education*. After the Supreme Court had remanded *Brown*, *Briggs*, and companion cases to the trial courts with instructions to implement its decree that state-prescribed segregation had no place in public schools, the trial court in *Briggs* construed *Brown* to mean that "the Constitution...does not require integration. It merely forbids discrimination." In 1965, Judge Floyd Gibson, a 1961 Kennedy appointee, concluded for an Eighth Circuit panel that "the dictum in Briggs has not been followed or adopted by the Circuit and it is logically inconsistent with Brown and subsequent decisional law on this subject." In a later school case, however, Judge Blackmun noted in a cover letter to his draft opinion that he saw "no occasion here to involve ourselves with the dictum in the Briggs case." Southern officials had often cited the *Briggs* opinion in attempting to prevent school integration. Conceding that his objections to Blackmun's preferred approach were "rather pointed and direct," Judge Lay expressed regret that Blackmun's draft opinion was not an "emphatic rejection of *Briggs*," particularly since the school board in the case was still relying on the *Briggs* dictum. "Your proposed opinion," asserted Lay, "*sub silentio* could lend countenance to the *Briggs* dictum by members of the panel." In his response to Lay, Blackmun stressed that he in no way had intended to imply that *Briggs* was the law in the circuit by not mentioning it in his opinion. He questioned, in fact, whether Lay, by his emphasis on *Briggs* in the concurring opinion he had drafted, was not actually "weaken[ing] your desired end of rejecting Briggs. Sometimes such emphasis in a separate concurrence or in a dissent has this effect." Blackmun also took issue with his colleague when Lay, again referring to *Briggs*, contended that later decisions had "completely refute[d] the theories of a southern district judge in that case." *Briggs*, Blackmun pointed out, was decided by a three-judge panel, not a single judge, and two of the three judges on the *Briggs* Court were "highly regarded." Ultimately, Blackmun did not mention *Briggs*, while Lay's concurrence stressed that it had been "la[id] to final rest" in earlier cases.[58]

Blackmun was also unwilling to find racial animus in every southern school board decision prompted by a desegregation ruling. In a case involving the termination of several African American teachers following the closing of an inferior all-black school, he resisted the "tempt[ation] in this sensitive time to try to put a case together on inferences that a school district's every move and failure to move has a racial overtone." Instead, with respect to one of the discharged teachers, he asserted that "vague implications of racial impropriety do not offset studied inaction on the complaining teacher's part." That teacher had not been terminated because of his race. "He just refused to comply with reasonable rules and procedures which were expected of all teachers and which were met and complied with by each and every one of his faculty colleagues....[Yet] he now seeks to excuse himself and to place his noncompliance under the protective shield of unallowable racial discrimination." The facts involving the other black teachers who were terminated also did not "add up to a showing of discrimination." They simply lacked the credentials of their white counterparts. Those adversely affected by school decisions, he concluded, "should not immediately jump to the conclusion that their predicament is necessarily the result of racial considerations."[59]

Blackmun's reluctance to attribute racial bias to every action of southern officials was not limited to school cases. Speaking for a divided panel rejecting jury discrimination and related challenges to the rape conviction and death sentence imposed on a black defendant, he minimized the weight to be assigned use of the epithet "nigger" by a state prison warden and the prosecutor during a hearing on defense motions outside the jury's presence. Those references, he concluded, were "unfortunate but only two in number and no objection was made to either." His colleague Pat Mehaffy, a Little Rock native, applauded Blackmun's "usual, fine opinion." Mehaffy found his treatment of the "nigger" issue particularly impressive. "When I say 'nigger,' I mean no reflection whatever on the colored race, and I know that the same is true of all native Southerners....I am quite sure that the day will eventually come when the decent Negro will reach the realization that the best friend he has ever had was from this section of the country." Little Rock, he added, recalling the city's desegregation crisis several years earlier, "is a dirty name throughout the world as is the State of Arkansas because we were chosen as a guinea pig in one of the original interracial movements (and in a manner which would really make your blood boil), nevertheless, without any attendant publicity and despite its lack of popularity with extremists, Little Rock has long since quietly desegregated its hotels, eating places, in fact, absolutely everything except its public swimming pools, and all of this prior to introduction or passage of the Civil Rights Act. As for the swimming pools, they were recently voluntarily desegregated."[60]

In his response, Blackmun took no issue with what Mehaffy had written. Instead, he expressed his view that the position of the defense in the case had been "crusading and offensive in many respects, that in a certain way it was representative of the times and added a kind of questionable 'color' to the case." Blackmun hoped that his opinion did not "indicate any sympathy with [defense] remarks about your State." In his judgment, Arkansas had "taken tremendous strides in these troubled days." He added, "You may not believe it but I find myself continually carrying the torch for the State when, in polite conversation, people ask the usual question about tender race issues which may confront us. In fact, I had a substantial dose of this last week when we were in Massachusetts."[61]

The Supreme Court reversed Blackmun's opinion for a circuit panel in *Jones v. Alfred H. Mayer Co.*, a significant fair housing case. But his opinion and other documents make clear that Blackmun had no objections to being overturned in that case. In *Mayer*, a black couple denied the opportunity to buy a home in Paddock Woods, an all-white St. Louis development, contended that their exclusion violated a provision of the 1866 Civil Rights Act, a remnant of Reconstruction, which gave all citizens the same rights as white citizens in property transactions. When Blackmun wrote his Minnesota friend Leland Scott that the case, which had been dismissed by a federal district court, was pending in the Eighth Circuit, Scott was appalled. "The fact that an issue can be made of this…shocks me, although I suppose it shouldn't.…By what right or authority can a man be *forced to sell his property* to another if he chooses not to do business with the other? I am so hopelessly out of date that I know I should retire into silence and complete capitulation to the social service workers and bureaucrats." But Blackmun was unlikely to have shared his friend's sentiments. In his opinion for a unanimous panel affirming the trial court, he bowed to Supreme Court precedent limiting congressional power under the Fourteenth Amendment's equal protection guarantee to state rather than private discrimination, and declining to extend the Thirteenth Amendment's ban on slavery to the sort of discrimination at issue in the case. "It is not for our court, as an inferior one," he observed, "to give full expression to any personal inclination any of us might have and to take the lead in expanding constitutional precepts when we are faced with a limiting Supreme Court decision which, so far as we are told directly, remains good law." When circulating his draft opinion to his colleagues, he asserted that a reversal of the trial judge had "its theoretical, logical and moral appeal," but concluded that, "at this late date, [it was] a matter for Congress [or the Supreme Court] and not for the lower federal courts to accomplish." "Perhaps, in this field I am not alert to the times or as 'progressive' as some of our 'brethren,' whom we could name, would be." In a letter to Judge Lay, moreover, he favored "fair housing [as] one of the factors for the elimination of the Ghetto."[62]

When the *Mayer* case was argued in the Supreme Court, Solicitor General Erwin Griswold, a longtime friend through their Harvard Law School ties, wrote Blackmun, applauding his opinion as "an able and illuminating one. I do not see how you could reach any other result in the place where you are sitting." He added, however, "It may be different, though, in the Supreme Court." Blackmun soon replied. "I expect, as you do, that the case will be reversed. From the language and tenor of my opinion you know, I think, that this would not displease me in the least." Blackmun was not disappointed with either the high Court's decision or its rationale. A majority held that Congress, via its authority to enforce the Thirteenth Amendment, could outlaw every form of racial discrimination, public or private, as a badge of slavery. Earlier, Blackmun had written Judge Gerald Heaney that a Supreme Court decision based on an expanded construction of the Thirteenth Amendment "could provide [a] fascinating way out of the state action dilemma" that a ruling based on the Fourteenth Amendment would pose.[63]

Criminal Justice

In most criminal justice cases, Judge Blackmun sided with the state, probably with some encouragement from Judge Sanborn. Early in his tenure, he sent Sanborn a copy of his proposed opinion upholding the automobile theft conviction of one Harry Floyd Brown, a habitual criminal whom he termed Sanborn's "old and persistent friend." Earlier, Sanborn had been on a panel that had reversed a trial court holding that Brown's appeal was frivolous and that he was thus not entitled to appointed counsel on appeal. In his reply to Blackmun, Sanborn indicated that, were he participating on the panel, "I should heartily concur" with the court's decision affirming the conviction. "Probably," he added, "we should have denied leave to proceed in forma pauperis [with an appointed attorney], but the Supreme Court seems so sensitive about the rights of such as Brown that we resolved all doubts in his favor."[64]

Blackmun shared Sanborn's concerns. After the Supreme Court ruled in *Escobedo v. Illinois* (1964) that suspects who become the focus of a police investigation are entitled to counsel during questioning, Blackmun circulated a letter with his proposed opinion in a case challenging use of a confession in a rape case. "For me, the present trend of the Supreme Court is in the direction of admitting no confession into evidence whatsoever. I suspect that about four of the Justices would be willing to reach this result right now. I personally do not favor this and I certainly do not wish to anticipate it in [this] case."[65]

At the same time, however, he scrupulously followed *Escobedo*, as well as traditional due process standards of voluntariness and the high Court's holding in *Miranda v. Arizona* (1966) that confessions were still admissible, but only if accompanied by the now familiar *Miranda* warnings safeguarding the rights of suspects subjected to custodial interrogation. He reversed the defendant's conviction in a brutal child rape-murder case, for example, even though the Supreme Court had declined to give *Escobedo* and *Miranda* retroactive application. Due process, Blackmun concluded, required a hearing on the voluntariness of the defendant's statements.[66]

Blackmun remained skeptical, however, of the expanded rights accorded suspects and defendants. In upholding one conviction based on evidence seized in a warrantless police search of a vehicle, he declared, "We are not willing, even in this day of critical review of all police operations, to hold that this highway investigation was improper, or not in line with the trooper's duty, or violative of any fundamental right possessed by [the defendant]." "As is common in these cases," he noted in another opinion, "no assertion is made here that [the defendant] Miner was innocent of the state crime with which he was charged." Speaking for a divided panel in that case, Blackmun affirmed Miner's waiver of counsel and plea of guilty to charges that he had molested his two young nieces. But in a vigorous dissent, Judge Lay declared that he was "unaware of another case where the law has shown such calloused insensitivity to the denial of basic constitutional rights of an individual." Miner was an illiterate American Indian and chronic alcoholic with forty-one prior arrests for intoxication. Lay seriously doubted that he had "knowingly" waived his right to counsel and pled guilty to the charges.[67]

On one occasion after his appointment to the Supreme Court, Blackmun would have the pleasure of joining a majority in overturning a Warren Court decision expanding the rights of a defendant in an Eighth Circuit case. In *Kaufman v. United States* (1965), he spoke for a unanimous panel in affirming the conviction of a defendant in a bank robbery case. Later, Kaufman filed a federal habeas corpus suit in which he contended that his conviction had been the product of an unlawful search and that such claims could be raised in habeas proceedings as well as on direct appeal of a defendant's conviction. The Eighth Circuit had consistently rejected such claims, and both the district court and the circuit refused to review Kaufman's contentions. A divided Supreme Court reversed, holding that search and seizure claims could be raised in federal habeas proceedings. In *Stone v. Powell* (1976), however, Justice Blackmun joined a ruling rejecting the Supreme Court's *Kaufman* rationale and holding that defendants could not raise search and seizure claims in federal habeas proceedings if they had been given a full and fair opportunity to raise them at trial and on direct appeal of a conviction.[68]

Usually Blackmun was also reluctant to anticipate a Supreme Court expansion of criminal procedure rights. In *Ashe v. Swenson* (1960), a defendant was convicted of robbing one of six participants in a poker game after earlier being acquitted of robbing another player. Citing *Hoag v. New Jersey*, a 1958 Supreme Court ruling with similar facts, an Eighth Circuit panel, per Judge Blackmun, rejected Ashe's double jeopardy and due process claims. In a letter to the other judges on the *Ashe* panel, Blackmun speculated that, given changes in the Supreme Court's membership since *Hoag*, the current Court would no longer embrace that precedent. "Thus our question is whether we adhere to *Hoag* as controlling authority and let them overrule it, or whether we are 'progressive,' as some judges would call it and be inclined to do, and flatly say that we think *Hoag* is no longer the law and reverse." Blackmun suggested that the panel follow *Hoag*. "I just am inclined generally to the view that it is not for us to change Supreme Court rulings, and that that is their function and not ours. As a matter of fact, in my view, a Supreme Court Justice ought really to expect this and ought to be annoyed, at least mildly, whenever a lower court ventures a guess that the law has changed because the Court's personnel has changed."[69]

The panel followed Blackmun's suggestion, and the Supreme Court reversed, as he had expected. By that point, Warren Burger had become chief justice. Over Burger's lone dissent, a majority concluded that Ashe's second prosecution violated the Fifth Amendment guarantee against double jeopardy, which the Court had made binding on the states the previous year via the Fourteenth Amendment's due process clause. Speaking for seven members of the Court, Justice Potter Stewart reasoned that the double jeopardy guarantee embodied the federal rule of collateral estoppel, under which any issue of fact that had been finally resolved in a case could not be relitigated in a suit involving the same parties. Ashe's first trial, according to Stewart, had resolved the only factual issue: whether Ashe was one of the gunmen who robbed the six poker players. But in his dissent, Burger contended that the charge against Ashe in the second trial required proof of a fact (robbery of another poker player) not at issue in the first trial. Scrawled across the front page of the slip opinion in the case that he sent Blackmun, the chief justice wrote that in a three- to four-minute summary from the bench he had suggested that the constitutional guarantee against being placed in jeopardy twice for the "same offense" be amended to read "for the same or similar offenses."[70]

Judge Blackmun was not invariably unwilling, however, to anticipate changes in Supreme Court construction of criminal procedure guarantees, at least when the evidence reflecting a likely shift in the Court's stance was substantial. In *United States v. Kahriger* (1953), the high Court had upheld provisions of the federal gambling law requiring gamblers not only to a pay a tax, but also to provide federal revenue officials with information about their operations, which could then be turned over to state officers, the law provided, for possible use in state gambling prosecutions.

The Court had not yet overruled *Kahriger* in 1967, when Blackmun spoke for a unanimous panel in striking down similar registration provisions in the National Firearms Act. Noting, among other things, that the Supreme Court had recently overturned registration requirements in a federal anticommunist statute and granted certiorari in two cases raising self-incrimination challenges to the gambling provisions *Kahriger* had upheld, he concluded that his court "would no longer be justified in declining to decide the Fifth Amendment issue" raised against the federal firearms statute. In 1968 and 1969, of course, the Supreme Court struck down both the gambling and the firearms registration provisions, as well as those in a federal marijuana tax law.[71]

Insanity Defense

With respect to another criminal justice issue, Blackmun made it clear early in his circuit tenure that he, like Warren Burger, did not embrace the expansive version of the insanity defense that the Court of Appeals for the District of Columbia had endorsed in *Durham v. United States* (1954). Under the old *M'Naghten* insanity rule, first announced in an 1843 British case, defendants could be declared legally sane only if they were unable to distinguish right from wrong at the time of their offense. Federal courts had applied the *M'Naghten* rule, supplemented by a requirement that the defendant's crime had also been the product of an "irresistible impulse," after the Supreme Court approved that version of the rule in an 1895 case. But in 1954, the D.C. circuit court adopted the *Durham* rule, declaring that defendants were not criminally responsible for crimes that were the product of "mental disease or mental defect." After his appointment to the D.C. bench, Warren Burger wrote a concurrence in *Blocker v. United States* (1961), in which he rejected the *Durham* rule and noted that two other judges joined him in recognizing "the need for a change in the standard of criminal responsibility" applied in the District of Columbia.[72]

In *Dusky v. United States* (1959), an appeal of a kidnapping conviction raising insanity and related claims, Judge Sanborn had asserted for a unanimous Eighth Circuit panel, "Our views as to the test of insanity...do not conform with [the] views of the Court of Appeals for the District of Columbia Circuit." Sanborn also suggested that "it would, no doubt, be helpful if the Supreme Court would grant certiorari…and clarify the law relating to the test of insanity." The Supreme Court granted review, reversed the lower courts, and remanded the case for further proceedings on the issue of whether the defendant had been competent to stand trial. But the high Court did not provide the assistance Sanborn had hoped for. After the trial court again rejected Dusky's claims, a unanimous Eighth Circuit panel, speaking this time through Judge Blackmun, affirmed, rejecting, among other things, the defendant's insanity claim. Like Judge Sanborn, Blackmun declined to invoke the *Durham* rule, noting instead "the very recent provocative and interesting opinions" in the *Blocker* case, which "show[ed] the breaking away from Durham of one-third of the membership of" the court that had created the rule. If a judge's charge to a jury on the insanity issue emphasized three "elements— knowledge, will and choice—… as essential constituents of the defendant's legal sanity," he declared, "we suspect that the exact wording of the charge and the actual name of the test are comparatively unimportant and may well be little more than an indulgence in semantics. We think this approach to be sound because it preserves and builds upon those elements of M'Naghten and of irresistible impulse which are acceptable in these days and yet modernizes them in terms which a jury can grasp and apply."[73]

When Blackmun shared a draft of his *Dusky* opinion with Warren Burger, his friend pronounced it an "excellent job." But Blackmun soon became suspicious of the position his Mayo friend Dr. Howard Rome was taking on the issue, writing Burger shortly before *Dusky* was announced that Rome "recently had a long conversation with Judge B. [presumably, David Bazelon, author of the D.C. Circuit's *Durham* opinion] in Chicago on Durham, et al. This merits investigation. I am beginning to wonder exactly where he stands." But other courts declined to adopt the *Durham* rule, and several years later, Burger had the satisfaction of scrawling across the first page of the *Blocker* ruling, "In 1960–61 an attack on *Durham* was like a parish priest endorsing birth control in 1900. This climate is largely forgotten now that *Durham* as such has been interred—but the original un-hinging took a lot of documentation."[74]

The Supreme Court would not directly confront its most vexing criminal justice issue, the constitutionality of the death penalty, until Blackmun had become a justice. But his circuit record reveals his deep personal distaste for capital punishment, particularly his concerns about racial disparities in its imposition and his preference for abolition of the death penalty through legislative and executive action rather than via judicial intervention.

In *Feguer v. United States* (1962), decided relatively early in his circuit tenure, Blackmun spoke for a unanimous panel in rejecting the insanity defense and upholding a death sentence imposed on a man convicted of kidnapping a physician who was later found shot to death. In his opinion, he emphasized the diligence and care with which appellate courts were obliged to review death sentences. "When a criminal case involving the ultimate penalty which the law can impose comes before an appellate court for review," he declared, "that court has an obligation, serious and profound, to examine with care every point of substance raised by the defense and acquaint itself intimately with the details of the record. This is especially so where, as here, the case concerns both an emotionally offensive act and many facets of the criminal law which today are particularly sensitive."[75]

While *Pope v. United States* (1967), another case involving insanity issues and the death penalty, was pending before the full circuit, Blackmun wrote Warren Burger, "I can't bring myself around to favoring capital punishment but I am not sure that our group would go along with a strong-arm reduction…to a life sentence." Ultimately, he spoke for a unanimous court in upholding Pope's conviction and death sentence for a bank robbery in which three employees were killed and a fourth seriously wounded. In high school, Pope had been a student leader. He was enrolled in college at the time of his crime. Moved by the defendant's exemplary background, Blackmun ended an initial draft of his opinion in the case with the suggestion that Pope might be a suitable candidate for executive clemency and a life sentence, rather than execution. "You may perhaps feel," he noted in a cover letter to his draft opinion, "that my closing comments about capital punishment and executive clemency should be omitted. If you do, please say so. Heretofore I have been rather neutral about capital punishment, but *Feguer* and this case have convinced me that its efficacy is questionable." Judge Lay "request[ed] that [Blackmun's] thoughts concerning executive clemency…be retained." But Judge Vogel recommended the passage's deletion, noting that it did "not express my thinking [about]…capital punishment, particularly in this case. I merely suggest the omission. If the other judges desire to go along…I shall not protest further." But Judge Matthes was not so sanguine. "I am opposed…to the gratuitous comments," he wrote Blackmun. "It is my view that these remarks add nothing to the opinion and have no effect." Blackmun obligingly removed the paragraph. But Judge Lay then added Blackmun's suggestion to the end of his concurring opinion in the case, and in more aggressive language than his cautious colleague had employed. "The ends of criminal justice," Lay declared, "would be served by a life sentence for Duane Pope. I fully recognize that clemency is not within the power of the judiciary, yet the overall circumstances of this case and need of humaneness in laws of criminal procedure require me to speak."[76]

Blackmun reiterated his concerns about capital punishment the next year in *Maxwell v. Bishop*. Maxwell, an African American, had been convicted by a jury and sentenced to death for the rape of a white woman in 1962. After the Arkansas Supreme Court affirmed his conviction, his counsel brought a habeas corpus proceeding in his behalf in federal district court. The suit alleged a host of constitutional violations, among them unlawful search and seizure, police mistreatment of the defendant, extraction of coerced confessions, racial discrimination in jury selection, and a challenge to the constitutionality of the death penalty. The district court rejected each of the petitioner's contentions, and in 1965 the Eighth Circuit affirmed. After the Supreme Court denied a writ of certiorari to review the Eighth Circuit ruling, Maxwell's counsel filed a second habeas proceeding in 1966. The district judge again denied his petition, and neither that court nor the Eighth Circuit agreed to grant a further stay of Maxwell's execution. After the Supreme Court granted a stay and ordered further review of Maxwell's case, a three-judge panel, speaking through Judge Blackmun, rejected his claims that a prima facie case had been established that the death penalty for interracial crimes was racially discriminatory in Arkansas, that Maxwell's conviction and death sentence via a single jury verdict permitted juries to render irrational sentencing decisions, and that the Arkansas system of jury selection was racially biased. Rejecting the statistical evidence purporting to demonstrate that the death penalty was racially discriminatory, Blackmun pointed out that the data were drawn from a county other than the one in which Maxwell's offense had occurred and where he had been tried and convicted. Those statistics, he added, also did not show that Maxwell's own jury was racially biased. "We do not say," he conceded, "that there is no ground for suspicion that the death penalty for rape may have been discriminatorily applied over the decades in that large area of states whose statutes provide for it. There are recognizable indications of this. But…improper state practice of the past does not automatically invalidate a procedure of the present.…We do say that nothing has been presented in Maxwell's case which convinces us, or causes us seriously to wonder, that, with the imposition of the death penalty, he was the victim of discrimination based on race." Nor would the panel accept Maxwell's contention that he was the victim of racial bias in the jury selection process.[77]

Even though Blackmun spoke for the court in affirming Maxwell's conviction and death sentence, he found the case unusually troublesome. On the circuit bench, Blackmun had begun a practice, which he would continue on the Supreme Court, of preparing one or more summaries of his impressions about each case he heard. In a summary for *Maxwell v. Bishop*, he indicated that he was bothered about the single verdict system in which the jury decided on a punishment as well as guilt or innocence following a trial. To that point, the Supreme Court had not ruled that a two-stage trial—one to determine guilt or innocence and a separate proceeding to assess punishment—was constitutionally required in capital cases. "One wonders about this," Blackmun wrote. "I personally could plump for it. Only by two trials does one preserve the right [of the defendant] not to take the stand [during the determination of a verdict] and the right of allocution" (that is, the right of defendants to speak out in their defense before punishment is imposed). He was further bothered by the imposition of capital punishment for rape. "I think we are not far from the point," he correctly predicted, "where the Supreme Court will hold that capital punishment for rape, or at least for interracial rape, is a cruel and inhuman punishment in violation of the Eighth Amendment."

Blackmun doubted that the Court was "yet ready" to outlaw capital punishment for homicide, but added, "It may reach that point." On the issue of racial discrimination in the imposition of death sentences, he was more ambivalent. "One senses, wholly apart from proof, that there has been unequal application of the death penalty in the southern states. [But] it is almost impossible to prove that this is so." Were the court to agree that Arkansas death sentences in interracial cases were racially biased, he added, "the State of Arkansas would really be in turmoil."[78]

Blackmun concluded his summary by noting that he had always found the case "troubl[ing], ... not from the viewpoint of guilt, for I think this man is unquestionably guilty, but from the moral aspect of capital punishment and the innate feeling that this is a rough area of southern justice. Maybe this is the case where I say what I should have said in *Pope* and express my opposition to capital punishment. Vogel and Matthes [the other two members of the panel] will not join me in this but the time may be ripe."[79]

Characteristically, whether out of innate modesty or deep-seated feelings of insecurity stemming from his childhood, Blackmun typically referred to the opinions he circulated to his colleagues as "feeble" efforts or in similar, self-deprecating terms. He submitted his draft in *Maxwell* to Judges Vogel and Matthes "with diffidence." Anthony Amsterdam, the aggressive lawyer and law professor, headed Maxwell's large legal team, and Blackmun also conceded to his colleagues that he had "difficulty ... reading and really understanding a professor's brief," adding, "I suspect I am too far removed from academic days to understand the professorial mind any more."[80]

He was now firm, however, in his commitment to state emphatically his misgivings about capital punishment, although he knew that his colleagues would not concur. "I admit," he wrote Vogel and Matthes, "that I have always regretted my withdrawal, in the Pope opinion, of my remarks about capital punishment which resulted in correspondence of sad memory and in Judge Lay's separate concurrence. But I do struggle with these capital cases, particularly the rape ones, and I feel compelled to indicate my anguish here."[81]

At the end of his draft *Maxwell* opinion, Blackmun observed that efforts on the petitioner's behalf would not have been so persistent had he received a life sentence rather than death. "This fact," declared the judge, "makes the decisional process in a case of this kind particularly excruciating

for the author of this opinion who is not personally convinced of the right-
ness of capital punishment and who questions it as an effective deterrent."
In his earlier personal summary of the case, he had written, "I am convinced
that the answer to this case is for the Governor to exert executive clemency
and commute this sentence to life imprisonment." In his draft opinion, however, he merely observed that "the advisability of capital punishment is a policy matter ordinarily to be resolved by the legislature or through executive
clemency and not by the judiciary." Anticipating the likely reaction of Vogel
and Matthes, he also attached a footnote at that point in his draft. Footnote
11 read, "Judges Vogel and Matthes do not join in this comment."[82]

Both Blackmun's statement and footnote 11 were in the final opinion. When the decision was announced, Judge Lay praised his colleague's
"superb job with a tough case!" In indicating his preference that footnote
11 be retained, however, Judge Matthes had written Blackmun, "I am fully
aware of your attitude in regard to capital punishment in a case of this
kind. If I were charged with the responsibility of imposing the penalty
for a rapist I would probably be hard put to mete out the death penalty,
but as a judge of a reviewing court, my position is that since the penalty is
authorized, no useful purpose is served in expressing my distaste for the
policy....The statement has a tendency to detract from the force of the
opinion and may furnish some ammunition for the Supreme Court."[83]

On June 1, 1970, the Supreme Court did vacate the decision, but
without challenging the death penalty directly. Instead, it remanded the
case to the district court for reconsideration in light of its 1968 ruling in
Witherspoon v. Illinois, which held that prospective jurors could not be
removed from a capital trial merely because of their general objections to
the death penalty, but only if their scruples were so deep-seated that they
would be unable to render a guilty verdict in a capital case. Two weeks
earlier, Blackmun had taken his seat on the high bench.[84]

The "Hide"

Whatever the complexities of Blackmun's feelings about capital punishment
and the role of the courts in such cases, he had no qualms about attacking
brutality in Arkansas's archaic penal system. Barbaric conditions at that

state's prison farms were to become a national scandal and the target of class action prisoner suits. Before Blackmun left the circuit bench he also played a significant part in that campaign. After a consolidated hearing in three suits by white inmates, two district judges had outlawed the use of crank telephones to send excruciatingly painful electrical shocks through the genitals of inmates as punishment for disciplinary infractions, as well as the requirement that inmates who broke prison rules stand for hours on a teeter board. The trial judges also barred the whipping of prisoners unless adequate safeguards were established to regulate such punishment. Speaking for a unanimous panel in *Jackson v. Bishop* (1968), Blackmun went further, barring all use of corporal punishment in Arkansas's prisons, regardless of the "safeguards."[85]

The whip of choice in the state's prisons was the "hide," as inmates called it, a strap about five feet long, four inches wide, and a quarter inch thick, attached to a wooden handle. Inmates subject to the hide lay face down while the blows, usually no more than ten lashes, were applied to their buttocks. The inmates were supposed to be fully clothed, but the evidence indicated that they were often required to remove their trousers and that the lashes frequently caused deep bruises and bleeding. Because inmates enjoyed few privileges that could be withheld as punishment, the hide was the primary form of discipline on Arkansas's prison farms.

Tracing the history of judicial constructions of the Eighth Amendment's ban against cruel and unusual punishments, especially the evolving nature of its meaning, Blackmun had "no difficulty in reaching the conclusion that...the strap's use, irrespective of any precautionary conditions which may be imposed, offends contemporary concepts of decency and human dignity and precepts of civilization which we profess to possess; and...also violates those standards of good conscience and fundamental fairness enunciated by this court in [other] cases." He was simply not convinced that any regulations governing the strap's use, "however seriously or sincerely conceived and drawn, will successfully prevent abuse." The prison system, in fact, had belatedly adopted such rules, but they had already been subjected to "misinterpretation and obvious overnarrow interpretation." Such rules were also often ignored, easily circumvented, vulnerable to abuse "in the hands of the sadistic and unscrupulous," and difficult to enforce when granted, as in Arkansas, to low-level officials (typically prison trusties). Distinguishing acceptable from unconstitutional whipping was equally problematic, Blackmun concluded, and its use was "degrading to the punisher and punished alike," frustrating the "correctional and rehabilitative goals" of criminal justice. Only two states, Arkansas and Mississippi, officially authorized the whipping of inmates, and Blackmun rejected any suggestion that they needed the strap as a disciplinary tool and were "too poor" to provide acceptable alternatives. "Humane considerations and constitutional requirements are not, in this day," he declared, "to be measured or limited by dollar considerations or by the thickness of the prisoner's clothing."[86]

Arkansas's attorney general decided not to appeal the ruling, and Blackmun's opinion in the hide case became one of the most widely applauded of his circuit tenure. Hans W. Mattick, a criminal justice specialist at the University of Chicago Law School, wrote, "It is not often that men have the opportunity to contribute to the relatively small store of rationality and decency in an over-burdened criminal justice system, but you have done so." The decision was announced on December 9, 1968, two weeks before Christmas. "It is particularly fitting and timely considering the season of the year," Mattick observed. "You have given the inmates of the Arkansas Prison System a gift of justice and, whether they know it or not, you have contributed to the humanity of the prison administrators, as well." The district judges whom Blackmun's panel had partially reversed were also complimentary. Judge Gordon E. Young termed the decision "a step that I think should have been taken, and I thoroughly agree with it," and Oren Harris praised Blackmun's "excellent opinion" and the "correct decision" the court had reached. Judge Young forwarded to Blackmun a letter he had received from Little Rock lawyer Edward L. Wright, one of two court-appointed counsel in the case. "I have always regarded Judge Blackmun," Wright wrote Young, "as a scholar's scholar and his opinion in this appeal adds even greater stature to his height. It is obvious that he spent a tremendous amount of time in developing what is truly an opinion of historic significance." The next year, when Blackmun wrote Wright congratulating him on his nomination as president-elect of the ABA, the lawyer wrote the first letter he had "ever written a judge on an opinion in any case in which I was counsel." Noting the opinion's "beauty and depth," Wright declared, "Quite apart from my naturally partisan interest, I regard the opinion as a landmark of the law. It is simply a classic."[87]

The trial judges, and no doubt others, were naturally concerned that Blackmun's opinion appeared to reject the use of all corporal punishment in Arkansas's prisons, but did not define that term. "In the next similar case," Judge Young suggested, "you may be called on to give a definition of 'corporal' punishment. Now pending is a prisoner's petition claiming that solitary confinement is a 'cruel and unusual' punishment." Judge Harris wrote Blackmun that "the terminology 'corporal punishment' gives me some concern." He "presume[d] that sooner or later the courts will be called upon for clarification." Rarely reluctant to concede his shortcomings, Blackmun wrote Young, "I am not so sure about that one." By the time he wrote Judge Harris in late January 1969, however, he admitted, "I share your concern....Clarification may be required in the future." He added, "Sometimes I think I have been too long on this court." Even so, his opinion would remain a powerful repudiation of prison barbarism.[88]

Religion and Expression

While zealous in his opposition to prison brutality, Judge Blackmun understandably was not so anxious to embrace expansive notions of inmate rights to religious liberty, at least not for maximum security prisoners with extensive histories of prison violence and related disciplinary infractions. *Sharp v. Sigler* (1969) involved the separate complaints of four white Nebraska inmates who contended that they should be allowed to attend religious services with the general inmate population in the prison chapel. One petitioner had been convicted first of armed robbery and then of assault on a prison officer; another was a three-time murderer whose last victim was a fellow prisoner; the third had been convicted of attempting to escape from prison, as well as assault, robbery, and automobile theft; the fourth was a convicted burglar who had assaulted another inmate. Such prisoners, Blackmun concluded, were "in a woefully weak position piously to proclaim their rights or desire for corporate worship with the general populations," particularly in view of the warden's efforts to provide for their religious needs, including an offer to make provision for services in a conference room within the prison's maximum security unit. "We do not underestimate an inmate's need for spiritual guidance in rehabilitation. But these petitioners expect and ask too much. Let them demonstrate by their continuing conduct that they are entitled to what they respectively seek. They will be entitled to enjoy what they earn. But until these four, with their miserable deportment records,...improve their conduct, they are in no position to demand...what they claim in the name of the free exercise of religion."[89]

In a conscientious objector case, Blackmun concluded that Congress could constitutionally grant CO status only to those whose opposition to combat was religiously based, while denying that status to those whose scruples were nonreligious, however sincerely and deeply felt. Brenda Barbara Weitzman, a native of South Africa, was prohibited from taking the oath as a naturalized citizen because her objection to combat was not grounded in her religious beliefs. Initially, she had claimed that her objections were religiously based. But later she abandoned that contention, characterizing her beliefs as entirely nonreligious and arguing that Congress could not constitutionally distinguish between religious and nonreligious objectors, denying CO status to the latter class of applicants.[90]

Over Blackmun's dissent, an Eighth Circuit majority reversed the district court and upheld Weitzman's petition for naturalization. The two members of the majority were split in their reasoning. Judge Lay concluded that Weitzman's objections to war were in fact religious in nature, despite her assertions to the contrary, and that she thus fell within the scope of CO regulations. Judge Gerald Heaney concluded, on the other hand, that the law must be declared unconstitutional or construed "as permitting all who sincerely object in conscience to bearing arms to be excused from the oath" requiring citizenship applicants to agree to bear arms. He preferred the latter course, under which Weitzman was entitled to CO status.[91]

In his dissent, Blackmun first emphasized his "profound respect for sincere personal conscience." At the same time, he saw "no reason to pamper Mrs. Weitzman and to say to her that she must not choose to abandon [her earlier position that her objections were religious] because, if she does, she may not achieve citizenship." Weitzman wanted naturalization, he asserted, "on her own precisely proposed terms, [wanted] the constitutional issue forced upon us and decided, and [was] capable of making [that] intelligent tactical choice." Blackmun was ready to oblige. Summarizing the history of CO regulations and relevant judicial interpretations, including early decisions declining to hold religious-based objections to combat unconstitutional, he contended that Congress had granted CO status only to religious objectors as a reasonable form of government accommodation to religious liberty. "The required separation of church and state [in the Constitution's religious establishment clause] does not compel the Congress to ignore religious beliefs or to be hostile to religion in the framing of legislation which implements a secular purpose. I regard the effort of the government to avoid an intrusion upon freedom of religion in the naturalization statute as one to remain neutral rather than to prefer religion." If Weitzman's constitutional arguments prevailed, he concluded, "our concepts of constitutionality have progressed far beyond [earlier days] when enunciated allegiance and devotion to the country had primary and significant meaning. As a member of an inferior federal court, I feel that we cannot go that far even in this permissive day."[92]

In the First Amendment field, as in other areas, however, Blackmun was willing to anticipate a new Supreme Court interpretation of the Constitution, given ample signals of the Court's likely shift in position. In *New York Times v. Sullivan* (1964), the Court had dramatically limited the power of trial courts to penalize libelous comment about the public activities of government officials. Under its decision, such comment could be punished only if made with malice, that is, with knowledge that the statement was false, or reckless disregard for its truth or falsity. Innocent falsehoods, even if damaging to an official's reputation, were protected by the First Amendment. In a 1966 ruling, a unanimous Eighth Circuit panel, per Blackmun, extended the *New York Times* rule to "public figures," prominent persons who, though not government officials, regularly thrust themselves into the public arena.[93]

The case involved Linus Pauling, the Nobel Prize–winning scientist and outspoken opponent of nuclear power. Pauling had organized a petition campaign calling for the United Nations to ban nuclear testing and refused to provide a Senate subcommittee with the names of those helping him to collect petitions. After 140 members of St. Louis's Washington University signed a petition supporting Pauling's defiance of the Senate, the *St. Louis Globe-Democrat* published a stinging editorial attacking the faculty and Pauling, whose nuclear views, the paper contended, were "identical with Russian policy." Anticipating a Supreme Court decision overturning Senate action against Pauling, the paper also declared that the "Court has been woefully weak in upholding the basic right of the nation to defend itself against the Communist conspiracy in recent years."[94]

Following the editorial's appearance, Pauling filed a libel suit against the *Globe-Democrat* based on a number of statements in the editorial that the paper conceded were "literally false." The Eighth Circuit panel affirmed a jury verdict dismissing the action. Citing the broad language of the Supreme Court's *Times* and other recent libel rulings, Blackmun could see little difference between the sorts of government officials to which the *Times* rule had been applied and a public figure such as Pauling, who, "by his public statements and actions, was projecting himself into the arena of public controversy...into the very 'vortex of the discussion' of a question of pressing public concern...and [was] attempting to influence the resolution of an [important] issue." The evidence Pauling had offered, he further concluded, "add[s] up to something far less than the definition of actual malice prescribed" by the *Times* rule.[95]

When Blackmun circulated his draft opinion in the case, he asked the other panel members whether they were "willing to be a little 'bold' with me in this case?" Judge Gibson fully concurred, asserting that he did not "think you could find a better factual situation to extend the doctrine of *New York Times* to persons of public prominence engaging in controversial public issues." Judge Vogel, the other member of the panel, thought Blackmun had written "a terrific opinion," adding, "While you may be a little bit 'bold,' I am in full and absolute concurrence with you all the way down the line." But Warren Burger, to whom Blackmun had also circulated a draft, was most gleeful, albeit more because of the personality involved in the case than the opinion's extension of libel doctrine. "The short of all this is that the Good Doctor wants to eat his public cake and have his private immunity. Perhaps Harry Truman would say if the damned fool can't stand the heat of the kitchen of controversy he should stay out! A gold star to you!"[96]

In 1967, the Supreme Court extended the *Times* rule to public figures and denied Pauling's petition for certiorari. One of the high Court's 1967 rulings involved retired general Edwin A. Walker, who had sued the

Associated Press and various television stations for their reporting on his bizarre activities during the 1962 desegregation riot at the University of Mississippi. In a 1968 ruling involving another of Walker's many libel actions, this one against the *St. Louis Post-Dispatch*, Judge Blackmun spoke for a unanimous panel in upholding the newspaper's motion for a summary judgment dismissing Walker's suit on "public figure" grounds.[97]

Whatever his personal feelings about the Supreme Court's expansion of First Amendment safeguards against libel laws, Blackmun was no doubt pleased when the Court, as he had expected, extended the *New York Times* rule to public figures. Early in his tenure, however, he and his colleagues had been singularly unhappy with the action of the U.S. solicitor general and the high Court in another case involving the press. In *Janko v. United States* (1960), Blackmun spoke for a panel in an income tax case that he considered minor, and certainly not deserving of the ten-year sentence imposed on the defendant. A majority remanded the case to the trial court with instructions to grant a motion of acquittal on one charge against Janko, but affirmed the trial court on other counts. Among constitutional claims that the panel rejected was the contention that prejudicial press publicity had tainted the jury. Janko had been granted a second trial based on the exposure of certain jurors to prejudicial reporting of the first trial. The trial judge had declined to sequester the jury for the second trial, but did caution jurors against exposure to media accounts of the case. When polled at the end of the trial, jurors said that they had not been influenced by anything but the evidence presented in the case. Based on the record of the proceedings, Blackmun concluded that "no prejudice to the defendant could possibly have resulted from ... news articles about the case."

On rare occasions, solicitors general file confessions of error with the Supreme Court, asking that the Court overturn a flawed lower court decision in favor of the government. When outgoing Eisenhower solicitor general I. Lee Rankin filed a confession of error in the *Janko* case based on Janko's prejudicial publicity claim, the Supreme Court summarily reversed his conviction and remanded the case to the district court for a new trial.[98]

Judge Sanborn had served on the *Janko* panel. "The action of the Supreme Court in Janko," he declared in a letter to Blackmun, "is ... ridiculous and settles nothing. I hope the new Solicitor General has some common sense." In his letter to Blackmun, Judge Matthes speculated that the "severe sentence that was imposed for what appeared to be a rather minor infraction of the law, was the motivating cause for the Solicitor General['s]" action. Blackmun agreed, writing "Of course" in the margin of Matthes's letter. "We had no trouble whatsoever on the publicity point," he wrote a district judge in Minnesota. A week after *Janko*, the high Court had overturned a conviction in another case on prejudicial publicity grounds. Scorning "inflammatory newspaper accounts" of criminal cases, Justice Frankfurter, citing *Janko*, declared in a concurring opinion that "again and again, such disregard of fundamental fairness is so flagrant that the Court is compelled, as it was only a week ago, to reverse a conviction in which prejudicial newspaper intrusion has poisoned the outcome." Convinced, and understandably so, that the publicity issue in *Janko* was "a minor one," Blackmun "really howled," he wrote Judge Matthes, when he read Frankfurter's comments.[99]

An important student rights case decided during Chief Justice Earl Warren's final term originated in the Eighth Circuit. In *Tinker v. Des Moines Independent School District* (1969), public school officials suspended students who wore black armbands to school as symbols of their opposition to the Vietnam War. A federal district court dismissed the students' complaint, through their parents, that the suspension violated their rights to freedom of expression. Following argument before a three-judge panel and reargument in the full court, the Eighth Circuit affirmed the trial court by an equally divided vote. Years later, Blackmun recalled that initially the vote was 5–3 to affirm the trial court but that one of the judges then changed his vote, remarking, "We'll make it four to four, and those jokers down in Washington can answer this question." Blackmun also remembered that he was one of the judges who favored reversing the students' suspension. But the justice's memory may have been playing tricks on him, because he appeared to side with the school officials in his private summary of the case prior to oral argument.[100]

In another case involving student expression in schools, the Fifth Circuit had concluded that any school regulation must be reasonable, with that question subject to case-by-case judicial review. Blackmun conceded that the Fifth Circuit's approach was "probably more immune against constitutional disapproval by the present Supreme Court than my view," then added, "I feel, however, that it is an apologetic [approach]. It makes each case depend on the existence of disruption and the extent of disruption [caused by student expression in schools]. It thus permits disruption to occur, rather than to prevent disruption before it occurs. This, to me, is a weakness in the Fifth Circuit approach. I think the school officials are entitled to protection at the point of prevention rather than later when tumult, disruption and chaos already occurred." Finally, he predicted that "Justices [William O.] Douglas and [Hugo L.] Black will be against this view and probably even against the Fifth Circuit. To them freedom of speech is an absolute and I suppose they would carry it even to the situation of school discipline."[101]

Blackmun was only partly correct, of course. Justice Douglas would join a 7–2 majority holding, per Justice Abe Fortas, that public school students were entitled to engage in expression, including "symbolic" speech "closely akin" to "pure" speech, on school property. School officials could not forbid expression based merely on a general, undifferentiated fear of disruption. Instead, they could control only substantial interferences with school discipline and the educational process. The wearing of the armbands had not created such a disruption of school operations.[102]

Justices Black and John Marshall Harlan dissented. Justice Harlan concluded that the suspensions were reasonable. But Justice Black, the First Amendment absolutist, argued, contrary to Blackmun's expectations, that people did not carry their First Amendment rights with them everywhere they happened to go, including the public schools. The Court, Black further contended, made a poor national school board.

Student protests during the period were hardly confined to the public schools or such mild activities as the wearing of armbands. On college campuses, mass demonstrations, armed takeovers of administrative offices, even the bombing of campus buildings became increasingly commonplace, as students and others protested against U.S. military involvement in Vietnam and other controversial government policies, including the military draft. In *Esteban v. Central Missouri State College* (1969), Blackmun spoke for a divided panel in upholding the suspension of two college students who participated in demonstrations involving hundreds of students and destruction of property. Alfredo Esteban, who was then on scholastic probation and had earlier been on disciplinary probation over a knifing incident with a fellow student, had refused a faculty member's request that he return to his dormitory during one of the demonstrations, then cursed a resident hall assistant who gave the faculty member Esteban's name. The other suspended student, Steve Roberds, claimed to be only a spectator at the demonstrations. But Blackmun was not convinced. He conceded that Roberds "may not have stopped any automobile or rocked it or forced out its occupants or damaged property," but he asserted that "these incidents took place and were aroused by the mob and he was a part of that mob. Mob action or, for that matter, the old style lynching action, always presents to the self-proclaimed 'spectator' the opportunity to claim that he was merely watching, that he did not participate, and that someone else did the job. But one may participate by being present and 'talking it up' as Roberds concededly did."[103]

Drawing a clear distinction between the "quiet and passive wearing by students of black armbands" at issue in *Tinker* and the disruptive conduct with which Esteban and Roberds were connected, Blackmun also administered the appellants a stern lecture on the responsibilities of adulthood:

> These plaintiffs are no longer children. While they may have been minors, there were beyond the age of 18. Their days of accomplishing ends and status by force are at an end. It was time they assumed at least the outward appearance of adulthood and of manhood. The mass denial of rights of others is irresponsible and childish. So is the defiance of proper college administrative authority... (gutter abuse of officials; the dumping of a trash can at a resident's feet [attributed to Esteban]... and being part of the proscribed college peace-disturbing and property-destroying demonstration). One might expect this from the spoiled child of tender years. One rightly does not expect it from the college student who has had two decades of life and who, in theory, is close to being "grown up."[104]

Although by somewhat different reasoning, Judge Lay concurred in the majority's disposition of Esteban's claims. But he found no evidence that Roberds had "in any way" materially and substantively interfered with school discipline, as required by *Tinker*. Roberds, asserted Lay, had merely attended the demonstrations and mentioned his "disgust with the college." Such activities were clearly within his First Amendment rights, in Lay's judgment.[105]

Blackmun's politically incorrect Minneapolis friend Leland Scott quickly noticed that the local press devoted more space to Judge Lay's dissent than to the majority opinion. "In a recent edition of the [Minneapolis] Tribune," Scott wrote Blackmun, "a rather long article appeared reporting your decision that colleges had the right and power to make rules. Since characteristically the paper devoted about all of its report to the lone dissenter's opinion, I am somewhat confused. For I had thought developments had established that colleges had no such power—that it was vested solely in militant negroes abetted by whites of the hippy variety." When Blackmun chided Gwenyth Jones, law reporter for the *Minneapolis Star*, about the relative attention given the majority and dissenting opinions in that paper, she "concluded that this was because the majority opinion was so clear and reasonable, it did not seem to require much exposition, while the minority opinion needed exploration. I suspect the result was a reaction to the question: 'Why would [Judge Lay] ever say that?' "[106]

Blackmun also had exchanges with his daughters regarding campus unrest and student opposition to the Vietnam War. During his oral history interviews years later, his former clerk Harold Koh turned at one point to that turbulent era. "It seemed to be a time of rebellion against authority. Did your daughters rebel against you?" At that twilight time in his life, Blackmun opted for a lighthearted reply: "Oh, they always are in a state of rebellion, Mrs. Blackmun and our daughters. They have enough votes to override a veto on my part all the time." After the *Esteban* decision was announced, however, his eldest daughter Nancy—"just to make myself thoroughly annoying"—had written her father a lengthy letter defending the protesters. Nancy, then a school counselor in Massachusetts, agreed that there were "certainly ridiculous and dangerous aspects to the student howlings and pressurings," but she also saw "a great deal of substance" in their concerns about civil rights and "the hypocrisy and smugness of our involvement in Vietnam." Social scientists had long recognized, she wrote, "that late adolescents and young adults...had something of very real substance to say to their elders, and that it would be to the general benefit of the whole civilization to listen to its youth carefully....I'm not saying that everything the kids say has value for the grown-ups...but a lot is worthwhile, especially these days when the kids have taken upon themselves very serious issues instead of foolishness." Nancy also thought it "*very* significant that...the activists and ones committed enough to get themselves arrested over what they believe in, are often the brightest and most involved kids, offspring of people like you, in fact, and your friends." Noting the turmoil at Harvard during the previous spring's commencement, she recalled how "shocking" it had been "to see how *upset* many of the very finest kids you could imagine were. They wanted to have faith in the institutions they'd grown up believing were divinely democratic, but were confronted by so much information proving...the selfish vested interest of a few powerful and wealthy people [involved in] immoral [conduct] (like American businessmen in places like South Africa)."[107]

By that point, Richard Nixon had won the presidency in a tumultuously divisive campaign that had been earmarked by appeals to a "silent majority" repulsed by the antiwar movement and the "hippy" lifestyles of its leaders. Soon, and somewhat ironically given Nancy's sentiments, Harry Blackmun was to become an indirect beneficiary of that campaign.

Chapter 4

"A Ton of Bricks"

Warren Burger and John Sanborn were clearly instrumental in Harry Blackmun's appointment to the Eighth Circuit. Judge Sanborn died in 1964. President Nixon chose Burger as chief justice in 1969, and the president's selection the next year of Burger's boyhood friend—the second Minnesotan in a row—to a seat on the high bench surely was not mere happenstance. Indeed, Blackmun appeared to acknowledge as much late in life. Asked who had urged the Nixon White House to choose him, the justice gave a sarcastic response: "At least a dozen claimed that they were separately responsible for it." But when asked whether Burger had ever claimed an influential role in Blackmun's selection, the justice replied, "No, I think he was content to let the facts speak for themselves. I think at the time he was pleased the nomination came along."[1]

President Nixon knew that he would have the opportunity to name a successor to Chief Justice Earl Warren even before his 1968 election. Hoping to enable Lyndon Johnson to fill the Supreme Court's center seat before a new president was inaugurated, Warren had submitted his resignation effective with the Senate's confirmation of a new chief. President Johnson selected as Warren's replacement his longtime friend and confidant Abe Fortas, the prominent Washington lawyer he had chosen as an associate justice in 1965. But a Senate filibuster by Republicans and conservative Democrats, armed with ethics allegations against the nominee, derailed Fortas's appointment.

Warren Burger appeared the perfect Nixon choice to replace Earl Warren. Much of Nixon's presidential campaign had been devoted to attacks on liberal Warren Court rulings, especially *Miranda v. Arizona* and other decisions expanding the rights of suspects and defendants. Such rulings, Nixon declared, had contributed to increases in violent crime and disrespect for law and order. If elected, he promised, he would restore the balance between the "peace forces" and the "crime forces" of the nation, in part by appointing "strict constructionist" judges who would interpret the Constitution, rather than legislate from the bench.

Burger's criminal justice record on the D.C. court of appeals and recent speeches certainly squared with the new president's campaign rhetoric and pledge to appoint "strict constructionists" to the federal bench. "Too many law professors," Burger had declared in a Columbus, Ohio, speech delivered in September 1968, "for a long time gave uncritical applause to anything and everything they could identify as an expansion of individual 'rights,' even when that expansion was at the expense of the rights of other human beings—the innocent citizens—presumably protected by the same Constitution.... Today we have the most complicated system of criminal justice and the most difficult system to administer of any country in the world. To a large extent this is a result of judicial decisions which in effect made drastic revisions of the code of criminal procedure and evidence, and to a substantial extent imposed these procedures on the states." In dissent from a 1969 D.C. Circuit decision overturning a defendant's conviction on *Miranda* and related grounds, Burger decried "the seeming anxiety of judges to protect every accused person from every consequence of his voluntary utterances." Such an attitude, he asserted, was "giving rise to myriad rules, sub-rules, variations and exceptions which even the most alert and sophisticated lawyers and judges are taxed to follow." Apparently, President Nixon was particularly impressed with a 1967 address that Burger had delivered to a college audience in Ripon, Wisconsin. Scorning a criminal justice system "in which it is often very difficult to convict even those who are plainly guilty," Burger applauded northern European systems in which justice was swiftly administered, "followed by a humane and compassionate disposition and treatment of the offender" in a prison system seriously committed to rehabilitation. After a lengthy trial and appeal process in the United States, by contrast, criminals tended to be regarded "as human rubbish." Shortly before his appointment as chief justice, moreover, Burger had told an audience at a judicial conference that close Warren Court civil liberties decisions could be undone "by so simple a happening as the advent of one or two new Justices."[2]

On May 21, 1969, the president announced Burger's nomination to the Supreme Court's center seat. Given the climate of the times, the Senate's favorable reception to Nixon's choice of a "law and order" chief justice was not surprising. After a brief, perfunctory hearing, the Senate Judiciary Committee unanimously recommended his confirmation. The full Senate concurred, and Earl Warren administered the oath of office to his successor on June 24, 1969.

The Blackmun Nomination

Harry Blackmun was present when Burger took the oath as chief justice. Soon he would follow his friend to the high bench. President Nixon had been given another vacancy to fill when Justice Fortas, under heavy fire from the White House and John Mitchell, the president's new attorney general, submitted his resignation. Blackmun was among those given early mention in the press as a possible successor to Fortas. Nixon, as part of his "southern strategy" to bolster Republican strength among whites in the South, instead chose Clement Haynsworth, a respected South Carolinian on the Court of Appeals for the Fourth Circuit. But following revelations that Haynsworth had sat in cases involving companies in which he had tiny stock holdings, that nomination went down to defeat in the Senate. Vowing to continue his campaign to place a southerner on the Court, Nixon next turned to G. Harrold Carswell, a Florida federal appeals court judge with mediocre credentials and a segregationist background. Nebraska Republican Roman L. Hruska made his now infamous attempt to defend Carswell in the Senate, declaring, "There are a lot of mediocre judges and people and lawyers, and they are entitled to a little representation, aren't they? We can't have all Brandeises, Frankfurters, and

Cardozos." But Hruska's effort was obviously to no avail. On April 8, 1970, the Senate also rejected Carswell's nomination.

Shortly after Carswell's defeat, President Nixon, accompanied by Attorney General Mitchell, heatedly told reporters that he was now convinced that the Senate would never confirm a nominee from the South and that his next choice for the Fortas seat would be a nonsoutherner. Several names of prospective nominees were mentioned in the press and by White House spokespersons, but the administration focused on Blackmun from the outset. Within hours of Nixon's announcement that he was now seeking a nominee from outside the South, Blackmun had managed to elude reporters and check into Washington's Cosmos Club, where he had been a nonresident member since his days at the Mayo Clinic. During that trip to the capital, he had lengthy sessions with John Mitchell, Deputy Attorney General Richard Kleindienst, and his future Supreme Court colleague William H. Rehnquist, then a member of the Justice Department's Office of Legal Counsel, as well as Johnnie Walters of the department's tax division. Next, he met with Mitchell and President Nixon at the White House. Years later, he still had vivid recollections of that visit with the president:

> After [the earlier] interrogation [by Mitchell and others],...I
> was told that we would go to the White House....No luncheon
> [had been] served up. I was hungry, but sure enough at two
> o'clock,...or whatever it was, why, Mr. Mitchell came in and
> got me where I was, and we went over in the attorney general's
> limousine to the White House...and were escorted up into the
> Oval Office. I well remember that conference with Mr. Nixon.
> It struck me as being a little unusual in some respects because
> Mr. Nixon sat on his side of the desk and Mr. Mitchell...on the
> other side. And they allowed as how I could sit in a chair at the
> end of the desk....I sat there silently [sipping a cup of coffee]
> while these other two spoke....Here were two former law part-
> ners who must have called each other by their first names all the
> time. There was none of that during that conversation. It was
> wholly formal. The President would say, "Mr. Attorney General,
> what is your recommendation?" and Mitchell would say,
> "Mr. President we recommend that the judge be offered the

nomination for the Supreme Court." I thought this was rather nice but certainly most unusual.

At one point during the meeting, Mitchell left the room. While Blackmun and the president were alone, Nixon asked two questions that the future justice found inappropriate and annoying.

> He said, "What kind of woman is Mrs. Blackmun?"
> I said, "What do you mean?"
> He said, "She will be wooed by the Georgetown crowd. Can she withstand that kind of wooing and resist it?" I said I thought she could. Then...he said, "Judge, what are you worth?"
> I said, "What do you mean, what am I worth?"
> "How many dollars do you have?"—which annoyed me at the time. I didn't know this was a factor to be considered, and it raised the hackles a little bit. He noticed my discomfort, and then I got a little lecture about how broke he had been when he left the vice-presidency and was strapped for funds. So I was on the receiving end of that. Otherwise, it was a happy enough conference.[3]

Given the somewhat dismissive treatment he had received at the White House, Blackmun could not have been surprised at what happened after his meeting with the president. "I was hoping that they'd take me out to the airport," he recalled in later years. "I had a five o'clock plane, or something, but they didn't. They just dropped me at the Cosmos Club. I grabbed my bag and scrounged for a cab. Fortunately, I found one."[4]

The announcement of Blackmun's nomination was equally unceremonious. He had met with Nixon on Friday, April 10. By that point, press speculation was focused on Blackmun and two federal district judges, Edward T. Gignoux of Maine and Alfred T. Goodwin of Oregon. Asked specifically about Blackmun at a Saturday briefing for reporters, Nixon's press secretary, Ronald Zeigler, answered, "It would be folly for me [to] imply that Judge Blackmun is not under consideration." The following Tuesday morning, April 14, Richard Kleindienst had a secret meeting with Republicans on the Senate Judiciary Committee, informing them that Blackmun was the president's choice. At the White House later that day, Zeigler announced that the Minnesotan was Nixon's third nominee for the Fortas seat, or "Old Number Three," as the justice would later refer to himself over the years. Still angry at the Senate for its rejection of his first two choices, Nixon was not present and had given his press secretary no statement for reporters or the nation. Instead, Zeigler told journalists that the president had met with Blackmun for forty-five minutes the previous Friday, had developed "great respect for his legal skills and his judicial temperament," and was "highly impressed by [his] personal qualities." Press reports were already speculating about Blackmun's long and close association with Chief Justice Burger and at least hinting at the possible impact of that relationship on the new justice. Perhaps for that reason, Zeigler also said that Blackmun's selection was not based on a recommendation from Burger. But he did concede that Attorney General Mitchell had talked with the chief justice prior to the nomination "because [Burger] was aware of Judge Blackmun's background."[5]

Blackmun was sitting on an Eighth Circuit panel in St. Louis when a note was passed to him on the bench, informing him that his nomination had been announced. When the morning court session concluded, he and his colleagues found the corridor filled with reporters. Judge Van Oosterhout was presiding over the panel that day. "He immediately came down," Blackmun later recalled, "and said, 'I think you should go home. And don't worry about the cases, we'll take care of them.' He did the same thing about other pending argued cases that had not yet been decided. It was a great boon to have him take things over."[6]

Before leaving St. Louis for Rochester, the nominee reluctantly agreed to talk with reporters. Emphasizing that he had not yet had any official word from the president or the White House, he said that he was "overwhelmed" by the news. "It's a very humbling thing....I feel as though a ton of bricks has landed on me." Identifying himself only as a "nominal Republican all my life," he gave what would become his stock answer to questions about his political and judicial leanings: "I've been called both a liberal and a conservative. I think labels are deceiving. I've tried to call them as I've seen them." Characteristically, he conceded that he viewed the nomination with "mixed emotions," but added, "No lawyer turns down a thing like this."[7]

Blackmun remained composed during the interview. But later, when he confronted reporters as he left his chambers, he appeared visibly shaken, tears glistening in his eyes. "No more, please," he told them, his voice reportedly choked and breaking. "I just don't feel up to it. You fellows have been so nice. I'm sorry you had to sit so long." He then caught a flight home with his law clerk and secretary.[8]

In Rochester, Dottie Blackmun reacted to the news, as anyone who knew her would have expected, with unconcealed joy. Dottie drove a green Ford Mustang, a striking contrast to her staid husband's aging, pale blue Volkswagen. She and a friend owned Designing Women, a dress shop featuring custom apparel. Pictured in news photographs wearing a stylish blouse, a skirt well above the knees, and modish, cream-colored leather boots, she informed reporters that her husband's nomination was not entirely a surprise. "Everybody all down through the years thought this would happen and people have been calling him 'Justice' for years." When the reports first came out, "there was a call every three minutes for six hours," she said. Her husband had told her to "disconnect the phone and get out of here, but I just can't." Acknowledging the obvious, that she and Blackmun were "just about opposites in a number of ways," she added, "If I'm gonna be his wife, he's gonna have to take me the way I am." She was hardly shy with reporters. Recalling the day in 1937 when they first met on a tennis court, she said, "I remember being very much interested in Harry, being struck by his poise and his way of speaking. I didn't look back when I walked to the [tennis] court, but he followed me." She also recalled their long courtship. "It took me four years to get him and now that I know him as well as I do, I've often wondered how I maneuvered it. Harry's not one to do things impulsively." When Blackmun arrived at the Rochester airport, he spotted Dottie "arm in arm with [legal reporter] Nina Totenberg, which upset me at the time a little bit. . . . [Totenberg] was on her way up, . . . trying to make a name for herself." Dottie, on the other hand, was hardly perturbed at the media attention her husband was getting.[9]

Reporters also contacted the Blackmuns' daughters. Nancy, then a school guidance counselor, assured a caller that her father was "a man of enormous personal and professional integrity." Sally was then living in Vestal, New York, where she and her husband, Richard Funk, were employed at IBM, Sally as a secretary. She was "a-bubble" that the nomination was finally official. Susie and her husband, Roger M. Carl, students at DePauw University, were "very proud," but, like her father, had "mixed feelings.

As dad said," referring to the upcoming Senate confirmation process, "you can't really tell what's going to happen in the next few months." Sally said that her father's "judicial mien...used to intimidate her friends." She and her sisters described him as a "serious, conscientious parent" with a "subtle" sense of humor. "We're pleased," Nancy said, "when we can make him smile." They portrayed their mother, on the other hand, as "delightful," "very cheerful," "friendly and alive."[10]

Other press coverage gave attention to the nominee's human side. He and Dottie lived in an attractive ten-room, redwood and brick home, designed and built by an architect and situated on an acre of land. But the trim on the house was three shades of green because Blackmun, according to Dottie, never finished repainting all the house at once. He had a stamp collection and enjoyed cutting the lawn; he studied and read late into the night. He had been an avid chess player, even playing opponents by mail. He was an ardent Minnesota Twins fan who "really knows baseball." His father had been so determined that Harry become a lawyer that he had written Harvard's president when his son decided to major in mathematics, asking what use math courses were to a future lawyer. Corwin Blackmun relented, apparently, only when told that there was "no better training [than mathematics] for teaching a man how to think." Harry was, at least one profile noted, "a quiet, withdrawn and somewhat aloof man...who is almost totally devoted to his work." He left his house every weekday morning at 7:15 for his chambers, which had been recently relocated to an apartment house after space needs obliged him to vacate the county courthouse in Rochester. Each weekday evening he returned home at 6:15. On Saturdays, he worked a somewhat shorter schedule, leaving home at 8 a.m. and returning at 3. On Sundays, he arrived at his chambers shortly after 8, where he worked until leaving for services at Rochester's First Methodist Church. After church, he returned briefly to his office, arriving home about 1:30 p.m.[11]

An examination of the nominee's professional career and judicial record quickly convinced the press that Blackmun, unlike G. Harrold Carswell, could not be dismissed as "mediocre." Even before the nomination was announced, the *Rochester Post-Bulletin* exclaimed editorially, "Judge Blackmun for High Court? He'd Be Superb!" National publications were seemingly unanimous in their approval of the selection. In an editorial entitled "A Turn toward Excellence," the *New York Times* concluded that President Nixon "appears finally to have met the exacting standards of excellence that the Senate has rightly demanded for one of the nation's most responsible and respected lifetime offices." Scorning Nixon's "strict-constructionist" pledge, the paper applauded Blackmun for "disavow[ing] such spurious attempts to prejudge a jurist," adding, "His record does reveal a meticulous reverence for the law and a thoughtful balancing of the prerogatives of legislators and jurists. That should be a comfort to all Americans, especially at a time when the Administration through its Attorney General has displayed a disturbing disposition increasingly to disregard fundamental individual rights as spelled out in the Constitution."[12]

Summaries of Blackmun's moderate Eighth Circuit record were typically complimentary. His opinion in the Arkansas prison whipping case received prominent play, as did his insistence on meaningful school desegregation. Yet, given the times, his cautious position on school busing and neighborhood schools was unlikely to cause him difficulty in the public mind or the Senate confirmation process. Only the previous month, for example, he had asserted for an Eighth Circuit panel, "We do not rule that the neighborhood school concept is constitutionally permissible or is constitutionally impermissible....We do not rule that busing is a constitutional imperative. Busing is only one possible tool in the implementation of unitary schools." In 1968, the Supreme Court had overruled his decision in *Jones v. Mayer*, in which he rejected use of a Reconstruction-era statute to outlaw private discrimination in housing, but he had merely bowed to established precedent rather than his personal preferences in that case, the press reported. In 1969, moreover, he had joined a unanimous panel in holding that racial discrimination in the St. Louis building trade unions violated the 1964 Civil Rights Act. The Court had recently rejected, over Chief Justice Burger's lone dissent, Blackmun's dismissal of the double jeopardy claim in *Ashe v. Swenson*, and he had regularly voted to uphold death sentences and generally assumed a conservative stance in other criminal justice cases. But he had also made clear his personal opposition to capital punishment, and in 1968 he had joined a three-judge district court decision ordering the addition of Communist Party candidates to the Minnesota ballot. Unlike certain lower court judges, newspaper readers and television viewers were informed, he had been reluctant to impose court-ordered reapportionment decrees on legislative bodies. But he had no qualms about enforcing the Supreme Court's reapportionment precedents. President Nixon's latest nominee, then, was depicted in the press as cautiously supportive of civil rights, reluctant to anticipate changes in the direction of Supreme Court decisions, and conservative in criminal cases, yet sensitive to prison brutality and personally offended by the death penalty.[13]

The Nominee and the Chief

Not surprisingly, Blackmun's long association with the chief justice received extensive press treatment. He had been, the media repeatedly reported, best man at Burger's wedding. When Blackmun's daughters were children, they referred to Burger as "Uncle Warren." Burger had been a trustee at the Mayo Clinic during Blackmun's tenure there. Reporters focused on the chief justice's role in Blackmun's nomination and the likely impact of their association on Blackmun's voting patterns on the high bench. *New York Times* reporter Fred Graham asserted in a profile of the nominee that Blackmun and Burger "appear[ed] strikingly similar in judicial philosophy." One newspaper headlined a reprint of Graham's article "A Man after Burger's Heart," another reprint was headed, "A Burger Majority?" and yet another asserted "Nixon Nominee Like Burger." The *Wall Street Journal* entitled a prenomination piece "Minnesota Friend of Chief Justice Burger Termed Leading Candidate for High Court." According to unnamed administration sources, the *Journal* reported, "Judge Blackmun...isn't known well by the President or Attorney General Mitchell, who has been quarterbacking the Administration's Supreme Court nominations. But the judge apparently has the high recommendation of the Chief Justice." According to those same sources, the White House thought Blackmun was "much the same kind of conservative as Chief Justice Burger."[14]

Whether in an effort to minimize any difficulties his relationship with Warren Burger might create for him in the Senate, or perhaps because he was already becoming irritated at any hint that Burger might exert an undue influence once he became a justice, Blackmun soon sought to establish his independence from his friend. During a two-hour interview in his Rochester chambers, he "warmly praised" Burger but also emphasized that they would not always agree on the Court. "We do not always see eye to eye. If by chance this thing should go through, he would be the first to expect that we would disagree." Over the years, the two had "argued a lot; we've never agreed on everything, by any means....This has been the history of our life, that we've been able to disagree on things and have fun doing it." They had never appeared in court together. "We used to joke about what we'd do if we ever went at it hammer and tongs." The Blackmuns' close friends, Dan and Ruth Connally, who were both on Mayo's medical staff, sought to underscore the nominee's independence from the chief justice. "I have met Judge Burger in Judge Blackmun's home," Dr. Ruth Connally told a reporter, "and Judge Burger has been in our home when these two men would argue violently about being on different sides of a case—differing opinions on the same case. They don't always see eye-to-eye."[15]

Even before Blackmun's remarks appeared, however, journalists and legal scholars were beginning to suggest that the nominee might well not be a Burger clone. Within a few days of the nomination, Fred Graham, who had been among the first reporters to suggest close Blackmun-Burger philosophical ties, wrote that the nominee seemed "much like" Potter Stewart, a judicial and constitutional moderate "in philosophy and style." Graham also quoted University of Michigan law professor Yale Kamisar, who, he said, had "cheered the Warren Court on to its most liberal criminal rulings." Kamisar was well acquainted with Blackmun and his record. He termed the nominee—for President Nixon, at least—a good choice. "All the evidence," Kamisar said, "supports Judge Blackmun's own statement that he can't be classified as a conservative or a liberal." The professor "wonder[ed] if Nixon might have been misled."[16]

The Vetting Process

As the press and legal community speculated about the sort of justice Blackmun might prove to be, the Nixon administration sought to avoid a repeat of the Haynsworth and Carswell fiascoes in the Senate, especially through close scrutiny of the nominee's finances and any possible conflict of interest claims that might arise from cases in which he had participated on the circuit. The day after the nomination, Deputy Attorney General Kleindienst sent Senate Judiciary Committee chairman James Eastland a lengthy letter summarizing Blackmun's biography, financial holdings, and Eighth Circuit record. In the letter, Kleindienst conceded that the nominee had participated in three cases in which he had a financial interest in the companies involved, but declared that Blackmun's holdings were so "microscopic" that they raised no question that he had violated federal law or the American Bar Association canons of judicial ethics. The letter listed Blackmun's net worth as about $125,000, including $75,000 in stocks, bonds, and bank accounts and about $50,000 equity in his Rochester home. In 1957, two years before his appointment to the Eighth Circuit, he had purchased fifty shares of Ford Motor Co. stock valued at $2,500. Six months after his appointment, he participated in a case involving Ford, but that decision reinstated a jury verdict of $24,500 against the company, which the trial court had set aside. Moreover, Blackmun had told Kleindienst that he sat on the case only after conferring with Chief Judge Harvey Johnsen "and concluding that his interest in the case was *de minimis*." In 1964 he joined the court in upholding a district court that had set aside a jury verdict of $12,500 against Ford. But in January 1970 he recused himself from another Ford case based on the national attention given the disqualification issue in the Senate debate over Judge Haynsworth. In 1967 he also sat in a case dismissing on procedural grounds a suit against a subsidiary of the American Telephone & Telegraph Co., even though he owned twenty-two shares of company stock, purchased at a total cost of about $1,350. But those twenty-two shares, wrote Kleindienst, were a tiny portion of the nearly 540 million AT&T shares outstanding in 1967, and the $35,000 sought by the plaintiff in the case was "an infinitesimal portion" of the company's $1.5 billion net income that year.[17]

Kleindienst's letter to Senator Eastland also disclosed income the nominee had received as a corporate director and as executor of two estates after going on the bench. For four years following his appointment, he had been given a $1,500 annual fee as director of the Kahler Corporation, which operated a Rochester hotel and had close connections with the Mayo Clinic. But in January 1964, Kleindienst noted, Blackmun resigned as director after the Judicial Conference of the United States, the body of federal judges responsible for overseeing operations of lower federal courts, had recommended that judges not hold offices or directorships in for-profit corporations. With respect to income Blackmun had received from service as coexecutor of two estates following his Eighth Circuit appointment, Kleindienst explained that Blackmun had been specifically named in the will of each deceased, which the ABA had held to exempt judges from the requirement that they hold no fiduciary appointments after going on the bench. There also was no indication, he added, that the executorships had interfered with the performance of his duties on the Eighth Circuit.[18]

Just as the Nixon administration was determined to avoid the sorts of conflict of interest concerns that had derailed the Haynsworth nomination, the ABA was also seeking to overcome criticisms raised over its handling of Haynsworth and Carswell. At the time of those nominations, the ABA's Committee on Federal Judiciary was rating prospective nominees as either "qualified" or "not qualified." Initially, the committee had given both Haynsworth and Carswell positive ratings. But after damaging allegations about Judge Haynsworth during the confirmation process, four of the committee's twelve members withdrew their support of the nominee, and although voting committee members remained unanimously behind Carswell's initial positive rating, three committee members did not attend the meeting in which support for Carswell was reaffirmed.

Although the ABA had given negative ratings to about a quarter of lower court nominees since it first began reviewing and rating candidates after World War II, it had never opposed confirmation of a Supreme Court nominee, and its handling of the Haynsworth and Carswell nominations provoked intense criticism. As a result, while Blackmun's nomination was pending in the Senate, the committee met to revamp its review procedures. Following that session, Lawrence E. Walsh, the former Eisenhower deputy attorney general then serving as the committee's chairman, announced that Blackmun would be subjected to closer investigation than previous nominees. Members of the committee had already contacted the nominee's Eighth Circuit colleagues, as well as many federal district judges and lawyers in the circuit. Now, said Walsh, they would also seek the impressions of law professors and attorneys elsewhere in the nation. Then, after the confirmation hearing had been concluded in the Senate, the committee would again meet to review its initial recommendation. The ABA, added Walsh, was also replacing the current two-category rating system with a formula rating a candidate as either "meeting high standards of professional competence, temperament and integrity," "not opposed," or "not qualified." Walsh emphasized that the ABA would continue, as in the past, to evaluate nominees purely in terms of their judicial temperament, integrity, and professional competence, rather than on the basis of their likely judicial and constitutional philosophy. Whether the committee would continue its evaluation process with later nominees had not yet been decided, said Walsh, but the committee had concluded that "the association owes the Senate an answer" on Judge Blackmun. Walsh gave no indication, of course, that the committee's decision to subject Blackmun to more rigorous scrutiny than previous candidates related at all to the nominee personally rather than to the criticism directed at the ABA's recent investigations.[19]

Blackmun's Senate confirmation proceedings were scheduled to begin April 19. Before the hearing, the nominee granted additional interviews with the press. Shortly after Deputy Attorney General Kleindienst sent Senator Eastland the letter about the potential conflict of interest allegations that might be raised against Blackmun in the Judiciary Committee, the nominee met with reporters for what the *Washington Post* termed a "remarkably candid" news conference. In that setting, he emphasized that neither President Nixon nor Attorney General Mitchell had inquired about his "legal philosophy" during their White House meeting prior to the nomination. "Relaxed and almost loquacious," according to one reporter, he also touched on his Harvard years, characterizing his judicial philosophy as following in the tradition of Felix Frankfurter, his favorite law professor, he said, and a leading advocate of judicial self-restraint during his years on the Supreme Court. Responding to questions about racial issues confronting the nation, he was general, saying only, "Everyone is in the struggle [and] we're all in the process of trying to grow up." He also defended his membership in the Minneapolis Club, which once had banned blacks and Jews from membership, saying that the club gave courtesy memberships to many public figures, including former vice president Hubert Humphrey.[20]

The nominee devoted most of his attention, however, to the possible conflict of interest concerns that were certain to be raised during his confirmation hearing. In "retrospect," as he put it, he should have resigned as a director of the Kahler Corporation following his appointment to the Eighth Circuit, but he considered those board meetings merely friendly monthly dinners with "cherished" old friends. In addition to the matters Kleindienst had discussed, Blackmun disclosed that he had been executor of the estate of Dr. Donald C. Balfour, the son-in-law of William J. Mayo, but he assured reporters that he had received no fee from that estate. His fees as executor in the estates Kleindienst had cited were, he added, "low." He acknowledged that he had also been a director of an airport company the Mayo Clinic had set up to assure transportation for patients, another matter not disclosed in Kleindienst's letter. But he saw that as an issue of minor importance because the airport was operated at a loss as a community service. He further acknowledged that he had purchased thirty shares of Minnesota Mining and Manufacturing stock at about the time he sat on a 3-M patent case. But that case, he pointed out, had been decided adversely to 3-M before his stock purchase.[21]

In other interviews with reporters, Blackmun provided mixed cues to the stance he might assume in cases he was likely to confront on the high bench. Suggesting that "we are progressing in our attitudes toward criminal law," he declared that he would not be "shocked" if the Supreme Court soon declared the death penalty unconstitutional as a form of cruel and unusual punishment, and he again reiterated his personal distaste for capital punishment, declaring, "If I were a legislator having to vote on it, I'm sure I would plump for its repeal." He also stressed, however, that the issue fell "on the legislative side of our three-legged stool." At the same time, he seemed unconcerned that courts might overturn precedents of long standing. "Law," he said at one point, "is, in part, social. Man is a social being. I can't get alarmed when they overrule a prior decision, especially if it is 5–4. Who is to say that five men 10 years ago were right whereas five men looking the other direction" were wrong? Responding to a question about student protests then rocking the nation, he was equally equivocal. He professed great faith in the "younger generation," terming it more idealistic and involved than youth of the past. But, he added, "I have no sympathy with violence. We can't bring the structure tumbling down around our ears." His initial reaction to his nomination had not changed, however. "I [still] feel like a load of bricks has landed on me."[22]

Blackmun's nomination to the Supreme Court long predated the extensive White House coaching, or vetting, of nominees that became routine after the Senate's defeat of Robert Bork, President Reagan's controversial 1987 choice for a seat on the Court. Dan Edelman, a Minneapolis native who was then clerking for Blackmun on the Eighth Circuit and would follow the justice to Washington, did prepare a list of constitutional provisions pertaining to the appointment process. Edelman also compiled the names of the Dorsey firm's corporate clients during Blackmun's tenure there to assure that the judge had not sat on cases involving clients he had personally represented while practicing law.[23]

On another trip to Washington prior to the Senate hearing, the nominee made courtesy visits to the offices of each member of the Judiciary Committee. In the company of John Deffner, a member of the Justice Department staff, Blackmun "spent a whole day," he later said, "calling first upon one and then upon another of the Judiciary Committee....It was a long and wearing day. I never did get lunch, and they didn't offer anything. But, Mr. Deffner got a doughnut at every congressman's suite. I think he must have put on about four pounds that day, and I lost about four pounds."[24]

Blackmun came away from those sessions uncertain about the impression he was making on committee Democrats. Senator Birch Bayh of Indiana had led the fight against Haynsworth and Carswell. Blackmun left Bayh's office "with a sense of antagonism on his part. I think he was suspicious of all [the Nixon] nominees." But, Blackmun later recalled, "I had to respect him. He was able. He was interested." When he walked into the outer office of Massachusetts senator Edward M. Kennedy, he "felt a distinct sense of hostility." But he found his conversation with Kennedy "very pleasant...generally. We had some things in common. Both had gone to the same law school and the like....I came out of that conversation with Senator Kennedy feeling fairly comfortable. He was nice to me."[25]

As the Senate hearing date approached, Blackmun's confirmation appeared all but certain. In contrast to their cautious approach at the time of his Eighth Circuit appointment, Minnesota's Democratic senators were on the nominee's Supreme Court bandwagon from the start. Enthusiastically, if not altogether truthfully, former Senator Hubert Humphrey endorsed Blackmun even before his nomination was announced. "He's a fine man,"

Humphrey told a reporter. "He was appointed by President Eisenhower [for the circuit bench] and I was one of those who recommended him at that time." Walter Mondale, who had replaced Humphrey in the Senate, also endorsed the appointment. Before takeoff on the flight back to Minnesota after Blackmun's prenomination White House meeting with Nixon and Mitchell, the judge had overheard a conversation between Mondale and a major contributor to the senator's campaign. The press had already begun speculating about Blackmun's nomination, and the Mondale supporter asked, "Who is this guy, Blackmun?" Mondale, not realizing that Blackmun was seated nearby, responded, "Oh, he's just another old conservative." When Blackmun gently alerted Mondale of his presence ("Walter, I'm here"), the senator was clearly embarrassed. Later, when the flight was under way, Mondale hurried back to Blackmun's seat. "I want you to know," he said, "that I'm all for you, but can't always say so in public." He was true to his word, as was Senator Eugene McCarthy.[26]

In fact, President Nixon and Attorney General Mitchell, not the nominee, were the primary target of press criticism and the playful jabs of editorial cartoonists for their bungling efforts to gain political capital in the South with the Haynsworth and Carswell nominations, as well as their repeated references to the ill-defined "strict constructionist" as the Nixon model for Supreme Court nominations. One editorial cartoon depicted a black-robed Blackmun shaking hands with the president, while John Mitchell, his arm around the nominee's shoulder, declares, "Not Only a Strict Constructionist, But He Lives in SOUTHERN Minnesota." In another, Nixon, Mitchell, and Vice President Spiro Agnew, the latter carrying a "Blackmun is Beautiful" sign, push a reluctant Blackmun toward the Senate hearing room. "Courage, Judge!" Nixon is saying. "We feel humble too, by now" In a column devoted to the confusion created by "strict constructionist" and related terms, the *New York Times* columnist Tom Wicker concluded that "such labels are usually too restrictive to encompass any man's views and are seldom a guide to their soundness."[27]

Perhaps in an effort to arouse President Nixon's core electoral base, Vice President Agnew, the administration's principal "attack dog," declared a few days before the confirmation proceedings were to begin that the "public will arise in wrath" if the Senate rejected Blackmun, based on the same arguments of "learned idiocy" that had been used to defeat

Haynsworth and Carswell. By that point, though, Agnew's rhetoric seemed entirely misplaced.[28]

Even so, the nominee was taking no chances. With characteristic caution, he compiled a collection of note cards, or "crib" sheets, for use in the hearing. Years before, while preparing for his confirmation as circuit judge, he had been told that Senator William Langer of North Dakota, an irascible conservative Republican on the Judiciary Committee, invariably asked nominees about the rule in *Shelley's Case*, a sixteenth-century British decision about estates that had become part of the common law but had long been repealed by statute in most states. Langer died in 1959, shortly after Blackmun took his seat on the Eighth Circuit. But one of the cards the nominee prepared summarized the rule established in *Shelley's Case*. Others provided information about capital punishment, Blackmun's youth, the Senate's officers, charities to which he had contributed, and the names of Judiciary Committee members.[29]

The Hearing

The April 29 hearing lasted only that day and was perfunctory for the most part. Minnesota's Democratic senators introduced the Republican nominee to the committee. Perhaps because he was one of the Democratic presidential hopefuls who had seen his party go down to defeat in the 1968 election, Senator McCarthy was unusually restrained in his remarks about the latest Nixon choice for the high bench. Having voted against the president's previous nominees, McCarthy told committee members that he was "glad [finally] to have a nominee whom I can vote for." Were he to vote against confirmation again, added McCarthy, "I am afraid I would be accused of general prejudice against the Supreme Court. That has never been the case." During the 1968 presidential campaign, Blackmun had joined a unanimous panel in denying the petition of McCarthy's supporters that the Supreme Court's one person, one vote reapportionment rule be extended to Minnesota's Democratic-Farmer-Labor party caucuses in the selection of national convention delegates. McCarthy said that he objected only to that decision among Blackmun's Eighth Circuit votes, jokingly adding, "I hope that when he is on the court and has more time to reflect, if that same issue comes before him, that that principle may be extended to the beginning of democracy."[30]

Compensating in part perhaps for Senator McCarthy's seemingly lackluster endorsement, Walter Mondale was effusive in his praise of the nominee. "Scholarly," Mondale said, "was an apt description." By the time of his appointment to the Eighth Circuit in 1959, the nominee had "established a reputation as one of Minnesota's most brilliant attorneys." He had also served with "great distinction" on the circuit court, where he had compiled a record "as an able, fair, and understanding judge," whose opinions were "carefully written,...demonstrat[ing] a clear respect for judicial precedents." Entering into the record two Rochester newspaper editorials that praised the nominee and warned against misleading attempts to label his judicial philosophy, Mondale pronounced himself "proud of the fact that such a qualified nominee is a resident of my State." Not surprisingly, two Minnesota Republican congressmen outdid Mondale. Albert H. Quie had never sensed in Blackmun "the faintest suggestion of bias or prejudice toward any man or toward any principle of law and justice." Clark MacGregor knew of no other jurist "who has the intellectual equipment, the ability, the industry and the fairmindedness of Judge Harry A. Blackmun." North Dakota GOP senator Quentin N. Burdick quoted Judge Charles J. Vogel, who had recently assumed senior status on the Eighth Circuit, and Vogel's replacement, Myron H. Bright. Vogel had termed Blackmun's nomination "tremendous" and thought the president could have made no "finer choice," while Bright called the nominee "an exceptional scholar" with "a fine legal mind" who produced "well written" opinions.[31]

Also entered into the record was a letter from Minnesota federal district judge Miles W. Lord, who generously ranked the nominee "the finest appellate judge in America" and recalled a conversation he and Blackmun's mentor Judge Sanborn once had regarding the nominee. "Harry," Judge Sanborn told Lord, "is the best legal scholar I have ever known. Every opinion or memorandum is a treatise in itself. He is deliberate, courageous and moderate. He is the single person who, I believe, would be the ideal appellate judge."[32]

In a letter to Senator Eastland, Lawrence Walsh informed the Judiciary Committee that the ABA's Standing Committee on Federal Judiciary had assigned Blackmun its most favorable evaluation. Seeking to avoid any complaint that its investigation was less than thorough, the ABA committee had not only surveyed the nominee's circuit opinions and interviewed Blackmun, but had also interviewed all his Eighth Circuit colleagues, the chief judge of each federal district court as well as a number of other federal and state judges in the circuit, over a hundred of the circuit's lawyers, the deans of four law schools in the circuit and at more than twenty-five other schools, and a substantial number of judges and lawyers outside the circuit. One lawyer in the circuit had asserted that Blackmun was against labor unions, and a recently appointed law dean declined comment on the ground that he did not know the nominee. Otherwise, Walsh reported, those interviewed were uniformly complimentary. Some of those interviewed remarked that Blackmun was not nationally known, but the committee concluded that "lack of national reputation [was] not unusual for highly competent federal judges whose work [was] primarily in their own circuit." Nor was the committee concerned about the remarks of some that the nominee's opinions tended to be "unduly extended," slowing the pace with which he disposed of cases. "We were reassured in our interview that Judge Blackmun recognizes the need for an Associate Justice of the Supreme Court to work rapidly and deal with an enormous volume of work under great time pressure and we believe that he would be able to meet the challenge." Based on its investigation, Walsh concluded, the committee was "unanimously of the view that Judge Blackmun meets high standards of professional competence, temperament and integrity"—its highest rating.[33]

Letters and documents entered into the record dealt in part, of course, with the stock holdings and off-the-bench activities Deputy Attorney General Kleindienst had addressed in his April 15 letter to Senator Eastland and in a later letter, dated April 28, which Kleindienst had sent Eastland after several Judiciary Committee members requested additional information. In his ABA report, Walsh indicated that none of that information had altered his committee's "favorable conclusion" about Blackmun's fitness for elevation to the nation's highest court. Martin D. Van Oosterhout, the Eighth Circuit's chief judge, wrote the committee that he and his colleagues were of the unanimous and "unqualified" opinion that Blackmun was exceptionally well qualified to be a justice.

In a separate letter, Judge Van Oosterhout also addressed the question of the nominee's participation in cases involving companies "in which he held a very minor stock interest." Until the issue had been raised with respect to Judge Haynsworth's confirmation, Oosterhout wrote, it was the policy of the Eighth Circuit that a minor stock interest in a corporate litigant should not disqualify a judge from sitting in a case. Given the Haynsworth matter, Oosterhout "realize[d] that a serious difference of opinion now exists whether a judge should sit in any case in which he has a stock interest, however trivial his interest may be. Since this controversy has developed, our judges have been uniformly disqualifying themselves from sitting in any case in which they hold stock ownership in one of the litigants and Judge Blackmun has followed this policy." But when Blackmun sat in the earlier cases about which questions had been raised, Oosterhout declared, he had only been following his circuit's policy and the recommendation of the chief judge with whom he was serving at the time.[34]

Judge Blackmun was the only witness to testify at the hearing. Committee members appeared relatively unconcerned about the conflict of interest issue, but that line of inquiry gave the nominee the opportunity to have entered into the record an excerpt from a letter he had recently received from Harvey Johnsen, the circuit chief judge from whom he had initially sought advice whether he should recuse himself from cases involving companies in which he held stock. The major question in Johnsen's mind at the time, the chief judge had written Blackmun, was why his colleague's "broker had sold you on Ford stock as an investment instead of General Motors." As for the conflict of interest question, added Johnsen, "you are free to state before the Senate Judiciary Committee and anywhere else that I expressed the view that you should not disqualify yourself from sitting on the basis of this trifling Ford-stock interest."[35]

Senator Bayh questioned Blackmun fairly extensively on the issue, at one point quoting Justice Hugo Black's assertion in a 1968 Supreme Court case that judges "not only must be unbiased but must also avoid even the appearance of bias." Bayh was clearly impressed, however, with what he termed Blackmun's "very candid presentation of your financial interests and how you dealt with them and how you anticipate dealing with them in the future." Indeed, when the nominee suggested that it might be best for him simply to sell all his securities, the senator stressed that he in no way intended "to suggest that all judges ought to sell all their stock," but only that jurists must "be very careful not to have a conflict of interest where [they] do own stock and sit on a case. And you suggested that this is the way you feel now and you by your own personal example did do this in [the 1970] case" involving a company in which Blackmun had a small stock interest.[36]

Blackmun's testimony offered clues as to the sort of justice he would ultimately become. At the request of unnamed Senate colleagues, Senator Eastland asked the nominee whether the Supreme Court's "only proper function" was to "interpret" the Constitution and laws. When Blackmun replied "most definitely...in the affirmative," Eastland next asked "to what extent, if at all," Blackmun thought it "proper for a Justice of the Supreme Court in interpreting the Constitution and laws of the United States to take into account his own personal idea of what constitutes enlightened social, economic or political policy?"[37]

Blackmun's responses to that and related questions were intriguing. He assured the committee chairman that he would do his "best not to have my decisions affected by my personal ideas and philosophy, but would attempt to construe [the Constitution] in the light of what I feel is its definite and determined meaning." He added, however, "Of course, many times this is obscure." He had begun his response, moreover, with the observation that "this is a changing world"—an observation often made by judges who contend that they must adapt constitutional provisions to the needs of a changing society. When North Carolina's Sam Ervin asked the nominee whether the Constitution's meaning should be based on the intent of its framers, Blackmun also concurred in that proposition, but hastened to add that evidence of the framers' views was merely "the *starting* point of constitutional interpretation and construction." Michigan Democrat Philip A. Hart, repeating Blackmun's observation that the framers' intent was at times "obscure," asked whether the work of a justice "by its very nature requires some interpretations beyond the words of the Constitution and this interpretation requires an understanding of the contemporary society which gives rise to the concrete problem that is presented." The nominee readily agreed. "This again is why we have courts. Conditions are different today than they were even 10 years ago. I see this in cases that come to us. This is one reason the Constitution has endured, that it is in a way a rigid instrument and in a way a very flexible one. We search for its meaning." Asked by Senator Hart what President Nixon meant when he professed to be seeking "strict constructionist" nominees, Blackmun replied, "I suppose—I do not mean to sound facetious—I suppose the President would be the best man to answer that." But he then referred Hart to the answers he had given to questions Senators Eastland and Ervin, among others, had raised, declaring, "[Whether] some would interpret that as a strict constructionist or as a loose one I do not know. I can say no more than that."[38]

The nominee also used his appearance before the committee to underscore his empathy for society's most vulnerable citizens and their problems. The previous evening, Senator Edward Kennedy had participated in a B'nai B'rith ceremony honoring former Chief Justice Warren and his contributions to the expansion of human freedom. During his remarks at that event, Kennedy had decried a long list of Nixon administration policies signaling the beginning of what he feared would be "an era of inaction and retrogression and repression"—among them, the relaxation of safeguards against illegal searches and improper police interrogation of suspects, support for preventive detention of suspects deemed dangerous and "likely" to be guilty, use of "scare tactics" to discourage peaceful protest, opposition to the extension of the Voting Rights Act for additional years, obstruction of school desegregation, and the selection of judicial nominees who were, the senator claimed, "chosen for their willingness to resist Constitutional mandates, rather than for eminence or leadership." Reading a lengthy excerpt from his remarks, Kennedy asked Blackmun for his "views of the Supreme Court as the protector of our basic liberties and our basic freedoms in the face of this challenge."[39]

The judge declined to comment about matters in the senator's list that he considered "essentially political or economic," declaring that he was "not well versed in those fields." Nor would he speculate about issues that might come before the Court. He did assert, however, that his "record and the opinions that I have written and which are spread upon the law books will show, particularly in the civil rights area and in the labor area and in the treatment of little people, what I hope is a sensitivity to their problems." Later he referred to "the utter respect which the little person has for the Supreme Court," adding, "I think that the little person feels this is the real bastion of freedom and protection of strength in this Nation."[40]

Because some of the charges Kennedy had raised against the administration involved alleged harassment of student protesters, Blackmun spoke, too, about the alienation of youth from the political system, which the senator characterized as "one of the real crisis areas…in our country and our society today." Ever self-deprecating about his place in the Blackmun household, the nominee referred to his role as a "parent," quickly adding, "I was going to say father, but maybe I have not qualified much more than [as] a general parent to three daughters." One of his daughters, he conceded, at times referred to him as an "old crock," and he declined to report what his youngest daughter, Susie, "calls me when she wants to insult me." But he was hardly despairing of his children or, presumably, young people generally. He and Mrs. Blackmun, he said, had "tried to communicate" with their daughters, Dottie more successfully than he had been; he thought they had "broken through whatever barrier there" was in their relationship with them. He and his daughter Nancy had "had many long talks about, in particular, things that have happened at Harvard Square and the environs in the last 2 or 3 years because she lives still in Cambridge, and I respect her opinion. I respect her attitude toward some of these problems. I do not always agree, but she thinks." The "emotional and traumatic days" since his nomination, he believed, had "brought us closer together as a family than ever before." In fact, Susie, "who is on the surface the most flip," had recently said, "Daddy, I think I understand you better now than I ever have before." To Blackmun, all his daughters were "good citizens. One has to work at it and sometimes go a little farther than half way but I believe that they feel that maybe the old man could be a lot worse than he is."[41]

Blackmun's appearance before the committee also gave him a further chance to separate himself from Chief Justice Burger and attempt to dispel any notion that Burger would exert an undue influence over his boyhood friend on the bench. Senator Kennedy asked, "Will you feel completely comfortable in disagreeing with the Chief Justice? I know you have been longtime friends and have had a good deal of mutual respect for each other." He and Burger, the nominee answered, had known each other since "our respective mothers packed us off to Sunday School at age 4 or 5."

But the two had only attended grade school together, not high school, college, or law school. During their seven years of college and law school, their "association necessarily was one of very limited relationship." Blackmun had practiced law in Minneapolis, Burger in St. Paul, and lawyers in one of the Twin Cities rarely practiced in the other. He and Burger, in fact, had never been associated in a case. They had both served on the board of the William Mitchell School of Law, which Burger had attended, but never together until the previous year. Blackmun had left Minneapolis to become counsel at the Mayo Clinic twenty years earlier; Burger had moved to Washington in 1953. Since that time, Blackmun had been in Washington and Burger in Minnesota, many times when their paths did not cross. Blackmun acknowledged that he had been best man at Burger's wedding and stressed that he "would not wish to conceal in any way the fact that he and I have been friends a long time, in our childhood and adolescent years particularly." He emphasized, however, that "as we grew up together I think we indulged more in arguments than we did in agreement...I would have no hesitation whatsoever, and he is the first person to be aware of this, in disagreeing with him, or...in his disagreeing with me. I think we respect each other."[42]

Kennedy termed Blackmun's response "a very good answer" and later remarked that the nominee had "been extremely responsive to [all] my questions." Committee liberals would probably have preferred different responses to certain of their questions. Asked about capital punishment, for example, Blackmun repeated his by now well-known personal opposition to its infliction, but also his belief that its use was essentially a matter for legislative judgment. Even his positions on controversial issues appeared balanced and reasonable, and members of the Judiciary Committee seemed uniformly pleased with his performance and qualifications. Recalling the contentious Haynsworth and Carswell nominations, Senator Bayh declared at one point, "The fact that a man of your caliber, of your excellence, is before us today may indeed give some salve for the wounds which have been incurred because of past confrontations and very distasteful disagreements. Perhaps these old battles have been worth while."[43]

His Judiciary Committee appearance having produced no surprises, Blackmun's confirmation was assured. Indeed, the conservative *National*

Review entitled an item on the process, "Will He (Yawn) Make It?" On May 5, the committee voted 17–0 to recommend his confirmation to the full Senate. Three days later, West Virginia Democrat Robert C. Byrd filed a supplementary statement to the committee's report, quoting approvingly from Blackmun's recent opinion regarding disruptive students at Central Missouri State College, especially the judge's observation, "One might expect [such behavior] from the spoiled child of tender years" but not from a college student "who, in theory, is close to being grown up." Especially given the climate of the times, that opinion did the nominee no harm. On May 12, the Senate voted 94–0 to confirm Harry Andrew Blackmun as the Supreme Court's ninety-eighth justice.[44]

Awaiting news of the Senate vote in Rochester, Blackmun soon met with reporters, Dottie at his side. In a prepared statement, the Court's latest addition, to the surprise of no one who really knew him, admitted that he was "troubled by an awareness of the awesome responsibility of this new assignment." "I sincerely hope that I have the character and the strength and the intellectual capacity adequately to fulfill it." The president, he told reporters, had telephoned to congratulate him. Nixon, who signed Blackmun's judicial commission on May 14, exactly a year after Fortas's resignation under fire, obviously was relieved that the lengthy process was finally over. Indeed, an editorial cartoonist may have exaggerated only slightly when he pictured a weary and disheveled president sitting in a maternity ward waiting room. "Congratulations," a doctor announces, "it's an associate justice."[45]

At the Supreme Court on June 9, Dottie, their daughters, and his mother and sister watched with others as a beaming Warren Burger administered the oath of office to his boyhood friend in a simple, seven-minute ceremony. The new justice then joined his colleagues on the bench for a brief, ceremonial session of Court, after which Blackmun and Burger paid a noontime courtesy call on the president at the White House.[46]

During the ceremony, the chief justice remarked that he "look[ed] forward to many years of work [with Blackmun] in our common calling." For the Court's newest justice, the feeling was obviously mutual. But Theo Blackmun predicted that the appointment would affect her son's relationship with his longtime friend. Years later, Blackmun recalled his response: "Mother, it just can't. We've been friends for a long time." But Theo was insistent. " 'Well,' she said, 'you wait and see.' " Then he explained what his mother meant: "[She knew] that we would disagree on certain issues, and Warren Burger was always impatient with disagreements. He didn't like disagreements. But that's the way multi-judge courts operate, and she was wiser than I was."[47]

Chapter 5

The Chambers

Adjusting to a seat on the nation's highest tribunal was to be no easier for Harry Blackmun than were other significant changes in his life. Asked at the end of his tenure to describe his emotions when he first joined his new colleagues, his painful response reflected the humility and insecurity so characteristic by that point of the man and the jurist. Rather than feeling a sense of exhilaration or triumph, the new justice had been nearly overcome by desperation and excruciating doubts about his fitness for his new position.[1]

Nor was the new justice given the luxury of easing into his responsibilities, even though he had taken his position near the end of the Court's 1969 term. The day after his Senate confirmation, Chief Justice Burger sent him two huge mailbags containing forty-seven certiorari petitions that had been held over for a full Court. A vote of four justices was required for the Court to agree to grant a writ of certiorari and thus review of a case appealed from a lower court. Pending Blackmun's arrival, the other justices were divided 5–3 to deny certiorari in the cases sent to their latest colleague, and a positive vote would be needed to grant review in each. Complaining to Burger that he had unfinished business to complete on the Eighth Circuit, he first attempted to avoid participating in those cases.

But the chief justice was insistent, and Blackmun's circuit court colleagues graciously offered to take over his unfinished assignments on that bench. With his vote, the justice later said, certiorari was granted in seventeen of the forty-seven cases held over for his arrival in Washington.[2]

Whatever anxiety his new post caused Blackmun, the die was now cast. Fortunately, he detected absolutely no "feeling of despair or misgivings" on Dottie's part. "I think it was exciting for her," he later said. When they went to Washington for the swearing-in ceremony, Chief Justice Burger had optimistically predicted they would be there only a few days before being able to return to Minnesota to make arrangements for their permanent move east. As it turned out, they were in Washington well into July. They had no trouble, however, selling their Rochester home to a next-door neighbor who had long expressed an interest in purchasing the property. In what Blackmun and Dottie thought would be a temporary arrangement, they also leased Apartment 306 at the Normandy House, 1701 North Kent, in Arlington, one of the original high-rises built across the Potomac from Washington. When the justice retired in 1994, they were still living there.[3]

The Justice and Company

The Court's newest member was also obliged, of course, to recruit a staff. Considering the importance of their work, justices have a very small support staff. When Blackmun took his seat on the high bench, each of the eight associate justices was allotted one secretary, three law clerks, and a messenger, or aide, as they were later designated. After failing to persuade his Eighth Circuit secretary to leave Rochester for Washington, Blackmun hired Shirley J. Bartlett, who had been working at the Court since 1964, including four and a half years as a second secretary to John Marshall Harlan, whose growing blindness had placed additional burdens on his staff. Following Warren Burger's appointment, Bartlett had become the second secretary to the chief justice, who was allotted two secretaries. In her first letter to Blackmun, she misspelled "presumptuous," which the meticulous justice quickly brought to her attention. When the justice asked that she submit a resume, she obliged, albeit noting the obvious:

"We have been very busy at the office with the term drawing to a close and I am afraid this was done somewhat hurriedly, as was my first letter, but I do hope I spelled all the words correctly this time." She also expressed hope that she would not be given any "special consideration because I am working in the Chief Justice's office" and, of course, that her current position would not "go against me." Her modesty and "team" spirit may have impressed Blackmun. "I know you must have heard from numerous applicants by now, and I am just one of many. In any event, even if I turn out to be one of the 'rejects' I would consider it a privilege to assist you in any way I can during this difficult period of transition."[4]

Bartlett became, in the justice's words, a "splendid" secretary. But in 1974, Blackmun and other associate justices were each assigned a second secretary for their chambers. Given the talent available in the nation's capital, the justice's choice of an assistant to Bartlett may have surprised others at the Court. Wanda Syverson Martinson grew up on a farm near Benson, Minnesota, over a hundred miles west of the Twin Cities. Following high school and secretarial training at a vocational school, she got a job at the Mayo Clinic. "I was happy as a lark there," she later said, "thought I'd be there the rest of my life." But in the summer of 1974, while visiting the clinic for his annual physical, the justice mentioned that he was looking for a second secretary, and someone introduced him to Wanda. "He interviewed me right there, and two weeks later I got the call that the job was mine. I had never been out of the state of Minnesota except on a high school band trip to Winnipeg." She later realized why she had been chosen: "I was pretty green, but I had excellent skills, and I wasn't old enough—I was 20—to have any bad habits. I think he looked at me and thought, 'I can mold her into just what I need.' And that's really what he did. He was a perfectionist in many ways and not always an easy man to work for. But he taught me everything I know and really became like a father to me."[5]

The justice's solicitude for his new young secretary quickly became apparent. He and Mrs. Blackmun drove from Rochester to Washington in early September for the beginning of the 1974 term. The next week he mailed Wanda the maps he had used, along with a detailed letter of directions and suggestions. "A classic HAB piece,... so like him," she later said. Wanda, he recommended, should "take along a supply of quarters and nickels to cover the tolls in Illinois.... The usual toll is $.30 and is collected by a drop box." The toll routine across Indiana, Ohio, and Pennsylvania would be less burdensome, he assured her, with drivers picking up a ticket at the entry point of a stretch of road and paying at the exit. "The tolls across the four States," he helpfully added, "will amount to about $13." The total distance would be "about 1,080 miles." To enjoy beautiful scenery along the route, the justice suggested that Wanda restrict her driving to daylight hours. The Chicago traffic, he cautioned, would be a problem: "heavy and fast.... They do not believe in the 55 mile speed limit." Northwestern Indiana was "highly industrial and ... usually immersed in a heavy smog. [But] from then on, it's really very pleasant." She should not attempt "to come into Washington after dark.... It is not the easiest town to get around in the very first time one encounters it." The justice realized that he "seem[ed] paternalistic in saying all this, but I want you to have a pleasant trip."[6]

During her first weeks in Washington, Wanda was "truly shell-shocked." On her first day at the Court, she was told to wait outside the building until Justice Blackmun's messenger, Coleman Williams, came down to escort her to the justice's chambers. "Coleman tells the story of how I was standing there in bib overalls with braided pigtails. I do think he embellished that a bit. But I was truly in a different world." She also had trouble with the southern accents that dominated the capital. Blackmun had arranged for her to stay with Justice Lewis Powell's secretary, Sally Smith, until she found an apartment. Smith drove Powell to the Court each day, and Wanda rode with them. Smith, like Justice Powell, was from Richmond. "The most difficult adjustment I had," Wanda remembers, "was understanding Sally and the justice. I [particularly] had trouble with words like 'am-bu-lance.' "[7]

But Blackmun was "a patient teacher," Wanda "like a sponge ready to absorb all that was before me," and Shirley Bartlett "an incredibly gifted person in terms of running the chamber."[8] Wanda adapted quickly to the routine, and she and Shirley worked well together.

In early 1979, however, tragedy struck the chamber. While dining at a restaurant, Shirley suffered a cerebral hemorrhage. "[She] and the justice were very much alike, both perfectionists," Wanda later recalled. "It was quite traumatic for the justice and me.... The justice and I would go to the hospital independently and together. And we would keep [the justice] advised while he was on the bench. It was a difficult time emotionally and [in terms of] keeping the chambers afloat...without her steady hand." After a month in the hospital, Shirley died. "It was very hard on the justice; he was very fond of her. But we got through it."[9]

Most senior secretaries at the Court were at least forty. But Blackmun decided to make Wanda, then twenty-five, Shirley's replacement. "With Shirley's departure," he later explained in a letter to the chief justice, "my choice was either to employ as my first secretary a woman of mature years and experience...or to give Miss Syverson an opportunity in return for her loyal and willing service over several years....I chose to go with youth and made this choice consciously. I have not regretted my decision....Miss Syverson has exceeded my expectations. She is willing, works overtime constantly, never hesitates to come in for extra hours when I ask, and is, I am convinced, popular around the building."[10]

As his second secretary, the justice hired Wannett Smith, a young North Carolina native working in the Court's secretarial pool. Perhaps in part because of the similarity in their ages, the two secretaries worked effectively during Wannett's decade in the chambers. Justice Blackmun was clearly impressed with their work, seeking increases in civil service grade and salary for them and pointedly informing the chief justice early in Wannett's tenure that, "while perhaps the fact is not 'compelling,' as we are accustomed to say in some opinions, I know that [their] two salaries together are substantially below (several thousand dollars) the combined salaries for the two secretaries in each other chamber in the building." Wanda and Wannett, he told prospective law clerks, perhaps only half-jokingly, had a veto power over his choices.[11]

The justice apparently maintained a close relationship with all his secretaries, especially Wanda, who remained with him until his death in 1999. When she married Ronald Martinson in 1981 at Washington's National Presbyterian Church, he was asked to offer remarks. Recounting Wanda's decision "to leave the more quiet life of the Midwest to seek a place in a city that is great in power and great in weakness, a city of high pressure and of cross pressure, a city of gains and of disappointments," he assured those present that Wanda had "served well in a confidential and confining secretarial capacity ever since," then added, "In that kind of relationship, one comes to know the other person very well. I say freely and candidly to Wanda's parents, who are here, that what I have come to know about their daughter is all good. They should be very proud of her." When Wannett Smith, who married Blackmun clerk David Ogden, decided to leave the chambers following the birth of their son, the justice invited Court personnel to attend a "Farewell to Wannett/Hello to Jonathan" party.[12]

For years, all messengers to the justices were African American and regarded by many as essentially personal servants, performing all sorts of duties at the Court and in the justices' homes that went well beyond the call of their official duties. As the change in title from messenger to aide during Blackmun's tenure suggests, the status of messenger/aides has improved over the years. But during Justice Blackmun's tenure and since, certain justices continued to hire aides as permanent members of their chambers staff. Blackmun had a different approach. He preferred to employ aides who had some interest in going to law school or furthering their education in other ways, and thus would view the position as a stepping stone to a professional career rather than a permanent job with little potential for advancement. "He wanted to hire very qualified young people, [including] women," for the position, Wanda Martinson remembers, and "typically had aides who would serve for two or three years, or less." For example, Todd Gustin, Blackmun's aide at the time of the justice's death, transferred to Justice David Souter's chambers, then attended Georgetown University Law School and joined a Washington firm.[13]

Extremely critical to the effective functioning of a justice's chambers are the clerks, outstanding recent law graduates who do research, play a major role in screening cases for possible review by the Court, assist their justice in preparing for oral argument and discussion of cases in the justices' conferences, and increasingly draft opinions. Throughout his tenure Blackmun had ninety-three clerks, including thirty-one women, the largest number of women clerks among the justices with whom he served. Initially, he and other justices were allotted three clerks each term, then four beginning with the 1976 term. All but four of Blackmun's clerks had also clerked on one or more lower courts before going to Washington, and those four served early in the justice's tenure. One of the justice's first three clerks, Daniel Edelman, had clerked for him the previous year on the

Eighth Circuit; another, Michael LaFond, had been selected to serve on the circuit the following term. Two Blackmun clerks clerked on the high courts of Illinois and Massachusetts before going to the justice's chambers. The rest had clerked on lower federal courts: fourteen for U.S. district court judges immediately before going to the Supreme Court and the others for members of the federal courts of appeals. Most, though not all, were graduates of elite law schools.[14]

Unlike certain other justices, Blackmun had no law professors or lower court judges who regularly served as "feeders" of clerks to his chambers. But several clerks interviewed for this book indicated that their clerkship with a judge whom the justice respected probably worked in their favor. A prospective clerk's association with a revered former Blackmun clerk could also be helpful. Geoffrey Klineberg, who clerked during the 1992 term, was convinced, for example, that both lower court judges for whom he had earlier clerked were instrumental in his selection, and that former Blackmun clerk Harold Koh was also "extraordinarily helpful." After clerking for the justice during the 1981 term, Koh had joined the Yale law faculty, where he later would serve as dean. Klineberg was one of Koh's research assistants. "Although I've certainly never seen the letter he wrote [the justice], I am sure he wrote a very nice letter for me, and I know the justice thought extremely highly of Harold. I have no doubt that made a huge difference."[15]

The screening of prospective clerks culminated in an interview with the justice—or, more precisely, in interviews with Blackmun, his secretaries, and current clerks. Early in his tenure, Blackmun had found the justices' library, on the second floor of the Court, an excellent and isolated place for his work. When candidates for a clerkship arrived for the interview, they would wait in the office with the secretaries until the justice came down from the library. Clerks quickly realized after joining the chambers, if not before, that those sessions with the secretaries were at least as important as the interview with the justice. "They played an important role in screening out people who would not be fun to have in chambers," recalled Edward Lazarus, who clerked during the 1988 term.

It's a very hardworking year in very close quarters, and there was a heavy emphasis put not only on legal acumen—presumably, if you got as far as the interview, you had the credentials...—but that you would be someone who would work as part of a team....Wannett left in the middle of my year....But Wanda was there the whole year, and she was with the justice for the duration of his time at the Court. These were people who were much more than secretaries; they were an essential part of his life and of the chambers....He was a meticulous man, and he would time [his appearance for an interview] so there was plenty of time for conversation [and] a real interchange with Wanda and Wannett.[16]

Asked about the secretaries' role in the screening of applicants, Wanda Martinson observed, "Well, the justice always said that we had veto power. But I don't know that we ever vetoed anyone. I think if they didn't pass muster with us, it was clear that they weren't passing muster with the current crop of clerks or with the justice himself....But he was always very thoughtful that way, to have the applicant come to the chambers early and, on the premise that they were waiting for him to come down from the library, give us ten or 15 minutes to visit with the people. It's a close working relationship; chambers are small and pressures are great....The clerks become family. I still stay in touch with many of them."[17]

Justice Blackmun's interviews with applicants followed a familiar pattern. Characteristically, he asked questions from a prepared list. Rarely did he inquire about issues of law or constitutional doctrine. Instead, he focused on the applicant's background, education, and family, on whether the candidate, as he put it, had "ever had any trouble with the law," and related matters. If a candidate had children, he emphasized the incredibly long hours the clerkship would require and his reluctance to put such a burden on someone with family obligations. Applicants who shared his love for baseball were likely to volunteer that fact to the justice.[18]

Some element in a candidate's background might also have pricked the justice's interest. On the Court and earlier, Blackmun had displayed a sincere interest in the plight of the American Indian. Several years before Edward Lazarus applied for a clerkship, his father had represented the Sioux tribe in *United States v. Sioux Nation* (1980), in which the Court, per Blackmun, sided with the elder Lazarus in a dispute over government confiscation of tribal property. Lazarus thought that association, as well as a book he was writing on the case, might have worked in his favor. But he also recalled that, during his interview, he picked up beanbags from a secretary's desk and ended up juggling them, much to Blackmun's amusement.[19]

At times, the justice revealed a whimsical side during interviews. On her flight from Los Angeles to Washington for her interview, Cecilia Wang, one of Blackmun's last clerks, had a stopover in St. Louis, where the justice had sat as an appeals court judge. During her interview, she noted seeing St. Louis's famous arch as the plane was landing. The justice then related "a little story," she remembers, "about how, when he was sitting on the Eighth Circuit, they were building the arch. And they built it from both ends up. And [the judges] all were worried that the last piece wouldn't fit."[20]

Blackmun's modesty and insecurities regularly surfaced in the interviews as well. He often made self-deprecating remarks, identifying himself, for example, as the Court's "dumbest" member and describing his humble roots. After *Roe v. Wade* became a subject of intense national debate, he often asked applicants whether they were aware of *Roe* and would be comfortable working with the justice who was the principal target of antiabortion invective. Naturally, applicants were surprised when asked such questions. "I almost thought he was joking," remembers Pamela Karlan, who clerked for Blackmun in the 1985 term. "How could you get through law school and not know this! But he was actually very sincere." David Ogden, who clerked in the 1982 term, agrees: "I think he was a truly, supremely modest human being. Whatever he privately thought of himself, he considered it to be incredibly important to project to others…a presentation of self that was not grand,…not great, or that assumed anything about what others thought about him.…He didn't want to [assume you knew about *Roe*], because if he assumed that you knew about it, that would somehow or other say that he was a great man, and you were the neophyte, and that wasn't the tone or the spirit [that he wanted].…I think it was really sort of part of his effort not to elevate himself."[21]

In certain of his clerks' eyes, Blackmun's humility appeared to extend to the clerk selection process. Alan Madans, who clerked for Blackmun in the 1982 term, recalls that the justice almost declined to interview Anna Durand, who clerked the next term, because of the long distance she would be obliged to travel for an interview. Durand was then clerking in Hawaii for a judge of the Ninth Circuit. "Justice Blackmun thought it was just too much of an imposition to fly all the way from Hawaii....He said, 'How can I ask her to do that? It's expensive. It's far.' And we [clerks] had to basically talk him into giving her an interview, to convince him that she would be delighted to come in for an interview even if she didn't get the job....I would like to think that she didn't get the job simply because he felt guilty. She was clearly a great candidate; we all liked her. But he felt terribly guilty about the idea of asking somebody to come that great distance and to incur that expense."[22]

The timing of the justice's offers of clerkships was equally revealing. Blackmun did not interview a large number of applicants, limiting interviews to two or three candidates for each slot to be filled. Often an applicant would be called with an offer of a clerkship within a few days of an interview; sometimes, in fact, the justice would make an offer during his session with the candidate. And the justice never seemed to assume that a candidate would actually be enthusiastic about accepting an offer immediately. At the end of his interview, William McDaniel recalls, the justice said, " 'Now, you think about this overnight and talk to your wife about it, or your parents, or whomever you want to talk to about it. And you call me back tomorrow and let me know.' And, of course, I [was thinking], 'You've got to be kidding! I'll surely call you back tomorrow morning!' "[23]

But Blackmun's modesty was not the only factor at work. Among his Court contemporaries, he typically chose his clerks last, usually around the middle of the term before those selected began their time in his chambers. That pattern enabled the justice to secure more informed impressions about clerk prospects from the lower court judges for whom they were clerking. But it meant that he was obliged to move fast. It may also have meant, Pamela Karlan said, "that we had the gratitude of pound puppies." Most had applied to other chambers without success. "If he hadn't hired us, we wouldn't have gotten the job at all!"[24]

Of course, not all those offered a clerkship accepted. Applicants were not only interviewed by the justice and informally screened by his secretaries; Blackmun also had candidates spend time with his current clerks and apparently valued their assessments. The term William McDaniel clerked, he recalls, the justice interviewed Maureen Mahoney, who ended up clerking for William Rehnquist, later served as deputy solicitor general in the first President Bush's administration, and became a frequent advocate before the Supreme Court. Blackmun and his clerks were impressed. But after the justice offered Mahoney a clerkship, "she called back and said she didn't want it. He was shocked!"[25]

Breakfast with Harry

Clerks usually leave the Court with deep respect and affection for the justices they served. The Blackmun clerks were clearly no exception, and a ritual going back to the earliest days of Blackmun's tenure no doubt enhanced his clerks' feelings of closeness to the justice. Each morning Blackmun had breakfast with his clerks in the Court's cafeteria. "That started very early" in the justice's first term, Robert Gooding recalls. "I remember it being from the very first days or weeks that we [clerks] were there. He would be having breakfast in the cafeteria, and he would say, 'Why don't you come join me?' And...it became a regular practice....Then, from time to time, clerks from other chambers would join us as well. [Subjects discussed were] a mixture of baseball, sports, politics, what was going on in Washington at the time. Not so much about cases before the Court [in that public setting]. It was more free and open conversation about whatever seemed to be the topic of the day. Often it was sports-related. But sometimes it was what was in the *Washington Post* that morning." Randall Bezanson, who clerked during the 1972 term, had similar memories: "It was very free-flowing....We couldn't talk about cases if there were a lot of people around. But, occasionally, we would talk about cases....And, of course, Watergate was going on. So we would talk about Watergate and what was going on with Nixon, and all that. And we'd talk about baseball [and] about our kids, because he loved the clerks' children. A lot of us were propagating."[26]

Nor was breakfast with the justice limited to clerks and former clerks. William McDaniel's wife, a high school teacher, occasionally brought her students to the Court to have breakfast with the justice. "My wife taught way down in Charles County, Maryland, which is really country. And these country kids would come and have breakfast with him, and he would make them feel like they were special guests.... I've sat there and marveled at him do this at breakfast.... 'What do you want to do? What's been the important thing in your year?' And these kids are just babbling away."[27]

On occasion, the justice would use these breakfast sessions to gently chastise a clerk. Throughout his career, Blackmun remained extraordinarily alert to errors of spelling and grammar. Commenting on a draft opinion Justice John Paul Stevens circulated in a 1982 case, he testily observed, "I am convinced that this generation of law clerks never learned how to spell 'accommodate.' The misspelled form appears twice on page 31." During breakfast toward the end of the 1988 term, the justice asked Edward Lazarus to spell "vacuum." "A slight panic set in," Lazarus later wrote, "yet somehow I got it right. The justice looked at me a little quizzically. 'You misspelled it in one of the memos I read last night,' he noted gravely. I muttered a sheepish apology. 'I wouldn't have mentioned anything,' he continued, 'but you misspelled it in November as well.' "[28]

Not surprisingly, perhaps, when a journalist pointed out a grammatical error in a statement issued by the justice's chambers, a former clerk could not resist bringing it to Blackmun's attention. Robert Eastabrook, a former *Washington Post* foreign correspondent turned columnist for a small Connecticut newspaper, praised Blackmun's record in one column, but also noted that a letter from the justice's chambers correcting a supposed press inaccuracy had stated, "I apologize for what the media *has* done." Blackmun, wrote Eastabrook, "better apologize to the English and Latin teachers too: *media* is the plural of *medium*." Professor Ruth Glushien Wedgwood, a 1977–78 Blackmun clerk teaching at Yale, lost no time in mailing a copy of the column to the justice. "I thought you might enjoy this one which mentions you with such affection, as 'notable for [your] independence and moderation.' " She added, "All journalists like to play Mrs. Grundy [a comic book English teacher], as you will see. No need to reply, just thought [Dottie] would like this one." Perhaps Mrs. Blackmun had been the target of her grammarian husband's continuing crusade as well.[29]

Justice Blackmun's contacts with his clerks outside his chambers were not limited to breakfasts in the Court cafeteria. Annual reunion dinners with former and current clerks were standard ritual among the justices, and Blackmun was no exception, even inviting his circuit court clerks and current clerks to a reunion during his first term on the Court. Once or twice a year, the current clerks also visited the Blackmuns' apartment for dinner. A visit to a Marine Band concert was a regular affair as well. After William H. Webster, who served on the Eighth Circuit following Blackmun's tenure there, became FBI director in 1978, Dottie Blackmun also regularly took her husband's clerks on a private tour of the FBI building, complete with a visit to the firing range and the opportunity to be photographed with a variety of large weapons. In one of several chambers romances, the justice's secretary Wannett Smith married his clerk David Ogden, with Blackmun participating in the ceremony, as he had done at Wanda Martinson's wedding. The Smith-Ogden marriage ultimately ended in divorce, but during their marriage, they were frequent visitors to the Blackmuns' apartment.[30]

The Blackmuns took a genuine interest in the private lives and families of their clerks and secretaries. All four of the justice's clerks for the 1985 term were Jewish. When they told him they would not be coming to the office on Yom Kippur, Blackmun mentioned that the *New York Times* reporter Linda Greenhouse had once invited him to a Passover Seder, which he had been unable to attend. Later that term, Pamela Karlan and other Jewish clerks at the Court decided to have a Seder and invited the Blackmuns to attend. Initially, the justice offered them the use of the justices' dining room, but Chief Justice Burger, he reported, vetoed that plan. Blackmun, Karlan later recalled, "kind of shook his head and said, 'I don't know; we had a Christmas tree in the front hall of the Court. But I think it might be better if you just borrowed some tables and chairs.' "[31]

With folding tables borrowed from the Court, Karlan and the others had the Seder at the apartment of one of Justice Marshall's clerks. "And the justice and Mrs. Blackmun came. He showed up, and he's wearing a yarmulke, he's carrying a prayer book, the whole thing....We were all very reform and would have done a kind of truncated [ceremony]. But he wanted to see the whole thing done, and done in Hebrew. So we did the whole thing."[32]

Later, while having dessert, Dottie Blackmun began talking about their wedding and marriage. "There we were on our honeymoon," Karlan remembers her reporting. "Trust Harry to pick the longest day and shortest night of the year, June 21. And there we were; it was the most frightening night of my life. The waves crashing against the shore [at the beach]." The justice, Karlan recalls, "was just mortified, I think. He just wanted to climb under the covers and die." But Blackmun himself was not entirely reluctant to reveal his human side to his clerks. On that same occasion, one clerk brought up *The Love Connection*, a television show in which couples shared with the viewing audience their experiences on a date. Someone was amazed stations would air such a show. "Oh, yes, they do," the justice promptly responded. "Sometimes when I can't sleep late at night, I put on my little headphones...and I watch this show. It's really fascinating!"[33]

Whatever mild embarrassment the justice's uninhibited wife might have caused him, his clerks were invariably charmed. "She was a stitch," Karlan remembers. "She was very outspoken and kind of perky." She also remained entirely spontaneous. Cecillia Wang remembers that "when you greeted her, she would kiss you on the lips. She was just so warm and spunky." During his clerkship, William McDaniel had the habit of wandering about the Court late at night when trying to work through a difficult case. One evening, he discovered a spiral staircase leading up to the catwalks below the roof of the Court. When McDaniel told Dottie of his discovery during one of the clerks' reunion dinners, she asked him to take her on a tour. "So, we got up and went up there. She's got on a long gown and these high-heeled shoes. And we're up there walking around on the catwalks...behind the 'Equal Justice Under Law' edifice" above the entrance to the Court. "The justice never would have gone up here. She was right up there." But their very different personalities, his clerks suspected, probably did as much as anything to draw the couple closer together. William Block, who clerked for Blackmun in the 1975 and 1976 terms, put it this way: "They each knew the other had foibles and liked the foibles as much as anything else."[34]

Chambers Routine

Whatever the extent of their social relationships, Justice Blackmun and his clerks and secretaries devoted incredibly long hours to the Court's work, with his clerks quickly becoming known as the hardest working among the justices' chambers. David Van Zandt, a clerk during the 1982 term, agrees that the justice worked extremely long hours but doubts that he expected such dedication from his clerks. "He was a hard worker, but I don't think he ever wanted the clerks to work that hard. I think it was the kind of thing that simply developed in the clerk lore. When I got there, I actually said, 'I'm not going to write bench memos [summarizing a case for the justice before oral argument] longer than 25 pages, and opinions longer than ten or 15 pages.' And he was thrilled with that." But that, as Van Zandt agrees, was not what most clerks thought was expected of them. "The history was that you worked there all weekend long."[35]

Early in his tenure, Justice Blackmun established a daily schedule and system for processing cases that would persist throughout his career. A man of great routine on the Court, as before, he typically arrived at his chambers between 7 and 7:30 a.m. and worked until 8 a.m., when he went to breakfast with his clerks. After an hour in the Court cafeteria, William McDaniel remembers, "he'd go back upstairs.... He might stand and talk for a few minutes with [the secretaries]. But then he would take his suit coat off and put his sweater on.... He was now at work, and he did not like to be interrupted." "I was pretty close to the justice by the typical standards," Edward Lazarus remembers. "And he could walk past me in the hallway and not even know I was there. That's how intensely focused [on his work] the man was.... Every other justice during my year would lunch with the clerks [from other chambers].... Blackmun did not participate.... He was so deep into his own thinking. When you got him in a social moment, you could not have found a gentler or kinder person to his clerks. But when he was working, he was working."[36]

Fairly soon after joining the Court, as noted earlier, Blackmun began doing most of his work in the justices' library rather than in his chambers. "I liked [that] for two or three reasons," he later explained, "the main one being that it's a splendid library. Everything's up there, and what isn't there, I can just call [for]...and it comes.... There's a telephone, but for some reason when I'm up there, the telephone is not as disturbing as it is downstairs.... The secretaries would bother me only if a telephone call they felt was important had to be answered right away." Another advantage was that the library was generally deserted. "One time, Justice [Sandra Day] O'Connor came up for a day or so, and used it. But evidently my presence was bothersome, or she didn't find it convenient." Justice O'Connor apparently thought her presence disturbed Blackmun. But whatever her motivation, she quickly stopped using the library. "No one, since then," said Blackmun, "has ever come up. So I almost had a private library to myself. It was great."[37]

The remainder of the justice's day followed a precise pattern as well. "The messenger would get his lunch every day," Wanda Martinson said. "He would eat at 12 o'clock on Court days,…about half an hour later on non-Court days, sitting at a window looking out at the capitol from his corner office." While having lunch, he read a newspaper: "the sports page first and then the rest of the paper." Some of the other justices typically gathered for lunch in the justices' dining room. Blackmun "would join them…when they celebrated a justice's birthday or another special occasion. But for the most part, he preferred the solitude of having his lunch time to himself. Then, at 5 o'clock every day, he went downstairs to exercise in the Court's physical therapy room, where he would take a steam bath, do stretching exercises, and ride an exercise bicycle. You could set your watch by Justice Blackmun's coming and going." Following an hour in the exercise room, he returned to his chambers for another hour's work. By that point, the secretaries might have left for the day, but not the clerks. "The clerks never left," Wanda only half-jokingly recalls; "they were there morning, noon, and night. It was a sad story, but they only did it for one year, and they loved it." At 7 p.m., Frank Holleman, who clerked during the 1981 term, remembers, "he would come in and say [to the clerks], 'I'm deserting you now,' and go home."[38]

But the justice's workday was hardly over. "He would go home," Holleman says, "and enter the apartment and start working. About thirty minutes to an hour later, Mrs. Blackmun would ring a bell, the five-minute warning for dinner. They would eat dinner, and then he would start working again. If there was a [ball]game [broadcast] on, supposedly he would have that on in the background. He would go to bed and then get up and do it again. And this [when Holleman clerked] was a 70-year-old man!" Nor were weekends an exception. "He worked Saturday what we consider a normal day, often at home, but sometimes in chambers. And on Sunday, my impression is, he worked half a day. That reflects both his dedication and how seriously he took issues" before the Court.[39]

Processing Cases in Chambers

Supreme Court cases, of course, potentially go through several stages of Court review. First, the justices must decide whether to review a case. Even at the time Blackmun joined the Court, the justices were obligated to review only a relatively small number of cases appealed from lower courts. Instead, most litigants were obliged to petition the Court for a writ of certiorari, which, if granted, directed the lower court to send a case up for review; a grant of certiorari lay entirely with the Court's discretion. If four or more justices considered a case worthy of review, a writ of certiorari was granted. But in the overwhelming majority of cases, litigants were denied review. Litigants surmounting that formidable screening hurdle then submitted briefs to the Court, after which their cases were scheduled for oral argument before the justices. Following argument, the justices discussed and voted on the case in one of their private conferences. If in the majority on a case, the chief justice, by long-standing tradition, has the prerogative of drafting the Court's opinion in the case or assigning that task to another member of the majority. If the chief justice is among the dissenters, the senior associate justice in the majority has the opinion-assignment prerogative. Justices in the majority were free to file concurring opinions, and dissenters could file opinions underscoring their differences with the majority.

When Blackmun arrived at the Court in 1970, each chamber was responsible for reviewing all petitions for writs of certiorari. "When I walked in the door [to the justice's chambers]," first-term clerk Robert Gooding recalls, "there was a stack of cert petitions [as they are commonly called], practically from floor to ceiling. It was amazing! ... There was a lot of work to do. I think we felt we were getting our feet wet together. The justice, too." During the 1972 term, however, the Court began using a pool arrangement to expedite the review of certiorari petitions. The idea for the "cert pool" is generally attributed to Justice Powell, who had begun his tenure on the Court during the 1971 term; but in his oral history, Justice Blackmun said that the idea originated with four law clerks, including John Rich, one of Blackmun's clerks in the 1972 term.[40]

Under the pool approach, all certiorari petitions were divided among the clerks of justices participating in the pool, and one clerk would be responsible for reviewing each petition and recommending a grant or denial of review. A "super clerk" with various managerial responsibilities in Chief Justice Burger's chambers became responsible for dividing the petitions among the chambers. Several justices declined to join the cert pool, preferring instead to have their clerks review all certiorari petitions. But that actually improved the pool arrangement by ensuring that more than one clerk would examine each petition. When the pool went into effect, Justice Blackmun joined. But in an effort to make more certain that those cases recommended for a denial of review were truly unworthy of the Court's attention, he also required his clerks to divide up, review, and annotate the cert memos that came in from other chambers.[41]

Blackmun was also among those justices who had their clerks prepare bench memos in advance of oral argument in cases granted review. The clerks themselves devised a sort of round-robin method for determining which clerk would write the bench memo for each case. That rotation arrangement gave the clerks some preference in the selection of cases over the term. "While generally we just took them as they came," William McDaniel remembers, "there was a little horse-trading, and we accommodated each other's special [case] interests. But I would say 80 percent of it was on a rotating arrangement."[42]

The bench memos Justice Blackmun's clerks prepared typically included questions the justice might wish to raise at oral argument. Throughout his career, Blackmun was not among the Court's more prolific questioners. In fact, late in life, he noted with some disapproval the number of questions raised by Justices Ruth Bader Ginsburg and Antonin Scalia, among others, during oral argument. "One time in a couple of related cases that were argued in tandem during a morning for two hours," he said, "I, just out of mischief, kept track of the number of questions asked, and between Justice Ginsburg and Justice Scalia there were over a hundred questions asked of counsel.... The result was often that counsel never could get his case argued.... It was a little disturbing at times." When Blackmun did ask questions, moreover, they tended to be relatively random in content. Once, during argument in a case about the status of Haitian refugees, he asked whether counsel had read Graham Greene's novel *The Comedians* (1966), set in Haiti during the dictatorship of "Papa Doc"

Duvalier. Apparently, he also took a relatively limited role in the justices' conference discussions of pending cases.[43]

Blackmun, however, regularly provided his clerks with information about the Court's conferences that was usually denied clerks in other chambers. Immediately following a conference, he met with his secretaries and clerks to summarize the business transacted there. Then, after the secretaries had left the room, he gave his clerks a detailed account of the justices' deliberations. "It was a performance really," according to David Ogden, among other clerks.

> He had this great desk in that wonderful office of his up in the front corner of the Court. And he'd be behind the desk and the four of us…would come in and gather around it. And he would describe the conference from the beginning to the end, with each of the comments by each of the justices delivered…in impressions.…He was [a] phenomenal [impressionist].…He had an O'Connor, and a Marshall, and a Burger, of course, and a Powell, all of them. He had their inflection and their tone. It really was not mocking at all. It was affectionate, really, for all of them, even the chief.…The amazing thing about it was that it truly was a verbatim rendition, so we knew more about what each of the justices on the Court thought about these cases, frequently, than their own clerks did.

Clerks from other chambers regularly pumped the Blackmun clerks for early information about the positions their justices had taken on the cases reviewed.[44]

Once, during Pamela Karlan's year at the Court, another commitment prevented Blackmun from holding his usual postconference session. Instead, he told his clerks to go to Justice William J. Brennan's chambers for a review of the conference. "We sat down, and Justice Brennan said, 'Well, in this case we voted to affirm, and in this case we voted to reverse.' And one of my co-clerks asked, 'Well, what was the…reasoning?' Brennan responded, 'Oh, the usual, you know.' Which was just completely different from Justice Blackmun, who would spend 20 minutes summarizing what had happened [even] in some incredibly boring case."[45]

Author or Editor?

Through much of the Court's history, justices generally prepared their own first drafts of opinions. During Justice Blackmun's tenure, however, clerks in most chambers increasingly prepared first drafts of opinions, with the justices becoming more editors than authors of the opinions that would carry their names. During his first term, clerk Robert Gooding remembers, Blackmun attempted to draft many of his opinions. But the process was slow. He was new to the Court and less familiar than other justices with the seventeen cases carried over from the previous term and reargued during his first year on the bench. Soon justices and clerks in other chambers were grumbling about the slow pace of output from the Blackmun chambers in terms of both producing opinions and responding to the work of other chambers.[46]

On January 11, 1971, Justice Black, the justice Blackmun perhaps admired the most, registered his concerns in a letter to Blackmun (misspelled "Blackman"), which the elder justice also circulated to their colleagues. His letter called attention primarily to *Baird v. Arizona* and *In Re Stolar*, two First Amendment cases challenging state loyalty oath requirements for prospective lawyers. Blackmun had written Black that he expected to write a dissent in the cases but was waiting until Chief Justice Burger circulated an opinion in a related case. Pointedly noting that he had first circulated his opinions in the cases "more than two months earlier," Black was more than mildly irritated, writing his colleague, "I think it would not be inappropriate, without criticizing anyone on the Court, to state that I believe we are further behind in handing down opinions at this time of year than we have ever been since I became a Justice, more than 33 years ago." Stricken, the junior justice quickly responded, also with copies to the other justices. Characteristically defensive, Blackmun pointed out what "some of us are inclined to forget, I suspect, that this term thus far has been a very difficult one for me personally, and for reasons which are applicable to me alone." Unlike his colleagues, he wrote, he had not had the advantage of being thoroughly familiar with the cases carried over for reargument from the previous term. He also realized that the justices were closely divided, perhaps tied, in each of them. "This made the cases weigh particularly on me for I felt that in many of them my vote might be the decisive one. As a result, I have taken what may appear to the rest of the Court to be an excessive amount of time on those particular matters. I merely remind the Justices that each of these cases is a new decision for me, and is not ground which I am covering for the second or even the third time." In defending himself "to a degree," he added, he was "anticipat[ing] criticism which I feel might otherwise be forthcoming as the year moves along."[47]

That afternoon, Justice Black sent his colleague a conciliatory note, this time spelling Blackmun's name correctly. "I appreciate very much the extra work that was put on you by the number of cases in which you have had to cast the pivotal vote....If you obtained any idea of any kind or character that what I said was critical of you, please remove such thoughts from your mind." That incident, however, may have helped to persuade Blackmun to begin delegating most opinion drafting to his clerks. Robert Gooding recalls this sequence of events during the 1970 term: "Typically what happened in our chambers, at least through the first two-thirds of the year, [was that] Justice Blackmun did his own [drafts]. He did not ask a clerk to do a first draft of an opinion. The justice typically would disappear up into the justices' library. You'd go up there, and you'd see him surrounded by books. He would literally go through them, reading the cases, reading the briefs, and doing a first draft of an opinion on his own. We [clerks] typically wouldn't see an opinion until it was pretty far along. Then, he'd give it to us, and ask us to comment, make suggestions, do edits. But the first draft typically came from him."[48]

Following complaints from Justice Black and others that the Blackmun chamber was slow in producing opinions and responding to those of other justices, Gooding went to the justice and offered to draft an opinion in a case. "I remember the case,... *Graham v. Richardson*," in which the Court, speaking through Blackmun, for the first time added alienage to the types of government classifications considered constitutionally "suspect," and thus subject to close judicial scrutiny, in discrimination cases. "[Justice Blackmun] said, fine, that would be great. So I think I did the first [clerk's] first draft of that term. Then...the other two clerks started doing drafts of opinions....We clerks were itching to draft opinions; we wanted to have that opportunity. I remember talking to my co-clerks and saying, 'well, what do you think?...Should [I] just offer to do it?' And they said, 'Sure, why not?' And I did. And he seemed to be very open to that [suggestion] and…pleased with it."[49]

From that point, clerks did the first drafts of most of Justice Blackmun's opinions. The clerk who had prepared the bench memo for a case prior to oral argument generally drafted the opinion also, if the justice wished to file an opinion in that case. The clerk next circulated the draft to coclerks for their reaction and possible revisions, then submitted the draft to Blackmun. The degree to which the justice edited the clerks' work varied considerably from case to case, with certain drafts undergoing virtually no changes and others rather extensive modification. When Blackmun or a clerk had questions about an opinion or, for that matter, other inquiries, the justice clearly preferred paper exchanges to verbal communications. Some of Blackmun's clerks, Wanda Martinson remembers, had previously served with lower court judges accustomed to discussing opinion drafts and related matters with their clerks. Certain other justices also found such exchanges productive. "Justice Blackmun did not. He really discouraged that." The justice's clerks prepared a manual of helpful hints for each generation of clerks. "One of the things that they would pass along," says Martinson, "was that he just [wasn't] a banter-things-about kind of man. If you had a thought, even if only a paragraph, send a note, a 'Mr. Justice' note."[50]

The clerks interviewed for this book had the same recollections. Exchanges with the justice, recalls one, were "principally done on paper; any verbal discussions were handled…at the justice's initiative.…We would not go in and say, 'Mr. Justice, I want to talk to you about the changes you made in the [bench] memo.'" Remembers another, "The longest sustained oral interchange about cases would be when he read to us, while going over his conference notes, what his view of a case was. Otherwise, almost everything of a really substantive nature would be done in writing. I think, in part, he was more comfortable with having it in writing; and in part also [later in his career] he was often worried that he didn't hear everything" said to him. "We talked to him a lot. But not about the substance of opinions." "He became very hands-on once the written document got into his hands," yet another clerk said. "I'm sure you've seen the marked-up documents, down to the commas." But not before the bench memos were converted into draft opinions.[51]

Each term, Blackmun did assign himself the first drafts of opinions in a number of cases. Not surprisingly, given his expertise as a tax lawyer, he frequently offered to write opinions in tax and related statutory cases, to the relief of most of his clerks. "It is genuinely true," David Ogden remembers, "that cases everybody else thought were 'dogs' were cases he loved. He loved the tax stuff, for example."[52] Ordinarily, however, Blackmun served as editor rather than initial author of opinions coming from his chambers.

"Casey at the Bat"

That did not mean, of course, that the justice never made major contributions to his opinions in widely publicized cases. In *Flood v. Kuhn* (1972), during his second term, the unabashed baseball fan spoke for the Court when a majority reaffirmed precedents exempting professional baseball from the antitrust laws. In an effort to underscore the majority's nostalgic, if unrealistic, notion that baseball was a game, not a business, Blackmun began his opinion with an affecting history of the sport, including a lengthy list of notable players, as well as references to "Casey at the Bat" and other homages to the "national pastime." Justice Powell, who did not participate in the case, applauded Blackmun's "splendid opinion" as "a classic summary of the history of organized baseball which will delight all old fans—as it did me." Potter Stewart asked only that his favorite Cincinnati Reds player of the past be included in Blackmun's honor roll of baseball greats. But Justice White made the "gentle suggestion" that his colleague delete the entire section from his opinion; when the justice declined, White and Burger, who had already listed himself as only a "reluctant affirm," refused to join that part of the *Flood* opinion.[53]

Thereafter, Blackmun always cited *Flood* as perhaps his favorite case, mildly castigating himself only for failing to include Mel Ott, "the great [New York] Giants' outfielder," in his list. (An official Mel Ott bat, a gift of the justice's clerks, hung in his chambers with an accompanying plaque, which read, "I'll Never Forgive Myself.") Commenting late in life on the unwillingness of White and Burger to join his "sentimental journey," Blackmun suggested that they probably thought it was "beneath the dignity of the Court." Justice White, he added, might also have "disagreed with my listing of the famous greats.... One day maybe I'll ask him. I'll get some blunt answer."[54]

An Abdication of Responsibility?

When Justice Blackmun's papers became available in 2004, the pattern of decision making in his chambers, particularly the extensive participation of his clerks in the preparation of opinions, attracted scholarly attention. The historian David Garrow was appalled at what he thought the papers revealed about the justice. Garrow realized that justices during Blackmun's tenure were increasingly delegating more opinion drafting and related work to their clerks. But Blackmun had taken that practice, he asserted, to an "indefensible" extreme, virtually abdicating his constitutional responsibilities to clerks. In "The Brains behind Blackmun," an article for *Legal Affairs* magazine, the historian offered up a scathing account of "a justice who ceded to his law clerks much greater control over his official work than did any of the other 15 justices from the last half-century whose papers are publicly available." Blackmun had become especially "disengaged," Garrow declared, after 1990, with his last-term dissent rejecting capital punishment in *Callins v. Collins* (1994) almost completely the work of his clerks, while the justice, always largely indifferent to the nuances of constitutional doctrine, seemed "most concerned with whether he should 'recheck the cites.'" According to Garrow, Blackmun's clerks had begun playing an inordinate role in producing his opinions as early as 1971, when *Roe v. Wade* and *Doe v. Bolton*, the landmark abortion cases with which his judicial reputation would be most closely associated, first came to the Court.[55]

Blackmun's papers revealed, observed Garrow, that at times the justice's clerks would refer to their opinion drafts as "my opinion" and note that they were unaware of Blackmun's views about a case. They even considered themselves free to make highly disparaging remarks about other members of the Court in their memos to the justice. Such comments, Garrow declared, "should not have been tolerated by any justice, liberal or conservative, and no similarly intemperate statements appear in clerks' memos [contained in the papers of Justices] Brennan, Marshall, or Powell. In addition, the hostile and sometimes harshly sarcastic references to other justices—and Blackmun's failure to stop such comments—appear to indicate that the justice himself lacked respect for some of his colleagues." Blackmun, concluded Garrow, "must now be seen not only as a justice who evolved toward a more compassionate jurisprudence but as a justice who increasingly ceded far too much of his judicial authority to his clerks."[56]

In the same issue of *Legal Affairs* in which Garrow's attack on the justice appeared, the magazine's chairman and three of Blackmun's clerks came to the justice's defense. Seth Waxman, the magazine's chairman, who had served as solicitor general in the Clinton administration, dismissed the issue as a "jarring anomaly" to *Legal Affairs'* avowed goal of "providing insightful discussion of issues at the intersection of law and policy." Garrow's "sweeping, condemnatory assertions…[that] Justice Blackmun did neither his own writing nor thinking," Waxman declared, stood in marked contrast to recently published excerpts from a forthcoming biography of the justice by the *New York Times* reporter Linda Greenhouse, which revealed "that while Justice Blackmun…encouraged his law clerks to write freely and forcefully within the confines of his chambers, he often rejected their recommendations and indeed composed his own analytical memos for each of the several thousand cases in which he participated over a 24-year tenure." Waxman's work before the Supreme Court and its justices left him "certain, and saddened, that this issue of *Legal Affairs* departs from its worthwhile mission."

One of the Blackmun clerks responding to Garrow was Edward Lazarus. Lazarus agreed—"notwithstanding my enormous affection and admiration for the justice"—that Blackmun "delegate[d] too much of the original design for the intellectual content for his opinions to law clerks." Thus, an article of the sort Garrow had written could provide "a useful counterpoint to the usual claptrap minimizing the role that clerks play in fashioning the law." The difficulty with Garrow's analysis, as Lazarus saw it, was that the historian had exaggerated and "caricature[d] Blackmun…compar[ing] him unfavorably with other justices," when actually "the problem of excessive clerk delegation was less serious in Blackmun's chambers than Garrow suggests but is also more commonplace among justices."

By focusing purely on Blackmun's papers and "apparently failing to augment his research with interviews and other perspective-enhancing tools," Garrow, charged Lazarus, had "painted an unnuanced, unfair, and ultimately inaccurate portrait." In criticizing the justice's failure, for example, to police his clerks for harsh comments about other justices—comments that could not be found in the papers of Blackmun's contemporaries—Garrow had not taken into account Blackmun's preference for having his clerks communicate with him almost entirely in writing. The author of *Closed Chambers*, a disturbing and highly controversial account of Court intrigue during Blackmun's last years, Lazarus doubted that the level of clerk decorum was much different in other chambers, especially given the "poisonous atmosphere that existed inside a deeply divided court in the late 1980s through the mid-1990s," when a number of Blackmun's clerks were most critical of other justices. "It's just that elsewhere the partisan sniping commentary was spoken instead of written." Finally, noted Lazarus, if Blackmun appeared to provide his clerks with less direction in later years than earlier in his tenure, that no doubt reflected the large body of Blackmun opinions relevant to issues facing the Court that were available to his clerks, opinions the justice insisted that they read closely.

In his reaction to Garrow, William McDaniel emphasized Blackmun's postconference discussions and breakfast sessions with his clerks as evidence that they were indeed familiar with his views about cases and the sorts of opinions he expected them to produce. McDaniel also ridiculed the extremely small sampling of case files on which Garrow had based his assertions: "barely 12 of [the 835] opinions" the justice authored during his tenure. "Justice Blackmun deserves better," McDaniel declared. For his part, David Ogden, the third clerk responding to Garrow, stressed the justice's incredibly rigorous work schedule and the care with which he reviewed and edited the clerks' work. "The justice literally read every case cited in every draft opinion to ensure the opinion was properly grounded. I can guarantee that is not a practice followed by every other judge."

Perhaps of greatest weight in undermining Garrow's thesis was a practice of the justice that Seth Waxman and Linda Greenhouse noted, but about which at least most Blackmun clerks may have been unaware, even at the time of the *Legal Affairs* exchange. On the Supreme Court, Blackmun continued his Eighth Circuit practice of preparing his own independent, initialed memos summarizing most of the cases before the Court and his tentative reaction to the issues raised. Garrow noted dismissively one such memo in the original abortion cases as evidence of the justice's indifference to the doctrinal underpinnings of the Court's decisions. Throughout his career, Blackmun did display considerable skepticism about the jurisprudential rhetoric in which the Court's rulings were wrapped, even though his opinion for *Roe v. Wade* appeared to take such doctrinal constructs to an unprecedented extreme. But the justice's personal case analyses clearly demonstrate that Blackmun was not simply ceding to his clerks his responsibility for reviewing cases.

None of the clerks interviewed for this book was aware of the justice's case summaries, but his secretary Wanda Martinson remembered them well. "They were memos to himself....He loved the printed word. He wanted to get his thoughts down on paper while they were fresh, and then he would go back and review those [memos] after the [clerks' drafts] came out, and use what had been his initial reaction [to a case] to weigh against what his clerks had told him, and what [views] other justices were expressing....He mostly dictated them on tape....Sometimes when I would come in, in the morning, there'd be two or three tapes sitting on my desk, or Wannett's desk. We would share [the typing] back and forth."[57]

Nor was it surprising, or reflective of indifference to the Court's work, that Justice Blackmun generally deferred to his clerks in the crafting of opinions, especially the doctrinal rhetoric they incorporated. After all, his postconference and breakfast sessions, as well as previous opinions, exposed them to his views. Moreover, given his training as a mathematician and that science's emphasis on precision, he probably attached little weight to judicial doctrine, considering it often ambiguous and little more than legal window dressing for the Court's conclusion that a particular government action was or was not reasonable. As a modest person wracked by feelings of insecurity throughout his life, as well as a lawyer whose legal expertise was in taxes and estates rather than public law, the justice may also simply have had more confidence in his clerks' familiarity with the nuances of constitutional doctrine. When a prominent law professor argued a death penalty case before the Eighth Circuit, it may be recalled, the justice confessed difficulty in following the arguments of "professors," speculating that his law school years were too far behind him. His tenure on the bench, following a long career in fields of law far removed from what are considered the most significant part of federal court caseload, may have done little to bolster his confidence as a constitutional craftsman.

In his rebuttal to Garrow, William McDaniel noted Blackmun's personal handling of a number of cases each term. At times, too, the justice disagreed with a clerk's recommendation for disposing of a case. When *Marsh v. Chambers* (1983), upholding state-funded legislative chaplains, was before the Court, David Ogden wrote a bench memo recommending that the practice be overturned. "If you took a doctrinal approach to the question," Ogden later recalled, "and asked yourself the questions that, under the leading line of [religious establishment] cases, one asks, then you had to say that [government funding of chaplains] was a [constitutional] violation. It had a religious purpose, and [there] couldn't have been a more symbolic way of tying the state to religion, and it potentially created [excessive church-state] entanglement." Ogden also outlined in his memo the rationale that the Court, speaking through Chief Justice Burger, ultimately invoked to uphold legislative chaplains—reasoning based essentially on uninterrupted practice going back to the Congress that proposed the Bill of Rights and its religious establishment clause. But Ogden recommended that the justice not take that stance, "because I think," he later said, that "the principle and the doctrine are important, and the fact that the first Congress [had] done it, or even that it's been done forever and ever, shouldn't be sacrosanct." Ultimately, though, Blackmun declined his clerk's advice and joined the majority.[58]

Blackmun did not readily defer to his clerks on the death penalty issue either. For more than a decade before his final-term dissent in *Callins v. Collins*, he resisted their entreaties that he reverse himself on capital punishment after years of deferring to legislative will, despite his personal distaste for the practice. Finally he yielded, but not until his last term.[59]

Ultimately, then, David Garrow's portrait of a justice grossly insensitive to his constitutional duties is overdrawn, especially given the growing reliance of most justices on their clerks during Blackmun's tenure. Instead, the pattern of decision making in his chambers was not substantially different, for better or worse, from that in the chambers of most of his contemporaries. The memos Blackmun personally prepared for cases demonstrate that he was hardly disengaged from the Court's work. So, too, do his extensive postconference briefings, daily breakfasts with his clerks, and the extraordinarily long hours he devoted to reviewing their work and the cases on which they relied.

Whatever the extent of Blackmun's involvement in the decision-making process within his chambers, of course, there is considerable irony to Garrow's complaint after his death that he had deferred unduly to his clerks. When he joined the Court years earlier, after all, the fear was that Blackmun would be little more than a pawn for his boyhood friend, Warren Burger, that he and Burger, in fact, might well prove to be the "Minnesota Twins."

Chapter 6

The Minnesota Twins

Harry Blackmun was aware of the more unappealing elements in his boyhood friend's personality even before he joined Warren Burger on the Supreme Court. Their mutual associates were also. Burger's appointment as chief justice "reminded" their Minnesota friend Leland Scott of a story about Leslie M. Shaw, Theodore Roosevelt's treasury secretary. Shaw, Scott wrote Blackmun on learning of Burger's appointment, had returned to the New England village of his birth. While taking a wagon from the train station to his hotel, he attempted to engage the elderly, taciturn shuttle driver in conversation. "[Shaw] introduced himself and asked if the Shaw family was remembered there? 'Yep.' Did they remember a Shaw boy named Leslie? 'Yep.'... Did they know that Leslie had risen in life to be Governor of Iowa and was now Secretary of the Treasury under President Roosevelt? 'Yep.' 'Well what do they say?' 'Oh, they just laugh.' " Blackmun promptly relayed Scott's anecdote to Burger. "I thought this was great. We need this kind of thing every now and then to help us not take ourselves too seriously."[1]

Blackmun's gentle reminder of the need for humility on the part of those in high places had no effect on the new chief justice. Burger's predecessor, Earl Warren, had been a master of negotiation and compromise, as well as unusually solicitous of his colleagues and their feelings. The new chief, by contrast, displayed from the beginning a domineering and pugnacious temperament and an inability to suppress his personal preferences in the interest of Court collegiality. Seemingly more preoccupied with the appearance of the building and grounds—even the shape of the bench and the justices' conference table—than with the substance of the Court's work, he quickly became the butt of pointed comments and jokes in the other chambers. Drawing in part on the anonymous observations of Burger's own colleagues, unflattering accounts of the Court's dissatisfaction with its new leader regularly appeared in the press and culminated in publication of *The Brethren*, the highly critical assessment of Burger's first decade as chief justice. The rate of concurring and dissenting opinions during his tenure was the highest in the Court's history.[2]

Particularly in light of the criticism the chief justice attracted on and off the Court, he undoubtedly relished Blackmun's arrival in Washington. In his own way, Burger was a very sentimental person who looked forward to this resumption of a close relationship. At the beginning of the October 1970 term, for example, the chief justice wrote his new colleague:

> When we had those dreams of "doing it together" neither of us ever dreamed it would be this way or in this place. It was the practice we wanted.
>
> ...For me it is the beginning of a great career for you—and an association which, whatever the decisions, will be a source of constant strength to the Court, the country and the C. J.[3]

Blackmun obviously looked forward to their new association as well, whatever his misgivings about his friend's personality. Over the years, he had successfully resisted Burger's repeated proposals that the two of them take an extended tour of Europe alone, reminiscent of their long hiking trip into Canada years before. But Blackmun's reticence was probably dictated more by his perennial concerns about finances than by any developing strains in their friendship. They had joined each other, after all, on family vacations to Florida. On one occasion, Blackmun wrote Burger that he and Dottie were planning a trip to Lido Beach, timed for April 1, "when the rates drop." Noting that their daughters were to be "left at home," he added, "It would be wonderful if we could spend some days together in Florida at that time, and nothing would please us more than to have you there. If you can get away and if this appeals to you, I think it would be well for us to make reservations [soon]."[4]

Blackmun also shared, to some degree, the chief's inordinate interest in what other justices would dismiss as housekeeping details. After becoming a justice, for example, Blackmun discovered, "much to my surprise," that the Court had no paper shredder for disposing of "sensitive material," but instead simply sealed paper in cartons, which the Court police then burned at the DC incinerator. He promptly recommended to Burger that two or three shredders be purchased for the chambers. Then, unimpressed with the quality of equipment available through government purchasing, he contacted his friend J. W. Harwick at the Mayo Clinic, inquiring about the source and cost of the presumably superior shredders used in Mayo's administration section.[5]

A Break with Tradition

Of course, Warren Burger's desire to have Blackmun join him on the bench was not dictated purely by sentimentality or their mutual interest in administrative minutiae. He undoubtedly thought his new colleague would become an important ally, sharing his thinking on many issues facing the Court, or easily molded in that direction. It was not surprising, then, that the chief justice broke with tradition in assigning Blackmun his first opinion of the Court. Customarily, new justices write their maiden opinions in noncontroversial cases decided by a unanimous vote. Burger, however, assigned Blackmun one of the most contentious cases of the 1970 term.

At issue in *Wyman v. James* (1971) was the constitutionality of a requirement that recipients of public assistance under New York's version of the federal Aid to Families with Dependent Children (AFDC) program submit to home visits by social workers or forfeit their eligibility for assistance. Barbara James, the mother of three-year-old Maurice, refused to comply and filed a suit challenging the regulation on a number of constitutional and statutory grounds. A divided three-judge federal district court struck down the home visit regulation, declaring it a violation of the Fourth Amendment right against unreasonable searches and seizures, made binding on the states through the Fourteenth Amendment's due process clause. Speaking for a majority over the dissents of Justices William O. Douglas, William J. Brennan, and Thurgood Marshall, Justice Blackmun reversed the district court.[6]

A number of Warren Court rulings had held administrative searches subject to a warrant requirement. But Blackmun refused to equate the home visits with a search, declaring, "We are not concerned here with any search by the New York social service agency in the Fourth Amendment meaning of that term....The visitation in itself is not forced or compelling, and...the beneficiary's denial of permission is not a criminal act. If consent to the visitation is withheld, no visitation takes place. The aid then never begins or merely ceases, as the case may be. There is no entry of the home and there is no search."[7]

But even on the assumption that home visits bore "some of the characteristics of a search in the traditional sense," they were not, in Blackmun's judgment, "unreasonable" and thus did not violate the Fourth Amendment. Not only did the visitations further the state's important interest in protecting children; they also helped to assure that public funds were being put to the purposes for which they were intended. "One who dispenses purely private charity naturally has an interest in and expects to know how his charitable funds are utilized and put to work," asserted the justice. "The public, when it is the provider, rightly expects the same. It might well expect more," because such funding constituted a public trust, "and the recipient, as well as the case worker, has not only an interest but an obligation."[8]

Terming the home visit "the heart of welfare administration" and emphasizing that AFDC recipients received ample notice of home visits, the justice further asserted that Mrs. James had raised "no specific complaint of any unreasonable intrusion of her home....What Mrs. James appears to want from the agency that provides her and her infant son with the necessities of life is the right to receive those necessities upon her own informational terms, to utilize the Fourth Amendment as a wedge for imposing those terms, and to avoid questions of any kind." Blackmun could not accept that proposition, observing at one point, "There are indications that all was not always well with the infant Maurice (skull fracture, dent in the head, a possible rat bite). The picture is a sad and unhappy one." At the same time, he refused to equate the home visit and case workers with criminal searches and police. "The caseworker is not a sleuth but rather, we trust, is a friend to one in need." To him, the situation was more "akin" to an Internal Revenue Service audit, in which the agency declines a questionable deduction if the taxpayer refuses to produce proof that the deduction is warranted. "The taxpayer is within his 'rights' in refusing to produce the proof, but in maintaining and asserting those rights a tax detriment results and it is a detriment of the taxpayer's own making. So here Mrs. James has the 'right' to refuse the home visit, but a consequence in the form of cessation of aid, similar to the taxpayer's resultant additional tax, flows from that refusal. The choice is entirely hers, and nothing of constitutional magnitude is involved."[9]

Even at this early stage of his Supreme Court career, Blackmun seemed sincerely sensitive to the problems of society's less fortunate. He had gone out of his way to make that point during his Senate confirmation proceedings. Earlier, in a letter of reference to a legal services agency for his Eighth Circuit clerk Dan Edelman, who ultimately would become one of his first-term Supreme Court clerks, he praised Edelman as "a person of sensitivity and possessed of deep sympathy for the unfortunate," adding, "He is desirous of doing what he can to adjust social inequities which are apparent.... He comes from a family which is socially conscious and active in fields similar to those to which any legal assistance program is directed." It is thus very likely that Blackmun's sanguine attitude about AFDC home visits reflected his fear that Maurice James and other children of recipients were vulnerable to abuse that home visits might, to some degree, deter.[10]

In dissent, however, Justice Marshall, joined by Justice Brennan, emphasized that Mrs. James had offered to provide AFDC officials with any information they desired and to be interviewed anywhere other than her home. AFDC officials, he added, had made no claim "that any sort of probable cause exists to suspect [Mrs. James] of welfare fraud or child abuse." Marshall also questioned Blackmun's characterization of social workers, declaring, "Of course, caseworkers seek to be friends, but the point is that they are also required to be sleuths.... Time and again, in briefs and at oral argument, appellants emphasized the need to enter

AFDC homes to guard against welfare fraud and child abuse, both of which are felonies." Although agreeing that abuse and exploitation of children were "heinous crimes," Marshall asserted that such tragedies were "not confined to indigent households," adding, "Would the majority sanction, in the absence of probable cause, compulsory visits to all American homes for the purpose of discovering child abuse? Or is this Court prepared to hold as a matter of constitutional law that a mother, merely because she is poor, is substantially more likely to injure or exploit her children." In a separate dissent, Justice Douglas was even more direct: "If the welfare recipient was not Barbara James but a prominent, affluent cotton or wheat farmer receiving benefit payments for not growing crops, would not the approach be different?"[11]

Members of the majority, of course, had a different reaction to Blackmun's first Court opinion. Justice Harlan judged it "excellent," Potter Stewart praised it as "thoroughly considered and clearly expressed," and Chief Justice Burger applauded his boyhood friend's "solid and workmanlike job [as] an excellent 'opener' for your long season here," adding, "More power to the Frankfurter School." Across a slip copy of the opinion, the chief justice wrote, "A great start and an event long looked forward to by me—clear and to the point and in an important case."[12]

A number of citizens disgruntled with social assistance programs sent Blackmun letters praising his maiden opinion. The decision had "renew[ed]" one writer's "faith in the 'system.'" A veteran medical social worker, "appalled at the abuses that have taken place since 1933," declared that, as a supervisor of cases in New York, she had "found people making more money on welfare than they had ever made by their own efforts." As an emergency health services officer in Georgia, she claimed, she had observed "negro women driving Cadillac cars attending free pre-natal clinics." Blackmun's opinion made her more optimistic that such "abuses" could be eliminated. A twenty-two-year employee of the Minneapolis welfare department applauded the justice for "not permit[ting] welfare mythology to destroy the nation." A Riviera Beach, Florida, physician who described himself as "one of the no longer 'silent majority'" and a "Little Man" who had "been silent too long!" sent Blackmun his congratulations, declaring, "Stand Up and be counted Americans!" And a Washington, DC, woman with a Watergate West address observed, "The growth of crime among our young seems to coincide with the growth of welfare programs for the benefit of the unwed mothers and their children." In her judgment, "proper American citizen[s] would be so grateful for receiving the assistance, they would not object to any inspection intended for the protection of their children."[13]

Not surprisingly, a large number of newspapers commented editorially on the opinion and its author, and the justice asked his secretary Shirley Bartlett to mail a number, both "pro and con," to his daughter Sally. To the *Albuquerque Tribune*, Justice Blackmun had simply "pointed out what should be obvious—that the taxpayers have a right to know how their money is being spent." The paper, among others, also found it "hard to accept the logic" of Justice Douglas's assertion that Mrs. James would have been treated differently had she been a defense contractor or wealthy farmer. The *Tribune* was confident that "anyone who receives public monies…is subject to examination." Along similar lines, the *Chicago Tribune*, which saw the ruling as a welcome development for "states facing bankruptcy as a result of the rapid growth of the welfare rolls," challenged Justice Douglas, declaring, somewhat ingenuously, that "government employees can and do go upon the land receiving farm subsidies, making inspections to determine if aid recipients are eligible." (Justice Douglas no doubt would have responded that going "upon the land" was quite different from government visits into the cramped quarters of most AFDC recipients' homes.) The *Saint Paul Dispatch* reasoned that, "despite some sociological theories to the contrary, the fact remains that some members of the human race are less than 100 percent honest." The need for home visits was thus obvious to that paper. Although recognizing that home visits "have an element of snooping that can be degrading to the receiver of public aid," the *New York Times* found "the manner and purpose of such visits…both legal and essential." For the *Times*, the "key passage" in Blackmun's opinion was his emphasis on the "paramount" nature of the dependent child's needs. "It did not escape the Justices…that the James infant had at various times suffered a skull fracture, a dent in the head and a possible rat bite." Given the adequate notice required before visits could be made, "the Court logically declined to regard them as…'unreasonable searches.'…As long as the state provides money specifically for the care of dependent children, it has an obligation to see that such care is adequate, consistent and continuing. To that end, the visiting privilege is still a regrettable necessity."[14]

But the press was hardly unanimous in its reception of Blackmun's maiden effort. To the *Washington Post*, the opinion had "a kind of dry toughness about it, and its reach seems to exceed its grasp; it says more than it needs to say, and its implications may go beyond its intent." Blackmun's suggestion that home visits were, in his words, "perhaps, in a sense, both rehabilitative and investigative," the *Post* contended, "ignore[d] the fact that the latter looms much larger than the former." By the same token, the justice's conclusion that home visits were "not forced or compelled…ignore[d] the harsh reality that the denial of permission entails for the beneficiary nothing less than the loss of her livelihood, not really a very free choice."[15]

A number of Warren Court decisions had required warrants for administrative searches of homes and businesses. Blackmun held for the *Wyman* Court, however, that "the warrant procedure, which the plaintiff appears to claim to be so precious to her," was "out of place" in the home visit context. Warrants, he noted, seemingly solicitous of AFDC recipients, could be served without notice and would justify forced entries. "Of course," he added, "the force behind the warrant argument, welcome to the one asserting it, is the fact that it would have to rest upon probable cause, [which]…requires more than the mere need of the caseworker to see the child in the home and to have assurance that the child is there and is receiving the benefit of the aid that has been authorized for it." Scorning that portion of Blackmun's opinion, Justice Douglas had characterized as "strange…indeed" a jurisprudence "which safeguards the businessman at his place of work from warrantless searches but will not do the same for a mother in her *home*." The *Washington Post* agreed: "Why should caseworkers dealing with relief clients not take the trouble to get a judge's authorization in advance when they deem intrusion into a home to be necessary? That degree of trouble-taking would not impede the operation of a welfare program; and it would afford invaluable protection to the right of privacy."[16]

A lawyer with a California agency providing legal services to the poor found a footnote in the justice's opinion especially offensive. In footnote 9, Blackmun drew on social service case files to outline Maurice Wyman's abuse and neglect, as well as his mother's uncooperative attitude toward social service personnel: "The record is revealing as to Mrs. James' failure ever really to satisfy the requirements for eligibility; as to constant and repeated demands; as to attitude toward the caseworker; as to reluctance to cooperate; as to evasiveness; and as to occasional belligerency." In a letter to Blackmun, Martin Spiegel, a lawyer with California Rural Legal Assistance, contended that the footnote "bode ill for the nature of future litigation concerning public welfare." Citing his considerable experience representing welfare recipients "in their effort to be treated with the dignity and respect that our country claims to guarantee to all of its citizens," Spiegel argued that a major problem with the system was "the tendency of welfare officials to answer assertions of the legal rights of recipients by referring to their case records in order to find examples of morally reprehensible conduct...a kind of administrative *ad hominem* brush off." Those case records, he claimed, consisted largely of "self-serving declarations by Welfare administrators," often made Spiegel's clients appear "reluctant to cooperate, evasive and belligerent, [and] even when...true...were generally irrelevant to the legal problems [involved]." Footnote 9, he declared, would encourage judges and welfare workers "to decide cases according to their moral judgments concerning the welfare recipients, rather than the legal doctrines that apply to our society as a whole." The insertion of such "morality" considerations into a determination of AFDC eligibility would be especially tragic, he asserted, given a 1968 Supreme Court ruling striking down an Alabama "substitute father" regulation that denied aid to the dependent children of a mother "co-habiting" in or outside her home with a man, regardless of whether the man was the children's father, legally obliged to support them, or providing support. In vain, Spiegel urged the majority to delete footnote 9 before the case was added to the Court's official reports.[17]

Only One Part of the Constitution

The week after *Wyman* appeared, at least one newspaper headlined an Associated Press profile of Blackmun's early Court voting record "Blackmun Rated More Conservative Than Burger," and the media began to discuss a new "Burger majority" or a "Burger-Blackmun Court." Nor, of course, were the two jurists' positions on home visits the sole basis for such speculation. Years later, Blackmun said that Justice Brennan had come to him, apologizing that the new justice's maiden opinion in *Wyman* was not unanimous. But Brennan must have been at least mildly appalled at Blackmun's early stance in a number of free speech cases.[18]

For his very first opinion as a justice, Blackmun had chosen to file a dissent in *Hoyt v. Minnesota* (1970), an obscenity case from his home state. Beginning with *Redrup v. New York* (1967), the Warren Court, hopelessly deadlocked in its efforts to define what erotica was "obscene," and thus beyond the First Amendment's protection, had begun summarily reversing obscenity convictions and civil penalties imposed on distributors of such materials. Justice Harlan had argued on numerous occasions that the Constitution did not impose a uniform, national obscenity standard on the states and their laws; Burger had assumed the same stance in two recent cases. In his *Hoyt* dissent, Blackmun, joined by Burger and Harlan, indicated that he, too, was "not persuaded" that the Constitution required national uniformity and allied himself "generally" with his two colleagues in what he termed "this still, for me, unsettled stage in the development of [the] state law of obscenity in the federal constitutional context."[19]

Blackmun, joined by Burger and Black, also registered a brief, caustic first-term dissent in *Cohen v. California* (1971), overturning the breach-of-peace conviction of a young man who wore a jacket bearing the words "fuck the draft" in a county courthouse. Justice Harlan, *Cohen*'s author, had originally favored denying review of the case, then voted to uphold Cohen's conviction. But under pressure from his clerks, the justice eventually relented, announcing an opinion now considered a classic survey of possible justifications for the regulation of offensive public speech. Emphasizing that "one man's vulgarity is another's lyric," Harlan rejected each of the arguments raised in defense of Cohen's conviction and declared that government had no authority to "make the simple public display here involved of this single four-letter expletive a criminal offense."[20]

In his personal analysis of the case prior to oral argument, Blackmun dismissed *Cohen* as a "troublesome little case [that], in my view, should not be here at all." His initial draft dissent included a paragraph devoted to that theme. "The importance of the litigation escapes me. I do not understand the Court's eagerness to take a case such as this. After all, this Court cannot decide every case or right every imagined wrong. With the burdens under which this Court labors, Cohen's case should be dismissed for want of a substantial federal question. I suspect that more deserving litigants, whose cases have been refused, will not understand, and may resent, our taking this one." In the draft as in his final dissent, he also scornfully declared, "Cohen's immature and childish antic, in my view, was mainly [unprotected] conduct and little speech."[21]

In his preargument summary, the justice predicted that his "sympathies in favor of conviction" would, "of course,…offend most of the law clerks around here." He was right. After reading his draft opinion, his clerk Dan Edelman took issue with every part of Blackmun's effort. The justice was wrong, he declared, to conclude that Cohen was convicted essentially for conduct rather than speech, without attempting to explain why. "Instead of trying to explain," you dismiss and downgrade what Cohen did as an 'immature and childish antic.' " Under the Warren Court's ruling in *United States v. O'Brien* (1968), involving the burning of draft cards by antiwar protesters, even an "antic" could be speech or conduct, depending on whether it included nonspeech elements the state had legitimate interests in prohibiting. "The mere facts that Cohen's message was written rather than spoken, and written on his jacket rather than elsewhere," declared Edelman, did "not place it in the 'nonspeech' category," and "in the absence of convincing articulation of non-speech aspects" in what Cohen did, the prosecution could properly be viewed only as directed at speech rather than an indirect regulation of speech as part of a broader course of conduct.[22]

Nor could Edelman concur with the justice's rejection of the case as unworthy of the Court's attention. "The fact that one may disagree with Cohen's message or be repelled by the word he chose render[ed] the case," asserted Edelman, "more—not less—important." Emphasizing that expression "popularly acceptable in both substance and form [would] not have to look to this Court for protection," the clerk further declared that free speech was "essential to a free society," and thus that "*every* speech [was] important."[23]

In his draft, Blackmun recommended that the case be remanded to the California courts for reconsideration in light of a recent state case that narrowed the state breach-of-peace law, in the justice's view. But that case, Edelman contended, had cited *Cohen* as one in which violence was "likely—despite the total lack of any evidence of threatened violence, let alone evidence of [the] clear and present danger" necessary to justify criminal punishment of speech.[24]

But Blackmun persisted in his position. Although deciding to remove the paragraphs in which he ridiculed what he considered the trifling nature of Cohen's claim, he kept the rest of his draft in his final dissent. If the justice's stance frustrated his clerk, the other two dissenters were clearly pleased. Despite his absolutist interpretation of the First Amendment, Hugo Black had long recognized broad governmental authority over speech on public property, and his seemingly conservative stance in protest cases during his last decade on the bench had attracted both new admirers and critics to the justice and his jurisprudence. After Blackmun modified certain language in his first draft, Black joined his dissent, exclaiming, "The amendment you have made to your dissent in this case suits me precisely. You hit the jugular and then stop!"[25]

Warren Burger was even more pleased with his longtime friend. Initially, the chief justice had circulated a brief dissent of his own, calling it "the most restrained utterance I can manage." Burger thought it "nothing short of absurd nonsense that juvenile delinquents and their emotionally unstable outbursts should command the attention of this Court." But when Blackmun's dissent appeared, Burger withdrew his own opinion.[26]

The dismay of Blackmun and Burger over the time and resources the Court had devoted to Cohen's case was soon to be more than matched by their frustration at the Court's resolution of the most momentous First Amendment case of 1971. That summer, a 6–3 majority hastily rejected the Nixon administration's efforts to persuade the courts to bar further publication of the so-called Pentagon Papers, the classified, multivolume Defense Department history of U.S. involvement in the Vietnam War. In a brief *per curiam* opinion filed for *New York Times Co. v. United States*, the majority concluded that the government had not met the heavy burden of justification traditionally required of prior restraints on the press. Burger, Harlan, and Blackmun dissented, with the Minnesotans filing particularly caustic opinions.[27]

As First Amendment absolutists, Justices Black and Douglas had opposed the Court's decision even to hear oral argument, urging instead an immediate, summary rejection of the administration's position as an obvious affront to the Constitution. In his personal summary of the cases prior to argument, however, Justice Blackmun stated that his "general reaction, contrary to that of some of the Justices, is that a litigant is entitled to his day in court." While "recogniz[ing] the demands of the First Amendment," he also wrote that he, "unlike some others," did "not regard it as an absolute," adding, "If the proposed publication would be a means whereby the code is broken, or if it were otherwise demonstrated that publication would jeopardize national security, then, I think, restraint is in order. The presumptions, of course, are against the Government and the United States has a very heavy burden. Nevertheless, if it alleges national jeopardy, it should at least have an opportunity to prove it."[28]

In his dissent, Blackmun, like Burger and Harlan, attacked what Harlan, in his opinion, termed the Court's "almost irresponsibly feverish" speed in disposing of the cases—a pace that stood in marked contrast to the deliberate manner in which the newspapers had received and prepared the material at issue for publication. "The New York Times," wrote Blackmun, "clandestinely devoted a period of three months to examining the 47 volumes that came into its unauthorized possession.... [But] seemingly, from then on, every deferral or delay [of publication], by restraint or otherwise, was [considered] abhorrent and...violative of the First Amendment and of the public's 'right immediately to know.'...Two federal district courts, two United States Courts of Appeals and this Court—within a period of less than three weeks from inception until today—have been pressed into hurried decision of profound constitutional issues on inadequately developed and largely assumed facts." To the justice, that was "not the way to try a lawsuit of this magnitude and asserted importance. It is not the way for federal courts to adjudicate, and to be required to adjudicate, issues that allegedly concern the Nation's vital welfare."[29]

Blackmun also objected to the special significance certain of the majority justices, especially Black and Douglas, assigned the First Amendment in the concurring opinions each had filed. "The First Amendment, after all, is only one part of an entire Constitution. Article II of the great document vests in the Executive Branch primary power over the conduct of foreign affairs and places in that branch the responsibility for the Nation's safety. Each provision of the Constitution is important, and I cannot subscribe to a doctrine of unlimited absolutism for the First Amendment at the cost of downgrading other provisions. First Amendment absolutism has never commanded a majority of this Court." Blackmun preferred, instead, a "weighing, upon properly developed standards, of the broad right of the press to print and of the very narrow right of the Government to prevent."[30]

The haste with which the Court moved had prevented, in Blackmun's judgment, that proper weighing of competing interests. Based on his study of affidavits filed by the government and some of the materials at issue, however, the justice feared that further publication could result in serious harm to the nation. The newspapers, he pointedly concluded, should "be fully aware of their ultimate responsibilities to the United States of America....I hope that damage has not already been done. If, however, damage has been done, and if, with the Court's action today, these newspapers proceed to publish the critical documents and there results therefrom 'the death of soldiers, the destruction of alliances, the greatly increased difficulty of negotiation with our enemies, the inability of our diplomats to negotiate' [which a court of appeals judge had predicted], to which list I add the factors of prolongation of the war and further delay in the freeing of United States prisoners, then the Nation's people will know where the responsibility for these sad consequences rests."[31]

After reading the justice's draft opinion, Michael A. LaFond, the most conservative of Blackmun's first-term clerks, promptly concurred "with the views expressed," adding, "I am glad that you are expressing them." LaFond, like Blackmun, favored "tipping the balance in the direction of the elective Executive and the checks provided to the Congress and the voters by the Constitution, rather than to an absolute First Amendment rule and newspaper editors whom I cannot vote out of office and whose primary interest...is to sell newspapers." LaFond could not "believe that the First Amendment licenses the jeopardizing of national security."[32]

In a column entitled "Why Were the Courts Stampeded?" William F. Buckley, the leading conservative pundit of the period, applauded Blackmun's "telling point" that the New York Times "had taken to using the argument of time pretty much as it served its convenience. Sometimes it gave the impression that every second counted. Other times, that, what the hell, we are dealing in matters that are ancient history." Reciting Blackmun's litany of the harms publication might cause the nation, Buckley called them "a high price to pay if we are to pay it, for one scoop, and one stampeded decision."[33]

The mail that Blackmun's dissent attracted, however, was decidedly negative. One man exclaimed, "Strict Constructionist, *bah*! More a strict Nixonist." A recent Harvard law graduate and Boston attorney, whose birth date and educational background Blackmun duly recorded in the margin to the young man's letter, found it "incredible that a man such as yourself, with a reputation (perhaps overrated) for intelligence and intellectual integrity, could have the temerity to suggest" that the media, "rather than the discredited Government officials, bureaucrats, generals, and 'intellectuals,'…deserve the blame" for the prolonged war. But a letter from Robert L. Bernstein, the president of Random House, probably drew the justice's closest attention. Blackmun had devoted the last paragraph of his dissent to his suggestion that the press would be responsible for any further prolonging of the war and resulting human and attendant costs to the nation. Scoring that paragraph as "more shocking and depressing than I can possibly tell you," Bernstein declared, "I must tell you how sad I felt to see a moral judgment passed by you, one that I believe to be wrong but even if correct, can do nothing but hurt the citizens' picture of the Court and make us feel it is becoming a political tool. I love this country very much and I beg of you to keep the Supreme Court out of the political picture."[34]

A Pack or Two of Cigarettes

During the early years of his tenure, Blackmun and Burger regularly allied in other cases as well. As in *Wyman*, the justice's stance in certain of those cases appeared to belie his professed sympathy for society's unfortunates. In *Boddie v. Connecticut* (1971), he joined Justice Harlan's majority opinion striking down a filing fee required for initiating divorce proceedings as a violation of due process. But two years later, in *United States v. Kras* (1973), he spoke for a 5–4 Court in refusing to extend *Boddie* to a bankruptcy filing fee as applied to an indigent would-be bankrupt.[35]

Robert William Kras lived in a two-and-a-half-room apartment with his wife, two children, ages five years and eight months, his mother, and his mother's six-year-old daughter. His younger child was undergoing hospital treatment for cystic fibrosis. Except for odd jobs, he had been unemployed since 1969, when he was discharged from his job as an insurance agent after he claimed that premiums he had collected were stolen from his home and was unable to make up the loss. His sole income was $366 in monthly public assistance payments. His only assets were $50 in clothing and essential household goods. All of his monthly income went to a $102 rent payment and what Justice Potter Stewart termed in dissent "the most basic necessities of life." Kras petitioned for leave to file for bankruptcy without prepaying the filing fee.[36]

In his preargument analysis of the case, Blackmun referred to *Kras* as a "little case" and found "some merit in the principle that those utilizing bankruptcy should pay for it." As for the filing fee, creditors, not Kras and other indigents, were, in his judgment, "the only ones who really suffer by the imposition of fees, for the fees reduce the bankrupt estate accordingly." Speaking for the majority, he sought to distinguish *Boddie* primarily by contending that divorce proceedings were the only means for legally dissolving a marriage, "while bankruptcy [was] not the only method available to a debtor for the adjustment of his legal relationship with his creditors." He also pointed out that would-be bankrupts were permitted to pay the filing fee in monthly installments for up to nine months, an average weekly payment of only $1.28. "This," observed Blackmun, "is a sum less than…the price of a movie and [only] a little more than the cost of a pack or two of cigarettes." Under that arrangement, the justice added, payment of the filing fee and the advantages of bankruptcy surely "should be within [Kras's] able-bodied reach."[37]

In a brief concurrence, Chief Justice Burger stressed what he saw as the significant differences in government control over divorce and bankruptcy. He agreed that there were strong policy arguments supporting change in the bankruptcy system, but declared, "The Constitution is not the exclusive source of law reform, even needed reform in our system."[38]

The dissenters, however, saw no meaningful difference between *Boddie* and *Kras*. "In the unique situation of the indigent bankrupt," Justice Stewart, joined by Douglas, Brennan, and Marshall, argued, "the Government provides the only effective means of his ever being free of…Government-imposed obligations" to pay one's debts. "While the creditors of a bankrupt with assets might well desire to reach a compromise settlement, that possibility is foreclosed to the truly indigent bankrupt. With no funds and not even a sufficient prospect of income to be able to promise the payment of a filing fee in weekly installments of $1.28, the assetless bankrupt has absolutely nothing to offer his creditors.... Unless the Government provides him access to the bankruptcy court, Kras will remain in the totally hopeless situation in which he now finds himself. The Government has thus truly pre-empted the only means for the indigent bankrupt to get out from under a lifetime burden of debt," just as the government totally controlled the divorce proceedings at issue in *Boddie*. By refusing to extend *Boddie* to bankruptcies, declared Stewart, a justice known for the apt turn of phrase, "the Court today holds that Congress may say that some of the poor are too poor even to go bankrupt."[39]

In a separate dissent, Justice Marshall scorned Blackmun's assumption that Kras could easily come up with installment payments on the filing fee—payments amounting to less than the price of a movie ticket or cigarettes. For poor persons, Marshall declared, "a pack or two of cigarettes may be...not a routine purchase but a luxury indulged in only rarely. The desperately poor almost never go to see a movie, which the majority seems to believe is an almost weekly activity. They have more important things to do with what little money they have—like attempting to provide some comforts for a gravely ill child, as Kras must do. It is perfectly proper for judges to disagree about what the Constitution requires. But it is disgraceful for an interpretation of the Constitution to be premised upon unfounded assumptions about how people live."[40]

Justice Marshall's dissent disturbed Blackmun deeply. According to Randall Bezanson, who was clerking for the justice when *Kras* was decided, Blackmun suspected that "it was kind of a set-up case" initiated by people interested in challenging filing fees for indigent persons, and not "a case that involved any real person who had a problem and couldn't go to court." The justice, Bezanson remembers, was "pretty upset" by Marshall's "scathing dissent.... He didn't think that was fair. He wasn't being insensitive...he clearly wasn't."[41]

A 1974 letter from the attorney who had argued *Kras* for the government convinced Blackmun that his skepticism about the case had been warranted. "On February 22, 1973, a little more than a month after the decision," Edward R. Korman reported in a letter to the justice, Kras had "paid the $50 filing fee in full."[42]

The justice's reply was prompt. "The payment of the fee really does not surprise me very much. I always had a feeling that there was something wrong with this case and that, when known, it would serve to counteract the critical comments evoked." Nor did the justice lose any time conveying the news to Justices Douglas and Stewart—although, interestingly, apparently to neither Marshall nor Brennan, another *Kras* dissenter. Like Stewart, Douglas had filed a dissent in the case. In his recently published autobiography, Douglas also discussed his work in Washington on the problems of bankruptcy during the early days of the Depression. "Never did I dream," he observed at one point, paraphrasing Stewart's *Kras* dissent, "that I would live to see the day when a court held that a person could be too poor to get the benefits of bankruptcy." After receiving the letter from Korman, Blackmun wrote Douglas and Stewart, gloating, "Because each of you has given me a hard time on this one (Potter's dissent; Bill's comment [in] his last book), I thought you might be interested in knowing that Mr. Kras, within six weeks of the rendition of our decision, paid the $50 filing fee in cash, in full. He discharged in bankruptcy on March 15, 1973. So it goes."[43]

Kras's prompt payment of the filing fee soon after the Court's ruling was hardly evidence that he had been able to pay it from the beginning; the money may well have come from a charitable group or individual. But Blackmun always considered Kras's full payment of the fee vindication of his stance in the case. Years later, when his reputation for empathy with society's unfortunates was secure, the justice conceded that the language of his *Kras* opinion "probably...was too strong." But he could not resist adding, "One interesting development afterwards is that Mr. Kras, who was regarded as such an indigent, paid his $50 within six weeks after the opinion came down, so either somebody paid it for him or he had it tucked away somewhere."[44]

The Scope of Equal Protection

In part, *Kras* was simply another episode in the Burger Court's effort to rein in the Warren Court's expansive construction of the constitutional guarantee to equal protection of the laws. Under Earl Warren's leadership, the Court had not only aggressively attacked racial discrimination in public schools and other government institutions, as well as private facilities permeated with significant state involvement; building on cases going back to the 1940s, the Warren Court had also come close to holding that laws based on wealth and illegitimacy were suspect classifications as well, to be upheld as constitutional only if found necessary to further a compelling government interest. In a related line of cases, the Court had assumed the same stance with respect to discriminatory laws that interfered with "fundamental" rights or interests, even those, such as interstate travel and welfare benefits, that were mentioned nowhere in the Constitution's text. Using such reasoning, sometimes in combination with "suspect classifications" doctrine, the Warren Court invalidated state poll taxes and laws restricting access to public assistance, among other regulations.[45]

Not surprisingly, given his Eighth Circuit record, Justice Blackmun had no difficulty joining early Burger Court decisions confirming broad authority for federal courts to eliminate school segregation rooted in law and other official action. Although he joined decisions contrasting de facto and de jure segregation, limiting the remedial power of federal courts to the latter, and rejecting racial balance as an independent constitutional requirement, he also sympathized with Justice Powell's contention that the distinctions between de jure and de facto segregation were unduly artificial and should be eliminated. While the Denver school desegregation case, which raised such issues, was pending in 1973, he wrote Justice Brennan, "I am not at all certain that the de jure–de facto distinction in school segregation will hold up in the long run. Segregation may well be segregation, whatever the form."[46]

Blackmun remained somewhat concerned, as he had been on the Eighth Circuit, about the Warren Court's conclusion in *Jones v. Alfred Mayer Co.* (1968) that Reconstruction-era civil rights laws extended to private discrimination via congressional power to enforce the Thirteenth Amendment's ban on slavery and involuntary servitude, which the *Jones* majority had construed to include, as "badges" of slavery, all forms of racial discrimination. But he accepted the *Jones* precedent, nevertheless. Speaking for the Court in a 1973 case subjecting a neighborhood association's segregated swimming pool to federal law, he was able to avoid, in a sense, the *Jones* issue by concluding that the association was not truly a private club exempt from the law's coverage. Later he did join the Court in *Runyon v. McCrary* (1976), which upheld, as within Congress's Thirteenth Amendment enforcement power, a Reconstruction provision giving all citizens the same contractual rights accorded whites, as applied to a private school's whites-only admissions policy. But he remained clearly uncomfortable with *Jones*, noting in his preargument *Runyon* analysis, "[*Jones*] I am convinced was a policy decision, not a legal one....It has been made and we go on from there. [But] this, I think, is the reason for the very positive [*Jones*] dissent by Justice Harlan joined in by two others that the Court's decision in *Jones* was 'clearly wrong.'" Blackmun was also reluctant to embrace an expansive notion of the "state action" doctrine, under which private action permeated with state influence was subject to constitutional requirements. In *Moose Lodge v. Irvis* (1972), for example, he joined the Court, over the dissents of Douglas, Brennan, and Marshall, in refusing to hold that a private club licensed by the state to serve liquor violated the equal protection guarantee when it refused to serve food and beverages to the African American guest of a member.[47]

The justice found *Palmer v. Thompson* (1971), a first-term race case from Jackson, Mississippi, particularly difficult. In the face of a lawsuit, Jackson's city officials agreed to desegregate its public parks, auditoriums, golf courses, and zoo, but decided to close the city's swimming pools rather than operate them on a desegregated basis. Over the dissents of Justices Douglas, Brennan, White, and Marshall, the Court, per Justice Black, upheld the city's decision, even though one of the five city pools, previously leased from a private association, apparently became a whites-only private facility. Initially, Blackmun had been "inclined" to rule against Jackson, although anxious to assure that any opinion in the case "be carefully drawn...so as not to contain statements which will spawn all kinds of new litigation." On the day after the justices discussed *Palmer* in conference, he told Black his "inclination," at that point, was to join the senior justice in affirming the city's action. He later wrote Black, however, that his vote in the case was "tentative." Then, when his clerk Robert Gooding ran across the Court's summary affirmance, a decade earlier, of a lower court decision striking down a Louisiana statute that had given that state's governor the authority to close any school ordered to integrate, the justice again wrote Black, asking whether the Louisiana school ruling created a "contrary implication to the affirmance" of Jackson's decision in *Palmer*. Because the Louisiana case involved schools rather than swimming pools, Blackmun "suspect[ed]" that case could be distinguished from *Palmer*, but the justice was "interested in [Black's] own reaction." In a separate letter that same day, Blackmun also wrote Black that he found the case "one of the most troublesome ones" of the term.[48]

Justice Black minced no words in his response. Black had joined the decision in the Louisiana school case, the elderly justice declared, but would "never have voted to affirm" in that case had he "ever entertained an idea that any part of the decision in that case would stand for the principle that the United States Constitution compels a State to tax its citizens to run public schools." The same rule, he added, "would apply with more force to a situation where for any reason a State through its legislature decided not to tax its people to operate swimming pools." Nor did Black share Blackmun's anxiety about the case. During oral argument, Blackmun had asked counsel for those challenging the pool closing whether Jackson would be "locked in" to providing swimming pools permanently, should the Court rule against the closing, even if their continued operation would cause the city serious economic hardship. The attorney had responded that the city would indeed be "locked in forever" if "racial problems...cause[d] a rise in economic difficulties in operating the pool." Reminding Blackmun of that exchange, Black found "no closeness or troublesomeness whatever in [the] case" because he "agree[d] with the counsel...that if the judgment [of the lower court upholding Jackson] is reversed the city will be 'locked in' and must continue to operate swimming pools so long as a majority of our Court declines to let them free themselves from that burden."[49]

But seemingly in all things, Blackmun lacked Black's certitude. In fact, language in the *Palmer* concurrence he first circulated reflected such turmoil on his part that it provoked a reaction from Chief Justice Burger. "For me," Blackmun's draft began, "this is perhaps the most excruciatingly difficult case of the present Term. I frankly admit that I find myself close to dead center. In isolation the litigation may not be of great importance; it could have, however, significant implications." On his copy of the draft that he returned to his fellow Minnesotan, Burger lined through the entire paragraph, explaining in the margin, "This will lead to press speculation that on the 'next' case, etc., etc., you will do thus and so." In a dissent joined by Justices Brennan and Marshall, Justice White was charging that the decision of Jackson officials to close the pools smacked of invidious racial bias. "Detect[ing] a sense of punitiveness in the approach and tone of [White's] dissent," Blackmun expressed the "judgment, inadequate and hesitant though it may be,…that this is neither the time nor the occasion to be punitive toward Jackson for her past constitutional sins of segregation." Burger crossed out that passage, too. In a separate note, moreover, he expressed the "hope" that Blackmun would "consider some 'muting'…of your…concurrence," adding, "I suppose this is because I am always uncomfortable—and I think most readers are—with our speaking too much of the difficulties of close cases.…I hope you will 'settle' for a simple statement that you find it a close and hard case."[50]

In the second draft of his concurrence, Blackmun followed much of Burger's advice. He also ended up joining Justice Black's opinion as well as the Court's judgment. But he declined to "read into the closing of the pools an official expression of inferiority toward black citizens, as Mr. Justice White and those who join him repetitively assert," instead dismissing White's conclusion as mere "speculation." He also repeated his opposition to any "punitive" attitude toward Jackson, despite its racial past. And he found "disturbing" the notion that the city would be " 'locked in' with its pools for an indefinite future, despite financial loss of whatever amount, just because at one time the pools of Jackson had been segregated." Finally, he thought it meaningful that Jackson had not closed its other recreational facilities and that the case involved a "municipal service of the nice-to-have but not essential variety," indeed, "perhaps a luxury, not enjoyed by many communities."[51]

Alienage Classifications

In nonracial cases, Blackmun generally joined Burger Court decisions restricting the scope of the equal protection guarantee. During his first full term, he spoke for the Court in *Graham v. Richardson* (1971), which added alienage to the list of constitutional suspects to be given strict judicial scrutiny. But *Graham* arguably was only a modest extension of the

The infant Harry and his emotionally fragile mother, Theo Blackmun. Courtesy of Collection of the Supreme Court of the United States.

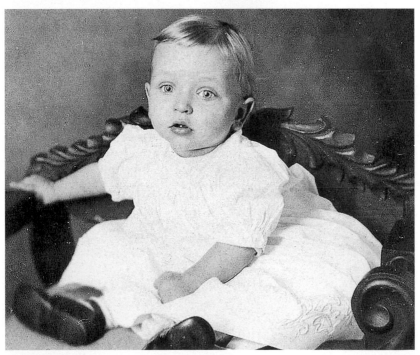

Harry A. Blackmun (1908–99). Courtesy of Collection of the Supreme Court of the United States.

A rare, unidentified newspaper photograph of Blackmun's father, Corwin Manning Blackmun, at right, who served as a National Guard major during World War II. Corwin Blackmun was always a disappointment to his son. Harry A. Blackmun Papers, Manuscript Division, Library of Congress.

Harry and his maternal grandfather, Theodore Reuter. Courtesy of Collection of the Supreme Court of the United States.

A patriotic Harry, at left, with unidentified playmates. Minnesota Historical Society.

The first—and favorite—of the many jobs Blackmun had while working his way through college: driver of the launch for the Harvard rowing crew. Courtesy of Collection of the Supreme Court of the United States.

To help defray college expenses, Blackmun also worked on a Wyoming dude ranch. In later years, he said his clerks were "amazed" to see photographs of the justice "on a horse [wearing] chaps and all the rest." Courtesy of Collection of the Supreme Court of the United States.

When his boyhood friend Warren Burger married Elvera Stromberg, Blackmun was best man. Courtesy of Collection of the Supreme Court of the United States.

Blackmun, standing in the rear at far right, with members of the Mayo Association in 1951. The justice considered his years as resident counsel to the famed Mayo Clinic (1950–59) the happiest of his life. Courtesy of Mayo Clinic.

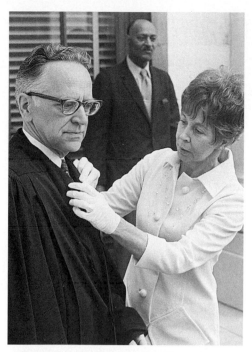

Dottie Blackmun adjusts her somber husband's robe as the justice, in his words, "almost desperate" and overwhelmed by feelings of inadequacy, begins a nearly quarter century tenure on the nation's highest tribunal. Courtesy of AP Images.

The Supreme Court in 1970, when Justice Blackmun took his seat on the high bench. Seated left to right: Justice John Marshall Harlan, Justice Hugo L. Black, Chief Justice Warren Burger, Justice William O. Douglas, and Justice William J. Brennan. Standing: Justice Thurgood Marshall, Justice Potter Stewart, Justice Byron White, and Justice Blackmun. Photograph by Robert Oakes and Vic Boswell, National Geographic Society. Courtesy of Collection of the Supreme Court of the United States.

An informal portrait of the Rehnquist Court in 1991, the year before a majority narrowly averted reversal of *Roe v. Wade*, Justice Blackmun's signature opinion. Standing left to right: Justice Clarence Thomas, Justice Byron White, Chief Justice William Rehnquist, Justice Anthony Kennedy, Justice Sandra Day O'Connor, Justice Antonin Scalia, and Justice David H. Souter. Seated: Justice John Paul Stevens and Justice Blackmun. Photograph by Joseph Bailey, National Geographic Society. Courtesy of Collection of the Supreme Court of the United States.

Justice Blackmun meets with President Clinton as the justice prepares to retire from the Court in 1994. Photograph by the White House. Courtesy of Collection of the Supreme Court of the United States.

Court's position in race cases. In his preargument summaries of *Graham* and a companion case, the justice made clear his view that treating alienage as a suspect was a more limited way of disposing of the law at issue than by reliance on a Warren Court precedent expanding the reach of equal protection. *Graham* struck down a state statute imposing a fifteen-year residency requirement on aliens' eligibility for welfare benefits. In *Shapiro v. Thompson* (1969), the Warren Court had struck down a one-year residency requirement before newcomers to a state could receive nonemergency welfare benefits, with the majority subjecting the law at issue to strict judicial review as a restriction on the fundamental right of interstate travel. Blackmun opposed a decision in *Graham* based on *Shapiro*, observing in his summary, "Frankly, I would just as soon stay away from comment on the right to travel and to stick instead to discrimination which is invidious." He also conceded "some trouble with the basic philosophy of *Shapiro*."[52]

The justice sought to pursue a narrow, cautious approach to alienage issues in later cases as well. In *Sugarman v. Dougall* (1973), he spoke for the Court, over Justice Rehnquist's lone dissent, in striking down a New York law limiting eligibility for permanent state civil service positions to U.S. citizens only. He agreed that states had a significant public interest in making aliens ineligible for positions involving "direct participation" in the "formulation and execution of important state policy." But the challenged law, he concluded, swept too broadly, bringing within its reach typists and other office workers.[53]

Even though declaring New York's law unconstitutional, the justice also embraced a more flexible equal protection standard than he had appeared to invoke in *Graham*. Noting once again that alienage classifications were subject to close judicial scrutiny, he made no reference in *Sugarman* to alienage as a constitutional "suspect." Probably because he was recognizing state power to exclude aliens from the electoral process and certain public jobs, he also declined to insist that alienage classifications be necessary to a "compelling" governmental interest. "We hold only," he observed at one point, "that a flat ban on the employment of aliens in positions that have little, if any relation to a State's legitimate interest, cannot withstand scrutiny under the Fourteenth Amendment," but did not specify the degree of judicial review that should be imposed in such cases. Later he reiterated the state's authority to impose a citizenship requirement not only for voting and elective office, but also for nonelected officers "who participate directly in the formulation, execution, or review of broad public policy [and thus] perform functions that go to the heart of representative government." Although agreeing that "such state action ... is not wholly immune from scrutiny under the Equal Protection Clause," he concluded, "Our scrutiny will not be so demanding where we deal with matters resting firmly within a State's constitutional prerogatives."[54]

In language if not outcome, Justice Blackmun's *Sugarman* opinion differed meaningfully from Justice Powell's majority opinion in another alienage case decided that day. *In Re Griffiths* (1973) involved a Dutch national and law school graduate who had once clerked for Justice Arthur Goldberg and, according to Blackmun's conference notes, was "pretty, they say." Ruling for Griffiths, the Court, per Powell, struck down a Connecticut rule limiting law practice to citizens. Quoting *Graham* and other cases, Powell termed alienage "suspect" and also declared that such discrimination must be "necessary" to accomplish a "compelling" governmental interest. After reading drafts of both *Sugarman* and *Griffiths*, Blackmun's clerk Randall Bezanson dismissed as "not really important at all" the fact that "*Griffiths* explicitly mentions the word 'suspect' classification [whereas] we do not." But Bezanson considered Powell's requirement that the means selected by the state to accomplish a compelling interest "be *necessary* to the accomplishment of its purpose" an "important aspect of Justice Powell's standard." The clerk thought it wise that Blackmun's *Sugarman* draft had avoided declaring that the alienage classification at issue, or such classifications generally, must be "necessary" to the state's purpose in restricting civil service jobs to citizens only. "Whatever the concerns of the State with respect to aliens," he reasoned, "they could in most cases be resolved by individualized examination—albeit in depth and extensive and burdensome—of the applicant rather than wholesale exclusion of the class of aliens." By requiring that an alienage classification merely be "narrowly confined" to the state's asserted objective rather than "necessary" to its purpose, the Blackmun draft avoided that pitfall.[55]

The chief justice also preferred "the narrow basis" of Blackmun's opinion to Powell's approach in *Griffiths*. Although "agree[ing] generally" with the dissent Justice Rehnquist had filed for both cases, Burger joined Blackmun's *Sugarman* opinion but registered a biting dissent in *Griffiths*. Emphasizing that the question before the Court was "not what is enlightened or sound policy but rather what the Constitution and its Amendments provide," Burger found nothing in those documents to support the Court's "expansive reading" of the Fourteenth Amendment, declaring, "I am [thus] bound...to reject the good policy the Court now adopts." But the chief justice reserved most of his ire for the *Griffiths* Court's expansive reading of the suspect classification doctrine. "In recent years," asserted Burger, "the Court, in a rather casual way, has articulated the code phrase 'suspect classification' as though it embraced a reasoned constitutional concept. Admittedly, it simplifies judicial work as do 'per se' rules, but it tends to stop analysis while appearing to suggest an analytical process." The Rehnquist dissent, with which Burger "generally" agreed, completely rejected the suspect classification doctrine outside the field of race, which, even Rehnquist conceded, the Fourteenth Amendment's framers "plainly" intended to treat as a suspect.[56]

Equal Protection Doctrine

Blackmun, like Burger, embraced a moderately narrow approach to equal protection doctrine in other cases as well. For example, he joined Justice Powell's majority opinion in *San Antonio Independent School District v. Rodriguez* (1973), in which the Court limited the fundamental rights branch of Warren Court equal protection standards to rights stated or implied in the Constitution rather than also including interests considered important or basic, whether or not grounded in the Constitution's text.[57]

Although Blackmun filed no opinion in *Rodriguez*, his preargument analysis makes clear his support for the majority's approach in the case. At issue in *Rodriguez* was a scheme under which public schools were funded largely through local property taxes, which produced substantial variations in per capita student educational funding from district to district. The plaintiffs contended, among other things, that the system interfered with each student's fundamental right to an equal education.

While assuming that the Constitution did grant some degree of educational opportunity to children, Justice Powell refused to recognize any fundamental right to equal schooling—and thus subject the challenged funding scheme to strict judicial scrutiny. Instead, he evaluated the system under the traditional requirement that discriminatory laws based on no suspect classification and interfering with no fundamental right merely be rationally related to a legitimate governmental purpose. Powell found such a relationship between the challenged funding arrangement and the state interest in local control of education.

In his case summary, Blackmun also indicated that "rationality rather than compelling state interests" should be the standard, asserting, "I am inclined to feel that education is not a fundamental interest any more than health [and] social welfare are fundamental interests." He had "the general feeling that education [was] a matter for the legislature and not for the courts," and he feared the daunting potential impact of a decision upholding the plaintiffs' challenge. "I wonder where we draw the line. If education is to be distributed with equality throughout the state, why does not the same thesis apply to police protection, hospitals, fire protection, and other such services?... The decision below," striking down the funding scheme, "would be just another step leading toward big government and centralized control in another field, to wit, education. If a state wants to do this, that is its privilege. If it does not want to do it, I wonder whether it is constitutionally required to do so."[58]

Blackmun initially assumed that the Court would overturn the Texas school-funding system and that a contrary stance would "be a very unpopular posture to assume." A clerk who prepared a bench memo for the case recommended affirming the three-judge district court decision declaring the program unconstitutional. But the justice had at least one ally in the case among his clerks. James W. Ziglar Jr., a Pascagoula, Mississippi, native who was to serve as an aide to Senator James Eastland and hold a succession of positions in the administrations of GOP presidents, including George W. Bush, clerked for Blackmun during the 1972 term. Ziglar faulted the author of the *Rodriguez* bench memo for recommending that "this Court should 'try' to affirm [the trial court] because he considers the Texas system of school financing to be unfair." To Ziglar, "what may or may not be wise social or education policy should not determine whether this Court 'finds' a constitutional violation." Ziglar stressed that he had "no idea how you intend to vote in this case, and [was] not undertaking a blitz campaign to persuade you that my position is correct." He also conceded that he was "in a very small minority among the [justices'] clerks on this question," but added, "I do feel strongly about it and this memo must be read in that light." By that point, of course, the justice and Ziglar were essentially of one mind on *Rodriguez*.[59]

Blackmun's willingness to join Powell's *Rodriguez* opinion did not mean that he would invariably defer to the government in cases involving claims of discrimination against the poor. In *James v. Valtierra* (1971), for example, he and Justice Brennan joined Justice Marshall's dissent from the Court's decision upholding a California constitutional provision forbidding the development of low-income housing projects until they were first approved in a voter referendum. Speaking for a majority that included Chief Justice Burger, Justice Black declared that such referendum measures "demonstrate devotion to democracy, not to bias, discrimination, or prejudice." But Marshall, in the dissent that Blackmun joined, charged that "singling out the poor to bear a burden not placed on any other class of citizens tramples the values that the Fourteenth Amendment was designed to protect."[60]

Sex Discrimination

Ultimately, Blackmun also declined to join justices urging the addition of sex to the list of constitutional suspects, and thus subject to the strict judicial scrutiny given racial and related forms of discrimination. But he took a complicated route in reaching that decision. In *Reed v. Reed* (1971), a unanimous Court, speaking through Chief Justice Burger, declared a gender classification unconstitutional for the first time in the Court's history. The statute at issue gave men preference over women when two persons (in this case, the parents of a child who had died without a will) were otherwise equally qualified to administer an estate. In his opinion striking the law down, Burger appeared to invoke the lenient, rational basis equal protection standard, but actually applied a more rigorous formula. The state had argued that the challenged preference was reasonably related to its interest in reducing the workload of probate courts by eliminating one type of dispute in estate cases. The chief justice conceded that the state's objective was "not without some legitimacy," yet he found the sexual preference used to advance that interest "the very kind of arbitrary legislative choice forbidden by the Equal Protection Clause."[61]

Two years later, in *Frontiero v. Richardson* (1973), the Court invalidated an Air Force regulation under which married servicemen were automatically granted a dependency allowance and medical benefits for spouses, while servicewomen were obliged to establish that they were actually providing over half a spouse's support. In a plurality opinion, Justice Brennan, joined by Justices Douglas, White, and Marshall, concluded that sex, like gender, was constitutionally suspect and that gender discrimination should be subjected to essentially the same judicial scrutiny as racial classifications. The regulation at issue was based on the stereotypical assumption that the spouses of servicemen were so likely to be dependent on their husbands for over half their support that no case-by-case determination of eligibility was needed. Such "mere administrative convenience," Brennan asserted, was hardly adequate to justify discrimination based on a suspect classification.[62]

Brennan's position, however, did not command a majority. Citing the *Reed* decision, Justices Stewart and Powell concurred only in the Court's judgment. Finding the challenged Air Force regulation "abundantly" inconsistent with *Reed*, Powell concluded that it was "unnecessary for the Court in this case to characterize sex as a suspect classification, with all of the far-reaching implications of such a holding." The proposed Equal Rights Amendment then before the state legislatures for ratification was, for Powell, another, and "compelling," reason for the Court to avoid embracing the Brennan plurality's thesis. Adoption of the ERA, he wrote, would resolve the debate over the status of gender classifications in a way clearly "prescribed by the Constitution": the constitutional amendment process.[63]

Like Burger, Justice Blackmun joined Powell's *Frontiero* concurrence without filing an opinion of his own. While *Reed* was pending before the Court, however, Blackmun had indicated in his preargument summary of the case that he was "inclined to feel that sex can be considered a suspect classification just as race and...alienage." Nevertheless, he made clear, as he did with alienage in his opinion for the Court in the *Sugarman* case, that he favored subjecting nonracial suspect classifications, at least, to somewhat less rigorous judicial scrutiny than the modern Court had invoked in such cases—an approach that, in the Court's hands, was almost invariably fatal for challenged statutes. After terming sex a suspect classification in his *Reed* summary, he immediately asserted, "This does not mean that every statute which makes a distinction based on sex is automatically invalid. It merely sets as the starting point the proposition that such a distinction is suspect and strong justification is needed to uphold it. There can be no question that women have been held down in the past in almost every area."[64]

In his bench memo for the *Frontiero* case, Blackmun's clerk James Ziglar had also argued, somewhat surprisingly, that sex should be considered a suspect classification. But when the first draft of Brennan's opinion was circulated, Ziglar changed positions because, he explained in a memo to Blackmun, "I believe, and I still believe, that an unyielding application of the suspect classification standards in the sex area would render unacceptable results. My feeling was, and is, that sex is not of the same character as race, and, indeed, biological difference [between the sexes] might justify certain classifications." When Brennan circulated his second draft, however, Ziglar recommended that Blackmun join Brennan. "Justice Brennan's [latest] circulation seems to give us the best of both worlds. While sex is treated as a 'suspect' classification and thus invokes...strict scrutiny, Justice Brennan makes it clear...that 'frequently' there is no basis for classifications based on sex. I read this to mean that the traditional [and almost invariably fatal] 'rigid scrutiny' will not be blindly applied in sex classification cases." The opinion that Randall Bezanson had prepared for Blackmun in *Sugarman v. Dougall,* the alienage case, added Ziglar, also embraced the "soften[ed]" version of strict scrutiny that Ziglar thought should be followed "in all suspect classification cases." The clerk was thus "inclined" toward Brennan's latest draft.[65]

Ultimately, however, Blackmun wrote Justice Brennan that, "after some struggle," he had "concluded that it is not advisable, and certainly not necessary, for us to reach out in this case to hold that sex, like race and national origin and alienage, is a suspect classification." To the justice, *Reed* provided "ample precedent" for striking down the Air Force regulation at issue in *Frontiero*, and there was thus no need to "enter the arena of the proposed Equal Rights Amendment."[66]

In *Stanton v. Stanton* (1975), Blackmun spoke for the Court when it again declined to decide whether sex classifications were "inherently suspect," yet struck down a Utah law under which females were no longer eligible for child support on reaching age eighteen, whereas twenty-one was the age of majority for males. Although finding *Reed* controlling, the justice declared "that under any test—compelling state interest, or rational basis, or something in between—[the challenged law,] in the context of child support, does not survive an equal protection attack." Even so, he cited state justifications for the sex distinction at issue in the case that were clearly "rational" in the traditional sense of that term.[67]

The next year, in *Craig v. Boren* (1976), Justice Brennan, now convinced that he could not put together a majority for the proposition that sex was constitutionally suspect, opted for the "in between" formula to which Blackmun had referred in *Stanton*, a standard remarkably similar to the "softened" version of strict scrutiny that the justice had begun embracing privately as early as *Reed* and had also invoked in the alienage cases. *Reed* and other cases, Brennan observed for the *Craig* Court, had "establish[ed] that classifications by gender must serve important governmental objectives and must be substantially related to achievement of those objectives." In *Stanton*, for example, the Court had held *Reed* to be controlling, yet declared Utah's differential age-of-majority law unconstitutional, "notwithstanding the statute's coincidence with and furtherance of the State's purpose of fostering 'old notions' of role typing and preparing boys for their expected performance in the economic and political worlds." The Oklahoma statute at issue in *Craig* allowed women to purchase "near beer" at age eighteen, while requiring males to wait until age twenty-one. Statistics offered by the state to defend the law, Brennan concluded, did not establish a sufficiently close connection between the discrimination at issue and Oklahoma's important interest in highway safety.[68]

Blackmun joined most of Brennan's opinion, including the portion subjecting sex classifications to heightened scrutiny. Chief Justice Burger, on the other hand, dissented, based on his "general agreement" with the lengthy dissent of Justice Rehnquist, the staunchest critic of the Court's growing willingness to subject discrimination based on sex, illegitimacy, and other "quasi-suspect" classifications to more rigorous review than required by the traditional rationality standard, under which virtually all nonracial classifications would survive constitutional attack. The chief justice saw no "independent constitutional basis" for the Court's decision to make "gender a disfavored classification." Thus, since he and most of his colleagues had not found the challenged law "irrational," he could "see no basis for striking [it] down...as violative of the Constitution simply because we find it unwise, unneeded, or possibly even a bit foolish."[69]

Illegitimacy as a "Quasi-Suspect"

State laws drawing lines based on status of birth gave Blackmun even greater difficulty than classifications based on sex. In *Levy v. Louisiana* (1968), the Warren Court had purported to invoke the rational basis test in striking down a state law denying illegitimate children the right to recover damages for the wrongful death of their mother. But during Blackmun's first full term, a majority, speaking through Justice Black, a *Levy* dissenter, in *Labine v. Vincent* (1971), upheld a Louisiana statute that barred an illegitimate child who had been acknowledged but not legitimated from sharing equally with legitimate heirs in the father's estate. Black, who had been increasingly critical of the Court's expansive constructions of what he termed the "vague generalities" of the equal protection and due process clauses during his last decade on the bench, cited the state's rational interest in promoting family life and establishing rules for the disposition of property within the state. But in a vigorous dissent, Justice Brennan, joined by Douglas, White, and Marshall, scorned the Court's failure to mention "the central reality of the case: Louisiana punishes illegitimate children for the misdeeds of their parents."[70]

When Justice Black circulated a second draft of his opinion, Blackmun clerk Dan Edelman declared it "disturbing and unsatisfying to say the least." Under *Levy*, the clerk wrote his justice, a " 'rational basis' *at the very least* [was] required to justify discrimination against illegitimates," yet Black had simply cited legitimate state purposes "without attempting to show that the Louisiana classification bears any rational relationship to those ends whatever." Under Black's formula, asserted Edelman, "the result would be the same if Louisiana denied intestate inheritance to persons with blue eyes or red hair, or to blacks. In spite of the presumable absence of rational basis for those discriminations, the Black approach would sustain the classification as occurring in an area where the states have traditionally had power to act. It is difficult to see what meaning remains to the equal protection clause given such an approach."[71]

Edelman's memo, however, had little effect on Blackmun. The justice's preargument analysis reflected considerable ambivalence toward illegitimacy classifications. His "general leaning" was "in favor of the acknowledged child." But he also noted the state's argument "that this is basically an area for state legislation, and not federal legislation," adding, "This, of course, is true." Apparently unaware, at that point, of *Levy* and a companion case, he mentioned that "evidently, there are two cases, somewhat old, from this Court, which held as unconstitutional any statutory attempt to exclude an illegitimate child from such rights as children have under wrongful death statutes." While "not exactly the same," he thought those cases "certainly afford[ed] a precedent." Ultimately, though, he joined Black in distinguishing *Levy* and upholding the state. When the Court changed course yet again the next year, observing, per Justice Powell, that the Court "exercise[d] stricter scrutiny" when state classifications "approach[ed] sensitive and fundamental personal rights," including familial interests, Blackmun concurred only in the judgment. Resting his vote in the case on a narrow ground, he refused to join in an opinion that he saw as "flatly granting dependent unacknowledged illegitimate children full equality with dependent legitimate children and striking down the Louisiana statutory scheme even for the situation where the father has the power to acknowledge his illegitimates but refrains from doing so."[72]

Two years later, the justice joined the Court, speaking through Chief Justice Burger, in again declining to declare illegitimacy a suspect, purporting to apply the rationality standard yet striking down a social security regulation restricting the survivors' rights of children born out of wedlock. "By and large," Blackmun wrote in his preargument analysis on this occasion, "I would not favor making illegitimacy a suspect category. We have been somewhat hesitant in expanding the suspect class....I see no need to do it here, for these particular appellants probably will prevail whatever standard we accept. I certainly could approach this case on middle tier [heightened scrutiny] or lower tier [rational basis] equal protection and come out to reverse." Yet he continued to be torn, observing, "There would be no problem at all if a compelling state interest on the basis of a suspect classification were the approach taken." But then he concluded, "In summary, I would reverse and would do so on absence of rationality.... I would refrain from the compelling state interest test and from the suspect classification [approach]." When the Court later appeared to tighten up on the scrutiny accorded illegitimacy classifications, he joined Burger, Stewart, and Rehnquist in reaffirming his approach for the highly deferential stance Justice Black had taken in the *Labine* case.[73]

Minnesota Twins?

During their early years on the bench, Blackmun and Burger occasionally parted company on issues facing the Court. Perhaps as a result of his avid love of the outdoors, Blackmun differed with the chief justice on the question of standing to sue in environmental cases. Burger joined the majority in *Sierra Club v. Morton* (1972), dismissing the environmental group's challenge to federal authorization for construction of a ski development in the Sequoia National Forest. The Court based its decision on the ground that the Sierra Club had alleged injury to the environment but not to the organization and its members, contrary to the traditional requirement that litigants allege injury to personal legal rights in seeking standing to sue. In a vigorous dissent, Justice Blackmun contended that the case was not "ordinary, run-of-the-mill litigation," in which traditional rules of standing should apply. Instead, the suit "pose[d]—if only we choose to acknowledge and reach them—significant aspects of a wide, growing, and disturbing problem, that is, the Nation's and the world's deteriorating environment with its resulting ecological disturbances." He then asked, "Must our law be so rigid and our procedural concepts so inflexible that we render ourselves helpless when the existing methods and the traditional concepts do not quite fit and do not prove to be entirely adequate for new issues?" Blackmun recommended "an imaginative expansion of our traditional concepts of standing in order to enable an organization such as the Sierra Club, possessed, as it is, of pertinent, bona fide, and well-recognized attributes and purposes in the area of environment, to litigate environmental issues."[74]

But such divisions were rare during their early years together on the Court. Both generally opposed expansive notions of standing to sue. Both favored limiting federal district court intervention in state judicial proceedings, intrusions that Justice Black termed, in the leading case on the issue, an affront to "Our Federalism" and the respect due state judges absent extraordinary circumstances. Both supported opinions limiting the scope of the exclusionary rule in search and seizure cases and the *Miranda* restrictions on the use of confessions. Both dissented when a 5–4 majority in *Furman v. Georgia* (1972) declared a state death penalty statute unconstitutional. In fact, until the Court's 1977 term, Burger and Blackmun voted together in about 90 percent of nonunanimous civil liberties cases.[75]

Even at that point, though, differences in tone and emphasis could be detected in their responses to issues facing the Court. When Blackmun, for example, drew on his extensive mathematical background and recent statistical data to conclude in *Ballew v. Georgia* (1977) that reduction of a jury's size to below six members promoted bias in the jury deliberation process, only Justice Stevens joined his opinion announcing the Court's ruling, while Chief Justice Burger joined Justice Powell's separate concurrence emphasizing the difficulties inherent in such line drawing. In his *Furman* dissent, moreover, Burger acknowledged that, "possessed of legislative power," he would vote to eliminate the death penalty entirely "or, at the very least, restrict [its] use…to a small category of the most heinous crimes," but immediately added that the Court's review of capital punishment "must be divorced from personal feelings as to the morality and efficacy of the death penalty."[76]

As he had on the Eighth Circuit, Justice Blackmun assumed essentially the same stance in *Furman*, but only to a point. He got off a few caustic shots at the other side. Noting that only a year earlier the Court had upheld the very type of capital punishment scheme it was now invalidating in *Furman*, the justice questioned "the suddenness of the Court's perception of progress in the human attitude since decisions of only a short while ago." He also accused the majority of taking the "easy" road. "It is easier to strike the balance in favor of life and against death. It is comforting to relax in the thoughts—perhaps the rationalizations—that this is the compassionate decision for a maturing society; that this is the moral and the 'right' thing to do;...that we are less barbaric than we were...a year ago." There was a difference, however. Blackmun's dissent reflected an anguish about state executions that Burger's opinion did not. "Cases such as these," he declared, "provide for me an excruciating agony of the spirit. I yield to no one in the depth of my distaste, antipathy, and, indeed, abhorrence, for the death penalty, with all its aspects of physical distress and fear and of moral judgment exercised by finite minds...[a] distaste...buttressed by a belief that capital punishment serves no useful purpose that can be demonstrated. For me, it violates childhood's training and life's experiences....It is antagonistic to any sense of 'reverence for life.' Were I a legislator, I would vote against the death penalty."[77]

There is simply no evidence to support the notion that Blackmun and Burger were ever the "Minnesota Twins" in the sense that the chief justice exerted an undue influence over his boyhood friend. In fact, given Blackmun's resentment of early press references to "Hip Pocket Harry" and other insinuations that he might be a Burger pawn on the Court, the justice was probably particularly alert—and resistant—to any Burger overtures in that direction from the beginning of their tenure together. There is also evidence from early in Blackmun's Court years that the chief justice had begun to try his friend's patience well before they began to be less frequently allied on issues confronting the justices. Blackmun's earliest clerks, for example, went to the Court assuming that the two were the closest of friends, but quickly sensed their justice's irritation with Burger's highhanded approach to the position of chief justice.

Years later, Justice Blackmun would trace the permanent breach in his relationship with Chief Justice Burger to the Watergate scandal and *United States v. Nixon* (1974), the tumultuous Court battle that brought down a president. The Court's role in bringing an end to the Nixon presidency has been told well and often elsewhere. Following oral argument, eight justices—with Justice Rehnquist, a former member of the administration, not participating—voted in conference to reject Nixon's claim to executive privilege over the Watergate tapes and documents. The chief justice then assigned himself the task of writing the Court's opinion. But when he circulated a draft extremely deferential to presidential authority, inviting suggestions for revisions, most of his colleagues readily obliged, gently but firmly converting Burger's draft into a collegial document that carried the chief justice's name and accorded the president broader powers than certain justices preferred, but that firmly rejected Nixon's claims to an absolute privilege not even subject to judicial review. When the Court announced its decision on July 24, Justice Blackmun's daughter Susie, an outspoken Nixon critic and opponent of the Vietnam War, left her father a one-word telephone message: "Thanks."[78]

Initially at least, Justice Blackmun was less than enthusiastic about the Court's intervention in the case, or use of the dispute as a vehicle for a major ruling on presidential privilege. He and Justice White voted to deny review, and in a July 9 conference, according to Justice Powell's notes, Blackmun urged the justices to avoid a broad constitutional pronouncement, preferring instead a "pragmatic, narrow decision based on [the case's] special facts." To Burger's likely dismay, however, he readily joined what he later termed the "palace revolution" against the chief justice.[79]

Blackmun's contribution to the Court's opinion was a substantially revised statement of the facts of the case, which Justice Brennan immediately pronounced "excellent" and urged Burger to incorporate into the Court's opinion. In a cover letter to the chief justice, Blackmun sought to soothe his friend's feelings. "Please believe me," he pleaded, "when I say that I do this in a spirit of cooperation and not of criticism. I am fully aware of the pressures that presently beset all of us." But the chief justice was hardly consoled. "I think he was upset, and understandably so, with the way the thing was working," Blackmun remarked in 1995, the year Burger died, "because very little of his opinion was automatically accepted, and I'm sure he resented my restatement of the facts, but I personally felt, and so did everybody else, that the facts needed revision, so we went about it that way. It was the kind of a situation that was ready-made for resentment and misunderstanding....Chief Justice Burger, understandably, is a very proud person, as all of us are, and he must have resented it, and, I suppose, to this day resents it to a degree. It must have been as difficult a summer as he's ever lived professionally. ...I'm sure that this case was a factor in the divergence from our former rather close relationship."[80]

Strains in their relationship had begun to surface, however, at least as early as the 1972 term and the Court's disposition of *Roe v. Wade* (1973), the signature case of Blackmun's career. Randall Bezanson, the clerk assigned to *Roe* that term, sensed the onset of a "breaking down or formalizing of the relationship between the chief and Justice Blackmun" during his year at the Court. Bezanson "thought that [it] was a function [primarily] of the chief's general way of doing things as chief. There was a certain officiousness there that Justice Blackmun, I think, didn't particularly care for. The chief justice would often play his power, and not just toward Justice Blackmun." Burger would withhold his votes at conference, for example, to assure that he was ultimately on the winning side of a case, and thus, as chief justice, had the prerogative of assigning the Court's opinion to the justice whose views were closest to his own. "I think it was that kind of thing more than anything else." The two clearly "were dear friends," but Bezanson doubts "that their relationship was a tight relationship [even] at that point" in their careers. "When I was there, they worked out together [in the late afternoon]. Justice Blackmun would go down [to the exercise room], and the chief was down there....Sometimes, he would come back and say, 'I wish he could make up his mind' or 'Sometimes, he drives me crazy!'" Arguably, Burger's handling that term of *Roe v. Wade*, to which we now turn, was the primary cause of Blackmun's frustration.[81]

Chapter 7

Roe and Beyond

Despite its civil libertarian reputation, the Warren Court largely confined its expansive constructions of civil liberties guarantees to rights specifically mentioned in the Constitution's text. In *Griswold v. Connecticut* (1965), a 7–2 majority invoked an unstated right of marital privacy to strike down that state's broad ban on the use of contraceptives. But Justice Douglas, *Griswold*'s author, sought, however unpersuasively, to tie the Court's decision to specific constitutional provisions. Marital privacy rights, declared Douglas, lay within the shadow or penumbra of several Bill of Rights provisions. Only in the opinions of concurring justices was the guarantee at issue based on what Justice Black in dissent derided as the "vague contours" of the due process clauses and inferences drawn from the Ninth Amendment's reference to unenumerated rights.[1]

It was thus ironic that in the *Roe* case, a 7–2 Burger Court majority, with only Justice Rehnquist of President Nixon's "strict constructionist" appointees in dissent, would throw caution to the winds and embrace substantive due process as the linchpin of its newly discovered abortion right. Even more ironic was the author of the Court's pronouncement, the Nixon justice personally endorsed by Nixon's new chief justice himself for a seat on the high bench. Citing *Roe* and other rulings seemingly inconsistent with the president's agenda, one newspaper aptly entitled a profile of the justices, "The Nixon Court vs. Richard Nixon."[2]

Prelude to *Roe*

Chief Justice Burger would never be comfortable with the direction the Court took in *Roe*. Initially, Justice Blackmun also seemed reluctant to expand on the right of privacy announced in *Griswold*. In *Eisenstadt v. Baird* (1972), a majority, speaking through Justice Brennan, invalidated on equal protection grounds a Massachusetts law prohibiting the distribution of contraceptives, or medical prescriptions for their use, to unmarried persons. Justice Douglas joined Brennan's opinion, but given the context of the case, also based his vote on First Amendment grounds. Following a lecture on overpopulation and contraception, Baird had invited members of the audience to come to the stage and help themselves to contraceptives; he also personally handed a package of vaginal foam to a young woman. In that setting, Douglas reasoned, display and distribution of the contraceptives was comparable to the use of visual aids in a lecture and thus, in his judgment, a permissible adjunct to free speech.[3]

Chief Justice Burger declared in dissent that Baird was properly convicted for dispensing medical material without a license and that the marital status of the woman to whom he had given the contraceptive had no bearing on the case. Justice Blackmun concurred in the Court's judgment but joined an opinion in which Justice White concluded that there was nothing in the record indicating whether the woman to whom Baird gave the vaginal foam was married or unmarried, and thus no reason to reach the constitutional question whether a state could validly restrict or forbid the distribution of contraceptives to unmarried persons. Blackmun thus avoided joining some of the more expansive passages in Justice Brennan's opinion for the Court, including the following assertion with enormous implications for the abortion issue: "If the right of privacy means anything, it is the right of the *individual*, married or single, to be free from unwarranted governmental intrusion into matters so fundamentally affecting a person as the decision whether to bear or beget a child."[4]

In his preargument written summary of a case decided the previous year, however, Blackmun had expressed few qualms about extending *Griswold* to the abortion arena. Milan Vuitch, a District of Columbia physician, was indicted under a DC law that forbade all abortions except those necessary to preserve a pregnant woman's life or health and performed under a doctor's direction. The lower court dismissed the indictment on vagueness grounds, pointing out that there was no indication in the law that abortions permitted to protect the woman's health included her mental as well as physical health. Speaking for the majority and drawing, characteristically, on the "general usage and modern understanding of the word 'health,'" as well as on other recent lower court constructions of the challenged statute, Justice Black rejected the vagueness challenge to the law.[5]

In conference, according to Justice Brennan's notes, Black had asserted that he could not "go with [a] woman's claim of [a] const[itutional] right to use her body as she pleases," and only Justice Douglas would suggest in dissent that abortion was part of the right of privacy he had announced for the Court in the *Griswold* case—a right, Douglas now seemed poised to declare, that needed no strained grounding in the specifics of the Bill of Rights. Brennan's notes include no mention of Blackmun, who apparently chose to remain silent in conference on the issues raised in *Vuitch*. Ultimately, Blackmun filed a brief separate opinion arguing, along with three other justices, that the case was not properly before the Court for decision, but he also joined Black's opinion on the assumption that the Court had jurisdiction to hear the appeal. Like most members of the Court, therefore, Blackmun was content to put off to another case the substantive issues raised by abortion laws.[6]

The justice's preargument analysis of *Vuitch* indicated, however, that he might already be leaning toward the stance he ultimately assumed in *Roe*—or could be easily pushed in that direction. In his summary, he noted that *Griswold* and *Stanley v. Georgia*, the 1969 case recognizing a right to possess obscenity in the privacy of one's home, provided "potent precedence in the privacy field." Significantly, he then added, "I may have to push myself a bit, but I would not be offended by the extension of privacy concepts to the point presented in the present case." He was "inclined" at that time to reverse the lower court holding that the abortion law at issue in the case was vague and remand for retrial. "If, on the other hand, the majority is not inclined in that direction, then I think I could go along with any reasonable interpretation of the problem [based] on principles of privacy."[7]

Mike LaFond, the clerk assigned to *Vuitch*, clearly gave the justice no encouragement in that direction, however. Commenting on the dissent Justice Douglas was preparing in the case, LaFond wrote Blackmun, "I think the state has a legitimate interest in regulating the practice of abortion for I am not persuaded that *Griswold* and the Bill of Rights grants the woman an automatic right to an abortion. At this point, I would say that the legislature is the appropriate body to weigh and balance the rights of the unborn child with those of the pregnant woman." The jurisdictional argument that the case was not properly before the Court on direct appeal from the DC district court, without intermediate review in the DC court of appeals, struck LaFond as "a good way to get rid of this difficult case."[8]

For the straitlaced justice, though, making a jurisdictional decision simply "to get rid of" a troublesome case was out of the question. In the margin next to LaFond's suggestion, Blackmun penciled in, "Not, however, the purpose" of a jurisdictional ruling.[9]

Roe: Round One

The justices had dodged the bullet in *Vuitch*. But *Roe v. Wade* and *Doe v. Bolton* would soon embroil the Court in the most contentious litigation since *Brown v. Board of Education*, with Harry Blackmun at the center of the storm. The story of *Roe* and *Doe* has been well and often told; the focus here is on Justice Blackmun's role and evolving position in the cases. Norma McCorvey, a young carnival worker, claimed in 1969 that she became pregnant as the result of a rape, but her physician refused to perform an abortion on the ground that Texas law forbade all abortions except those necessary to save the mother's life. Eventually, McCorvey was referred to Linda Coffee and Sarah Weddington, two lawyers interested in challenging the Texas statute. They filed a federal class action suit, and a three-judge district court declared the law unconstitutional on Ninth Amendment grounds but declined, for a variety of reasons, to issue an injunction against the statute's enforcement. Both McCorvey, under the pseudonym Jane Roe, and the state then appealed to the Supreme Court.[10]

The Georgia abortion statute at issue in *Doe v. Bolton* was typical of more modern state regulatory schemes. Under that law, abortions were to be performed by a duly licensed Georgia physician and only when necessary, in the physician's judgment, to protect the woman's life or health, when the fetus was likely to be born with a serious defect, or when the pregnancy resulted from rape. The statute also required that patients be Georgia residents, that abortions be performed in an accredited hospital, that the procedure be approved by a hospital abortion committee, and that two other licensed physicians confirm the attending doctor's judgment. An indigent, married, pregnant woman who had been denied an abortion, along with several physicians, nurses, clergymen, social workers, and two Georgia abortion reform organizations, filed a federal suit challenging the law. When a district court struck down certain provisions of the statute but upheld others, *Doe* also went to the Supreme Court.[11]

During what would be the first round of oral arguments in the cases, on December 13, 1971, Justice Blackmun assigned Sarah Weddington a "C+" in his notes, then described her as "large, blond hair, rather pretty, plump." At the Court's conference several days later, the justice, according to Brennan's notes, conceded that states would have the authority to outlaw all abortions were the Court to accept the "fetal life thesis"—the notion that a fetus is a person in a legal sense immediately upon conception. But he appeared to reject that theory out of hand, referring to "opposing interests," such as the "right of [the] mother to life and mental and physical health, [the] right of parents in case of rape, of [the] state in case of incest." At the same time, he also rejected the contention that "there is an absolute right to do what you will with your body."[12]

At that point, Justices Powell and Rehnquist, President Nixon's replacements for Justices Black and Harlan, were not yet hearing cases, and Chief Justice Burger was thus presiding over a seven-member Court. Of the seven, Justices Douglas, Brennan, Stewart, and Marshall favored striking down the abortion laws at issue in the cases. According to Brennan's *Roe* conference notes, Douglas pronounced the Texas statute "unconstitutional," Marshall "[went] with Douglas," as did Brennan, and Stewart termed the right at issue a Fourteenth Amendment due process right, "as John Harlan said in *Griswold*." Although somewhat ambivalent, Chief Justice Burger leaned toward reversing the lower court, declaring, "I can't find [the] Texas statute unconstitutional, altho[ugh] it's certainly archaic and absolute." Justice White, again according to Brennan's notes, rejected recognition of abortion rights. It appeared, then, that only Burger, White, and possibly Blackmun were in dissent. As the Court's senior member, Justice Douglas thus had the prerogative of writing the Court's opinions or assigning them to another justice in the majority.[13]

When the chief justice instead assigned the *Roe* and *Doe* opinions to Justice Blackmun, the crusty Douglas immediately protested. In a letter to the chief justice regarding the conference in *Doe*, Douglas declared, "My notes show there were four votes to hold parts of the Georgia Act unconstitutional.... There were three to sustain the law as written—you, Byron White, and Harry Blackmun." Douglas pointedly recommended "that to save future time and trouble, one of the four, rather than one of the three, should write the opinion."[14]

Burger soon responded, asserting that "at the close of discussion of [*Doe*], I remarked to the Conference that there were, literally, not enough columns to mark up an accurate reflection of the voting in either the Georgia or the Texas cases. I therefore marked down no votes and said this was a case that would have to stand or fall on the writing, when it was done." Burger remained convinced that was the best way "to handle these two...sensitive cases, which," he meaningfully added, "are quite probable candidates for reargument." The chief justice attempted to assure Douglas, however, that he had "no desire to restrain anyone's writing even though I do not have the same impression of views."[15]

On May 18, 1972, Blackmun circulated to the conference a first draft of his *Roe* opinion. Whether as a result of lobbying by Burger or otherwise, he had elected to invalidate the Texas statute as unconstitutionally vague, thereby avoiding the substantive privacy issues the cases raised. "With its sole criterion for exemption as 'saving the life of the mother,' " he declared, the law "is insufficiently informative to the physician to whom it purports to afford a measure of professional protection but must measure its indefinite meaning at the risk of his liberty." Given disposition of the case on vagueness grounds, he added, "There is no need in Roe's case to pass upon the contention that under the Ninth Amendment a pregnant woman has an absolute right to an abortion, or even to consider the opposing rights of the embryo or fetus during the respective prenatal trimesters. We are literally showered with briefs—with physicians and paramedical and other knowledgeable people on both sides—but this case, as it comes to us, does not require the resolution of those issues."[16]

In his cover memorandum to the draft, the justice assured his colleagues that he was "still flexible as to results" and would "do [his] best to arrive at something which would command a court." On the "more complex" Georgia case, he noted, he was "still tentatively of the view, as I have been all along," that *Doe* merited reargument "before a full bench." But he promised also to produce a draft in *Doe* before the justices made a decision regarding reargument.[17]

In his first *Doe* draft, circulated on May 25, Blackmun gave some constitutional weight to an abortion right bottomed on substantive privacy claims. Declared invalid were provisions of the Georgia law limiting abortions to Georgia residents, requiring confirmation of the attending physician's judgment by two other doctors, mandating advance approval by a hospital abortion committee, and limiting the procedure to nationally accredited hospitals. "What essentially remains," the justice observed in a cover memorandum, was the requirement that abortion decisions be based on the physician's "best clinical judgment" and performed only in a state-licensed hospital. As usual, he noted that the decision had not been "the easiest conclusion" for him to reach. "I have worked closely with supervisory hospital committees set up by the medical profession itself, and I have seen them operate over extensive periods. I can state with complete conviction that they serve a high purpose in maintaining standards and in keeping the overzealous surgeon's knife sheathed....I have also seen abortion mills in operation and the general misery they have caused despite their being run by otherwise 'competent' technicians."[18]

Blackmun's colleagues lost no time in responding to his *Roe* and *Doe* drafts. According to Brennan's recollections of the conference, a majority had voted to strike down all abortion statutes "save to the extent they required that an abortion be performed by a licensed physician within some limited time after conception." Blackmun, Brennan further recalled, had even indicated at conference that he "might support this view at least in" *Roe*. Brennan did not disagree with Blackmun's conclusion that the

Texas law was unduly vague, but he "prefer[red] a disposition of the core constitutional [privacy] issue." Brennan also saw no reason to schedule either case for reargument.[19]

Justice Douglas agreed that Blackmun "should meet what Bill Brennan calls the 'core issue.'" Citing his own conference notes, Douglas recalled that a majority of the seven took "the clear view" that abortion statutes were valid only to the extent that the state could require that they "be performed by a licensed physician within a limited time after conception." The chief justice, added Douglas, "had the opposed view," which "made it puzzling" to Douglas "as to why he made the [opinion] assignment at all except that he might affirm [the lower court] on vagueness." Douglas, too, opposed reargument of the cases.[20]

Because Blackmun's *Doe* draft came closer than his *Roe* effort to embracing what they hoped to see in the Court's opinions, Douglas, Brennan, and Marshall praised their colleague's draft opinion in the Georgia case. "I've just finished reading your very fine opinion," wrote Brennan. "I am going to be happy to join it." Even the irascible Douglas agreed that Blackmun had done "a fine job," and Marshall "wholeheartedly join[ed]" the opinion. After a telephone conversation with Blackmun, Justice Stewart wrote that he could also join the draft with modifications his colleague offered to make. By May 31, Douglas had even decided that he could join Blackmun's opinions in both cases, which he praised as "creditable jobs of craftsmanship [that] will, I think, stand the test of time."[21]

Douglas's rather sudden acceptance of Blackmun's opinions in both *Roe* and *Doe* hardly reflected any growing mellowness on the senior justice's part. By that point, Chief Justice Burger, with Justice Blackmun's strong support, had begun a campaign to have the cases reargued before a full Court the next term. William Rehnquist was already on record as opposing judicial recognition of abortion rights, and the chief justice assumed that Lewis Powell was similarly inclined. Reargument might produce a new majority opposed to any expansive ruling on the abortion issue.

In a May 31 memorandum to the conference, Burger asserted that he had encountered "a great many problems with these cases from the outset." Noting that they were "not as simple for me as they appear to be for others," he emphasized that the states, in his judgment, had "as much concern in this area as in any within their province," while the federal government (including its judiciary, he might have added) had "only that [authority] which can be traced to a specific provision of the Constitution." Part of his problem, Burger thought, lay with "the mediocre to poor help" that the Court had received from counsel in the cases. On reargument, amici curiae, or friends of the court, could be appointed on both sides to improve the quality of argument. "This is as sensitive and difficult an issue as any in this Court in my time and I want to hear more and think more when I am not trying to sort out several dozen other difficult cases." In short, concluded Burger, "I vote to reargue early in the next Term."[22]

When the justices were canvassing possible cases for reargument the next term, Justice Blackmun had also suggested that *Doe* at least be included. In a May 31 memorandum to the conference, he conceded that his earlier suggestion had not been "enthusiastically received," but he again recommended reargument of both cases. "Although it would prove costly to me personally, in the light of energy and hours expended," the justice, ever the martyr, asserted, he thought that "on an issue so sensitive and so emotional as [abortion], the country deserves the conclusion of a nine-man, not a seven-man court, whatever the ultimate decision may be." Despite working on the cases "with some concentration," he also remained uncertain about many "details":

> Should we make the Georgia case the primary opinion and
> recast Texas in its light? Should we refrain from emasculation of
> the Georgia statute and, instead, hold it unconstitutional in its
> entirety and let the state legislature reconstruct from the begin-
> ning? Should we spell out—although it would then necessarily
> be largely dictum—just what aspects are controllable by the
> State and to what extent?...These are some of the [considera
> tions] that have been [raised] and that prompt me to think
> about a summer's delay....I therefore conclude, and move, that
> both cases go over the Term.[23]

Justice White also favored reargument; most critically, the two newest members of the Court did, too. Because by that point Justice Powell had been on the Court more than half a term, he thought he now had a "duty" to participate in the reargument decision, "although from a purely personal viewpoint I would be more than happy to leave this one to others." Powell professed not to know how he would vote were the cases reargued, but he was persuaded to favor reargument, he wrote his colleagues, underlining his position for emphasis, "primarily by the fact that *Harry Blackmun, the author of the opinions, thinks the cases should be carried over and reargued next fall.* His position, based on months of study, suggests enough doubt on an issue of large national importance to justify the few months delay." Not surprisingly, Justice Rehnquist provided the fifth, and decisive, vote for carrying the cases over to the next term.[24]

Of justices opposing reargument, Justice Douglas was the most vehement. "If the vote of the Conference is to reargue," he promised, "then I will file a statement telling what is happening to us and the tragedy it entails." When the cases were carried over, he initially followed through on his threat. Recounting Chief Justice Burger's violation of Court protocol in assigning the Court's opinions in the cases, even though he "represented the minority view in the Conference and forcefully urged his viewpoint on the issues," Douglas charged that the reargument ploy was "merely another strategy by a minority somehow to suppress the majority view with the hope that exigencies of time will change the result. That might be achieved of course by death or conceivably retirement. But that kind of strategy dilutes the integrity of the Court." Responding to concerns that a decision in 1972, an election year, rather than later, would thrust abortion into the political arena, he declared, "Both political parties have made abortion an issue. What the political parties say or do is none of our business. We sit here not to make the path of any candidate easier or more difficult." The position of Blackmun and others prevailed, however, and Douglas circulated but did not file his opinion opposing reargument.[25]

Roe: Round Two

On October 11, 1972, the Court heard the second round of oral arguments in *Roe* and *Doe*. Justice Stewart emphasized during the proceedings that the Constitution's language seemed clearly to confer legal personhood on persons only after birth, and several justices pressed an assistant Texas attorney general to explain why, if a fetus was indeed a person in a legal sense, the state could allow any abortion, even to save a mother's life. At one point, Justice Blackmun questioned whether there would be "anything inconsistent" between the Court's recent decision striking down the death penalty for murderers and recognition of a woman's right to abortion. When an abortion rights lawyer complained about unreasonable "red tape" confronting women seeking abortions in Georgia, Blackmun pressed her to concede that the state had authority to limit abortions to licensed facilities. But she continued to insist that it was unreasonable to allow a medical committee to veto the decision of a woman's physician in abortion cases.

At conference two days later, Justice Rehnquist concurred with Justice White's rejection of any meaningful abortion right and refusal, as White put it, "to second guess state legislatures in striking the balance in favor of abortion laws." But Justice Powell, perhaps to the dismay of Burger and others, favored at least the sort of abortion right Justice Blackmun had alluded to in his original *Doe* draft. Moreover, unlike Blackmun, who continued to favor *Doe* rather than *Roe* as the lead case, Powell preferred *Roe* and, he meaningfully added, "wouldn't go on [the narrow] vagueness ground" in deciding the fate of Texas's restrictive abortion law. Powell was thus clearly on board with those who favored deciding both cases on substantive privacy grounds.[26]

Following the conference, the chief justice again assigned the task of drafting opinions to Blackmun, who noted during conference discussion of *Doe* that a revised draft of the opinion in that case had already been prepared. On December 17, 1971, following the first round of oral arguments in the cases, Blackmun had written Thomas Keys of the Mayo Clinic's library, asking, "Would your well equipped library have anything about the history of abortion? You can imagine why I ask." If Keys sent him a list of standard works on the subject, Blackmun "suppose[d] [he] could unearth the books at the Library of Congress." But, he added, "If you suggest that I come out for a week's research in your hallowed precincts, I would be tempted."[27]

In the subsequent months, Keys sent the justice a massive collection of materials on the subject, and Blackmun visited the library during a trip to Rochester the week of July 24, 1972. The justice's clerks largely drafted his opinions, however, after both arguments and conferences in the cases.[28]

In a cover letter to a *Roe* draft opinion that he circulated on November 21, 1972, Blackmun concluded that the end of the first trimester of a pregnancy was the critical point triggering state authority to ban or restrict abortions. Justice Powell professed to be "enthusiastic" about the opinions his colleague was circulating in both cases, commending their "impressive scholarship and analysis." But Powell questioned Blackmun's selection of the end of the first trimester as the point at which states could legitimately begin to regulate abortions. Instead, Powell recommended "viability," the point at which a fetus could survive independently of the mother's womb, as the preferred cutoff point. But the diplomatic Virginian chose not to send a copy of his letter to their colleagues. "No doubt," he explained, "we will discuss your opinion in Conference, and I thought it might be helpful—to you and certainly to me—if you had the opportunity in advance to consider my reservation as above expressed."[29]

Responding to Powell, Blackmun indicated that he had "no particular commitment" to the end of the first trimester rather than viability or some other point after which states would be free to regulate or prohibit abortions. He had selected the end of the first trimester, he explained, simply "because medical statistics and the statistical writings seemed to focus on it and to draw their contrasts between the first three months and the remainder of the pregnancy." He also thought the end of the first trimester was more likely to command a Court and that a state, after all, was free to make its decision on the liberal side and fix a later point at which its regulation of abortions would begin. Many physicians, added Blackmun, were probably concerned about abortion facilities, such as the need for hospitalization, after the first trimester. He wanted "to leave the states free to draw their own medical conclusions with respect to the period after the first three months and until viability. The states' judgment of the health needs of the mother, I feel, ought, on balance, to be honored."[30]

In a memorandum to the conference, Blackmun made some of the same points, but also made the case for drawing the line at viability, observing, "I am sure that there are many pregnant women, particularly younger girls, who may refuse to face the fact of pregnancy and…do not get around to medical consultation until the end of the first trimester is upon them or, indeed, has passed."[31]

Several days later, Justice Marshall made more explicit the state public health interest to which Justice Blackmun had alluded. In a letter to the justice, Marshall agreed that drawing the line at viability rather than at the end of the first trimester was best. But Marshall also shared his colleague's "concern for recognizing the State's interest in insuring the abortions be done under safe conditions. If the opinion stated explicitly that, between the end of the first trimester and viability, state regulations directed at health and safety [of the mother] alone were permissible, I believe that those concerns would be adequately met." Albeit in more flexible terms, Justice Brennan made essentially the same proposal. When Justice Douglas favored the end of the first trimester rather than viability as the cut-off point for state regulations, Justice Powell's clerk Larry Hammond was shocked: "The Justice, who more than anyone else on this Court stakes his judicial reputation on protection of the poor and the black…, cannot fail to recognize that a first trimester rule falls most heavily on those classes," declared Hammond in a note to Powell. But Douglas may simply have assumed that second trimester regulations would be limited to protecting the mother's health. Preferring to give states "more latitude to make policy judgments" in the abortion field than Blackmun's developing trimester approach appeared to allow, Justice Stewart indicated that he would prepare a "tentative" concurring opinion in the cases. For his part, Chief Justice Burger raised questions about the rights of fathers and of the parents of pregnant minors. "Then, too," he asserted, "since the Court gave 'illegitimate fathers' the same rights as a lawful parent, we must face up to that."[32]

Justice Blackmun's clerk, Randall Bezanson, also weighed in on the debate. When Justice Powell suggested viability rather than the second trimester as the point at which states could begin to regulate abortions, the clerk questioned whether Blackmun should embrace such an approach.

I am…of the opinion that during the "interim" period between the end of the first trimester and viability (about 6 months), the state might impose some greater restrictions relating to medical dangers posed by the operation, e.g., the operation would have to be performed in a hospital…and the like.…Justice Powell's approach seems to view the relevant state interests too narrowly and disregards the state's interest in assuring that the medical procedures employed will be safe. Your opinion, as I view it, rests on two state interests, which become compelling in varying degrees over time, and not simultaneously, the state's interest in preserving the life of the fetus [here the logical cutoff, as Justice Powell suggests, is viability], and the state's interests in assuring that the abortion procedure is safe and adequately protects the health of the patient [it is the interest to which I think Justice Powell gives too little weight].…Thus the state's interests may increase vis-à-vis this factor before "viability."[33]

Later, once Brennan and Marshall made their recommendations regarding the state's second trimester interests in protecting the woman's health, Bezanson wrote a memo essentially capsuling for the justice the approach that would provide the core of Blackmun's final *Roe* opinion. "I think it…appropriate," he wrote the justice, "to define some sort of threshold cutoff [such as]…the end of the first trimester…before which the state must leave the matter entirely within the medical judgment of the physician.…Thereafter, it might be useful, as part of the opinion, to articulate the two state interests, and the point at which they assume increasing significance. With respect to the state's interest in preserving the safety of the operation and the conditions surrounding it, regulation might be permissible somewhere between the end of the 1st trimester…and 'viability' or beyond. But with respect to the state's interest in preserving fetal life, the opinion might, for example, indicate that only after 'viability' does this interest become sufficiently compelling to support regulation in furtherance of this interest." Bezanson was not certain what Justice Stewart had been "getting at" in his memo suggesting that states be given greater "latitude" in the abortion field than Blackmun was suggesting in his draft. But if Stewart was suggesting that the cutoff point for regulation of abortion be left "completely vague," the clerk opposed that approach. "This Court must give some fairly certain guidance to the patients and doctors, as well as the legislators who will be spending much time drafting new legislation and who will be placing substantial reliance on this Court's opinion."[34]

As the drafting and circulation of his opinions progressed, Justice Blackmun also had exchanges with Justice Rehnquist, who, along with Justice White, had decided to file a dissenting opinion in the cases. In recent First Amendment cases, certain justices, including Blackmun, had sought to limit the scope of the overbreadth doctrine under which statutes were declared unconstitutional on their face if they were so sweeping in their scope that they covered much protected expression as well as conduct subject to governmental control. When Blackmun initially recommended that the government be allowed to restrict or ban abortions after the end of the first trimester, Rehnquist wrote his colleague asking whether, in light of the justice's opposition to a rigorous overbreadth doctrine, Blackmun should invalidate the Texas law at issue in *Roe* "only as applied to a litigant who seeks abortion within the first 'trimester,' rather than, as I understand you to do, invalidating [the law] *in toto?*"[35]

In his response, dated November 27, 1972, Blackmun indicated that he was "not now prepared to say that immediately after the first trimester a very restrictive statute of [the Texas] kind would pass constitutional muster." He reminded Rehnquist, moreover, that in his initial *Roe* opinion, he had proposed disposing of the law on vagueness grounds, but that most of their colleagues "preferred to get to what they called the 'core issue.'" At that relatively early stage of opinion drafting, Blackmun also assured Rehnquist that states would be entitled to "more latitude procedurally as well as substantively" after the first trimester, although he would later modify his opinions to limit second trimester regulations to procedures reasonably relating to protecting the mother's health.[36]

In the dissent that he circulated for *Roe*, Rehnquist accused Justice Blackmun of embracing the substantive due process formula that the long-discredited laissez-faire Court of the pre–New Deal era had invoked to strike down what those justices deemed to be "unreasonable" state and federal regulations of business and industry. Critics of the laissez-faire Court had charged it with acting as a "super legislature," and the analogy Rehnquist drew between *Roe* and the Old Court's rulings carried considerable force. Logically, after all, there was little difference between the use of due process to protect "liberty of contract" and other unenumerated economic rights from governmental control and the *Roe* majority's use of the same constitutional guarantee as the vehicle for recognition of abortion rights that also were mentioned nowhere in the Constitution. But Randall Bezanson recommended that the justice make no response to Rehnquist's dissent, which, in the clerk's judgment, "misses the point." Blackmun's opinion, asserted Bezanson, albeit not very convincingly,

> enunciates and defines an independent constitutional right, found before in *Griswold*...and other opinions, which is very much akin to the First Amendment speech and press right. The fact that that right rests in the "liberty" portion of the 14th amendment due process clause does not make the equal protection or "substantive due process" tests applicable. "Liberty" is a core value protected by the right, and the due process clause is therefore an appropriate source for the right. I should finally note that rather than confusing, as Justice Rehnquist suggests, this privacy right clears up a very muddled area. Indeed, in my view it is substantive due process and equal protection which are the more confusing areas.[37]

In an effort to deflect Rehnquist's complaint, Blackmun attempted in his first *Roe* draft to separate his approach from the Old Court's ventures into judicial legislation. At one point, for example, he quoted from Justice Holmes's celebrated dissent in *Lochner v. New York* (1905), the signature case of the laissez-faire era: "[The Constitution] is made for people of fundamentally differing views, and the accident of our finding certain opinions natural and familiar or novel and even shocking ought not to conclude our judgment upon the question whether statutes embodying them conflict with the Constitution of the United States."[38]

The justice also did his best to accommodate the recommendations and feelings of his colleagues and the public. For example, he asked Justice Brennan, a Roman Catholic, to pay "particular attention" to passages in *Roe* devoted to the Catholic Church's position on the abortion issue. "I believe they are accurate factually," he observed, "but I do not want them to be offensive or capable of being regarded as unduly critical by any reader. Your judgment as to this will be most helpful." In a footnote to his *Roe* opinion, he also addressed the concerns that Chief Justice Burger had expressed about the rights of fathers. As he noted, however, what he wrote was probably "not very satisfying" to Burger and others with such concerns. "I am somewhat reluctant," he explained to members of the conference, "to try to cover the point in cases where the father's rights, if any, are not at issue." In classic understatement, he added, "I suspect there will be other aspects of abortion that will have to be dealt with at a future time."[39]

In late December, Justice Stewart decided to drop his plans to file a "rather lengthy" concurring opinion in the cases, opting instead for a brief concurrence defending substantive due process as a respected constitutional doctrine, despite the use to which the laissez-faire Court had put that formula. Stewart had taken a number of swipes at the doctrine in his dissent for *Griswold*, but on further reflection had decided that substantive due process was in the mainstream of American constitutional law. By the second week of January, Warren Burger appeared to be the only justice seeking further delay in an announcement of the Court's decisions. On January 16, Justice Stewart passed Blackmun a bench note, asking whether "*Doe, Roe,* etc. [were] going to be announced tomorrow?" "Who knows?" Blackmun replied. "I doubt now that they will be announced tomorrow. He [Chief Justice Burger] says he may write. I hope for Monday, the 22nd at the latest," he added with dramatic flourish. "They *must* come down." Stewart soon responded, "I wholeheartedly agree."[40]

The day before, Burger had passed a bench note to Blackmun as well. "Can we chew on [the] 'abortion' cases after session today[?] Just ring me at 3:00 please if OK." Then, on January 16, the chief justice wrote Blackmun that he hoped to have "some concurrence" in the cases "circulated sometime tomorrow," but assured his friend, "I do not believe they will involve any significant change in what you have written."[41]

As the final touches were being put on the justices' efforts, Blackmun made plans for announcing his opinions in Court. The justice had never been comfortable speaking extemporaneously, even relying on notes when interviewing applicants for clerkships. On January 16, "anticipat[ing] the headlines that will be produced over the country when the abortion decisions are announced," he circulated to his colleagues an eight-page typescript of what he "propose[d] as the announcement from the bench" in *Roe* and *Doe*. He also suggested that copies be distributed "to the press if any reporters desire it." Given, in effect, a transcript of what he would say, he thought reporters might be less likely to go "all the way off the deep end" in their coverage of the rulings.[42]

Justice Brennan soon replied, praising Blackmun's proposed announcement as "indeed very well done," but also giving his colleague a short lesson in Court protocol. "Our practice in the past has always been not to record oral announcements of opinions," wrote Brennan, with copies to their colleagues, "in order to avoid the possibility that the announcement will be relied upon as the opinion or as interpreting the filed opinion. I think that policy is very sound and, important as the Abortion Cases are, I do not think we ought to depart from that policy." When Burger saw the memo, the chief justice conceded that Brennan's concern "had not occurred to me but precedent is [a] factor." Never a media friend, Burger "suspect[ed] we'd be better off to simply ignore [the] press birds entirely except as the Headnote [to advance copies of the opinions] can get the printed word to them."[43]

Blackmun had hoped the cases could be announced on Monday, January 21, or on Tuesday "at the latest." On January 22, he announced the rulings in Court, reading from the statement he had prepared for the occasion. Dottie Blackmun was among those attending the session. In a note to her, the courtly Justice Powell assured Mrs. Blackmun that "Harry has written an historic opinion, which I was proud to join. His statement from the Bench this morning also was excellent. I am glad you were here."[44]

The Opinions

Anxious to deflect the inevitable charge that the Court's recognition of abortion rights smacked of the judicial lawmaking of the discredited *Lochner* era, Justice Blackmun, as previously noted, quoted early in his *Roe* opinion from Justice Holmes's *Lochner* dissent and its celebrated defense of judicial self-restraint. As Justice Rehnquist contended in his *Roe* dissent, however, Blackmun's opinion was "more closely attuned to" the *Lochner* majority opinion than to Holmes's dissent. The extensive medical and medical-legal history to which the justice devoted much of *Roe* was intended, Blackmun asserted, to assist the Court in resolving the constitutional issues "free of emotion and of predilection." But that discourse ultimately demonstrated merely that, though abortion had been largely tolerated through much of recorded history, highly restrictive state abortion laws, such as the Texas statute at issue in *Roe* and similar laws in most other states, extended back to the Civil War, or earlier. It thus could hardly be argued, as Blackmun appeared to use the historic section of *Roe* to suggest, that a right of abortion was somehow deeply rooted in American tradition. Nor did he even attempt to tie his opinions to the specifics of the Bill of Rights. Instead, he simply declared that a right of privacy sufficiently broad to encompass abortion rights was implicit in the "liberty" guaranteed by the Constitution's due process clauses.[45]

As an exercise in judicial lawmaking, Justice Blackmun's abortion opinions put to shame the judicial legislators of the *Lochner* era, so widely repudiated since the 1930s. In his now-classic summary of the *Roe* ruling, the justice wrote:

1. A state criminal abortion statute of the current Texas type, that excepts from criminality only a *life-saving* procedure on behalf of the mother, without regard to pregnancy stage and without recognition of the other interests involved, is violative of the Due Process Clause of the Fourteenth Amendment.

   (a) For the stage prior to approximately the end of the first trimester, the abortion decision and its effectuation must be left to the medical judgment of the pregnant woman's attending physician.

   (b) For the stage subsequent to approximately the end of the first trimester, the State, in promoting its interest in the health of the mother, may, if it chooses, regulate the abortion procedure in ways that are reasonably related to maternal health.

   (c) For the stage subsequent to viability, the State in promoting its interest in the potentiality of human life may, if it chooses, regulate, and even proscribe, abortion except where it is necessary, in appropriate medical judgment, for the preservation of the life or health of the mother.

2. The State may define the term "physician," as it has been employed in the preceding paragraphs…, to mean only a physician currently licensed by the State and may proscribe any abortion by a person who is not a physician so defined.[46]

And all of that, of course, the justice found in a single word, "liberty," in the Constitution's due process guarantee.

In subjecting abortion laws to such strict judicial scrutiny, the justice drew not on modern due process precedents, but on Warren Court equal protection cases declaring that laws having a discriminatory impact on "fundamental" rights were unconstitutional unless necessary to further a "compelling" governmental interest. This approach was particularly ironic given recent Burger Court decisions purporting to restrict the scope of the fundamental rights branch of Warren Court equal protection doctrine. In his *Roe* dissent, Justice Rehnquist complained that the Court's "transplanting of the 'compelling state interest test' " from the equal protection field to due process would "accomplish the seemingly impossible feat of leaving this area of the law more confused than it found it." Rehnquist agreed that the Fourteenth Amendment's due process clause "embrace[d] more than the rights" enumerated in the Constitution, but asserted that such "liberty [was] not guaranteed absolutely against [government] deprivation." Instead, the post-1936 Court had accorded "social and economic legislation" claimed to violate the due process clause broad latitude, striking down such laws only if they bore no "rational" relation to a legitimate governmental objective. Had Texas forbidden abortions even to save the mother's life, the justice had little doubt such a statute would lack a rational basis. "But the Court's sweeping invalidation of any restrictions on abortion during the first trimester [was] impossible to justify under [the rational basis] standard, and the conscious weighing of competing factors that the Court's opinion apparently substitutes for the established test is far more appropriate to a legislative judgment than to a judicial one."[47]

Citing its inclusion of "extensive historical fact and ... wealth of legal scholarship," Justice Rehnquist conceded that Blackmun's opinion "commands my respect." The irascible Justice White, the other *Roe* and *Doe* dissenter, wasted no time with such amenities. Filing his dissent "with all due respect," White found "nothing in the language or history of the Constitution to support the Court's judgments," declaring:

> The Court simply fashions and announces a new constitutional
> right for pregnant women and, with scarcely any reason or
> authority for its action, invests that right with sufficient substance

to override most existing state abortion statutes. The upshot is that the people and the legislatures of the 50 States are constitutionally disentitled to weigh the relative importance of the continued existence and development of the fetus, on the one hand, against a spectrum of possible impacts on the mother, on the other hand. As an exercise of raw judicial power, the Court perhaps has authority to do what it does today; but in my view its judgment is an improvident and extravagant exercise of the power of judicial review.[48]

White was particularly concerned that the Court, through the second trimester of a pregnancy, "values the convenience of the pregnant woman more than the continued existence and development of the life or potential life that she carries." Declared the justice:

The common claim before us is that for any [reason] ..., or for no reason at all, and without asserting or claiming any threat to life or health, any woman is entitled to an abortion at her request if she is able to find a medical adviser willing to undertake the procedure.... Whether or not I might agree with that marshaling of values, I can in no event join the Court's opinion because I find no constitutional warrant for imposing such an order of priorities on the people and legislatures of the States. In a sensitive area such as this, involving as it does issues over which reasonable men may easily and heatedly differ, I cannot accept the Court's exercise of its clear power of choice by interposing a constitutional barrier to state efforts to protect human life and by investing women and doctors with the constitutionally protected right to exterminate it. This issue, for the most part, should be left with the people and to the political processes the people have devised to govern their affairs.[49]

As White indicated, Justice Blackmun's *Roe* and *Doe* opinions recognized rights for both women and physicians; women were freed from restrictive abortion laws but only doctors could perform abortions, and their professional judgments were thus critical to the woman's exercise of the abortion right. Given that element of the justice's opinions, his close ties to the medical profession, and his youthful aspirations to become a physician, some students of Blackmun's career have seen the right of physicians to make medical judgments free of unduly restrictive governmental regulations as the core of *Roe* and *Doe*, with the rights of women secondary to that central concern. In fact, some of the justice's more ardent admirers have argued that his increasing commitment to women's rights in later years was a significant and positive sign of his "growth" as a justice over the balance of his career.[50]

The clerk who worked with Blackmun on *Roe* disputes that assessment. "[Justice Blackmun] said at the time and he would say for years after," Randall Bezanson remembers,

> that this was the most important step on the way to the emancipation of women. And what he meant by that was that he saw the abortion laws...as treating women as people without moral agency, as unable to make their own moral choices. And the abortion cases for him asked the question, "Can a state deny a woman the ability to make the same kinds of moral choices as...men, in the sense of their being a whole moral being with free will?"...The physician thing was secondary. It was clearly there, but he saw the claim as the woman's ability to seek the advice of a physician in making this kind of decision, the way men seek the advice of physicians about surgery....There's just nothing to that claim that *Roe* was a physician-based opinion.[51]

The Fallout

Justice Blackmun obviously realized that the abortion decisions would be controversial. But he could not have anticipated how profoundly they would divide the nation, how protracted the national debate over abortion was to become, and how closely and personally he—rather than the Court as an institution—would be connected with the rulings and the deep divisions they spawned. Over the years, the boxes of mail the justice received on the issue would eventually occupy an entire room, the huge sampling in his Library of Congress papers amounting to only 5 percent of the total. Much of the mail was positive. "Some of the most beautiful letters he ever received," his secretary Wanda Martinson recalls, "[were] from women who had safe abortions [as a result of *Roe*], or had illegal abortions at a time when they weren't safe." But the justice also became the principal target of antiabortion protests and vicious hate mail, complete with full-color photographs of aborted fetuses.[52]

A number of signed, respectful letters opposing judicial recognition of abortion rights had reached the justice's desk even before the Court announced its decision in *Roe* and *Doe*. In one, an Ohio woman asked Blackmun to "use your influence to stop the cutting off of life for millions of children by voting to repeal the abortion-on-demand laws which are flourishing in some states," adding, "My feeling on this is not based on religion—this is not even a 'religious' issue, this concerns the right of a human being to life as guaranteed in the Fourteenth Amendment to our Constitution." Noting the recent judicial restrictions on capital punishment, a Maryland man questioned how the "death penalty for convicted criminals" could be considered cruel and unusual punishment, while "in our society…many of those alive in the womb are subjected to the cruel and unusual punishment of abortion. Are we creating an unjust society which annihilates the innocent and spares the guilty?"[53]

But the justice perhaps first became aware of what might be in store for him when, a few days after the rulings, he arrived in Cedar Rapids, Iowa, for a Chamber of Commerce speech and was greeted by fifty antiabortion picketers. He insisted to his audience there that the Court had "not authorized abortion on demand" and that the decisions had been preceded by many "bitter nights" of deliberation. But the opposition hardly subsided. A year later, when he traveled to St. Paul to receive a distinguished alumnus award from Mechanic Arts High School, he agreed to an informal chat with reporters. "The thing that interests me about the decision," he told them, "is the personal abuse heaped upon me. I've never seen such an outpouring of hate mail, a lot of it form mail. It chills me to think that someone can sit down and say, '40 of us must write letters.'" It was a "new experience" for him, he added, "to go places—not here, fortunately—and be picketed and called Pontius Pilate, Herod and the Butcher of Dachau and accused of being personally responsible for 500,000 deaths in the past year."[54]

At one point in his remarks, the justice hinted to the reporters that he might even retire the following November, when he had completed fifteen years on the bench, including his tenure on the Eighth Circuit, and could leave the Court at his full salary. When pressed on the matter, he insisted that the reporters should attach "absolutely no significance" to his comment. In typical Blackmun fashion, however, he stressed the burdens of his position. When asked by "little ladies" how he liked Washington, he said that he always replied, "Not at all. This is not the kind of job you enjoy," adding, "I've never worked harder in my life. It's 14 to 16 hours a day, and it's not five or six days a week—it's seven days a week. This is my fourth year on the court. That's not very long, but it seems like 100 years in some respects." Standing before a banner that read "WELCOME BACK, JUSTICE BLACKMUN," he could not resist confessing to Mechanic Arts students that he was "just as uneasy, frightened and scared up here as I was 50 years ago when the principal put me on the assembly program." Or that his status as President Nixon's third choice for the Court seat he now occupied had been "a very humbling experience [that] one never forgets." And now, he seemed to be suggesting, he had the added indignity of being the principal target of anti-*Roe* sentiment.[55]

Nor, of course, was criticism of *Roe* and *Doe* confined to anonymous hate letters and antiabortion pickets. Many newspapers and their columnists applauded the rulings. The *New York Times* declared editorially that the majority had "made a major contribution to the preservation of individual liberties and of free decision-making." The *Wall Street Journal* confessed "reservations" about the decisions, but, its editor concluded, "on the whole…the court struck a reasonable balance [on] an exceedingly difficult question." The *Washington Evening Star* pronounced the decisions the greatest "victory for women's rights since enactment of the 19th amendment," granting the vote to women; the *Washington Post* termed the rulings "both wise and sound," and the *St. Louis Post-Dispatch* praised Justice Blackmun's handiwork as "remarkable for its common sense, its humaneness and most of all its affirmation of an individual's right to privacy." Calling the Court "an amazing, and a uniquely American, institution," the *New York Times* columnist Anthony Lewis found it remarkable that the justices had decided such a deeply controversial issue; he declared that "no other court, anywhere, would undertake to speak for a society on such an issue." Noting the contention of Justice Rehnquist and others before him that the courts "should defer to the judgments of elected politicians, however foolish they may seem," Lewis thought the difficulty with "that self-denying formula" was that judges found "it so difficult to apply consistently." Even justices determined to avoid inserting their personal predilections into their decisions had no alternative, wrote Lewis; they had "sworn to defend 'liberty,' and can only fill that empty constitutional word with what [they think] are the basic beliefs of [their] society. [They have] to make judgments." Restrictive state abortion laws "were already being worn away by changed attitudes," and the Court was "the perfect institution to register [such] changed moral and social perceptions," just as it had in 1954, when it began the assault on state-imposed racial segregation.[56]

But such media sentiments were not unanimous. Not surprisingly, the Roman Catholic Church and its press organs were highly critical of the decisions and their author. Vatican Radio denounced the rulings and condemned abortion as "no more and no less than the killing of a human being." The *Catholic Standard* accused the Court of "tak[ing] an unparalleled step backwards. Sweeping aside the hard evidence of science and logic, it has repudiated the most fundamental right of all—the right to life itself." A conservative Catholic lay organization called for the excommunication of Justice Brennan as a member of the *Roe* majority, and a committee of Catholic bishops condemned the decisions as a "charter for abortion on request." After Justice Blackmun, during his 1974 visit to his high school, described the sort of hate mail he was receiving, the newspaper for a Catholic diocese in Minnesota came to his defense. The church's "justifiable" stand against abortion, the paper declared, "in no [way] approves or condones vicious attacks such as Justice Blackmun and the Court have suffered at the hands of extremists." The justice, added the paper, was "an honest person who deserves and demands respect." Most church leaders, however, attacked the rulings in the harshest terms.[57]

Minnesotans had mixed reactions to the rulings and their adopted native son's role in them. The head of the Mayo Clinic's obstetrics and gynecology section declared that "any quality physician would take a dim view of interrupting a pregnancy at the six-months stage simply at the request of the patient." A Rochester leader of the opposition to liberalized abortion laws called the decisions a "horrible regression," adding, "A constitutional amendment shouldn't be necessary to protect the unborn, but it appears it will be." The administrator of Rochester's St. Mary's Hospital announced that abortions would not be allowed under any circumstances at that facility and called *Roe* and *Doe* a "disaster to our society." A spokesperson for Mayo, however, said that the clinic would continue to practice medicine only in strict accordance with the law. A newspaper article cited a 1967 medical magazine report indicating that, at that point, thirty-six therapeutic abortions had been performed at Rochester's Methodist Hospital, with which Mayo was affiliated, but also noting that probably half of those abortions were performed merely under the "guise" of therapeutic reasons. Antiabortion Minnesota legislators began drafting new abortion measures that, one promised, would "be as restrictive as we possibly can make it."[58]

The justice had his Minnesota defenders as well. In 1971, when the state's Hamline University conferred an honorary doctorate on Blackmun, Hamline's president, Richard P. Bailey, told the justice, "You have honored law by your service and have helped keep the fountains of justice flowing for all mankind.... The little people of America found justice in your [Eighth Circuit] courtroom. In your court justice became truth in action." Writing in the Minneapolis *Star* less than a month after *Roe* and *Doe* were announced, Bailey reaffirmed his admiration for the justice. "Uninvited," he declared, "I stand...beside an embattled Justice Blackmun. Approximately half the nation, and [conservative gadfly] Bill Buckley, stand opposed. I strongly prefer 'our' group."[59]

A number of prominent legal scholars, even those sympathetic with the result the Court had reached, weighed in with harsh criticism of Blackmun's rationale and the legislative characteristics of his opinions. The Yale law professor John Hart Ely's scathing attack probably drew the most attention in the legal community and undoubtedly caused the justice the greatest distress. Ely found Blackmun's version of judicial lawmaking even more offensive than the laissez-faire opinions of the *Lochner* era. At least those justices had professed to accord legislative bodies wide latitude, even if in practice they had not. Blackmun, on the other hand, had created a right having no basis in the Constitution's text and history, conferred on it a "fundamental" status, and required a "compelling" interest to justify any abortion regulation whatever. Indeed, *Roe* had conferred on abortion, Ely contended, "a far more stringent protection...than that the present

Court accords the freedom of the press explicitly guaranteed by the First Amendment."[60]

For Ely, *Roe* was a truly daunting decision: "What is frightening about *Roe* is that this super-protected right is not inferable from the language of the Constitution, the framers' thinking respecting the specific problem in issue, any general value derivable from the provisions they included, or the nation's governmental structure. Nor is it explainable in terms of the usual political impotence of the group...protected. And that, I believe...is a charge that can responsibly be leveled at no other decision of the past twenty years."[61]

Ely realized that, perhaps with the exception of the unusual degree of policy detail they contained, Blackmun's opinions hardly reflected a novel approach to constitutional decision making. Both conservatives and liberals, including President Nixon, for all his talk about "strict constructionists," had largely accepted the "invitation, to get in there and Lochner for the right goals." But that formula, contended Ely, made for "bad constitutional law, or rather [no] constitutional law." If a constitutional principle, such as that *Roe* and *Doe* embodied, "lacks connection with any value the Constitution marks as special, it is not a constitutional principle and the Court has no business imposing it. I hope that will seem obvious to the point of banality. Yet those of us to whom it does seem obvious have seldom troubled to say so. And because we have not, we must share in the blame for this decision."[62]

When Ely's comment appeared, the justice discussed it with his clerks at breakfast. Blackmun's clerk Jim Ziglar also prepared a consoling memorandum for the justice. "Ely goes to great lengths," Ziglar wrote, "to distinguish *Roe* from all the supposedly good things which the Warren Court did. He does this by arguing that all of the Warren Court decisions were grounded on values which can be easily found in the Constitution. Thus, there was a textual commitment on which to base these decisions. *Roe*, however, cannot be justified on the basis of some value found in a constitutional provision. Rather, the Court reached out and found this nebulous right in the Due Process Clause."[63]

To Ziglar, Ely was simply attempting to provide "liberals a way of reacting adversely to the abortion decision while maintaining a firm hold on their dedication to such [Warren Court] decisions as *Miranda*."

The clerk conceded that the charge the *Roe* Court "acted legislatively" was the "soft underbelly" of the abortion right. But Ely could not, asserted Ziglar, condemn *Roe* on that point yet also approve of *Griswold*, which "Ely seems to believe has some textual" basis in the Constitution. In Ziglar's judgment, *Roe* and *Griswold* were clearly related, because "privacy and the right to control one's body are intertwined. Thus, the privacy rationale of *Griswold*…gives substance to the abortion opinions as well," and Ely's article was "basically ineffective because its major thesis is misdirected." Clearly, Ziglar concluded, "this article won't be cited as the definitive work by anti-abortion forces."

Whatever the analytical weaknesses of Ely's attack, Blackmun never forgot—or forgave—the sting of his article. "Professor Ely," he told Harold Koh during their oral history interviews, "could hardly wait. He got his first critical writing out before the ink was dry, on the opinion, actually." But Ely was not *Roe*'s or Blackmun's only contemporary scholarly critic. Laurence Tribe, a Harvard law professor, complained that, "behind its own verbal smokescreen, the substantive judgment on which [*Roe*] rests is nowhere to be found."[64]

Another World "Out There"

While the national debate over abortion grew in intensity, fissures also began to develop in the *Roe* majority. Chief Justice Burger had reluctantly joined Justice Blackmun's *Roe* and *Doe* opinions. But in a brief concurrence, he questioned the wisdom of certain elements in the Court's rulings, attempted to emphasize their limits, and became the first justice to suggest the more lenient "undue burden" approach to abortion regulations that the Rehnquist Court, in *Planned Parenthood v. Casey* (1992), would ultimately substitute for Blackmun's strict trimester formula. In his *Roe* concurring opinion, for example, the chief justice noted that he was "somewhat troubled" by the Court's use of scientific and medical data in its decision. While agreeing that the abortion statutes at issue in *Roe* and *Doe* "impermissibly" restricted abortions to protect the pregnant woman's health, he cited *Vuitch*, in which the Court had relied on the vagueness doctrine without reaching the substantive privacy issues ultimately confronted in *Roe* and *Doe*, and on which he and Blackmun originally preferred to rest those cases. Burger also would have upheld Georgia's requirement that two additional physicians confirm a doctor's judgment that an abortion should be performed; that provision, he concluded, was not an "unduly burdensome" requirement. Finally, he sought to give his colleague's opinions a narrow reading and thus minimize the "sweeping consequences" the dissenters feared *Roe* and *Doe* would produce. They were "discount[ing] the reality that the vast majority of physicians observe the standards of their profession, and act only on the basis of carefully deliberated medical judgments relating to life and health. Plainly, the Court today rejects any claim that the Constitution requires abortions on demand."[65]

It was hardly surprising, therefore, that when the Court decided its first major post-*Roe* abortion case, Burger parted company, at least to a degree, with his boyhood friend. In *Planned Parenthood v. Danforth* (1976), Justice Blackmun spoke for the Court in upholding a number of Missouri abortion regulations while declaring others contrary to *Roe* and *Doe*. But Burger joined *Roe* and *Doe* dissenters White and Rehnquist in objecting to the Court's decision to strike down two key provisions of the Missouri scheme: a requirement that married women secure their spouse's consent and a parental consent requirement for any unmarried woman under eighteen, except where an abortion was necessary, in her physician's judgment, to preserve her life. For Burger and company, the father's interest in participating in the raising of his own child outweighed the mother's interest in avoiding the burdens of child rearing. "It is truly surprising," Justice White declared for the dissenters, "that the State must assign a greater value to a mother's decision to cut off a potential human life by abortion than to the father's decision to let it mature into a live child.... These are matters which a State should be able to decide free from the suffocating power of the federal judge, purporting to act in the name of the Constitution." The parental consent requirement, added White, was designed "to vindicate the very right created in *Roe*... the right of the pregnant woman to decide whether *or not* to terminate her pregnancy." Traditionally, states have been allowed "to protect children from their own immature and improvident decisions." The abortion decision, White asserted, was "unquestionably important [with] irrevocable consequences whichever way it is made," and Missouri was entitled to require parental consultation and consent "to protect the minor unmarried woman from making the decision in a way which is not in her own best interests.... There is absolutely no reason expressed by the majority why the State may not utilize that method here."[66]

In general, Justice Blackmun was willing to uphold parental consent requirements that included a judicial bypass provision, under which an unmarried minor could secure a court order authorizing an abortion. But he insisted that such measures be limited to immature minors. In *Bellotti v. Baird* (1979), for example, Blackmun joined Justices Stevens, Brennan, and Marshall in rejecting a statute construed by Massachusetts's highest court to provide that no minor, however mature and capable of informed decision making, could secure an abortion without the consent of both parents or a judge. Such an absolute, third-party veto over a minor's abortion right, they contended, violated *Roe*.[67]

When a majority, speaking through Chief Justice Burger, upheld a Utah statute obligating a physician, "if possible," to notify the parents or guardian before performing an abortion on a minor, as applied to an unmarried fifteen-year-old girl living with and dependent on her parents, Blackmun and Brennan joined Justice Marshall in dissent. "Many minor women will encounter interference from their parents," declared Marshall. "In addition to parental disappointment and disapproval, the minor may confront physical or emotional abuse, withdrawal of financial support, or actual obstruction of the abortion decision.... Pregnant minors may attempt to self-abort or to obtain an illegal abortion rather than risk parental notification.... The possibility that such problems may not occur in particular cases does not alter the hardship created by the notice requirement on its face. And that hardship is not a mere disincentive created by the States, but is instead an actual state-imposed obstacle to the exercise of the minor woman's free choice." No interests cited by the state in defense of the challenged statute, he added, justified the burdens imposed on the rights recognized in *Roe* and *Doe*.[68]

Probably in an effort to draw attention away from his role in the abortion controversy, Justice Blackmun simply joined others, rather than file his own opinions, in the parental consent and notification cases. But when a majority decided abortion-funding cases in a way flatly contrary, in his judgment, to *Roe* and *Doe*, the justice could not restrain himself. In a number of cases decided at the end of the 1976–77 term, the Court upheld regulations denying indigent women public funding of abortions that were not medically necessary, even under programs providing assistance for medical care relating to pregnancy and maternal care. *Roe*, Justice Powell asserted for the Court, "did not declare an unqualified 'constitutional right to an abortion.'...Rather, the right protects the woman from unduly burdensome interference with her freedom to decide whether to terminate her pregnancy. It implies no limitation on the authority of a State to make a value judgment favoring childbirth over abortion, and to implement that judgment by the allocation of public funds." The regulations before the Court, observed Powell, "place[d] no obstacles—absolute or otherwise—in the pregnant woman's path to an abortion. An indigent woman who desires an abortion suffers no disadvantage as a consequence of [a state's] decision to fund childbirth; she continues as before to be dependent on private sources for the service she desires.... The indigency that may make it difficult—and in some cases, perhaps, impossible—for some women to have abortions is neither created nor in any way affected by the [challenged] regulation."[69]

The Court, Powell assured readers, was "certainly...not unsympathetic to the plight of an indigent woman who desires an abortion." But the Constitution, he declared, quoting from an earlier case, "does not provide judicial remedies for every social and economic ill." States had always enjoyed "a wider latitude in choosing among competing demands for limited public funds." Such regulations need have only a "reasonable basis," and "the state interest in encouraging normal childbirth exceed[ed] this minimal level" of reasonableness.[70]

After the justices had voted in conference to uphold the abortion-funding restrictions, Blackmun clerk Richard Willard wrote the justice a memorandum. The clerk conceded that some members of the majority were "simply hostile to *Roe v. Wade* and want to cut back on it as much as possible." Others, however, "agree[d] that it is unconstitutional for the government to prohibit abortion" but made "the simple distinction between negative and affirmative action: that just because the government cannot punish abortion does not mean it must provide subsidies" for indigent women seeking an abortion. That distinction, wrote Willard, reflected "a fundamental understanding of constitutional liberty, which I happen to share." In the clerk's view, the Constitution embraced a " 'negative' concept of liberty, which creates privileges against governmental coercion." The "positive" notion of liberty, on the other hand, imposed affirmative obligations on government, such as the "rights to health care, productive employment, and social security" found, Willard noted, in the "constitutions [of] Communist countries."[71]

In Willard's judgment, *Roe* was "squarely within the American constitutional tradition" of negative liberty. But the clerk rejected the broader view that the abortion right was not "real unless one has sufficient funds to pay for it." Such reasoning, he wrote, smacked of "egalitarianism," which he considered "ultimately incompatible with the individualistic concept of liberty.... We do not require the government to pay for publishing costs or travel expenses so that these constitutional liberties can be fully realized by the poor.... Thus I would also reject an argument that as a general matter the Constitution requires the government to pay for abortion for the indigent."

Willard did think, however, that Blackmun's opposition to restrictions on abortion funding could be supported on "a much narrower and less radical basis": in a "modern welfare state," he reasoned, "the denial of government largesse can be just as effective a means of coercion as criminal sanctions. When the spending power is used, not to save money, but to 'punish' conduct that the government cannot constitutionally prohibit, then I think the refusal to spend can properly be regarded as coercive." In fact, the exclusion of abortion from welfare funding of medical services "had no rational explanation except as an attempt to use the government's spending power in a coercive manner," because "in the long run it surely costs more to pay for the increased number of live births (not to mention extra welfare costs)."

Willard was respectful, expressing the "hope" that his " 'lecture' [had] not seemed too presumptuous," and the final dissent that Blackmun filed incorporated certain elements of his clerk's memorandum. But the justice was singularly unimpressed with Justice Powell's majority rationale. In fact, when Powell circulated the first draft of his opinion in one of the cases, *Maher v. Roe*, Blackmun scrawled "very disheartening!" on the first page of his copy. And the justice's brief but biting indictment of Powell's majority opinion clearly had a much broader sweep than his clerk would have preferred.[72]

The majority, Blackmun declared, was permitting states "to accomplish indirectly" what *Roe* and *Doe* had "said they could not do directly." The justice was incredulous. "The Court concedes the existence of a constitutional right but denies the realization and enjoyment of that right on the ground that existence and realization are separate and distinct. For the individual woman concerned, indigent and financially helpless,...the result is punitive and tragic. Implicit in the Court's holdings is the condescension that she may go elsewhere for her abortion. I find that disingenuous and alarming, almost reminiscent of: 'Let them eat cake.' "[73]

For Blackmun, too, the majority's argument that welfare funds were limited and that states must be given the discretion to decide how they could best be allocated was "specious" at best. "The cost of a nontherapeutic abortion is far less than the cost of maternity care and delivery, and holds no comparison whatsoever with the welfare costs that will burden the State for the new indigents and their support in the long, long years ahead."[74]

Concluding his dissent, the justice delivered the first of what was to be many moving sermonettes on the Court's constitutional obligations to society's "little people": "There is another world 'out there,' the existence of which the Court, I suspect, either chooses to ignore or fears to recognize. And so the cancer of poverty will continue to grow. This is a sad day for those who regard the Constitution as a force that would serve justice to all evenhandedly and, in so doing, would better the lot of the poorest among us."[75]

In an earlier draft of his opinion, his appeal on behalf of society's most vulnerable citizens had been even more emphatic. Richard Willard found nothing in the dissent "that struck me as intemperate or inappropriate for a judicial opinion." He did suggest, however, that Blackmun "reconsider the very last sentence in terms of your constitutional philosophy. I would not characterize the Constitution as a force to better the lot of the poor, but rather as requiring the government to deal evenhandedly with rich and poor alike." Blackmun acquiesced, but only to a degree, in Willard's suggestion.[76]

The justice was never able to persuade his colleagues to adopt his position on the abortion-funding issue. He continued to argue that the exclusion of abortions from welfare funding for poor women was tantamount to infringing on the abortion right directly, and thus a violation of *Roe*. Most of his colleagues, by contrast, saw a clear-cut distinction between the right recognized in *Roe*, which the Constitution guaranteed, and abortion funding, which they considered purely a matter for legislative discretion. In 1980, a majority upheld the so-called Hyde Amendment, a congressional enactment severely limiting the use of federal Medicaid funds for abortions. The justice filed another brief dissent, quoting key passages from his 1977 opinion. Given the Court's latest ruling, he observed, " 'the lot of the poorest among us,' once again, and still, is not to be bettered."[77]

Commercial Speech

Justice Blackmun was obviously frustrated with the Court's handling of the abortion-funding issue—and undoubtedly anxious about potential further judicial retrenchment in the abortion field. His authorship of *Roe* did lead, however, to opinion assignments in the only other extensive line of constitutional cases for which the justice would be the Court's principal spokesperson. When the Burger Court decided to overturn earlier precedents and confer First Amendment protection on commercial speech, it began the process in a case involving restrictions on the advertising of abortion services, for which Blackmun naturally seemed ideally suited to draft the Court's opinion.

Beginning with *Valentine v. Chrestensen* (1942), the Court for years, albeit without much thought and reflection, had excluded commercial speech from First Amendment coverage. In *Pittsburgh Press v. Pittsburgh Commission on Human Relations* (1973), decided the same year that *Roe* was decided, Justice Powell invoked *Valentine* in upholding a Pittsburgh civil rights ordinance construed to forbid newspapers from carrying sex-designated advertising columns. In dissent, Justice Stewart, joined by Justice Douglas, questioned the continuing validity of the commercial speech doctrine, even as applied to "purely commercial advertising," but flatly rejected any power of government to "tell a newspaper in advance what it can print and what it cannot." For Stewart, the First Amendment constituted a "clear command that government must never be allowed to lay its heavy editorial hand on any newspaper in this country." Only those who thought the amendment "should be subordinated to other socially desirable interests," declared Stewart, "will hail today's decision."[78]

When asserting that the First Amendment would "remain in grave jeopardy" while "members of this Court view [it] as no more than a set of 'values' to be balanced against other 'values,'" Stewart in his original draft cited opinions that Blackmun had joined as well as his colleague's *Cohen* dissent, in which the justice had asserted that the "Court's agonizing over First Amendment values seem[ed] misplaced and unnecessary" in that case. In the margin to Stewart's draft, Blackmun noted that the reference to *Cohen* was "out of context" and that, after all, Justice Black, hardly a First Amendment "balancer," had joined Blackmun's *Cohen* dissent. Blackmun shared his concerns in a letter to Stewart, offering to join the dissent "if you could see your way clear to omit that paragraph," but adding, "If you insist on its retention, I, of course, would not." Stewart deleted the reference to *Cohen* but retained the rest of the paragraph, including a citation to the *Pentagon Papers Cases*, in which Blackmun had also dissented. In a brief dissenting statement, Blackmun indicated that he "substantially" agreed with Stewart's opinion but did "not subscribe to the statements" in the paragraph to which he had objected.[79]

Over the next several years, Blackmun spoke for the Court in gradually dismantling the commercial speech doctrine. But earlier cases, including *Pittsburgh Press*, had already made it clear that expression was not to be automatically and entirely excluded from First Amendment protection simply because it was couched in the terms of an advertisement. When, for example, the Warren Court in *New York Times v. Sullivan* (1964) significantly limited governmental authority over libelous expression, the justices declined to dismiss a newspaper advertisement criticizing Montgomery, Alabama, police as the sort of commercial speech traditionally barred from First Amendment protection. The advertisement at issue there, Justice Brennan asserted for the *New York Times* Court, "expressed opinion, recited grievances, protested claimed abuses, and sought financial support on behalf of a [civil rights] movement whose existence and objectives are matters of the highest public interest and concern." In *Pittsburgh Press*, moreover, the Court had upheld the restriction on sex-designated want ad columns only because they did no more than propose a commercial transaction and thus resembled the advertisement (an ad for admission to a submarine) at issue in *Christensen* more than the ad in the *New York Times* case.[80]

In *Bigelow v. Virginia* (1975), Justice Blackmun invoked such reasoning to overturn the conviction of a weekly newspaper editor who ran an advertisement for a New York abortion referral service, in violation of a Virginia law that made it a misdemeanor to encourage abortions through the sale or circulation of publications. Abortions were legal in New York and, under *Roe*, nationally. But the Virginia courts held that advertisements were beyond the First Amendment's scope. Citing *New York Times* and *Pittsburgh Press*, Justice Blackmun rejected such a sweeping pronouncement. The mere fact that an advertisement had commercial elements did not deny it all constitutional protection, he held, and the advertisement at issue in *Bigelow* did more than offer a commercial transaction: "It conveyed information of potential interest and value to a diverse audience—not only to readers possibly in need of the services offered, but also to those with a general curiosity about, or genuine interest in, the subject matter or the law of another State and its development, and to readers seeking reform in Virginia." Given *Roe*, the subject of the advertisement also related to constitutionally protected interests. "Thus," declared the justice, "appellant's First Amendment interests coincided with the constitutional interests of the general public."[81]

The Court reserved for the time being the broader question to what extent commercial speech was entitled to constitutional protection "under all circumstances and in the face of all kinds of regulations." But Blackmun did observe that the validity of each regulation required a weighing of competing First Amendment and public interests; no interest cited by the state, he concluded, could outweigh the First Amendment interests at stake in *Bigelow*, particularly under a law applied to a newspaper editor rather than to the referral service itself.[82]

Personally, rather than as the Court's spokesman, Blackmun believed, as his clerk David Patterson put it in a memorandum to the justice, that "truthful information about wholly legitimate commercial activity [was] protected [from government regulation]. Period." No balancing of competing interests was necessary. Especially to accommodate Justice Powell, however, Blackmun continued to endorse a balancing approach in subsequent commercial speech cases. In *Virginia State Board of Pharmacy v. Virginia Consumer Council* (1976), a majority, per Blackmun, struck down a law forbidding pharmacists to advertise prescription drug prices. The state's interest in maintaining professionalism among licensed pharmacists, he concluded, was simply inadequate to justify keeping the public ignorant of variations in the prices pharmacists were offering for their products.[83]

As a former ABA president, Justice Powell was also concerned about extension of the pharmacy decision to "the traditional learned professions: medicine and law." In a letter to Blackmun, the justice reluctantly conceded that "pharmacy *is* a 'profession' and not an unimportant one." Noting, however, that 95 percent of the drugs dispensed by pharmacists was now prepackaged, he added, with an ample dose of condescension, "Today the typical function of a pharmacist is pouring pills or tablets from a larger bottle into a small bottle." It was thus in the public interest, in Powell's judgment, "for these essentially fungible 'commodities' to be retailed competitively [and] only advertising [could] achieve [that] end." But the services doctors and lawyers provided were "not fungible," and their situation was thus "profoundly different" from that of druggists. Powell did not oppose all advertising by physicians and attorneys, but he feared that Blackmun's draft opinion might prevent "a discriminating assessment—and balancing—of the public interest against First Amendment rights when we have the medical and legal professions before us."[84]

Blackmun's draft opinion, Powell suggested, had "elevate[d] [the pharmacist] to a professional status which he no longer enjoys," and he hoped that his colleague would revise the opinion "to deemphasize the current professional role of the pharmacist." The justice could "live with" the draft, however, if Blackmun simply added "something along the lines" of an attached paragraph, which read: "We have considered in this case the regulation by a state of commercial advertising by pharmacists. Although we express no opinion as to other professions, the distinctions—historical and functional—between professions may require consideration of quite different factors. Doctors and lawyers, for example, do not dispense standardized products; they render professional *services* of almost infinite variety and nature, with the consequent enhanced opportunity for confusion and deception if they were to undertake certain kinds of advertising."[85]

In his reply, Blackmun indicated that he had decided "not to try to downgrade the professional aspects of the practice of pharmacy." Justice Brennan had already cautioned the justice against following Powell's suggestion ("I'm not sure that I'd cast aspersions upon pharmacy as a profession"). Blackmun's clerk David Patterson concurred with Brennan, observing, "We should give the profession its due, particularly since we are dealing them what is (at least in their own eyes) a significant blow." But Blackmun did include Powell's suggested paragraph as a footnote to his opinion.[86]

Not surprisingly, Blackmun and Powell parted company even more fundamentally in 1977, when Blackmun concluded for the Court that a state could not prohibit the advertising of routine legal services, but left in place restrictions on in-person solicitations and advertisements "as to the *quality* of legal services." In dissent, Powell expressed fear "that today's holding will be viewed by tens of thousands of lawyers as an invitation—by the public-spirited and the selfish lawyers alike—to engage in competitive advertising on an escalating basis. Some lawyers may gain temporary advantages; others will suffer from the economic power of stronger lawyers, or by the subtle deceit of less scrupulous lawyers. Some members of the public may benefit marginally, but the risk is that many others will be victimized by simplistic price advertising of professional services 'almost infinite [in] variety and nature.' "[87]

Ultimately, however, Powell's balancing approach to all commercial speech issues would prevail. Speaking for the Court in *Central Hudson Gas and Electric Corporation v. Public Services Commission* (1980) Powell laid down a four-part test for evaluating restrictions on commercial speech. First, it must concern lawful activity and not be misleading. Second, the restriction at issue must serve a substantial governmental interest. Third, the regulation must directly advance that interest. Finally, the regulation must not be more extensive than necessary to serve that interest. Applying that formula, the Court struck down an energy conservation measure that completely banned advertising by an electric utility.[88]

Justice Blackmun filed an opinion concurring only in the Court's judgment. Noting that limitations on the content of expression were ordinarily subjected to the most rigorous judicial scrutiny, the justice argued that the intermediate level of review reflected in Powell's four-part test was appropriate only for cases involving "misleading or coercive speech, or [regulations] related to the time, place, or manner of commercial speech," rather than to its content. As the majority itself recognized, wrote Blackmun,

> we have never held that commercial speech may be suppressed
> in order to further the State's interest in discouraging purchases
> of the underlying product that is advertised....[Regulations]
> designed to deprive consumers of information about products
> or services that are legally offered for sale consistently have been
> invalidated....Even though "commercial" speech is involved,
> such a regulatory measure strikes at the heart of the First
> Amendment....It is a covert attempt by the State to manipulate
> the choices of its citizens, not by persuasion or direct regulation,
> but by depriving the public of the information needed to make a
> free choice....If the First Amendment means anything, it means
> that, absent clear and present danger, government has no power
> to restrict expression, because of the effect its message is likely to
> have on the public.[89]

Under the Court's approach, Blackmun argued, states would be permitted to ban all direct advertising of air conditioning on the assumption "that a more limited restriction on such advertising would not effectively deter the public from cooling its homes." In his judgment, however, government was required to attack such problems directly, through, for example, a ban on air conditioning or the regulation of thermostat levels, not, he asserted, quoting his *Virginia Pharmacy* opinion, "by keeping the public in ignorance."[90]

Justice Brennan joined Blackmun's *Central Hudson* opinion. By this point in his career, Blackmun was also joining Brennan and other Court liberals more regularly than he was allied with Chief Justice Burger. The justice's relations with his boyhood friend had continued to deteriorate. In Burger's original opinion for the *Virginia Pharmacy* case, the chief justice had equated the pharmacist who sold prepackaged drugs with the "clerk who sells lawbooks." A *New York Times* editorial applauding the Court's decision erroneously attributed Burger's remark to Justice Blackmun, who quickly drew the wrath of one Leslie Chrismer, a Pennsylvania pharmacist. In a letter to the *Times*, a copy of which he mailed to the justice, Chrismer termed "Justice Blackmun's statement...more than a gratuitous insult. It is a false analogy and an ignorant appraisal." Noting a poll indicating that "less than 30% of the public had a favorable opinion of the legal profession—that is, held it in trust and esteem," he also stressed the rigorous course of study pharmacists were obliged to complete and termed them "invaluable helpmates to physicians." "Every pharmacist catches errors in doctors' prescriptions—some serious enough to cause death."[91]

The justice soon responded, gently informing Chrismer that his letter had done him "a disservice," that his opinion in the case in fact "assumes the professional aspects of the practice of pharmacy," and that the statement found "offensive was made by another justice and not by me." When Chrismer was duly apologetic, Blackmun replied that he was "pleased to know that this, at least, has been straightened out to your personal satisfaction." But he could not resist a jab at the press, observing, "The media's error, of course, is seldom capable of repair."[92]

The next year, while working on his opinion for *Bates v. State Bar* (1977), striking down restrictions on the advertising of legal services, Blackmun learned from a law review article that Chief Justice Burger had deleted the offensive passage from his own *Virginia Pharmacy* opinion prior to publication of the Court's official report of the case—but without informing the author of the Court's opinion. Justice Blackmun was not happy. In a letter to the chief justice, he complained, "I think the change is substantial, and my file contains no information whatsoever that it was made. Is it not customary to notify the Conference of any substantial change in an opinion after it has been issued in slip form..., and, particularly, the author of the primary opinion?...I am advised...that certain members of the local academic community are aware that the change was made."[93]

Chapter 8

Liberal Icon

From the late 1970s through the end of Chief Justice Burger's tenure in 1986, Justice Blackmun was increasingly likely to embrace liberal civil liberties claims. He was clearly not the Burger Court's most liberal justice. According to one survey, he supported civil liberties claims 44 percent and 54 percent of the time in the 1978–80 and 1981–85 terms, respectively, compared with pro–civil liberties records of 24 percent and 23 percent for the chief justice during those terms, and 13 and 17 percent support rates for Justice Rehnquist. By contrast, Justice Brennan had a pro–civil liberties record of 81 percent and 80 percent for those terms, and Justice Marshall supported civil liberties claims 82 percent and 83 percent of the time. Justice Stevens, President Ford's only nominee, had pro–civil liberties records of 59 percent and 61 percent for the 1978–80 and 1981–85 terms. As a result of his connection with *Roe*, however, Blackmun had become something of a liberal icon in the media and the public eye.[1]

Gagging the Press

Given that image and his growing estrangement from the chief justice, Blackmun's involvement in the first important censorship suit to reach the

Court since 1971 must have come as something of a surprise even to those familiar with his dissent in the *Pentagon Papers Cases*. On October 18, 1975, six members of a Nebraska farm family, age five to sixty-six, were sexually assaulted and murdered in their home. After the arrest of a suspect, a county court issued a gag order against the press in an effort to preserve the defendant's right to trial by an impartial jury. Under that order, as modified by Hugh Stuart, a state district court judge, the media were forbidden, among other things, to report statements by the suspect or other evidence "strongly implicating" him in the crime. When the Nebraska Supreme Court announced that it would not begin reviewing the order until December 5, a group of Nebraska press organizations petitioned Justice Blackmun, as circuit justice for the Eighth Circuit and thus initially responsible for reviewing petitions to the Court from that circuit, to lift the gag. Initially, Blackmun declined to intervene, instead urging Nebraska's high court to act promptly on the matter. The state justices agreed to move up the date on which they would begin reviewing the case, but only by a few days. Concluding at that point that the state high court's delay had "exceed[ed] tolerable limits," Justice Blackmun lifted portions of the state gag order. But he left in place provisions forbidding the publication or broadcast of the accused's confession or other incriminating information.[2] The justice's action meant that reporting on the case in Nebraska would be restricted pending the full Court's review.

Media reaction was immediate and fierce. Columnist Tom Wicker of the *New York Times* was particularly vehement. Recalling the justice's *Pentagon Papers* dissent, Wicker declared, "Blackmun is still in the business of prophesying what dire things *might* happen if newspapers publish certain information." In his opinion in those cases, Justice Brennan had contended that, even in the national security field, "the First Amendment tolerates absolutely no prior restraint of the press predicated upon surmise or conjecture that untoward consequences may result." Yet Blackmun, declared Wicker, was now upholding a press gag based on the mere possibility that publicity about a criminal case "*might* render jurors unable to form an independent judgment as to guilt or innocence from the evidence adduced at trial."[3]

Terming the order "exceptionally ominous" for "those who believe, as we do, that the rights protected by the First Amendment are the core of American liberty," the *Washington Post* considered the justice's action, "to put it bluntly, a major step toward a judicially imposed system of censorship unprecedented in American history." To the *Post*'s knowledge "this [was]…the first time a member of the Supreme Court has ever sanctioned such an injunction." The *Los Angeles Times* entitled another critical editorial "Justice Is Blind—and Gagged." Sigma Delta Chi, the society of professional journalists, called the order a "dangerous precedent" and urged the full Court to reverse the justice "without delay." And conservative columnist James J. Kilpatrick, contending that the Nebraska gag rule posed a "far more serious" threat to press freedom than the *Pentagon Papers Cases*, predicted that a full Court ruling affirming Blackmun would "invite every defense attorney, in every important case, to move for a gag; and trial judges, thus encouraged, will stop our presses. We can't let it happen."[4]

A federal district judge in Tennessee came to Blackmun's defense, reminding Tom Wicker in a letter to the columnist of recent cases in which defendants' convictions had been overturned on prejudicial publicity grounds and also emphasizing that press gags only delayed, rather than prevented, publication of information about criminal cases. A grateful justice thanked the judge for a copy of the letter to Wicker—and vented his frustration at the press. "I appreciate your kindness in all this," he wrote, "for I have been subjected to a critical barrage from the media from coast to coast. No one seems to recognize the fact that initially I was endeavoring to get [the Nebraska] Supreme Court to act (having in mind the customary concern about federal-state relationships), and the additional fact that I did give the media at least part of the relief they requested. Such facts are lost in the overreaction. I suppose, however, that all this is the kind of thing you and I must expect in the jobs we have."[5]

On December 1, the Nebraska Supreme Court modified and reinstated Judge Stuart's gag order in the case. At that point, an official at the Supreme Court saw a way to extricate the justice from the controversy. Because the state high court had vacated the district court order to which Blackmun's partial stay had been directed, he wrote Blackmun, the pending press motion to vacate the justice's order "appear[ed] to be moot as a practical matter." He thought it might be best to dissolve Blackmun's order in light of the Nebraska Supreme Court's action. "Dissolution—as opposed to vacation—would indicate that your order has served its purpose. It unquestionably would wipe the slate clean and permit everyone to start anew." He also saw a tactical advantage in such an approach. "Such action would negate in large part the precedential authority your decision appears to have attained [in other lower court cases], an effect which I am not sure that you intended and which some members of the court may find troublesome even if the stay is as a practical matter moot."[6]

Blackmun followed the suggestion, but the full Court agreed to review a press challenge to the state high court's order. The justices declined, however, to grant the case an expedited review. Over the dissents of Brennan, Marshall, Stewart, and White, the Court also denied a motion to lift the gag while reviewing the case.

The Nebraska high court's intervention in the case had taken some of the media heat off Justice Blackmun. In his preargument summary of the suit, the justice wrote that he was "generally somewhat surprised that [the media briefs filed in the case] have not, anywhere so far as I can see, attacked me personally because of what I did or did not do in the two in chambers opinions I issued last November. The spleen now is directed at the Supreme Court of Nebraska."[7]

In the summary, the justice also made clear that he regarded "the First Amendment right of the press to be free and the Sixth Amendment right of a defendant to have a fair trial...as coequals," adding, "I do not place the First Amendment on a superior position to the Sixth." To the extent that the gag orders had prevented publication of information already revealed in public court proceedings, he acknowledged that "the Nebraska Court and I myself may have been wrong in our orders." But in another notation regarding the case, he asserted, "I have no apology whatever to make for last Fall's In Chambers opinions."

In its ruling for *Nebraska Press Association v. Stuart* (1976), the Court, per Chief Justice Burger, emphasized the heavy burden prior restraints on the press were obliged to surmount and struck down the Nebraska gag orders. The state courts, asserted Burger, should first have pursued less drastic means of neutralizing potentially prejudicial media publicity given the case before gagging reporters. It was doubtful, he added, that the orders were effective in any event. Potential jurors, after all, were undoubtedly exposed to outside media not covered by the gag, as well as local gossip in the rural community where the crime took place. Furthermore, declared the chief justice, under the Court's ruling in *Cox Broadcasting Corp. v. Cohn* (1975), striking down a state ban on publication of the names of rape victims, media reports of information revealed in court proceedings, such as much of the material covered by the Nebraska gag orders, enjoyed broad First Amendment protection.[8]

Opening the Courts

Perhaps to the surprise of certain of his media critics, Justice Blackmun joined the *Nebraska Press* ruling. Later, he also became one of the Court's staunchest defenders of open criminal proceedings, albeit on Sixth Amendment fair trial rather than First Amendment free press grounds. In *Gannett Press v. DePasquale* (1979), the trial judge closed a pretrial hearing on a motion to suppress a confession and certain physical evidence against two defendants charged with murder, robbery, and grand larceny. At conference, a majority voted 5–4 to overturn the trial judge's decision, and Blackmun was assigned to draft the Court's opinion in the case. But the resolve of Justice Powell, the fifth member of the majority, gradually weakened in the face of a fierce Stewart dissent. In a letter to Blackmun, Powell recalled that no majority had actually agreed in conference "exactly how the competing interests in the case should be resolved." Powell agreed with his colleague "that the accused [had] no constitutional right to close a trial or a pretrial suppression hearing." But the draft majority opinion Blackmun was then circulating created an unduly "strong presumption in favor of open proceedings," in Powell's judgment. "I am inclined to think that where both the defendant and the prosecution (representing the public) agree that cloture is necessary to protect the right of a fair trial, the burden would be on the press or a representative of the public to satisfy the court that this is not necessary."[9]

Powell insisted that his views were "quite tentative," the case "difficult," and Blackmun's "thorough consideration" of the issues in his lengthy draft opinion "impressive." But the justice could not be "sure where I will come down" until he had an opportunity "to write something out."

Soon Blackmun's clerk Bill McDaniel reported "some very bad news" from Powell's chambers. According to one of the justice's clerks, Powell and Justice Stewart had been "in frequent consultation" the previous weekend and, although "LFP has not yet finally made up his mind...it looked as though a deal has been swung with Justice Stewart....Justice Powell will concur in the judgment to affirm [closure of the suppression hearing]. He will write to say that there is a First Amendment right of access to such proceedings, but that all that is required under this right is that the trial judge listen to and consider the objections of the member of the press or public attempting to gain access to the hearing. He thinks that what was done in this case is adequate to meet the First Amendment requirements, since once the press requested access to the hearing it was heard out by the trial judge, and the trial judge considered their case."[10]

A week later, McDaniel had even worse news to report. "The axe," he wrote Blackmun, "is about to fall in *Gannett*, at long last." One of Justice Stewart's clerks had "stopped by...and could not resist crowing about their victory in [the] case." According to the clerk, Powell had agreed to join Stewart if he modified the draft opinion to assume a First Amendment right of access to pretrial proceedings, then find that right had "been satisfied" in *Gannett*. Stewart had obliged but, at Powell's suggestion, circulated the revised draft as a dissent, thereby permitting Powell to read it, "decide" that he could now join Stewart, and add a brief concurrence of his own. "Of course," McDaniel added, "that little concurrence has already been written and is ready to go out as soon as propriety will permit."[11]

The next day, McDaniel gave Blackmun another update. The latest version of Stewart's "dissent," he reported, "pick[ed] up almost exactly the First Amendment analysis" Powell had outlined in his letter to Blackmun. "I am told by Justice Powell's clerk that Justice Powell will be calling and giving you a visit soon to discuss his 'reaction' to the dissent circulated by Justice Stewart." But McDaniel remained convinced that Powell had already decided to join Stewart, and change the outcome of the case, when Stewart's revised opinion was circulated.[12]

Powell made his defection official with a letter to Blackmun and copy to their colleagues. Although Stewart had not reached the First Amendment claim in his latest effort, Powell wrote, his colleague had recognized the amendment's "possible relevance" to the case. "I therefore will join his opinion," Powell announced, adding, "I know that you have devoted a great deal of time and thought to your scholarly opinion, and I am sorry to end up being the 'swing vote.'...But upon a more careful examination of the facts, I have concluded that the trial court substantially did what in my view the First Amendment requires." Between "swing" and "vote" on Powell's letter, Blackmun scrawled "*changed* vote!" When Burger, originally a dissenter, then assigned the opinion for the new majority to Stewart, an angry Blackmun exclaimed on his copy, "How ridiculous! This, too, part of the charade?"[13]

Two months earlier, when what was to have been Blackmun's majority opinion in *Gannett* was circulated, the chief justice, according to Bill McDaniel, told his clerks "that he simply could not understand why your *Gannett* opinion was going to be so long. 'I could have knocked that one out in about 12 pages,' the Chief is purported to have said, 'but of course, I would have gone the other way.' "[14]

But Blackmun was hardly deterred. In one of the longest and most thoroughgoing dissents of his career, he contradicted the majority's rejection of any Sixth Amendment requirement of open proceedings. A copious survey of the history of the amendment and its common law antecedents convinced him that the public had a right to attend trials. The "critical importance of suppression hearings to our system of criminal justice" further persuaded him that such proceedings "must be considered part of the trial." The public's interest in open trials required that any exception be narrowly drawn; the facts in *Gannett*, in his judgment, were insufficient to mount that hurdle. "It has been said," he concluded, "that publicity 'is the soul of justice.'...And in many ways it is: open judicial processes, especially in the criminal field, protect against judicial, prosecutorial, and police abuse; provide a means for citizens to obtain information about the criminal justice system and the performance of public officials; and safeguard the integrity of the courts. Publicity is essential to the preservation of public confidence in the rule of law and in the operation of courts. Only in rare circumstances does this principle clash with the rights of the criminal defendant to a fair trial so as to justify exclusion...those circumstances did not exist in this case."[15]

Nor did Blackmun confine his criticism of the *Gannett* majority to the pages of his dissent. In the face of widespread media criticism of what

Newsweek called the "Gannett muddle," Chief Justice Burger issued a statement emphasizing, as he had in a *Gannett* concurrence, that the ruling applied only to pretrial proceedings, not trials; Justice Powell suggested to a reporter that press complaints might be "a bit premature," since the Court had not yet decided whether the press had a right to attend trials. In a speech at the August annual conference of Eighth Circuit judges in Rapid City, South Dakota, however, Justice Blackmun declared, "Despite what my colleague, the chief justice, has said, if the defense, the prosecution and the judge agree to close the trial itself, the courtroom shall be closed." He also termed the *Gannett* ruling "outrageous, totally in error."[16]

When the remarks were carried by the Gannett News Service in a South Dakota newspaper, Lyle Denniston, a reporter for the *Washington Star*, contacted Blackmun's secretary, Wanda Martinson, in an effort to confirm the justice's statements. Blackmun vouched for most of what the South Dakota paper had reported but told his secretary that, contrary to the news article, he had not said that the majority opinion was "simplistic," and he hoped Denniston would not include that statement in his coverage of the justice's speech. If the reporter pursued that issue, according to Martinson's notes, she could tell Denniston that he could quote Blackmun as saying that "the separate concurrence of the Chief Justice took a simplistic approach" to the case.[17]

Whatever its overall merit, Stewart's *Gannett* opinion cried out for clarification. Although, as Burger emphasized, the case dealt only with the closing of a pretrial hearing, Stewart had devoted most of his opinion to the Sixth Amendment's impact on *trials*. Not surprisingly, therefore, trial judges began citing *Gannett* as precedent for closing trial proceedings. Less than two months after the ruling, closure motions, by one count, had been filed on fifty-one occasions in various types of criminal proceedings, and more than half of those motions had been granted or upheld on appeal, even though many dealt with postconviction hearings and even trials rather than with pretrial proceedings.[18]

The justices got their chance to clarify the *Gannett* holding the next term in *Richmond Newspapers v. Virginia* (1980), in which a trial judge had granted a defense motion to close a murder trial after the defendant's first conviction had been reversed on appeal and two subsequent proceedings had ended in mistrials. Speaking for a plurality, Chief Justice Burger found a right of the public and press to attend criminal trials implicit in the First Amendment, absent an overriding interest in closing the proceedings. In a concurring opinion, Justice Blackmun reiterated his opposition to Stewart's *Gannett* rationale and his argument that the Sixth Amendment included a right of public trial. But he also felt "driven to conclude, as a secondary position," that the First Amendment provided some measure of protection for the right of access as well.[19]

In 1984, the justice joined a ruling extending *Richmond Newspapers* to the voir dire examination of prospective jurors. Earlier he had also joined the Court, per Burger, in holding that the televising of criminal trials did not necessarily deny the accused due process. Blackmun did not file an opinion in that case, but the suit did occasion another incident suggesting the degree to which relations between Blackmun and the chief justice had deteriorated. In his draft opinion for the Court in *Chandler v. Florida* (1981), Burger noted that seven opinions had been filed in *Estes v. Texas*, a 1965 case overturning a criminal conviction on the ground that the cumbersome presence of television cameras in the court had denied the defendant a fair trial. "Perhaps I can't count," Blackmun soon wrote his boyhood friend, with a copy to their colleagues, "but I am able to find only six [opinions in *Estes*]. Am I in error?" "Six it is," Burger replied later that same day, also copying the other justices. "You can count!"[20]

Revival of Dual Federalism

If Blackmun's actions as circuit justice in the Nebraska gag order case raised doubts, despite *Roe*, about the justice's growing commitment to civil liberties principles, his stance in another notable case of the mid-1970s appeared to fly in the face of the basic assumption of the post-1936 Supreme Court that federal-state disputes were to be resolved in the political arena, not the courts. In *National League of Cities v. Usery* (1976), a 5–4 majority that included Blackmun struck down a congressional statute on state sovereignty and federalism grounds for the first time since 1936. Overturning a law subjecting state and local governments to federal wage and hour standards, the Court, speaking through Justice Rehnquist, held the national government powerless to interfere with "integral" or "traditional" state functions.[21]

Except during the laissez-faire era, the Court had never held that an otherwise valid exercise of congressional regulatory authority was unconstitutional if it touched activities traditionally controlled by the states. In fact, the post-1936 Court had dismissed the Tenth Amendment as a mere "truism," reserving to the states powers not delegated to Congress but imposing no substantive restrictions itself on congressional authority. Justice Rehnquist's opinion for the *Usery* majority was thus a remarkable departure from precedents going back to the days of Chief Justice John Marshall and embraced a doctrine of dual federalism most closely associated with the long-discredited *Lochner* era—as Justice Brennan, joined by White and Marshall, effectively demonstrated in a lengthy *Usery* dissent.[22]

In his preargument summary of the case, Justice Blackmun readily recognized the broad reach of congressional regulatory authority, but also expressed concern about undue federal intervention in state policies. "We have emasculated state operations exceedingly in the past, and this could be another large step in that direction," he wrote. "Does the Tenth Amendment have any meaning at all? If we affirm [congressional power] here it has comparatively little meaning."[23]

Consistent with his concerns, Blackmun cast the controlling vote in *Usery*, but did so reluctantly. In a brief concurrence, he indicated that he was "not untroubled by certain possible implications of the Court's opinion" and attempted to give the decision a narrow construction. "I may misinterpret the Court's opinion," he observed, "but it seems to me that it adopts a balancing approach, and does not outlaw federal power in areas such as environmental protection, where the federal interest is demonstrably greater and where state facility compliance with imposed federal standards would be essential."[24]

Blackmun's suggestion of a balancing approach to diminish *Usery*'s "ominous implications" did not impress Justice Brennan. To the senior associate justice, it was only "a thinly veiled rationalization for judicial supervision of a policy judgment that our system of government reserves to Congress."[25]

Ultimately, Blackmun himself would abandon *Usery*, casting the deciding vote for its reversal in *Garcia v. San Antonio Metropolitan Transit Authority* (1985) and a companion case. At issue in *Garcia* was whether the city's mass transit system was immune from federal wage-hour regulations. Following initial argument in the case, a majority, including Blackmun, decided that mass transit services were a "traditional" government function and thus, under *Usery*, immune from federal standards. Chief Justice Burger passed when the case came up for a vote in conference, but later voted to affirm a lower court decision upholding the transit authority and assigned Blackmun to draft the Court's opinion.[26]

Attempting to prepare a draft for the justice, Blackmun's clerk Scott McIntosh soon began "to worry," as he put it in a twenty-two-page memorandum to the justice, "whether the distinction [between traditional and nontraditional state functions] on which the Court is relying is either sound in theory or workable in practice." The *Usery* doctrine reminded the clerk of the Court's effort, ultimately abandoned, to distinguish between "governmental" and "proprietary" functions in the intergovernmental tax immunity field. In *Transportation Union v. Long Island R. Co.* (1982), the Court's only post-*Usery* case involving the *Usery* doctrine to that point, he added, "the Chief's attempt to give nonhistorical content to the idea of 'traditional governmental functions' was not a rousing success...and none of the factors that come to mind for such an enterprise looks any more promising." Lower courts, in McIntosh's judgment, had been equally unsuccessful in applying *Usery* to specific contexts.[27]

To McIntosh, the problem with *Usery* was "that neither the governmental-proprietary distinction nor any other one that purports to separate 'integral' or 'necessary' governmental functions from other ones can be faithful to the role of federalism in a democratic society. The essence of this Nation's federal system is that within the realm of power left open to them under the Constitution, the States must be equally free to engage in any activity that their citizens choose for the common weal, no matter how unorthodox or unnecessary anyone else—including the judiciary—deems state involvement in that activity to be. If this promise of state sovereignty is to be fulfilled, it must be left to the citizens of each State rather than to federal judges to decide what policies the State should pursue and what means it should use to pursue them. Any rule of state immunity that looks to the 'traditional,' 'integral,' or 'necessary' nature of governmental functions is an open invitation for the judiciary to make *Lochner*-era decisions about which state policies they favor and which they dislike."

In place of "unworkable [and] misconceived" attempts to distinguish essential from nonessential governmental functions, McIntosh proposed a nondiscrimination principle for limiting federal control over the states: "Federal regulation that is otherwise within Congress' power under the Commerce Clause may extend to state [government] functions so long as it applies uniformly to private as well as public activities and does not discriminate against the States and their subdivisions." In McIntosh's opinion, the federal government was "unlikely to produce regulatory schemes that frustrate or obstruct state functions as long as those functions are shared by a range of private parties as well, and as long as Congress is forbidden from singling out States for regulatory burdens and thereby separating them from what otherwise would be similarly situated private interests." States were represented in Congress, but might still lack the political clout to protect themselves if acting alone. If congressional legislation were required to affect private interests and states equally, however, undue congressional interference with state autonomy would be unlikely.

Justice Blackmun ultimately would have much in McIntosh's memo, though not its nondiscrimination formula, incorporated into his opinion for the *Garcia* Court. But not before a good deal of debate among the justices over *Usery*.

In late May, McIntosh submitted a draft majority opinion to the justice. In a cover memorandum, the clerk noted that, at Blackmun's suggestion, his discussion of the *Long Island* railway case did "not reflect critically on the Chief," instead "simply highlight[ing] the difficulties posed by the 'traditional governmental function' approach." By embracing the nondiscrimination standard outlined in his earlier memo, he also avoided adopting the position of the *Usery* dissenters, who had contended "that Congress is subject to no limitations when it applies its Commerce Clause powers to the States." Particularly because Blackmun had joined the *Usery* majority, however, the clerk emphasized that adoption of the nondiscrimination formula would have required, of course, "a different result as well as a different analysis in" *Usery*. But his approach, McIntosh asserted, would "put state immunity doctrine on an even keel…by using an administrative rule that neither abandons the idea of state immunity nor uses unworkable and unprincipled standards like 'traditional governmental functions.' "[28]

After review of McIntosh's draft, Justice Blackmun informed his colleagues in a memorandum to the conference that he was changing his vote in the case. In conference, his vote in support of the transit authority's position had been "shaky," he reminded the justices. "I assume that it is because of this that the Chief Justice assigned the cases to me, on his frequently stated reference to the 'least persuaded.' " After spending "a lot of time on these cases," however, he had decided that there was "no principled way in which to affirm" the lower court. "It seems to me that our customary reliance on the 'historical' and the 'traditional' is misplaced and that something more fundamental is required to eliminate the widespread confusion in the area."[29]

The justice circulated his draft opinion with his memorandum, but also acknowledged that the case should be reassigned and that some of the justices might feel the case should be reargued the next term. Not surprisingly, Justice Brennan, who to that point had been among the *Garcia* dissenters, promptly responded that he agreed with Blackmun's opinion and saw no need for reargument. Marshall concurred with Brennan, but members of the original majority, of course, had a decidedly different reaction. "Needless to say," Justice O'Connor declared in her own memo to the conference, "Harry's circulation today supporting a reversal of the judgment below and offering a significant change in our approach to the Tenth Amendment [reserved state powers] question is unexpected. Because our summer recess is right around the corner, I, for one, would prefer that the case be reargued rather than reassigned." Burger readily agreed. "At this stage—almost mid-June—a 30 page opinion coming out contrary to the Conference vote on a very important issue places those who may dissent in a difficult position." Without editorial comment, Justice Rehnquist also quickly favored reargument.[30]

Somewhat less predictably, Scott McIntosh supported reargument as well. Among other things, the clerk predicted "a great deal of ill will on the part of the dissenters if the [new] majority is seen as 'steamrolling' these cases through without observing the usual courtesies." He thought that Justice O'Connor "in particular feels it simply unfair to circulate an opinion changing tack so sharply at this point in the Term." Unless given time for a "measured response" to Blackmun's shift, the "simple fact" that dissenting justices "will feel wronged will only complicate relations on the Court next Term and make life around here generally more unpleasant."[31]

Despite McIntosh's concerns, Blackmun opposed reargument, but lost that battle. Once the case was carried over to the next term, Justices Powell and O'Connor jointly proposed that briefs and reargument be devoted to the following question: "Whether or not the principles of the Tenth Amendment as set forth in *National League of Cities v. Usery*...should be reconsidered?" Blackmun quickly produced a pointed and prophetic response. "If the question [proposed] is to be presented, *National League of Cities* just might end up being overruled. In the opinion I prepared this Term, and as to which some took umbrage, it was not overruled."[32]

Justice Powell was characteristically conciliatory. Given Blackmun's criticism of *Usery* in his draft opinion, Powell wrote his colleague, he and Justice O'Connor simply thought it "desirable to focus the attention of the parties broadly on the principles followed by the Court in that case." Powell was "sure [he spoke] also for Sandra in saying that we would, of course, consider a different framing of the question."[33]

The Court retained the phrasing Powell and O'Connor proposed, but the pair perhaps miscalculated the majority's likely reaction to such a fundamental reexamination of *Usery*. After reviewing the original draft opinion, Mark Schneider, the new clerk assigned to *Garcia*, recommended that the nondiscrimination restriction on congressional power that Scott McIntosh had proposed be discarded and that the Court commit the resolution of federal-state regulatory conflicts once again to the political arena, albeit "leav[ing] open the possibility that there may be some laws which violate federalism principles independent of any limitation in the Commerce Clause...[should] the political process...go...[completely] awry."[34]

Blackmun readily agreed to Schneider's proposed approach. Underscoring the confusion the *Usery* distinction between traditional and nontraditional governmental functions had created for the lower courts, he observed in his final opinion for the Court that three federal courts of appeals and one state appellate tribunal had held, contrary to the trial court in *Garcia*, that mass transit was *not* a traditional government function, and thus *was* subject to federal wage regulations. Rejecting the *Usery* and related formulas as "unsound in principle and unworkable in practice," he concluded for the majority that the states' participation in national governmental action, reflected especially in each state's congressional representation, provided "the principal and basic limit on the federal commerce power" in the federal system. "The model of democratic decision-making the Court...identified [in *Usery*]," declared Blackmun, "underestimated, in our view, the solicitude of the national political process for the continued vitality of the States. Attempts by other courts since then to draw guidance from this model have proved it both impractical and doctrinally barren. In sum, in *National League of Cities* the Court tried to repair what did not need repair." The only hint in the justice's opinion of any independent constitutional limitation on congressional regulatory authority inherent in federalism was this statement: "Of course, we continue to recognize that the States occupy a special and specific position in our federal system and that the scope of Congress' authority under the Commerce Clause must reflect that position." But he quickly noted that *Garcia* did "not require us to identify or define what affirmative limits the constitutional structure might impose on federal action affecting the States under the Commerce Clause."[35]

In a vigorous dissent, Justice Powell, joined by Burger, Rehnquist, and O'Connor, recalled few other cases in which the Court had ignored a recent precedent "as abruptly as we now witness." But Powell was even more disturbed at the potential impact of Justice Blackmun's opinion on state authority and the federal system. "Despite some genuflecting in the Court's opinion to the concept of federalism," he declared, "today's decision effectively reduces the Tenth Amendment to meaningless rhetoric when Congress acts pursuant to the Commerce Clause." At least since *Marbury v. Madison* (1803), the courts had been obliged to enforce constitutional limitations against the political branches of government. Under *Garcia*, however, "federal political officials, invoking the Commerce Clause, [were] the sole judges of the limits of their own power," yet the majority offered "no explanation for ignoring the teaching of the most famous case in our history."[36]

In her rhetoric at least, Justice O'Connor seemed even more incensed at the Court's decision. "With the abandonment of *National League of Cities*," she asserted, "all that stands between the remaining essentials of state sovereignty and Congress is the latter's undeveloped capacity for self-restraint." She wondered, in fact, "whether any realm *is* left open to the States by the Constitution—whether any area remains in which a State may act free of federal interference." But she remained hopeful that the Court would "in time again assume its constitutional responsibility." In his own brief dissent, Justice Rehnquist agreed. Rehnquist wasted no energy lamenting the Court's decision, but expressed confidence that the principle embodied in his opinion for the *Usery* majority would "in time again command the support of a majority of this Court."[37]

Justice Blackmun's shift and *Usery*'s demise surprised certain Court observers. The Harvard University law professor Laurence Tribe wrote the justice that he was "amused by Justice Rehnquist's certitude that your landmark decision overturning [*Usery*] will not be long for this world." In a new book, Tribe noted, he himself had predicted that, given prospects for additional "Rehnquist-like" Reagan administration appointments to the Court, "an obituary [for *Usery*] could well turn out, like the early reports of Mark Twain's death, to be greatly exaggerated indeed." When those lines were written, joked Tribe, he "did not know…that, by the time they saw the light of day…, the subject of my remarks would already be officially interred. Congratulations!"[38]

In part because he had defended the law at issue in *Maryland v. Wirtz* (1968), a precedent *Usery* had overruled, Erwin Griswold also sent Blackmun a "fan letter." Griswold had been "distressed" when *Usery* was decided, "because [he] felt it pointed towards a sort of Balkanization of the United States." He found Blackmun's *Garcia* opinion "very persuasive."[39]

Some were concerned about the impact *Garcia* would have on state and local revenue and policy. The conservative Richmond *Times Dispatch* headlined an article on the ruling "Boosts U.S. at States' Expense." But much critical media attention was directed at the dissenters rather than the majority. Applauding what it termed the Court's return to a "sensible federalism," the *New York Times* scored the dissenters as justices who "like to be seen wearing the robes of judicial restraint" but in *Garcia* were "actually wearing the sweatier jerseys of judicial 'activists,' meddling in the political process." In her dissent, Justice O'Connor accused the majority of violating the "spirit" rather than letter of the Constitution. Her choice of language, common among those supporting flexible constitutional constructions, was not lost on the *Times*. Even George Will, the conservative columnist, considered the dissenters' rhetoric outmoded "Jeffersonian residue." The Reagan administration, Will observed, had submitted a brief supporting the position that prevailed in the Court.[40]

Following Justice Blackmun's retirement, a Rehnquist Court majority would again strike down a number of congressional statutes on state sovereignty grounds. But the position Blackmun belatedly embraced on the issues raised in *Usery* and *Garcia* would generally prevail for the balance of his career.[41]

"To Get beyond Racism"

However realistic in a modern, complex society Justice Blackmun's *Garcia* rationale might have seemed to George Will and other conservatives, they viewed with alarm the Nixon appointee's increasingly liberal stance on most civil liberties issues. When the Court first confronted affirmative action in higher education, Blackmun not only endorsed race-conscious admissions policies, which Justice Powell defended in the prevailing opinion for *Regents v. Bakke* (1978), but also voted to uphold the use of racial admissions quotas, which Powell found unconstitutional.[42]

Characteristically, though, Blackmun did not reach those conclusions quickly or easily. Allan Bakke, a white applicant denied admission to medical school in the University of California at Davis, had challenged a policy under which sixteen of one hundred first-year slots were reserved for disadvantaged minority applicants. After a trial court invalidated the program yet refused to order Bakke's admission, the California Supreme Court affirmed the lower court findings that the program was illegal and also ordered Bakke admitted to the medical school.

When *Bakke* reached Washington, Blackmun voted to deny certiorari and privately termed the Court's decision to review the case "for me… a matter of regret." He was, he explained in a personal memo, "sufficiently satisfied by the result reached by a liberal state court of high repute and by the briefs in opposition filed by ongoing organizations highly regarded for their sensitivity on civil rights." The justice had a hope, "perhaps a forlorn one," he conceded, "that with the passage of a few more years the Nation will mature in its attitude and practice in this area of admissions policy, and that all will come to accept the fact that applicants are to be evaluated and judged...according to ability and promise of accomplishment. Then racial and like considerations may be abandoned as outmoded tools temporarily utilized to meet a situation with respect to which maturity and basic fairness had yet to be achieved." But because the Court "in its wisdom," he resignedly added, had "chose[n] to plunge once more into what essentially is an issue of social policy,...the case must be decided."[43]

Successful prostate surgery at the Mayo Clinic sidelined the justice from November 11, 1977, until early January 1978. By late April, he had still not cast a vote in *Bakke*, much to the dismay of his colleagues. On May 1, he outlined his position—and defended his slow pace—in a thirteen-page memorandum to the conference. "The Chief, not inappropriately," he wrote, "has been pressing me for a vote." Although "constantly stewing about the *Bakke* case," he had "purposefully and I think properly" given priority to his other work. Except for *Bakke*, he assured his colleagues, with characteristic defensiveness, he had "held nothing off either for a dissent or for any other reason."[44]

The justice's memorandum furnished clear signals about the position he would ultimately assume in *Bakke*. If the nation were ever to realize its goal of a "society that is not race conscious," he asserted, it must first confront its exceedingly small percentage of minority doctors, lawyers, and medical and law students. He also found irony in the degree to which people were "so convulsed and deeply disturbed" over race-conscious admissions, yet "evinced [little] concern" about the "fact that institutions of higher learning for many years have given conceded preferences up to a point to the skilled athlete, to the children of alumni, to the affluent who may bestow their largesse on the institution, and to those having connections with celebrities and the famous."

Allan Bakke had contended that the admission scheme he was challenging violated not only the Fourteenth Amendment equal protection clause, but also Title VI of the 1964 Civil Rights Act, which prohibited discrimination by federally funded programs, such as the University of

California at Davis. In arguing that the Davis arrangement violated Title VI, Bakke and others had drawn on remarks made by Senator Hubert Humphrey, Blackmun's fellow Minnesotan, during congressional debate over the legislation. The justice was not convinced. "Hubert's emphasis was inclusive, not exclusive. I suspect, from what I know of the Senator, there could be only one answer for him to the *Bakke* case; indeed, I doubt he would find it very difficult at all."

On the equal protection issue, Blackmun argued that "racial and ethnic distinctions where they are stereotypes [were] inherently suspect and call for exacting judicial scrutiny." But affirmative action programs were "benign" and "free of stigma" directed at any race. Indeed, although the justice conceded that affirmative action conflicted with the sort of "idealistic equality" for which Justice Rehnquist had been arguing in opposing all race-conscious policies, Blackmun thought such programs were consistent with the Fourteenth Amendment's original purpose "until [true] equality is achieved. In this sense, equal protection may be used as a shield."

At that point, Justice Powell was circulating his opinion endorsing the admissions policies of Harvard and other elite universities at which "race or ethnic background is put forward as only one of many factors" considered in admissions decisions. Blackmun agreed that such "middle-road" schemes "seem[ed] to be much...better" than the Davis program, which was susceptible "to labeling as a blatant quota-system." But for the justice, the line between the two types of programs was "a thin one. In each, subjective application is at work. At worst, one could say that under the Harvard program one may accomplish covertly what Davis does openly....I think the Davis program is within constitutional bounds, though perhaps barely so."[45]

Remarkably in a document intended for his colleagues, Blackmun next engaged in a bit of sociological commentary. Yale law professor Alexander Bickel, among others, opposed affirmative action on the ground that equal protection prohibited all racial discrimination, regardless of skin color. Toward the end of his memorandum, Blackmun acknowledged that "Alex Bickel's elegant and shining words...speak of the idealistic and have great appeal." But ours, the justice insisted, was "not an ideal world, yet." Then he continued: "Of course, [Bickel's] position is—and I hope I offend no one, for I do not mean to do so—the 'accepted' Jewish approach. It is to be noted that nearly all the responsible Jewish organizations who have filed amicus briefs here are [on] one side of the case. They understandably want 'pure' equality and are willing to take their chances with it, knowing that they have the inherent ability to excel and to live with it successfully. Centuries of persecution and adversity and discrimination have given the Jewish people this great attribute to compete successfully and this remarkable fortitude."[46]

In closing, the justice thanked his colleagues for their patience but was by no means penitent. "For me," he wrote, "this case is of such importance that I refused to be drawn to a precipitate conclusion. I wanted the time to think about it and to study the pertinent material. Because weeks are still available before the end of the term, I do not apologize; I merely explain."

When the Court's ruling was announced at the end of the 1977–78 term, it was immediately evident that the justices were as divided as the rest of the nation over affirmative action. The classic swing justice of the Burger era, Justice Powell, joined by four justices, struck down the Davis quota scheme. Joined by four other justices, however, he held that institutions could consider race, among other nonacademic factors, in attempting to assure a diverse student body and the educational benefits such diversity was claimed to provide. As suggested by his memorandum, Blackmun joined Brennan, White, and Marshall in voting to uphold the Davis program on the ground that the chronic underrepresentation of minorities in the medical profession justified the remedial use of a racial admissions quota. Justice Stevens, joined by Burger, Stewart, and Rehnquist, argued, on the other hand, that any use of race in the medical school's admissions policies violated Title VI of the Civil Rights Act.

A separate opinion Justice Blackmun filed in the case largely tracked his earlier memorandum but also included what would become perhaps the most quoted passage from the various *Bakke* opinions. "In order to get beyond racism," the justice declared, "we must first take account of race. There is no other way. And in order to treat some persons equally, we must treat them differently. We cannot—we dare not—let the Equal Protection Clause perpetuate racial supremacy."[47]

Although not in the league with the enormous volume of mail the justice's *Roe* opinion continued to attract, *Bakke* drew its share of venom.

"You sir," one Nevada man wrote Blackmun, "are a lousy Supreme Court Justice. YOUR MIND IS CLUTTERED WITH CLAP TRAP." *Bakke* called for an answer only to the question "whether using RACE as a criteri[on] for anything be CONSTITUTIONAL," not whether that was "good or bad, desirable or not." The letter writer obviously had no doubt as to the response the Court should have given. "Anyone displaying an ounce of brains could answer with one word, NO." A Los Angeles writer ridiculed the Court for "believ[ing] that reverse racial discrimination, if not *too* obvious, is O.K., [and] that will make up to Uncle Amos, long since dead [and] buried by giving racist [and] racism points to young *un*discriminated against blacks of today!"[48]

Press coverage of Blackmun's opinion, however, was generally positive. The *Time* correspondent Simmons Fentress also took the time to write a letter to the justice, expressing his "admiration" for what Blackmun had written. Fentress, a North Carolina native, had found it difficult, "even in casual social intercourse," to support the university's position. "In my bones I knew that position to be responsible and right; I knew it took into account the sad story that is American history where race is concerned. Yet it was a position that was tough to argue, especially since it so clearly damaged Mr. Bakke." The journalist had been "frankly surprised," therefore, that four justices shared his views. "I was almost thrilled," he wrote, "when I read those words of yours: 'In order to get beyond racism, we must first take account of race.'... How true, and how eloquent."[49]

Fentress had recently discussed *Bakke* with a friend, a Georgia native and Baltimore lawyer who represented a steel company in race and sex discrimination cases. "He surprised me by saying that if he were a justice in the case he would vote to uphold the Davis plan. How so? I asked. 'It's a question of who pays for slavery, the blacks or the whites,' he told me." Fentress thought the justice and his lawyer friend were saying essentially the same thing. He predicted, moreover, that "yours is an opinion that will mean something fifty or a hundred years from now."[50]

For the balance of his career, Justice Blackmun would persist in his support of the use of race as a means of getting beyond racism. When the Court struck down a set-aside program for minority subcontractors, for example, he declared in a brief, biting dissent:

I never thought that I would live to see the day when the city of Richmond, Virginia, the cradle of the Old Confederacy, sought on its own, within a narrow confine, to lessen the stark impact of persistent discrimination. But Richmond, to its great credit, acted. Yet this Court, the supposed bastion of equality, strikes down Richmond's efforts as though discrimination had never existed or was not demonstrated in this particular litigation.... The Court today regresses. I am confident, however, that, given time, it one day again will do its best to fulfill the great promises of the Constitution's Preamble and of the guarantees embodied in the Bill of Rights—a fulfillment that would make this Nation very special.[51]

Going Public

When the justice's *Bakke* dissent appeared, William A. Holmes, the minister of Washington's Metropolitan Memorial United Methodist Church, which the Blackmuns faithfully attended, also wrote the justice an admiring letter. Blackmun had arranged for Holmes to attend the Court session at which the *Bakke* decision was announced and to visit the justice's chambers afterward. In his letter, the minister termed the experience "one of those 'special moments' in one's lifetime which will be recalled and savored for years to come." The letter also left no doubt where Holmes's sympathies about the issues in *Bakke* lay. "With as much objectivity as I can muster, it seems to me that the opinions rendered by you and your three colleagues clearly represented the most profound awareness of our nation's history in regard to race, as well as the most morally incisive interpretation of the Constitution as it pertains to the redress of that history. Being aware of the complexity and genuinely ambiguous dilemmas posed by Bakke, I would have honored and respected the integrity of your decision if you had arrived at some other opinion, but I confess to be deeply proud and grateful that you came out where you did." For Holmes, "being present to see a friend and member of my congregation declare himself unequivocally on one of the most difficult and far reaching moral issues of our time—that was the greatest privilege of all."[52]

Holmes and his congregation regularly assumed liberal and progressive positions on a variety of social, political, and legal issues. Some have suggested that the Blackmuns' close association with their church may have reinforced the justice's resolve with respect to abortion, affirmative action, and other controversial issues confronting the Court.

An enduring friendship the justice forged with a University of Chicago law dean may have played an even greater role, however, in bolstering Blackmun's confidence and the tenacity with which he defended his constitutional agenda. Blackmun met Norval Morris, a leading scholar on criminal justice and penology, when the justice first attended the annual Seminar on Law and Society at the Aspen Institute in 1975. In 1977, Institute officials approached Blackmun about moderating one of their two-week seminars. The justice's recuperation from prostate surgery—and anxieties over his adequacy for the task—prompted several delays. But he finally agreed to moderate his first seminar in August 1979. The "clinching factor" in his decision finally to yield to the Institute's repeated invitations, he wrote Morris, "was your presence as [co]moderator."[53]

Blackmun would continue to hold the August seminars—whose participants each year included some two dozen leaders in American business, law, and government—until 1995, a year after his retirement. Always a lover of nature, he and Dottie attempted to spend some time each summer at a cottage on Spider Lake in Wisconsin. He found the spectacular mountain setting of Aspen, Colorado, especially invigorating and the congenial, overwhelmingly supportive audience immensely gratifying. The sessions were wide-ranging and philosophical rather than narrowly jurisprudential, with one day each year devoted to *Roe* and its progeny. One year Pamela Karlan and her Blackmun coclerk Beth Heifetz visited the seminar for "*Roe* Day"; later, Karlan served two summers as moderator of other seminars. "For the most part," she recalls, "there weren't lectures. The moderator would give about fifteen or twenty minutes' worth of comments, and then throw it open to discussion among the participants. The one exception was *Roe* day, when the justice would talk much longer. He loved it. He liked being out there, and he liked the participants."[54]

The *Roe* sessions affected Blackmun and his audiences deeply, with the justice and those in attendance often becoming quite emotional. Ed Lazarus, among other former clerks, believes that the Aspen experience may have affected the justice's judicial decisions. "I think an aspect of his life that's underappreciated was the time he spent at the Aspen Institute.... To me, that experience was very important to the justice.... That was a couple of really happy weeks for the justice, away from the everyday pressures of the Court, where he could think about some of the broader issues.... I think that time was very meaningful for him as a time for reflection. The kinds of things that he talked about in those seminars may well have had a liberalizing influence on him."[55]

In a study of the justice's Aspen association, the law professor Dennis Hutchinson also suggests that the Institute may have been "a catalyst for [his] metamorphosis" as a liberal. At Aspen, writes Hutchinson, "The summa cum laude graduate in mathematics from Harvard College...was exposed to classical political theory and jurisprudence for the first time in more than four decades, and, perhaps really for the first time in his life. His interaction with Morris and the distinguished students in the yearly seminars, allowed Blackmun to redefine his job, as a jurist committed to espousing the standards of a just society rather than as a judge simply navigating case law."[56]

Others, including Professor Karlan, doubt that the Aspen experience had a significant substantive influence on the justice's positions. After all, "he was already as far left as any of them on issues like abortion." Indisputably, though, those summers in Colorado strengthened Blackmun's confidence as a justice and the stubborn resolve with which he defended his jurisprudence. As Hutchinson notes, the justice "redefined his image [at Aspen] as well, from the man out of his depth to the plain-spoken tribune of the people, armed with both candor and media savvy. Aspen always awaited at the end of each term as an intellectual and emotional safe house where he could return as a local hero."[57]

The beginnings of Blackmun's Aspen association, as Hutchinson correctly observes, also corresponded roughly with his increasingly consistent selection of "clerks who were eager to see law used as an instrument for social change," whose "support, both intellectually and emotionally, helped keep his transformation on course." Whether Blackmun substantially changed over time or, as he often claimed, the Court and issues did, the justice's papers suggest that his later contingents of clerks rather uniformly sought to push Blackmun in liberal directions. His association with

Roe probably accounted as much as anything else for that trend; liberal clerk applicants were drawn to *Roe*'s author—at least if they were unable to obtain clerkships with Brennan or Marshall. As in the past, the justice's passive management style continued to enhance the influence of his clerks as well. Clearly, he was not as disengaged from the substantive issues confronting the Court as David Garrow, among others, has contended. But the significant role the justice's clerks played in drafting his opinions undoubtedly had a meaningful impact on his judicial record and, even more important, constantly reinforced his positions on issues before the Court. To a greater degree perhaps than in most other chambers, Blackmun's clerks played a major part in the selection of their successors, thereby helping to assure slots for like-minded replacements—and the perpetuation of an essentially liberal mind-set in the justice's chambers.[58]

The Brethren, for which he agreed to be interviewed, appeared in 1979. Its authors, among others, claimed that several of Blackmun's colleagues, including Brennan and Stewart, considered him inadequate as a justice. Such unflattering accounts no doubt fueled his own considerable self-doubts. As Aspen and supportive clerks bolstered his confidence, however, Blackmun began to take his case to the public. As early as 1975 he had begun to suggest that members of the Court should stay attuned to grass-roots sentiments in the nation. "I think it's so easy," he told a reporter for the *St. Paul Pioneer* that year, "for us to stay in our ivory tower and not get out. I think we're too confined at times. It doesn't seem to me that we should hit the political circuit, but it's good to hear the voices of America from a different podium than the rostrum before us." Rating the Court from "conservative" (Rehnquist, Burger, White, and Powell) to "liberal" (Douglas, Stewart, Brennan, and Marshall), he characterized himself as "distinctly more near the middle than any of the others."[59]

By 1982, with several sessions at Aspen behind him, the justice had become even more outspoken. In an hour-long television interview on CNN with the reporter Daniel Schorr, whom he had met at Aspen, Blackmun displayed a new resilience. "Well, of course, it hurt at first," he acknowledged, referring to the abuse hurled at him after *Roe*. "[But] it doesn't hurt so much anymore, because I think one's hide gets a little…thick, to use the old phrase. On the other hand, I like to know what people are thinking. And the fact that 75 percent of the correspondence was critical doesn't mean that represents 75 percent of the population." On clashes with his colleagues, he was remarkably blunt. "If somebody's going to play hardball with me, I'll play hardball back if I firmly believe in the position, although I suppose that if I were completely a gentleman I wouldn't." But he also displayed the pixie side of his personality. The previous year, some of his colleagues had heard a faint electronic ringing sound in the justices' secret conference room and thought the room might be bugged. Blackmun realized that his hearing aid was the source of the noise but, "feeling mischievous," waited a few days before telling the others. "The secret was out and we all laughed about it."[60]

Only three other justices—Hugo Black, William O. Douglas, and Potter Stewart, when the last announced his retirement the previous year—had allowed themselves to be questioned before television cameras while still sitting judges. But Blackmun was exceptional in his willingness to comment during his interview with Schorr about other justices. He also became the first member of the Court publicly to praise *The Brethren*. After his daughter Susan read it, he said, she told her father, "For the first time in my life I think I have an idea of what your work amounts to and what you're trying to do." If *The Brethren* did that "for a lot of people," said the justice, "I think maybe it served a purpose." But he always told law classes, he added defensively and somewhat inaccurately, "that if you're going to read [it], don't stop after 30 pages because I smell pretty bad for those 30 pages, but read the whole thing....Maybe personally and from a very selfish point of view, I think I'm not so bad after the full number of pages."[61]

Several months after the CNN interview, the justice, pictured standing with arms crossed on the steps to the Court's main entrance, was the subject of a cover profile in the *New York Times Magazine*. "Just a few years back," the writer John Jenkins began, "Harry A. Blackmun was nearly an invisible Justice, widely dismissed, in his own resentful words, as 'a stepchild of others on the Court.'" Despite *Roe*, "his early years on the Court were mostly distinguished by what appeared to be indecisiveness." Recently, however, he had emerged "as the Court's most unlikely crusader, a jurist determined to make the Court responsive not only to individuals—'One has to be aware that human beings are involved in all these cases,' he says—but also to 'prevent it from plunging rapidly to the right.'"[62]

Jenkins attributed Blackmun's "unprecedented candor" during the interview as much to "personal resentment" as to concern about the future direction of the Court. "I have a little anger underneath it all," the justice said. "Anger from being categorized over the 12 years I've been here in a way that I think never fit." Presumably he was speaking of his characterization as Chief Justice Burger's "appendage," the "subordinate half of the 'Minnesota Twins,'" as Jenkins put it. In describing Burger, Blackmun made a half-hearted attempt to be charitable. The chief justice, he assured the writer at one point, "has a soft spot,…as everybody does—if one can find it!" Later he said that Burger "has a great heart in him, and he's a very fine human being when you get to know him, when the tensions are off. One has to remember, too, that he's under strain almost constantly. I think he's tired, as all of us are tired." But he insisted the two had enjoyed a close relationship only during Blackmun's first years on the Court. Since that time, he observed, "our closeness has lessened considerably. He doesn't come down here to the chambers, although others stop in on occasion. Socially, I don't see him at all." Did Burger feel that his boyhood friend had "betrayed" him? Jenkins asked. "It wouldn't surprise me if he felt that way," Blackmun replied. "But I'm not going to be a stand-in for anybody. I'm not going to be a No. 2 vote for anybody. I never have been, and I don't intend to be."[63]

Blackmun's resentment of the chief justice by that point was obvious. Burger, he declared, "was never very enthusiastic about joining the [*Roe*] majority," and since *Roe*, he observed "with exasperation," the chief justice had "gone the other way on abortion." Blackmun had also continued to fume over Burger's attempt in the *Gannett Press* case to confine Justice Stewart's prevailing opinion to the closing of pretrial proceedings only, not trials. "I [still] cannot understand it. He tried to make [the ruling] into a pretrial thing in the face of Potter Stewart's much broader language. I just think it doesn't fit in a scholarly way."[64]

The profile's assessment of Blackmun's own legal scholarship was far from flattering. Yale Kamisar, the University of Michigan law professor who had predicted years before that Blackmun might well prove to be a different sort of justice than the Nixon administration anticipated, thought much criticism of the justice's jurisprudence was simply a matter of style. "He's a plodder. No charisma. No commanding presence. No one would ever take him for a Supreme Court Justice. When I think of someone to compare Blackmun to, it's Harry Truman. Just like Truman, Blackmun has said in effect: 'What am I doing here? I didn't deserve the appointment, but I'm going to make the most of it, and I'm going to convince people by the time I leave that I deserved it.' "[65]

But others, Jenkins noted, questioned the quality of the justice's opinions, especially their general lack of rigorous analysis. In 1980, Burt Neuborne, a New York University law professor and national director of the ACLU, wrote an article in which he termed Blackmun "a significant centrist force on the court," whose opinions were "non-ideological, technically satisfactory, [and] intuitively fair." Neuborne sent the justice a copy of the manuscript. In a thank-you note that Blackmun ultimately chose not to mail, the grateful justice expressed his "appreciation for your considerateness and understanding and 'tender' approach," adding, "I am not used to this kind of thing, especially from New England or the East." But Neuborne had also expressed doubt in his article about Blackmun's "ability to express his results in a persuasive, doctrinally acceptable manner," prompting a humble promise from the justice to "do my best to fulfill the challenge which is implicit in your writing."[66]

In the *Times* profile, Neuborne lamented some of Blackmun's early opinions as "just wretched" and recalled that "in the civil-liberties community, we just despaired. We couldn't believe anyone could be that insensitive [to individual rights]!" At the time of Jenkins's profile, though, "the civil-liberties community looks to him as a very important third vote [along with Brennan and Marshall] on the Court." But Neuborne continued to have doubts about Blackmun's skills as a jurist. "To my mind, Blackmun is a terrific dispute resolver, but he is not a great teacher. He's a brilliant pragmatist, but only a passable theoretician." Another, unnamed constitutional law professor agreed. "What is lacking...is an explanation of how he decided as he did. Even some of his most important opinions and concurrences and dissents are just very personal statements without any law in them. They lack the reasoned foundation that a better justice would lay."[67]

In his interview with Jenkins, Blackmun professed to be entirely unconcerned about such criticism. "I'm not a 'jurisprude.' I couldn't be an expert in jurisprudence if I wanted to be....I don't have the intellect for it. [But] I do not think I've been inconsistent." Whatever his jurisprudential failings, moreover, Jenkins's portrait of the human qualities reflected in

Blackmun's opinions was entirely positive. His growing reputation as the justice most sensitive to the needs of society's outsiders got ample play. "We're dealing with *people*—the life, liberty and property of *people*. And because I grew up in poor surroundings, I know there's another world out there that we sometimes forget about." The profile also underscored his innate humility. Although his net worth was now "well into six figures," he still drove to Court in his old blue Volkswagen. He was "a favorite of Court clerks and staff" and even had a "well-developed mischievous streak." When President Reagan appointed Sandra Day O'Connor as the first woman justice in 1981, Blackmun soon heard the rumor that she and Justice Rehnquist, who were law school classmates at Stanford, had once dated. After taking the oath, the Court's newest member was seated on the bench next to Rehnquist, whom Blackmun promptly but playfully admonished, "No fooling around." A charming, intimate photograph of the justice and Dottie Blackmun, both grinning broadly, graced the profile as well.[68]

Finally, and inevitably, the justice touched on the controversy *Roe* had spawned, including the more than forty-five thousand letters he had received to that point since the decision was announced. Itemizing once again the hateful names with which he had been tagged, he described himself as "fatalistic" about his safety. "I'm in my 70's now. I've lived a good life.... If something's going to happen, it's going to happen."[69]

"Couldn't Care Less"

Whatever his growing visibility may have done for Blackmun's standing as a significant member of the Court, the justice obviously remained the principal target of the antiabortion movement. Perhaps as part of an effort to divert some of the heat to other members of the Court, Justice Powell was assigned to speak for the majority in *Akron v. Akron Center for Reproductive Health* (1983), substantially reaffirming *Roe* several months after the *Times* profile appeared. "I think," Blackmun's clerk David Ogden remarked, "that the justice may have thought in his private heart that Burger gave [Powell] the assignment to deprive Blackmun of the honor.... I am certain Justice Blackmun did not ask that it be done that way. I am sure that he would have relished [the assignment]....[But] for Justice Blackmun...that actually wasn't a bad thing because it did demonstrate that" he was not solely responsible for the Court's abortion rulings.[70]

Afterward, Justice Powell did receive at least one death threat. Even so, antiabortion extremists continued to consider Blackmun the chief "Architect of the American Holocaust," in the words of a New Jersey man who regularly bombarded the justice's chambers and home with the vilest sort of hate mail. Death threats were not uncommon either. Declaring that the justice's "tortured legal logic will cost millions their lives," one anonymous correspondent mailed Blackmun this chilling message: "I am preparing myself for sacrifice. You and I will enter eternity together before the year is over. It will happen outside Washington. It will happen when you least expect it. I dress well, belong to no political party, and have a pleasant middle-age prosperous appearance. I am ready to die."[71]

Shortly before that letter arrived at the Court, the justice received a death threat, purportedly from the "Army of God," a group that had claimed responsibility for recent attacks on abortion clinics around the nation. The threat contained no signature but bore the return address of "D. Maguire, Marquette University." Marquette professor Daniel Maguire told reporters in Wisconsin that his name had been forged on the letter.[72]

When Alfred Wong, the Supreme Court marshal, asked Blackmun "for some authorization...for personal protection," the justice reluctantly complied. "I have never been greatly concerned or alarmed by things of this kind and generally have gone my own way without too many incidents," he wrote Wong. "Your office and the FBI, however, undoubtedly know far more about all this than I do. I only know of the receipt of the letter and the persistent press inquiries. You have my authority to do whatever you feel is indicated under the circumstances. I must rely on your good judgment as to this. I do not wish to embarrass the Court in any way."[73]

While the justices heard oral argument in four cases that day, guards were doubled at the Court's two main entrances and three officers were posted inside the courtroom. But Blackmun's letter to Wong prompted a pointed response from the chief justice, who appeared primarily intent on underscoring just who was boss at the Court. "First," Burger informed Blackmun, "it should be clear that when there is any real threat to any

Justice or to the Court, security measures will be taken." But the "first step" in such situations was "to advise me of the problem and of any requests." The Blackmuns were planning a trip to Atlanta for a talk the justice was to give at Emory Law School and a visit to their daughter Sally, an Emory law student, who had given birth to their latest granddaughter a few days earlier. Wong and Burger, the chief justice wrote, had already decided that deputy marshals would meet the Blackmuns at the Atlanta airport and escort them to their hotel. "Depending on your moves in Atlanta and during your stay," added Burger, "other measures will be taken."[74]

But Burger was also quick to point out, somewhat pompously, that Blackmun was not the only target of threats. "Threats to me, as one may guess, are by no means uncommon, including 'sick' people coming out to the house." Jon Hinckley, the young man who had attempted to assassinate President Reagan in 1981, was "sick," after all, "when he shot the President, so caution is indicated." Apparently assuming that Blackmun's chambers were the source for news reports of the death threat against the justice, the chief justice emphasized, too, that "security experts" had advised him years ago "that threats should not be made public, in part because one 'nut' act [or] threat inspires and stimulates others." Blackmun had been provided a police escort to and from the Court. If the justice "wish[ed] to continue" that arrangement "and coverage at Atlanta," Burger concluded, "it will, of course, be provided."

Blackmun's rejoinder to the chief justice that same day was courteous but frosty. First, he vigorously denied any implication in Burger's letter that he or his staff had been the source of news reports about the death threat. A reporter had telephoned after the threatening letter arrived, asking for the justice's reaction. "My chambers did not acknowledge receipt of the letter in question but stated that I periodically receive letters of a threatening nature and those letters are routinely forwarded to the Supreme Court marshal." In fact, he added, it was his understanding that the Court's public information office, not his staff, had confirmed the letter in response to a reporter's inquiries. "This was followed by a barrage of calls from other reporters, including some who showed up at the apartment yesterday morning (Dottie refused to see them). To this moment," the justice insisted, "I do not know how or why information as to the receipt of this letter got into the hands of the media."[75]

The justice also made it clear that he had not initiated any request for additional security. Instead, "the note I gave Mr. Wong was in response to a request from his office that I write something. Why such a formal request was needed, I do not know." FBI Director William Webster, the Blackmuns' friend, had informed him that the threat should not be taken "lightly," and the justice saw no alternative other than to comply with the directions of the Court police and marshal, who had also decided to have a marshal accompany the Blackmuns on their flights to and from Atlanta. Ending his letter, the justice assured Burger that he was "grateful for all this and deeply appreciate the considerateness that has been displayed," yet he could not resist a parting shot. "In some respects," he wrote, "I couldn't care less."[76]

During security preparations for another trip to Atlanta in December, Blackmun wrote Burger again, reminding the chief justice of his earlier statement "about all this security business," and adding, "I still feel that way....I dislike the loss of my freedom and do not like to live this way." An escort between the airport and his daughter's home would be "acceptable," but he was, he emphasized, "mak[ing] no request" for security on the flight to and from Atlanta. He had "specifically" asked that "I be completely free when we are in Georgia for the few days next week." Apparently, Burger had informed the justices of security arrangements made for his travels. "What you do and how you are protected," wrote Blackmun, "is a different matter, for you are the Chief Justice and the rest of us are somewhat expendable." For some reason, he was particularly resistant to Burger's suggestion that he defer to the expertise of Marshal Wong. "I know nothing about what you say is Mr. Wong's great experience in these matters. He has offered me nothing." Any assistance Blackmun received, he informed Burger, had come from the Court police and marshals in the field.[77]

An incident in the winter of 1985 may have shaken somewhat Blackmun's professed indifference about his safety. As his secretary Wanda Martinson pulled into the Court driveway on Friday morning, March 1, a member of the Court police, "instead of waving me through to my parking spot from the kiosk, approached my car, an awful look on his face, and said, 'Now, everything's all right, but I want you to know that we were at the justice's apartment last night.'" The previous evening, a slug from a 9 mm handgun had shattered a living room window, showering Dottie Blackmun with glass and lodging in an apartment chair in which she had been sitting only moments before. Justice Blackmun had just left the room, and neither he nor his wife was injured. But the officer wanted Martinson to know "before I got upstairs, so ... I could get myself together before I saw the justice. By that point, I had been with the justice long enough to be family, so I was upset."[78]

On Monday of the following week, in response to a query from a wire service reporter, the justice's chambers issued a terse statement: "A shot went through the window of the Blackmun home last Thursday, February 28. No one was injured. The matter is under investigation." Martinson also told reporters that the justice had been placed under constant protection, and all his mail was being screened.[79]

The media, public officials, and friends assumed the worst. One editorial cartoon pictured two people driving by a roadside billboard. "I remember," the driver was saying, "when the lunatic fringe was satisfied with 'Impeach Earl Warren.'" The billboard read, "Shoot Harry Blackmun—The Army of God." Randall Bezanson, the clerk who largely drafted Blackmun's *Roe* opinion, found it "hard to express [his] feelings of outrage as well as regret and utter disappointment. I feel more sadness than anger. I have marveled at your strength over the years following *Roe v. Wade*, and I am certain this is testing your limits." Oregon senator Bob Packwood, himself a recent recipient of a death threat from the "Aryan Nations," another hate group, bemoaned the "tragedy that great leaders in history have had to live with fear for their lives simply by expressing and upholding a definition of liberty and freedom." In a letter to a newspaper, Peter Dorsey of the justice's old law firm decried the "new terrorism ... seemingly encouraged and sanctioned by a sanctimonious, special interest group." A medical friend even attempted to add some levity to the affair, expressing hope that the justice could "take some solace from Winston Churchill's statement, 'There is nothing quite so exhilarating as being shot at without result.'"[80]

The justice sought to reassure friends. "Mrs. Blackmun and I are fine, and that little incident is well behind us," he wrote one. "Dottie and I are fine," he wrote another. "All this is part of living in the Washington goldfish bowl." "We, indeed, shall 'hang in there' and not let those guys get us down," he assured yet another friend. But he also admitted to another that the incident had been "somewhat disturbing."[81]

And well he and his family should have been alarmed. Although initially suspicious that an antiabortion group was responsible for the shooting, the FBI ultimately found no conclusive evidence of foul play. In a statement released over ten months after the incident, the Bureau reported that "an examination conducted by the FBI laboratory determined that the shot was fired by a handgun, and, based on the trajectory and velocity, was probably fired from a location across the Potomac River under circumstances that greatly exceeded the accuracy of a handgun."[82]

Even so, the shooting, combined with the continuing onslaught of hate mail, must have been unnerving to the justice, and undoubtedly to his family. Shortly before the incident, a typewritten letter had arrived at his chambers. The sender vowed to kill the justice and "laugh" at his funeral. The previous January, a Rochester, Minnesota, man, identified by the local police chief as a "complete kook," telephoned the chambers, describing himself as an "angel of death." The caller, who gave his name, had no police record but was a suspect in a robbery and several rapes. Shortly after the shooting, a letter writer demanded $2 million or else the next bullet "will connect with your head." Most of the threats were the rants of disturbed but harmless persons. But the justice and his loved ones could never be certain which of the "crazies," as one law professor friend termed them, might represent a serious threat to the justice's life.[83]

The Reagan administration's attitude toward *Roe* was no help either. In January before the shooting, more than seventy thousand abortion opponents gathered at the steps of the Court. Speaking to the crowd from the White House via a telephone/loudspeaker hookup, President Reagan, in a manner reminiscent of southern segregationist politicians following civil rights murders, condemned recent violence at abortion clinics, as did Reverend Jerry Falwell of the "Moral Majority" and other speakers. But Reagan also encouraged his audiences to "end the national tragedy of abortion." Such rhetoric by the nation's highest official, like the earlier defiance of segregationist leaders in the South, undoubtedly added fuel to the flames of the abortion controversy and unfortunately may have encouraged those who saw violence as the solution to *Roe*.[84]

"The Right to Be Let Alone"

Opposition to *Roe* and whatever concerns Blackmun had about his personal safety in no way inhibited his commitment to causes he considered just. At the end of the Burger era, he unleashed one of his most memorable dissents when the Court refused to extend the right of privacy to homosexual sodomy. In Georgia, police arrested Michael Hardwick for violating that state's sodomy statute after discovering him having sex with another man in his apartment. When the local prosecutor delayed taking the case to a grand jury pending further investigation, Hardwick, fearing prosecution, brought a civil rights suit challenging the sodomy statute's constitutionality. An Eleventh Circuit panel struck down the statute on substantive due process and related grounds, and the state appealed. In *Bowers v. Hardwick* (1986), a 5–4 Court, per Justice White, upheld the law, as applied to homosexual relations. Emphasizing that sodomy was still forbidden in many states, White rejected Hardwick's contention that a right to engage in such conduct was deeply rooted in American legal traditions and fundamental to liberty. Nor did Hardwick's claim, declared White, find support in the Court's privacy precedents, which involved family relationships, marriage, and procreation, activities bearing little resemblance to any right to engage in homosexual sodomy. Also to no avail was Hardwick's reliance on *Stanley v. Georgia* (1969), the Warren Court decision affirming a right to possess obscenity in the privacy of one's home. That case, White concluded, was based on the First Amendment, not on privacy notions having no basis in the Constitution's text.[85]

For White, a *Roe* dissenter, the Court had an obligation to construe narrowly whatever power it possessed "to discover new fundamental rights imbedded in the Due Process Clause," and for reasons that were obvious to the justice:

> The Court is most vulnerable and comes nearest to illegitimacy when it deals with judge-made constitutional law having little or no cognizable roots in the language or design of the Constitution. That this is so was painfully demonstrated by the face-off between the Executive and the Court in the 1930's, which

resulted in the repudiation of much of the substantive gloss that the Court had placed on the Due Process Clause of the Fifth and Fourteenth Amendments. There should be, therefore, great resistance to expand the substantive reach of those clauses, particularly if it requires redefining the category of rights deemed to be fundamental. Otherwise, the Judiciary necessarily takes to itself further authority to govern the country without express constitutional authority.

Any notion that substantive due process included a right to engage in homosexual sodomy, declared White, was, "at best, facetious."[86]

Initially, however, White had been a *Bowers* dissenter. At conference, five members of the Court, including Justice Blackmun, had voted to uphold Hardwick's claims, with Justice Powell casting the decisive vote. In conference, Justice Blackmun praised the appeals court's "sound" decision sustaining Hardwick on substantive due process grounds. He also emphasized that the conduct at issue had been limited entirely to the home and construed *Stanley* to rest on privacy as well as First Amendment considerations. Powell, on the other hand, found Hardwick's privacy claims unpersuasive but thought the Georgia statute violated the Eighth Amendment guarantee against cruel and unusual punishment; ultimately, he rejected even that argument, changing his vote and the outcome of the case. Explaining his position in a *Bowers* concurrence, the justice reasoned that a prison sentence for "a single private, consensual act of sodomy...certainly a sentence of long duration—would create a serious Eighth Amendment issue." But Hardwick had not yet "been tried, much less convicted and sentenced." In fact, the Eighth Amendment issue had not even been raised in the lower court. Powell thus left that issue, and any relief for Hardwick, to another day.[87]

As he noted in the margin of a memo to his clerk, Powell obviously found *Bowers* "a most troublesome case." In 1990, after leaving the bench, he even told a law school audience that he had "probably made a mistake in that one." But Chief Justice Burger had no such concerns. At conference, Powell had suggested that criminal punishment of homosexual conduct was similar to prosecution of mere "status," which the Court in the past had declared a violation of the Eighth Amendment.

In a letter to the justice—which Powell found to contain "both sense and nonsense,...mostly the latter"—Burger ridiculed such thinking. "These homosexuals themselves proclaim this is a matter of sexual 'preference,' " he fumed. "Moreover, even if homosexuality is somehow conditioned, the decision to commit an act of sodomy is a choice, pure and simple—maybe not so pure!" *Bowers*, declared the chief justice, raised "the most far reaching issue" of his thirty years on the bench. "Incredible statement!" Powell noted in the margin of the letter.[88]

According to Pamela Karlan, the clerk assigned to *Bowers*, Justice Blackmun was "absolutely convinced" that Burger lobbied Powell vigorously to change his mind in the case. But Powell clearly did not share the chief justice's extreme views, much less his rhetoric, on the sodomy issue. Indeed, Burger's brief *Bowers* concurrence was only slightly more moderate in tone than his letter to Powell had been. Defending his contention "that in constitutional terms there is no such thing as a fundamental right to commit homosexual sodomy," the chief justice drew not only on the "ancient roots" of laws against sodomy, but on Blackstone's description of the " '*infamous crime against nature*' as an offense of 'deeper malignity' than rape, a heinous act 'the very mention of which is a disgrace to human nature,' and 'a crime not fit to be named.' " To hold that such conduct was somehow a constitutionally protected fundamental right, Burger declared, "would be to cast aside millennia of moral teaching."[89]

Although Karlan drafted Blackmun's dissent, which the justice then revised, Blackmun was very familiar with the issues *Bowers* raised. By that point he was devoting a portion of his annual remarks at Aspen to the historic debate between the British jurist Patrick Devlin and the legal scholar H. L. A. Hart, with Blackmun defending Hart's thesis, based on the philosophy of John Stuart Mill, that government had no business interfering with private acts that inflicted no harm on others merely because society considered such conduct "immoral."[90]

Blackmun, joined by Brennan, Marshall, and Stevens, began the dissent with the charge that Justice White's majority opinion reflected a fundamental misunderstanding of what *Bowers* was about. "This case," he declared, "is no more about 'a fundamental right to engage in homosexual sodomy,' than *Stanley*...was about a fundamental right to watch obscene movies, or *Katz v. United States* [extending the Fourth Amendment to electronic eavesdropping] was about a fundamental right to place interstate bets from a telephone booth." In fact, he found the majority's "almost obsessive focus on homosexual activity…particularly hard to justify in light of" the Georgia statute's ban on all sodomy, not merely homosexual intercourse. Instead, asserted the justice, *Bowers* involved what Justice Brandeis had termed " 'the most comprehensive of rights and the right most valued by civilized men,' namely, 'the right to be let alone.' " If that right meant anything, Blackmun exclaimed, it meant that "before Georgia can prosecute its citizens for making choices about the most intimate aspects of their life, it must do more than assert [as at least one Georgia case had claimed] that the choice they have made is an 'abominable crime not fit to be named among Christians.' "[91]

Blackmun also took issue with the majority's contention that earlier privacy cases were limited to family and procreation issues far afield from Hardwick's claim. That was true, he insisted, only in the most superficial sense. At bottom, they rested on the broad freedom of individuals to make choices in matters of sexual intimacy, including the selection of sexual partners. The *Bowers* majority erred, too, according to Blackmun, in construing *Stanley* as only another First Amendment case. The Court's opinion in *Stanley* made clear that that case rested squarely on privacy concerns central to the Fourth Amendment's meaning, not merely or even primarily on the First Amendment. "Indeed," he asserted, "the right of an individual to conduct intimate relationships in the intimacy of his or her home [was] the heart of the Constitution's protection of privacy."[92]

The justice found the state's arguments in support of the sodomy statute equally unimpressive. Georgia's position rested primarily on its authority to protect public morals. But such a rationale smacked of religious intolerance. Although "certain, but by no means all, religious groups condemn [sodomy]," the state had "no license to impose their [religious] judgments on the entire citizenry." The legitimacy of the state regulation, he asserted, "depend[ed] instead on…some [sort of] justification [going] beyond its conformity to religious doctrine." Yet there was none. "A State can no more punish private behavior because of religious intolerance than it can punish such behavior because of racial animus." In fact, added Blackmun, drawing on John Stuart Mill and H. L. A. Hart, the case "involve[d] no real interference with the rights of others," and "the mere knowledge that other individuals do not adhere to one's value system cannot be a legally cognizable interest,…let alone an interest that can justify invading the houses, hearts, and minds of citizens who choose to live their lives differently." Regulation of public conduct was one thing, but control of consensual conduct by adults in the privacy of the home quite another matter.[93]

During World War II, the Court had first upheld, then overturned, compulsory flag programs in the public schools. Concluding his *Bowers* dissent, Justice Blackmun recalled that historic dispute over compelled orthodoxy and declared, "I can only hope that here, too, the Court soon will reconsider its analysis and conclude that depriving individuals of the right to choose for themselves how to conduct their intimate relationships poses a far greater threat to the values most deeply rooted in our Nation's history than tolerance of nonconformity could ever do. Because I think the Court today betrays those values, I dissent."[94]

At the end of that term, Chief Justice Burger, always seemingly more interested in administrative matters than the substantive issues confronting the Court, left the bench to head the nation's celebration of the Constitution's bicentennial. Until his death in 1995, a year after Justice Blackmun's own retirement, Burger and his boyhood friend would continue to share greetings on special occasions, news about mutual friends, and other perfunctory exchanges. But whatever warm relationship they once enjoyed had ended years before. Blackmun had begun noting to clerks the chief justice's growing coldness toward him in the late 1970s, and his own remarks to clerks about Burger had grown increasingly caustic over the years.

At times, Blackmun's jabs at the chief justice were playful. As a sign of support for the Carter administration's austerity measures during the Mideast oil crisis of the late 1970s, the Blackmuns had begun driving to White House functions in the justice's old blue Volkswagen, often arriving immediately before or after Burger's chauffeured limousine. Blackmun delighted in pointing out the contrast to friends. When the chief justice, prompted by a lawyer in the solicitor general's office, suggested having counsel wear wigs during oral argument, Blackmun was appalled.

"He thought," Pamela Karlan recalls, that "wearing a wig to argue was the height of pompous lunacy. He used to call the chief the 'Great White Father,' sort of shake his head, and remark, 'he looks like a chief justice.' . . . I think he found the pomposity and the ceremonial stuff [very offensive]."[95]

At the end, Blackmun's estrangement from his childhood chum clearly ran deep. Each term, clerks in a justice's chambers traditionally took other justices to lunch. Once, while Blackmun was at lunch with Justice Marshall's clerks and began complaining about Burger, one of the clerks looked perplexed. "Weren't you best man at his wedding?" he asked. "You must have been friends." "The chief," Blackmun replied, "has no friends."[96]

When Burger died in 1995, Blackmun issued a gracious statement for the Court's public information office. The chief justice, he observed, had "served extraordinarily well as the head of our national judiciary." Burger's death after "a friendship that indeed was lifelong," he added, "instills a sensation of loneliness, not only for me but for the Court."[97]

The justice also contributed to a memorial issue of the law review at the William Mitchell College of Law, which the chief justice had attended. "Evaluators," he concluded, would find Burger's record "good," "a large 'plus' that the rest of us will be hard put to match." For such a tribute, however, Blackmun's statement was remarkably frank and revealing. It read in part, "Of course, Chief Justice Burger and I disagreed now and then as to the results to be reached in submitted cases. When we did, the disagreement often was basic and, on occasion, emphatic. He had little patience for disagreement. I do not know what he expected, but surely he could not have anticipated that I would be an ideological clone. He knew me better than that. But when disagreement came, his disappointment was evident and not concealed. The situation was not comfortable."[98]

Chapter 9

Changing the Guard

At least for the first several terms of William Rehnquist's tenure in the Supreme Court's center seat, Justice Blackmun apparently considered the new chief justice a decided improvement over his predecessor. Geoffrey Klineberg, one of the justice's clerks during the 1992 term, recalls Blackmun remarking "how terrific" Rehnquist was "at running the conference. And pretty clearly the point was, in marked contrast to [Burger]. He and Rehnquist were rarely together on matters of substance, but he had immense respect for him in terms of his ability to manage the Court and handle the conference."[1]

Edward Lazarus, who clerked for Blackmun in the 1988 term, substantially agrees. "Blackmun thought of [Rehnquist] as a positive force, and in large part I think that was because he wasn't Burger. The rap on Rehnquist coming in was that he was going to run a fair Court, that he wasn't going to manipulate the vote, that he was going to assign opinions fairly....When I was clerking, the Chief was seen as...a straight shooter. We don't think his opinions are [good], but this is someone who administratively is running a fair ship."[2]

Blackmun, Klineberg remembers, also appreciated the new chief justice's decided preference for brief conference sessions: "I think he was grateful they were over as relatively quickly as they were." Years later, the justice himself discussed contrasts in the Burger and Rehnquist conference styles. Asked whether he remembered the longest "speech" ever given at conference and who gave it, Blackmun responded, "No, I can't single one out," yet then added, "Chief Justice Burger was inclined to cover a case very thoroughly and would take a lot of time....Chief Justice Rehnquist, when he came on, employed much shorter preliminary comments. I think he felt that the justices knew the case and it wasn't necessary to state the facts in most cases, so his conferences, or the conferences over which Chief Justice Rehnquist presided, usually were much shorter."[3]

Whatever Blackmun's admiration for the new chief justice's managerial skills, however, he must have viewed with alarm the changing face of the Court during the Reagan years and the first President Bush's single term. Pro-life witnesses complained about Sandra Day O'Connor's Arizona abortion record during her 1981 confirmation hearing as Reagan's first nominee, but O'Connor quickly emerged as a *Roe* skeptic on the Court. Elevation of Rehnquist, a *Roe* dissenter, to chief justice enabled President Reagan to place Antonin Scalia, an avowed *Roe* opponent, on the high bench. The 1987 retirement of Justice Powell, a *Roe* supporter and constitutional moderate, raised further doubts about the future of abortion rights, and although the Senate rebuffed Reagan's efforts to replace Powell with Robert Bork, another outspoken *Roe* critic, Anthony Kennedy, the justice finally confirmed for the Powell seat, was by no means a certain vote to retain *Roe*. Nor was David Souter, President Bush's choice to replace Justice Brennan when he retired in 1990. And although Clarence Thomas, Bush's choice to fill Justice Marshall's seat the next year, testified at his confirmation hearing that he had never even so much as discussed *Roe*, Thomas would also be a vehement opponent of abortion rights.

Closed Chambers, Edward Lazarus's controversial insider account of relations among the justices and their clerks in the period following Senate rejection of Robert Bork, vividly portrays a Court plagued with internecine strife, particularly between liberal clerks and their conservative counterparts bent on exacting revenge for Bork's fate. However overdrawn, *Closed Chambers* undoubtedly captures the sense of malaise that must have permeated the Blackmun chambers and the justice himself as Reagan and Bush sought to remake the Court in their own image.[4]

Presidents, however, are rarely perfect prophets, as Nixon's selection of Blackmun so obviously demonstrated. Justice Souter would become one of the Court's most liberal justices. He and Blackmun also forged a close friendship that may have helped to relieve any sense of isolation that threatened to overwhelm the elderly justice as Reagan-Bush justices—especially Rehnquist, Scalia, and Thomas—challenged *Roe* and other precedents Blackmun held so important. During the justice's tenure, there was relatively little interaction, professional or social, among the justices, and that apparently was particularly true in Blackmun's case. Powell and Blackmun had shared adjoining chambers, and the affable Virginian occasionally dropped in for a chat with his colleague. But Powell's 1987 retirement left a void there. Blackmun clerks interviewed for this book uniformly recalled that their justice rarely visited other chambers, and drop-ins by other justices were equally rare. As noted earlier, Blackmun did most of his work in the Court library, and other justices sometimes visited him there, but rarely. He had breakfast each morning with his clerks, ate lunch in his chambers, regularly declined to participate in the lunches clerks traditionally had each term with justices from other chambers, and usually confined his interaction with colleagues to letters and memoranda. Personal contacts with his colleagues and their chambers had thus been extremely rare throughout his career, and the departure of Brennan and Marshall, combined with threats the arrival of Scalia and Thomas posed for *Roe* and its progeny, undoubtedly aggravated whatever sense of isolation and insecurity his own innate shyness and the largely solitary pattern of his daily routine had created over the years.

In that setting, Blackmun's warm association with Justice Souter no doubt bolstered the older jurist's spirits. The justice was never able to persuade his reclusive colleague to even attend the Aspen seminars, much less accept speaking engagements. "I know you get a kick out of these things," Souter explained to his colleague after declining yet another Blackmun-instigated invitation. "But you have to realize that God gave you an element of sociability, and I think he gave you the share otherwise reserved for me." Blackmun obviously enjoyed serving as the target of Souter's gentle wit, however. Soon after the elder justice recalled a family story that one of his ancestors had been hanged in New Hampshire, Souter produced a "report" from the state's attorney general, detailing the crimes of a long list of Blackmun miscreants, including Esmeralda Blackmun, who poisoned her lover with a raspberry tart, and Esmeralda's brother Jebediah "The Butcher" Blackmun, who decapitated several neighbors. A postscript to one of Souter's summer letters to Blackmun from New Hampshire read, "The sight of the N. H. State prison the other day reminded me of you and your family." On another occasion, Souter sent Blackmun a postcard depicting two fishermen, one in a boat, one wading. The caption read, "Roe v. Wade: the Great Western Fishing Controversy." Blackmun probably appreciated, too, the effective but affable way in which Souter deflected the sarcastic barbs with which Justice Scalia regularly attempted to skewer his colleagues.[5]

Fortunately for Blackmun, Justice Souter would be but one of the Reagan-Bush appointees to frustrate the presidents who chose them. Only Rehnquist, Scalia, and Thomas proved overwhelmingly faithful to the Reagan-Bush human rights agenda. O'Connor and Kennedy became moderately conservative swing voters and the most influential justices of the Rehnquist Court era. Justice Stevens, President Ford's only appointee, had also become a reliable member of the Court's liberal bloc, as would Justices Ruth Bader Ginsburg and Stephen Breyer, President Clinton's choices to replace Justices White and Blackmun in 1993 and 1994. The justice would thus be on the winning, as well as the losing, side of significant battles waged during his final years on the bench. He was also finally to reconcile personal abhorrence and constitutional judgment in his review of death penalty cases.

Blackmun and his colleagues confronted a wide range of civil liberties issues during his final terms on the bench. His dissent in one case would include language that became even more famous than his *Roe* ruling in capturing the justice's image as champion of society's underdogs. In *DeShaney v. Winnebago County* (1989), a majority, speaking through Chief Justice Rehnquist, held that the federal courts had no authority to intervene in a case challenging the failure of social workers to protect a four-year-old boy from his brutish father. The child and his mother, Rehnquist concluded, must look to the state for redress.[6]

In the last paragraph of his dissent, Justice Blackmun exclaimed:

Poor Joshua! Victim of repeated attacks by an irresponsible,
bullying, cowardly, and intemperate father, and abandoned by

respondents who placed him in a dangerous predicament and who knew or learned about what was going on, and yet did essentially nothing except, as the Court revealingly observes,...' dutifully recorded these incidents in [their] files.' It is a sad commentary upon American life, and constitutional principles—as full of late of patriotic fervor and proud proclamations about 'liberty and justice for all'—that the child, Joshua DeShaney, now is assigned to live out the remainder of his life profoundly retarded. Joshua and his mother...deserve—but now are denied by this Court—the opportunity to have the facts of their case considered in the light of the constitutional protection that [federal law] is meant to provide.[7]

Although a clerk drafted the dissent, Blackmun would later say that he contributed its lament for "Poor Joshua!" as a rebuttal to the majority's impersonal, procedural disposition of the case. "I thought they'd lost sight of the individual concern....Sometimes we overlook the individual's concern, the fact these are live human beings that are so deeply and terribly affected by our decisions." Asked about reports that his clerks had urged him not to include those words in his dissent, the justice replied, "They probably were embarrassed by my use of them and my stepping out into the crossfire....I couldn't get along without my clerks but that doesn't mean I had to agree with everything that they concluded."[8]

Whatever the attitude of his clerks that term or the continuing concerns of scholarly critics about his "personalizing" of constitutional issues, the justice's lament for "Poor Joshua!" undoubtedly struck a chord with those committed to law's human dimension, including prospective clerks. When Cecillia Wang sought a clerkship with the justice, she recalled his *DeShaney* dissent in her letter of application. "During my first semester of law school," she wrote, "I was struck by a curious phenomenon in the law. In many of the judicial opinions I studied, the real problems of real people had been boiled dry, until there was not much left but an abstract legal question or two. The real people themselves had been reduced to abstract ciphers....I was troubled by this harsh distillation, for I had chosen the law for what I had supposed was its connection to the real world." Later that semester, however, she had read the justice's *DeShaney* dissent.

" 'Poor Joshua!' became a touchstone and a lifeline for me—one adjective, one proper noun, and one punctuation mark that represented all the real people who had been left out of their own stories. Your dissent was a sign of life, and to me it represented everything the law can and should aspire to be. Whenever I find myself immobilized by disillusionment or doubts about the law's capacity for justice, I find myself turning once again to your retelling of Joshua DeShaney's story."[9]

Blackmun would also remain faithful to a broad construction of the First Amendment's religion clauses. In his first term, the justice had joined Chief Justice Burger's majority opinion in *Lemon v. Kurtzman* (1971), declaring that laws affecting religion violated the establishment clause unless they had a secular purpose and primary effect that neither advanced nor harmed religion and did not create an excessive entanglement between church and state. Over the years, Blackmun had maintained his allegiance to *Lemon* and other cases broadly construing the establishment clause, and when the *Lemon* test came under increasing attack in the Rehnquist Court, he held firm. In 1992, Justice Kennedy, speaking for a majority in *Lee v. Weisman*, suggested that the school commencement prayer at issue there was invalid only because students in essence were "coerced" to participate. Blackmun filed a concurrence citing *Lemon* and other cases to emphasize that proof of coercion was not necessary to establish a constitutional violation in church-state cases. Although much less elaborate and extensive than what Blackmun clerk Molly McUsic uncharitably termed the "grand essay on the Establishment Clause" that Justice Souter filed in the case, Blackmun minced no words, declaring, "When the government arrogates to itself a role in religious affairs, it abandons its obligation as guarantor of democracy. Democracy requires the nourishment of dialogue and dissent, while religious faith puts its trust in an ultimate divine authority above all human deliberation. When the government appropriates religious truth, it 'transforms rational debate into theological decree.' "[10]

Near the end of Chief Justice Burger's tenure, Blackmun had dissented when the Court in *Lynch v. Donnelly* (1984) upheld a Pawtucket, Rhode Island, Christmas display that included a crèche as well as a Santa house and other secular symbols of the holiday. In the original draft of his *Lynch* dissent, the justice decried the majority's "relegat[ing] the crèche to the same secular status as Santa Claus and equat[ing] the purpose of the Christ Child with that of the bearded old gent who merrily inspires shoppers to spend beyond their means. The city has its victory—but it is a Pyrrhic one indeed.... I cannot join the Court in denying either the force of our precedents or the abiding message of Christian love and hope that is at the core of the crèche." At the suggestion of two clerks, one of whom thought that the justice's language "may sound more evangelical than you want to in the U.S. Reports," Blackmun modified the text of the dissent, but not its message. He was willing to uphold seasonal displays with religious overtones, but only where religious symbols were clearly subordinated to secular features of the display. In 1989, he announced the Rehnquist Court's judgment in companion cases from Pittsburgh, one upholding display of a menorah and Christmas tree, the other striking down a crèche display in the lobby of a public building. Chanukah, for which the menorah was the primary visual symbol, had both secular and religious meaning, he reasoned, and no predominantly secular symbol of that Jewish holiday was available as an alternative to the menorah. Its appearance with the Christmas tree was thus simply part of a secular seasonal display. Display of the crèche alone, on the other hand, amounted to state endorsement of an obviously religious message.[11]

Nor would Blackmun join the Rehnquist Court in diluting the First Amendment's guarantee to the free exercise of religion. For years, the Supreme Court had subjected governmental policies that interfered with religious practices to strict judicial scrutiny, striking them down unless they were found necessary to further a compelling state interest. In 1990, however, a majority upheld Oregon's denial of unemployment benefits to two members of the Native American Church who had lost their jobs as drug counselors when it was discovered that they partook of peyote as part of their faith's religious rituals. Distinguishing earlier cases, Justice Scalia held that people were obligated to obey generally applicable, religiously neutral, criminal laws, including drug laws, even if they impinged on religious practices. In dissent, Justice Blackmun, reaffirming his commitment to the strict standard traditionally applied in religious liberty cases, could find no compelling interest justifying Oregon's action, especially since twenty-three states and the federal government granted the religious use of peyote an exemption from their drug laws.[12]

"A Chill Wind"

Safeguarding and, if possible, expanding *Roe* remained, of course, the justice's principal priorities. On a number of occasions, the Burger Court had substantially reaffirmed *Roe* and its trimester framework. The justices also declined several opportunities to reassess and possibly overturn the controversial ruling during William Rehnquist's early tenure as chief justice. Even during the Burger years, however, a majority, to Blackmun's dismay, had refused to mandate public funding of abortions for indigent women and also upheld parental notification requirements so long as they included a judicial bypass option for minors seeking an abortion. In 1983, during her second term on the bench, Justice O'Connor, joined by *Roe* dissenters White and Rehnquist, filed a significant dissent, attacking *Roe* and proposing an alternative approach to abortion issues. Advancing medical technology reducing the period within which a fetus became viable and triggering governmental authority to forbid nontherapeutic abortions, meant, declared O'Connor, that Blackmun's trimester formula was "clearly on a collision course with itself." In its place, O'Connor proposed upholding abortion regulations at any stage of a pregnancy unless they imposed an "undue burden" on the woman's choice.[13]

Bolstered by the Reagan administration's antiabortion stance, many states adopted highly restrictive measures, providing the Rehnquist Court with ample opportunity to revisit *Roe*. For Blackmun and others committed to abortion rights, *Webster v. Reproductive Health Services* (1989) from Missouri, a state noted for antiabortion sentiments, was particularly ominous. In *Roe*, the Court had construed the Constitution to extend rights only to postnatal beings. But in the preamble to its abortion statute, Missouri declared that "life ... begins at conception" and conferred legal rights on the "unborn." The law also obliged physicians to perform viability tests before performing abortions on women believed to have been pregnant for twenty or more weeks, prohibited the use of public employees or facilities for abortions not necessary to save the pregnant woman's life, and banned the use of public funds, employees, and facilities for "encouraging or counseling" abortions except in life-saving situations. As Justice Blackmun wrote in his notes about the case, "Mo [Missouri] is Mo and will push and push."[14]

A federal district court and an Eighth Circuit panel, speaking through Blackmun's former circuit colleague Donald Lay, had struck the statute down. But the Supreme Court reversed. Speaking for a majority, Chief Justice Rehnquist dismissed the challenge to the counseling provisions as moot and held that the preamble, on its face, did not constitute an abortion regulation, but only a reflection of the state's values. A judicial decision on the preamble's constitutionality, reasoned the chief justice, would be appropriate only after it had been used to restrict abortions in some tangible way. Citing the Court's precedents, the majority also upheld the statute's ban on the use of public employees and facilities for nontherapeutic abortions.

In a portion of his opinion joined only by Justices White and Kennedy, Rehnquist conceded that the viability testing provisions conflicted with *Roe*'s trimester framework and urged the Court in an appropriate case to abandon Blackmun's formula, which, he argued, resembled more an intricate code of regulations than a body of constitutional doctrine and also interfered with the state's compelling interest in protecting fetal life throughout a pregnancy rather than merely after viability. According to Justice Marshall's notes, however, Rehnquist had indicated at conference that he did not favor overruling *Roe* "as such" at that point; he concluded for the plurality that the facts of *Roe* and *Webster* were sufficiently distinguishable that the viability testing provisions could be upheld without overturning *Roe*.[15]

Justice O'Connor was not prepared to go even that far. In her judgment, the viability testing and other provisions of the Missouri law did not conflict with *Roe* or the Court's other abortion precedents. "There will be time enough to reexamine *Roe*," she scolded the plurality, "when the constitutionality of a State's abortion statute actually turns on the constitutional validity of *Roe v. Wade*." But Justice Scalia, who saw *Webster* as the perfect vehicle for reconsidering and discarding *Roe*, had a lecture of his own for O'Connor. In declining to revisit *Roe*, she had cited the familiar principle that courts should issue rulings no broader than required by a case's precise facts. Noting sardonically that the rule had a "good-cause" exception, Scalia declared, "It seems particularly perverse to convert the policy into an absolute in the present case, in order to place beyond reach the inexpressibly 'broader-than-was-required-by-the-precise-facts' structure established by *Roe v. Wade*."[16]

Justice Blackmun was no doubt relieved that the *Webster* majority had ignored Scalia's proposal, but in every other way the case must have aggravated his growing sense of despair over *Roe*'s future. The justice had remained a central focus of the national abortion debate. In December 1986, he declined public comment on press reports that he had initially agreed to accept a public service award from the National Family Planning and Reproductive Health Association (NFPRHA), a pro-choice group, then declined the recognition in the face of criticism from the National Right to Life Committee, which had written the justice that acceptance of a "trophy" from a pro-choice group "litigating on controversial matters of public policy" would violate the ABA's code of judicial conduct. Geoffrey Hazard, the prominent specialist in legal ethics, told a reporter that acceptance of the award, even if the group had no cases before the Supreme Court, would indeed be inappropriate. Awards, said Hazard, are "a way of currying favor," and the justice should "stay a mile away" from any plan NFPRHA had to honor *Roe*'s author.[17]

Nor had personal attacks on the justice subsided. In 1987, after Blackmun suffered a recurrence of prostate cancer, a fundamentalist Baptist minister in Los Angeles asked his followers to pray for the justice's removal "in any way that God sees fit," adding, "I don't know if our prayers will be answered. The answer to that will come if he dies in time for President Reagan to appoint someone who is capable of the job."[18]

At times, the justice had publicly expressed concern about *Roe*'s future. As the Court was beginning the 1988 term, in which *Webster* was decided, he addressed first-year law students at the University of Arkansas. Originally, the event was to be closed to the press, but when university officials learned that two law students were also reporters, they opened Blackmun's speech to all media. During his talk, widely reported in the press, the justice asked, "Will Roe v. Wade go down the drain?" Then he answered his own question. "I think there's a very distinct possibility that it will, this term....You can count the votes." In an obvious reference to Justice Kennedy, President Reagan's latest appointee, he observed, "One never knows what a new justice's attitude toward *stare decisis* [precedent] is. [*Roe* is] now 15 years old." But he appeared clearly to fear the worst.[19]

As the justice prepared for conference following oral argument in *Webster*, Edward Lazarus provided him with a memorandum in which he attempted to anticipate arguments the justice's colleagues were likely to raise, including responses to attacks on *Roe* itself. The clerk realized the justice faced an uphill battle. Closing the memo, he wished Blackmun "Good luck tomorrow, Mr. Justice." Afterward, Blackmun reported to his clerks that *Roe* had survived, but barely so.[20]

As other justices circulated draft opinions in the case, Lazarus kept Blackmun abreast of each development. When circulation of Justice O'Connor's concurrence was briefly delayed, he promptly notified the justice. "Apparently, her tennis game with Barbara Bush this morning, and her luncheon appointment, had precluded her final pre-circulation review [of her draft]."[21]

In early June, Lazarus had informed the justice that he was "now full steam ahead on the [*Webster*] dissent and will work on it as hard as I possibly can—and be as tough as I possibly can." He also incorporated into his draft portions of passages Blackmun contributed, praising them as "powerful and moving in a way that I would not even hope to emulate." But the justice's pointed summary of the case's political context did not make it into the final opinion. "The two lone dissenters in *Roe* v. *Wade* and *Doe* v. *Bolton*, after 16 years, now have prevailed," he wrote, "with the assenting votes of the three newest Members of this Court, in rolling back *Roe* and *Doe*, for all practical purposes.... This, of course, is the result of the democratic process with the election of two administrations who have politicized, and thereby exacerbated, the issue."[22]

The dissent, joined by Justices Brennan and Marshall, was one of the most passionate and forceful of Blackmun's career. He was particularly provoked with the Rehnquist plurality, which, he complained, would overrule *Roe* "silently," while Justice Scalia would do so explicitly. "The plurality opinion," he declared,

> is filled with winks, and nods, and knowing glances to those
> who would do away with *Roe* explicitly, but turns a stone face
> to anyone in search of what the plurality conceive as the scope
> of a woman's right under the Due Process Clause to terminate
> a pregnancy free from the coercive and brooding influence of
> the State. The simple truth is that *Roe* would not survive the

plurality's analysis, and that the plurality provides no substitute for *Roe*'s protective umbrella.... Thus, "not with a bang, but a whimper," the plurality discards a landmark case of the last generation, and casts into darkness the hopes and visions of every woman in the country who had come to believe that the Constitution guaranteed her the right to exercise some control over her unique ability to bear children.[23]

To the plurality's contention that *Roe*'s trimester framework was "somehow inconsistent with a Constitution cast in general terms," Blackmun had a ready rejoinder: "The 'critical elements' of countless constitutional doctrines nowhere appear in the Constitution's text. The Constitution makes no mention, for example, of ... the standard for determining when speech is obscene" or of the rational basis test and other formulas applied in equal protection cases. "Rather, they are judge-made methods for evaluating and measuring the strength and scope of constitutional rights of individuals against the competing interests of government."[24]

Most infuriating of all for Blackmun was the extremely "deceptive fashion" in which the plurality, on the one hand, had not made "a single, even incremental change in the law of abortion," yet, on the other hand, was "implicitly invit[ing] every state legislature to enact more and more restrictive abortion regulations in order to provoke more and more test cases, in the hope that sometime down the line the Court will return the law of procreative freedom to the severe limitations that generally prevailed in this country before [*Roe*]." To the justice, the prospects for abortion rights were bleak, indeed.

> I fear for the future. I fear for the liberty and equality of the millions of women who have lived and come of age in the 16 years since *Roe* was decided. I fear for the integrity of, and public esteem for, this Court. ...
>
> For today, at least, the law of abortion stands undisturbed. For today, the women of this Nation still retain the liberty to control their destinies. But the signs are evident and very ominous, and a chill wind blows.[25]

Not surprisingly, Blackmun devoted little of his *Webster* dissent to Justice O'Connor's concurrence. In fact, in a footnote, he complimented a portion of her analysis. O'Connor, after all, had chided other members of the majority for revisiting *Roe* prematurely; her "undue burden" approach appeared to offer greater protection for abortion rights than the *Webster* plurality's essentially rational basis formula, not to mention Justice Scalia's enthusiasm for *Roe*'s reversal outright.

Perhaps as part of a strategy to marshal O'Connor's support for retaining at least a portion of *Roe*, Edward Lazarus, realizing the depth and intensity of Blackmun's feelings, apparently suggested that the justice forgo reading portions of his *Webster* dissent in Court. Three days before *Webster* was announced the clerk wrote the justice, "emphasiz[ing] that I in no way meant to discourage you from speaking from the bench. If I am cautious, it is only because I know what a strong impact the bench-statement will have, and because I have become so deeply committed to the dissent that I find myself fighting to keep a balanced head. Whatever you decide, I will never forget the experience of working on this case, and I will always be grateful to you for the opportunity."[26]

Whatever Lazarus's preference, when the decision was announced on July 3, Justice Blackmun, in what the *New York Times* described as "a weary and sorrowful tone," read portions of his dissent to the courtroom audience, including his apprehension that "the signs [of *Roe*'s demise] are evident and very ominous, and a chill wind blows." When the session ended, he left his seat alone through the curtains behind the bench. O'Connor and Kennedy, the other justices at his end of the bench, had not been present. A few days earlier, Randall Terry, head of the antiabortion group Operation Rescue, had suggested facetiously that, were he a justice, he would release the Court's inevitably controversial *Webster* ruling by throwing it from the window of a plane as he left the country. His words were almost prophetic. When *Webster* was announced, O'Connor had already flown to Great Britain for a legal conference and Justice Kennedy to the McGeorge School of Law in California, where he had taught before his appointment to the Court.[27]

Pro-choice leaders branded *Webster* a "total disaster," in the words of Molly Yard, president of the National Organization for Women. Tracking

Justice Blackmun's dissent, Judith Lichtman, director of the Women's Legal Defense Fund, observed, "Is it still legal to have an abortion? Yes. Is *Roe v. Wade* well on the way to unraveling? Yes." The director of the ACLU's reproductive freedom project conceded that "there is no longer a majority on the Court to support *Roe*," adding, "Now it's just a battle over details." *Roe* opponents were elated. President Bush's attorney general Richard Thornburgh, who had asked the Court to overrule *Roe*, welcomed the Court's willingness to "recognize an increased role for state legislatures in regulating abortion." The head of the National Right to Life organization exclaimed, "We're thumbs up all the way!" And in a parody of Justice Blackmun's expression of "fear for the future," the conservative columnist William F. Buckley declared, "There are those of us who fear for Blackmun's power to reason." Essentially equating fetuses with "human beings," Buckley noted the justice's vehement defense of a woman's "sovereignty" over her own body, then observed, "It is instructive to remember that exactly such thought was relied upon 150 years ago in asserting the rights of the slave master."[28]

Preserving *Roe's* Future

As *Webster* made clear, Justice O'Connor was key to *Roe's* future. Only Justice Scalia had urged its complete rejection. But the tone of the chief justice's plurality opinion, joined by Justices White and Kennedy, had been harshly critical of *Roe* and its trimester framework. And while O'Connor had assumed a harshly negative stance in earlier cases, her refusal to rush to judgment on *Roe*, as well as her undue burden standard, clearly signaled that she was unwilling to accord abortion rights no meaningful protection whatever. Blackmun and other justices committed to *Roe* thus hoped to coax O'Connor into their corner to the greatest extent they could realistically expect. Justice Scalia's continuing ridicule of O'Connor's undue burden formula as "irrational" did their cause no harm either.

In the term after *Webster*, Justice O'Connor voted to uphold a measure requiring a minor's physician to notify one of her parents before performing an abortion unless a juvenile court issued an order approving the minor's consent to the procedure. But O'Connor also joined Blackmun and company in holding an abortion restriction unconstitutional for the first time in her tenure. At issue in *Hodgson v. Minnesota* (1990) was a complicated two-parent notification requirement. O'Connor joined Rehnquist, White, Scalia, and Kennedy in upholding a two-parent notification requirement that included a judicial bypass option. But she also agreed with Blackmun and others that requiring notice to both a minor's parents, rather than only one, was unconstitutional.[29]

Gossip from O'Connor's chambers about her likely position in *Hodgson* had been both positive and negative. After initially appearing to lean toward striking down at least part of the Minnesota statute, Blackmun's clerk Anne Dupre reported to the justice after oral argument in late November, O'Connor was "back to being 'troubled' again." A recent newspaper article had tagged O'Connor's abortion jurisprudence "murky." "Perhaps she is concerned," noted Dupre in a memo to Blackmun, "that…to strike down the Minnesota statute would somehow add to the murkiness." O'Connor, she understood, was "receiving a lot of pressure from her [two] conservative clerks…to uphold the statute and to abandon even the 'undue burden' test."[30]

One of the first law review articles on *Webster*'s impact may have bolstered Blackmun's spirits, however, at least as Dupre digested it for the justice. The law professor Daniel Farber saw *Webster* as a major defeat for pro-life forces, with only Justice Scalia bent on " 'throw[ing] *Roe* on the scrap heap' " and Justice O'Connor "anxious to avoid that step." Even Rehnquist, White, and Kennedy "handled the issue gingerly and [could] be read to have affirmed some aspects of *Roe*." Were *Roe* overruled, Farber doubted that abortions would end, especially since, according to a recent poll, only 17 percent of the public favored a complete ban on abortions, and the number of illegal abortions performed before *Roe* was about "75% of the number of legal abortions now." Retention of *Roe*, observed Dupre, paraphrasing Farber and attempting to soothe Blackmun's concerns, would thus have important symbolic value, "but the true stakes are less than both sides claim."[31]

Justice Blackmun obviously saw *Roe*'s survival as more than symbolism and surely must have been relieved when Justice O'Connor told her colleagues that she was voting to strike down Minnesota's two-parent notification scheme, albeit approving the provision allowing a minor to avoid notifying either parent by resorting to the judicial bypass option provided in the law. In an unusual arrangement, Justice Stevens then drafted an opinion striking down the two-parent notification requirement, while Justice Kennedy drafted an opinion upholding the judicial bypass arrangement; Justice O'Connor provided the critical fifth vote for each position. As Justice Stevens maneuvered to retain O'Connor's vote, Blackmun wrote Brennan, Marshall, and Stevens, suggesting that they "join as much of Stevens' writing as is possible...[so] that the three of us should be together as much as possible and not apart." Brennan (and presumably Marshall as well) readily offered his "wholehearted agreement..., especially now that Sandra had agreed to invalidate at least part of an abortion law." A week later, the decision was announced.[32]

The next term, in *Rust v. Sullivan* (1991), Justice O'Connor dissented again when a majority upheld federal regulations forbidding federally funded physicians and agencies to provide abortion counseling services. Unlike Blackmun, though, she merely concluded that Congress had not authorized the regulations at issue and declined once again to reach the constitutional questions raised in the case.[33]

By that point, Justice Souter had replaced Justice Brennan. During oral argument, Souter appeared poised to invalidate the abortion counseling rules on the ground that they interfered with doctor-patient speech. Ultimately, he joined Chief Justice Rehnquist's majority opinion, but only after the chief justice revised his opinion to indicate that the challenged regulations did not "significantly impinge upon" that aspect of the doctor–patient relationship. Even so, Rehnquist did not fully comply with Souter, adding the adverb "significantly" to Souter's suggested language. "I do not really know if there is any one legally accepted definition of the doctor–patient relationship," he explained to Souter, "and if we say it doesn't impinge at all I am sure that Harry could find some examples, however obscure, indicating *contra*, to incorporate in his dissent."[34]

Blackmun circulated a vigorous *Rust* dissent, challenging the regulations on constitutional as well as statutory grounds. Just as in the abortion funding cases and *Webster*, he declared in his final paragraph, the majority was "technically leaving intact the fundamental right protected by *Roe*," but "once again has rendered the right's substance nugatory." To Blackmun, "this [was] a course nearly as noxious as overruling *Roe* directly, for if a right is found to be unenforceable, even against flagrant attempts by government to circumvent it, then it ceases to be a right at all."[35]

Justice Stevens praised his colleague's "powerful" dissent and expressed the hope that he could "join all of it." But Stevens found Blackmun's last paragraph troubling. "I think it may be poor strategy to assume that either Sandra [or] David—and certainly not both—are prepared to overrule *Roe* v. *Wade*. Your last paragraph implies that one who joins the majority opinion has that objective ultimately in mind." Stevens also doubted that the majority had done "quite [as] much damage" as Blackmun feared. "At least for the woman who can afford medical treatment, the right remains intact."[36]

Not surprisingly, Blackmun refused to delete his last paragraph, and Stevens declined to join that portion of his colleague's dissent. But a notation Blackmun made on Stevens's letter suggested that the justice's rhetoric may have simply been part of a campaign to convince O'Connor and Souter, especially the latter, that most abortion regulations ultimately constituted a threat to the survival of *Roe* itself. "Told JPS what I was doing," Blackmun noted at the bottom of Stevens's letter. "He OKs."[37]

As the justices began their 1991–92 term, then, Justice Scalia was the only member of the Court on record as favoring *Roe*'s outright rejection. It appeared highly likely, however, that Thomas would concur fully with Scalia, especially given early reports that Scalia and his clerks were closely "mentoring" the new justice and his chambers. Rehnquist, White, and Kennedy had already publicly rejected *Roe*'s trimester framework and indicated their support of broad discretion for state legislatures in the abortion field. In a March 1992 interview, Blackmun gave Souter an essentially positive preliminary assessment, observing, "His vote is conservative, but it's not an automatic knee-jerk vote. He doesn't do what some of the others do: 'I agree with the Chief' or 'I agree with Scalia,' something like that. He may agree with them, but he has his own reasons for doing it....I think this is good. And he's a very nice person." But Souter had upheld the abortion counseling regulation at issue in the *Rust* case. Given her undue burden approach to abortion issues, O'Connor was obviously unlikely to favor scrapping *Roe* entirely. In recent cases, moreover, she had not resurrected her contention that advancing medical technology had placed *Roe*'s trimester framework on a "collision course with itself."

In fact, when Hastings law professor David Faigman raised the question during a 1990 conference, Blackmun, according to Faigman, "bridled at that and referred to the phrase as a clever cliché written by a law clerk." Asserting that the charge conflicted with a "medical consensus" that there was no foreseeable prospect for keeping fetuses of less than twenty-three to twenty-four weeks old alive outside the womb, Blackmun reportedly added that O'Connor herself had told him that she no longer subscribed to her earlier assertion. Blackmun obviously was not certain, however, just what portion of *Roe* his colleague might vote to retain. Justice White, of course, had dissented in *Roe* itself, as had Rehnquist. Indeed, only Justice Stevens seemed substantially committed to Blackmun's position.[38]

Planned Parenthood v. Casey (1992) would resolve at least some of Blackmun's doubts about *Roe*'s future. A Pennsylvania statute provided that a woman must give her informed consent to an abortion and be provided, at least twenty-four hours before the procedure, with information enabling her to make that judgment. Minors were required to obtain the informed consent of a parent or guardian but were allowed a judicial bypass option. Ordinarily, a married woman was obliged to notify her husband. An exception from compliance with those provisions applied in cases of "medical emergency," and facilities providing abortion services were subject to various reporting and record-keeping requirements. Before the law took effect, five abortion clinics and a physician filed a federal suit alleging that each of its provisions was unconstitutional on its face. A federal district court agreed, but the Third Circuit largely reversed the trial court, striking down only the spousal notice provision.[39]

When a petition for a writ of certiorari reached the justices, it appeared for a time that review of *Casey* would be postponed a year. A sufficient number of justices favored review, but certiorari petitions must be formally approved at conference before oral argument can be scheduled in a case, and a move was launched to have the *Casey* petition "relisted" for approval at some uncertain time later in the term. As a practical matter, such a delay would have meant that *Casey* would not be reviewed until the 1992 term.

On January 16, 1992, each of Justice Blackmun's clerks signed a brief note "recommend[ing]" that the justice "take a clear stand at Conference tomorrow in favor of granting this case," adding, "We feel strongly that the case should be heard this spring, and that you should oppose efforts to relist the case any further."[40]

The justice agreed fully with his clerks. "The obvious reason for this" relisting effort, he hotly declared in a draft dissent, "is the political repercussion of a decision of this Court in the midst of an election year. But the issue already has been politicized by the present [Bush I] Administration and its predecessor [Reagan] Administration and, surely to some degree by this Court with its decisions in *Webster* and *Rust*....This Court stands less than tall when it defers decision for political reasons. This is a Court of justice, and I had thought it was the Supreme Court of the United States. We should conduct our business above the fray of politics."[41]

Ultimately, the relisting effort ended, and Blackmun never circulated his draft dissent. During oral argument on April 22, however, he was particularly feisty. When Pennsylvania's attorney general suggested that *Roe* allowed abortion on demand, the justice was incredulous. "*Roe* itself said that [it] does not provide for abortion on demand," he declared, adding, his voice filled with sarcasm, "Have you read *Roe*?"[42]

Neither Souter nor Thomas offered any clue to their likely positions in *Casey* during oral argument; Souter asked questions only for purposes of clarification, and Thomas said nothing. Especially in view of Thomas's marked tendency to vote with Justice Scalia in most major cases during his first five months on the Court, members of the press and legal community seemed confident that Thomas would vote to overturn *Roe*. The same suspicion, albeit less assuredly, appeared to prevail in their predictions about Souter. Aviam Soiefer, a Boston University constitutional scholar and abortion rights specialist, told a reporter, "I think it would be an overwhelming surprise if either Souter or Thomas did anything but what we would expect, which is to go along with the hard majority who would overrule *Roe*."[43]

Such speculation about Thomas, of course, would prove entirely correct. Well before oral argument in *Casey*, however, Justice Blackmun had become more sanguine about the stance Souter might ultimately embrace. In January, while the justices were considering what questions to have the parties address were the case granted review, Stephanie Dangel, the Blackmun clerk assigned to the case, had a piece of "possibly good news" for the justice. Peter Rubin, one of Souter's clerks, had told Dangel that Souter was "trying to write the question in such a way as to *avoid* overruling *Roe*." Souter's proposed question, Rubin reported, would focus on the standard of review appropriate for abortion cases "and/or what role should considerations of stare decisis play in this case." Souter had been among the justices who favored delaying the case for a term, but only, according to Rubin, because he wanted the summer to consider how best to frame the question raised in the certiorari grant. Dangel did not doubt Rubin's assessment of his justice's motives. "Unlike the Chief and SOC [Justice O'Connor]," she assured Blackmun, "DHS [Souter] is not concerned about the election." Souter, his clerk reported, "had also expressed a tremendous amount of interest" in knowing Blackmun's position on whether the Court should grant certiorari in *Casey* and assumed, at that point, that his colleague, fearing the Court might use *Casey* to overrule much or all of *Roe*, would vote to deny review in the case. "While I know that your final decision will depend on the questions presented" in any grant of certiorari, asked Dangel, "do you want me to pass on anything to DHS about your inclinations that might help in framing the question presented?"[44]

At conference after oral argument in April, Justice Souter, according to Blackmun's notes, endorsed O'Connor's undue burden formula. But Souter's strong commitment to stare decisis, even precedents he did not approve, extended back to his days as a New Hampshire jurist, and he attempted to ensure that the questions the Court raised in its grant of certiorari in *Casey* would avoid reconsideration of *Roe*. The undue burden standard O'Connor favored, as well as her repeated refusals to confront *Roe* prematurely, suggested that she was also unwilling to scrap *Roe* entirely. Kennedy's ultimate likely stance in *Casey* was more problematic. He had joined the chief justice's plurality opinion in *Webster*. As a young lawyer, the Roman Catholic jurist had also denounced *Roe* as the "Dred Scott of our time." With Thomas now on the Court, Kennedy could provide the critical fifth vote to scuttle *Roe*.[45]

On May 29, however, Kennedy sent Blackmun a cryptic but heartening note. "I need to see you as soon as you have a few moments. I want to tell you about some developments in Planned Parenthood v. Casey, and at least part of what I say should come as welcome news." The "news," Kennedy later told his colleague, was that he, O'Connor, and Souter were preparing a rare joint opinion in which they refused to overrule *Roe*.[46]

The "*PP* troika," as Stephanie Dangel promptly dubbed the trio, quickly produced a sixty-one-page draft. In it, as expected, they rejected *Roe*'s trimester framework, concluding instead that no undue burden could be imposed on a woman's decision to obtain an abortion prior to a fetus's becoming viable. They thus preserved what they termed *Roe*'s "essence," as well as its acceptance of state authority to forbid nontherapeutic abortions after viability. But the three also recognized the government's legitimate interests in protecting the woman's health and fetal life throughout a pregnancy, so long as such controls did not unduly interfere with the woman's choice. Under that approach, they found all the Pennsylvania statute's provisions except the spousal notification requirement valid. In an important section of the opinion, drafted primarily by Justice Souter, the troika emphasized the importance of stare decisis, especially in controversial issue areas. Determined to avoid any appearance that the Court was caving in to the intense debate *Roe* had provoked, the trio declared that "a decision to overturn *Roe*'s essential holding under the existing circumstances would address error, if error there was, at the cost of both profound and unnecessary damage to the Court's legitimacy, and to the Nation's commitment to the rule of law."[47]

Justice Stevens quickly pronounced the troika's effort "a fine piece of work...substantial parts" of which he could join, assuming his colleagues were "interested in a partial join by a non-author." Blackmun's clerk thought he would also be able to concur with much of the opinion, but had a number of concerns about the troika's draft, as did Stevens. Certain language in the stare decisis section indicated that "at least some of the three [believed] that *Roe* was wrongly decided," Dangel reported. "Obviously, we cannot join that language." She hoped that the trio could be persuaded "to tone down...language critical of *Roe*, or at least move it into a different [later] section of the opinion." Blackmun and Stevens, she added, also "obviously" could not join language outlining and embracing the undue burden approach to abortion controls. But "in our opinion," suggested Dangel, "we can...do our best to give the test a little more bite." In her judgment, Justice Blackmun, given his stance in earlier cases, also could not join portions of the troika's effort upholding the challenged statute's informed consent, parental consent, and reporting provisions, the last of which the trial judge had struck down, she suspected, because "he thought that the information was intended to make it easier for outfits like Operation Rescue to identify…offending clinics." Blackmun's own opinion, which his clerk was beginning to draft, should be used, she suggested, "to put the best possible spin on the SOC/AMK/DHS opinion and to attack the CJ's opinion, which…will probably end up only one vote short of a majority. We also need to criticize the undue burden test and the overruling of [portions of prior cases], although this should be done in such a way as to not make the undue burden test look completely toothless." Blackmun was leaving Washington for several days. "Have fun in San Francisco," Dangel concluded. "We'll do our best to hold down the fort."[48]

Blackmun had always delegated opinion writing almost entirely to his clerks, and *Casey* clearly was no exception. By the time the justice returned to his chambers, his clerk was nearing completion of a draft concurring and dissenting opinion for him to file in *Casey*. As Blackmun had recently remarked, the troika's opinion had taken "some of the pressure off" him to defend abortion rights. But Dangel had "little doubt," she wrote the justice, "that many people will be looking to the author of *Roe* to tell them what to think about this rather unexpected turn." Given the importance of Blackmun's views in the case, she "wanted to give [the justice] a brief summary of the approach I am taking in my draft." She also assured Blackmun that she had already cleared her approach with his other clerks, as well as the Stevens clerk responsible for *Casey*. She hoped, however, that he would inform her "if you think I'm headed down the wrong track."[49]

Before beginning the summary, Dangel conceded feelings of ambivalence about what the troika was doing; Blackmun penned "OK" in the margin to that portion of her memorandum. "Given the middle ground that they have taken," she wrote, "I fear the decision may have the effect of removing abortion from the political agenda just long enough to ensure the re-election of Pres. Bush and the appointment of another nominee from whom the Far Right will be sure to exact a promise to overrule *Roe*." Even so, she considered it important in the first section of Blackmun's opinion to put "a positive 'spin' on the troika's opinion…to 'congratulate' the troika on taking a principled stand." The position they were taking, after all, would "have its cost. Once this opinion comes out, there will be no more speculation about a Vice President O'Connor or a Chief Justice

Kennedy—and, as DHS himself recognized," much to the reclusive Justice Souter's relief, she might have added, "I suspect Barbara Bush will find herself another most-eligible-bachelor to include on her White House invite list." The trio also deserved praise, wrote Dangel, for their "principled stare decisis approach,... [which] provided a safe haven for conservatives on [the abortion] issue." Although conceding that there were "certainly better reasons to reaffirm *Roe*, [the troika's] middle position," in her judgment, might "be the best we can hope for in the next nominee, if Bush gets re-elected." Most important, Blackmun's positive assessment of the trio's opinion would enable the justice to put "as much 'bite' as possible" in the troika's undue burden formula, the standard lower courts would now be expected to follow. In fact, by using the spousal notification requirement, the only part of the challenged law the trio considered unconstitutional, as a model for application of the undue burden standard, Blackmun's opinion could "subtly indicate that under that standard, even the other provisions upheld today could be knocked down—it's simply a matter of compiling the factual record" showing that each regulation at issue unduly burdened the woman's choice.

In the opinion's second section, Dangel continued, Blackmun should reaffirm his commitment to *Roe* and its strict scrutiny approach to abortion regulations. But the tone of those passages, she advised, should not be "harsh." Instead, the section must reflect "the more consoling tone of an older, wiser uncle.... The bottom line should be that, while you think the troika's approach is wrong, you remain hopeful that they will see the light."

The third section of the draft attacked the "CJ and Co.," who were assuming essentially the same positions in *Casey* they had in *Webster*. "While the specifics of this section cannot be worked out," wrote Dangel, "until AS [Antonin Scalia] has circulated his monstrosity, the format of this section should be a parade of the ever increasing horribles: first, the CJ's opinion, which overrules *Roe* without admitting it; second, AS's opinion which, by calling for the overruling of *Roe*, takes the ridiculous position that the answer to a question as fundamental as the right to choose should vary from State to State; and finally," drawing on the stance of the Bush I administration during oral argument in *Casey*, a demonstration "that even the overruling of *Roe* will not suffice—pro-life forces will not be satisfied until the fetus is declared a person under the Fourteenth [Amendment] so that decisions on reproductive freedom can be made once and for all by some right-wing minority."

Then Dangel summarized what she proposed as the justice's conclusion: "In short, while there may be something to cheer in the troika's opinion, there is much more to fear from the right. And the difference between the two positions is a single vote—a single vote that is up for grabs in the coming election." The clerk hoped what she had drafted met with Blackmun's approval. "Nothing like ending the year with a bang." The justice was satisfied, penning his "OK" for each of the sections at the bottom of his clerk's summary. "I *must* write," he added, presumably meaning that he must file what Dangel had written.

At the request primarily of Justice Stevens, O'Connor, Kennedy, and Souter made modifications in their opinion's substance, and especially in its organization, enabling Stevens and Blackmun to join part of their effort. Dangel continued to refine Blackmun's opinion, albeit noting at one point that she had been delayed in "writing my 'parade of horribles' section by the absence of a rather important 'firetruck'—the evil nino has yet to circulate." Through one of his clerks, Justice Kennedy expressed concern about "references to the Chief Justice as 'the Chief' " in the Blackmun opinion. Dangel made the change, informing the justice, "While I have my doubts as to whether he deserves to be call[ed] 'Justice' on this one, I guess there's no need to ruffle feathers needlessly—we ruffle enough with our criticism already."[50]

In the final two paragraphs of Blackmun's draft dissent, Dangel tied the future of abortion rights closely to politics and the selection of the elderly justice's successor. Through their clerks, she soon wrote Blackmun, Justice Stevens had expressed concern that such an ending "undermin[ed] the attempt by the joint opinion to say 'S Ct Justices are above politics, Mr. Pres., so why don't you stop trying to influence us.' He also thinks it's important to encourage the troika." Dangel readily agreed that the trio deserved credit for their stand and thought the opinion she had drafted accomplished that goal. But she seriously doubted that *Casey* could "end the politicization of the [judicial] appointment process," adding, "Indeed, with the vote at 5–4, I think it highly likely that *Casey* will only push the Pres. to get a commitment to overrule *Roe* from the next nominee."

She could also understand Justice Stevens's efforts to "form an alliance" with the troika. After all, they were the Court's swing votes and "carr[ied] a lot of power." Even so, she was increasingly disappointed with Blackmun's colleague, who was not only voting in *Casey* to uphold abortion regulations he previously had opposed but, in her judgment, had been "distancing himself" from Blackmun in other cases as well. "I can't help but think," she asserted, "that JPS sees that there's power in the middle, and therefore that's where he's moving. In short, I think JPS is taking for granted that you will always be here to make the principled argument, so he's free to go off and build coalitions in the middle."[51]

To Dangel, however, abortion and related liberty issues were too critical to be brokered.

> At some point, on some issues, some people have to end the compromises and perpetuations of myths. Some issues are just too important—abortion is one of them, and like it or not, you are the person American women look to in order to find out what is really happening in this case. I can't but fear that without that last paragraph women are going to think they can rest easy, because *Roe* has been reaffirmed once and for all.
>
> And, quite honestly, this is not just about abortion or this Term. Justices who oppose *Roe* have a constricted view of most liberty interests. And the Justices who get appointed in the next few years are going to make up the Court *for most of my life*!

When the justice himself expressed some concern about the tone of the opinion's final two paragraphs, Dangel offered "a more muted ending," which now read, she assured Blackmun, "less as a battle cry, and more as a lament that an issue as important as this should be decided in such a circus atmosphere." She also expressed the "hope" that the justice did not think "that [she and other clerks] were pressuring you too much on the final section....You certainly should not include it if you feel uncomfortable." Dangel obviously also hoped, however, that the final paragraph could be retained. "The people of America need someone to tell them the truth," she declared. "And, as the author of *Roe*,...you're the only person who can do it." Jokingly, no doubt, Blackmun also questioned mention of his age (eighty-three) in the draft. But after Dangel suggested changing that language to "getting along in years," the justice decided to leave well enough alone.

The two final paragraphs did remain, becoming perhaps the most frequently quoted passages of the opinions filed in *Casey*:

> In one sense, the Court's approach is worlds apart from that of the Chief Justice and Justice Scalia. And yet, in another sense, the distance between the two approaches is short—the distance is but a single vote.
>
> I am 83 years old. I cannot remain on this Court forever, and when I do step down, the confirmation process for my successor well may focus on the issue before us today. That, I regret, may be exactly where the choice between the two worlds will be made.[52]

On June 29, the day the ruling was announced, Justice Blackmun had his customary breakfast with his clerks in the Court cafeteria. "He seemed bubbly and chipper," a reporter observed, "not the mood to expect if he was about to witness the demise of his cherished doctrine legalizing abortion." He had reason to be happy. In *Webster*, as he put it in his *Casey* opinion, "four Members of this Court appeared poised to 'cast into darkness the hopes and visions of every woman in this country,' who had come to believe that the Constitution guaranteed them the right to reproductive choice. All that remained between the promise of *Roe* and the darkness of the plurality was a single, flickering flame. Decisions since *Webster* gave little reason to hope that this flame would cast much light....But now, just when so many expected the darkness to fall, the flame has grown bright."[53]

The pleasure of the day, however, was also tinged with anxiety for the future. While praising the O'Connor-Kennedy-Souter joint opinion as "an act of personal courage and constitutional principle," the justice readily conceded that the troika's undue burden formula did not accord abortion rights "the full protection afforded by this Court before *Webster*," adding, "I fear for the darkness as four Justices anxiously await the single vote necessary to extinguish the light."[54]

Legal scholars and journalists agreed with Blackmun that abortion rights remained in serious jeopardy. The troika, after all, had rejected *Roe's* trimester framework and upheld all but one of the abortion controls at issue in *Casey*. They had also concluded that the state's interest in fetal life justified some degree of regulation throughout a pregnancy.

The outcome, though, obviously could have been much worse, as suggested by the shrill tone of the opinions Chief Justice Rehnquist and Justice Scalia filed in the case. The future scope of abortion rights would simply be subject to a more elastic standard than the trimester framework had permitted, but one hardly as deferential to governmental authority as Rehnquist, Scalia, and Thomas preferred. In any event, the justice's former clerks seemed pleased. Telephoning her congratulations, Pamela Karlan ridiculed Scalia's opinion as "near hysteria" and questioned pro-choice attacks on the ruling, which Karlan praised as "more than we ever could have hoped for out of this Court." Of Clarence Thomas's decision to join Scalia's opinion, she noted, "First we have the 'Minnesota Twins,' then we have the 'Arizona Twins' [Rehnquist and O'Connor], and now we have 'Ebony and Ivory.'" In her notes summarizing Karlan's message for the justice, Wanda Martinson explained, "The latter is a musical duo, but perhaps you know that."[55]

"The Machinery of Death"

In remarks at an Eighth Circuit conference the following month, Justice Blackmun expressed hope, although "it may take years," that the *Casey* troika "just may realize that [the undue burden] standard is unworkable and revert to the strict scrutiny approach." Noting that he had been discouraged—by whom, he did not say—from making such observations, the justice also offered his audience his impressions about a number of his colleagues. Justice Thomas, the Court's junior member, was "surely... trying to be an effective justice," he said, but "it's tough," given the controversy over Thomas's Senate confirmation. Alluding to reports that Thomas never asked questions during oral argument, he noted that he also was "generally silent," adding, "We leave the questions to Justice Scalia and some of the others." Characterizing Justice Souter, at that point in his career, as "conservative but…independent," a quality he said he had to "respect," he also told listeners that he and Mrs. Blackmun found Souter charming. "Dottie and I have also concluded that perhaps he's the only normal person on the Supreme Court. I won't expand on that."[56]

The justice made no mention of any plans for retirement. As he had in *Casey*, however, he mentioned that he was "very much aware" of his age. When Bill Clinton denied the first President Bush a second term in the fall elections that year speculation mounted that he might soon leave the Court.

For a number of Blackmun's clerks, however, there remained an important piece of unfinished business: persuading the justice to reject capital punishment. Although he had voted in *Furman v. Georgia* (1972) and other cases to uphold the death penalty, he had made clear his public abhorrence of legalized executions throughout his judicial career. Increasingly over the years, he had joined majorities limiting the scope of capital punishment and, more frequently, had dissented when the Court rejected challenges to death sentences. He had voted with the majority in overturning the death penalty for rape. But he dissented when the Court upheld execution of the mentally retarded and youths at least sixteen years old at the time of their offense, affirmed the use of victim impact statements during the penalty phase of capital cases, and rejected the contention that statistical evidence of racial disparities in state executions created a presumption of unconstitutional bias in imposition of the death penalty.[57]

Blackmun found one aspect of the penalty phase in capital cases especially disturbing: the use of psychiatrists' predictions about "future dangerousness" as justification for a defendant's execution. In *Barefoot v. Estelle* (1983), a Texas case, a majority upheld a death sentence that had been based in part on the testimony of two psychiatrists, including one Dr. John Grigson. Dr. Grigson, as one wire service report put it, had "been used by the state of Texas for dozens of sentencing hearings in death penalty cases and virtually each time had testified that the defendant was incorrigibly dangerous, thus permitting them to be sentenced to death. Texas newspapers have labeled him 'Doctor Death.'" Blackmun was appalled at the Court's deference to such testimony. David Ogden, the clerk assigned to the case, drafted a vehement dissent that clearly pleased the justice. One morning in the Court cafeteria, the clerk later recalled, he told Blackmun that he was revising the dissent to respond to passages in the majority opinion. "I remember his taking my arm in the breakfast line, waiting for his egg to be cooked, and saying, 'Just don't take the ginger out.'" The "ginger" stayed in. Drawing largely on an amicus curiae brief filed in the case by the American Psychiatric Association, the dissent exclaimed, "Psychiatric predictions of future dangerousness *are not accurate*; wrong two times out of three, their probative value, and therefore any possible contribution they might make to the ascertainment of truth, is virtually nonexistent."[58]

Most frustrating for the justice was the Court's growing reluctance to grant stays of execution and further habeas corpus review of death sentences, even in the face of new evidence that the defendant might well be innocent. In *Herrera v. Collins* (1993), a defendant pled guilty to the murder of one police officer and was convicted of a second officer's murder, receiving a death sentence on each charge. Ten years later, after direct appeal efforts and a round of state and federal habeas corpus proceedings had failed, he filed a second federal habeas petition, alleging that he was innocent of the second officer's murder and that his death sentence thus violated both due process and the Eighth Amendment's guarantee against cruel and unusual punishment. In support of his petition, he offered affidavits from two persons who claimed that the defendant's now-dead brother had told them he, not his brother, had killed both officers. Emphasizing the need for finality in criminal cases and principles of federalism, a majority, speaking through Chief Justice Rehnquist, denied the petitioner relief. Even "assuming for the sake of argument" that "truly persuasive" evidence of innocence with an "extraordinarily high" prospect of success might warrant a new trial for the defendant, Herrera, Rehnquist concluded, had not met that "extraordinarily high" threshold. The chief justice also rejected the petitioner's due process challenge to a Texas rule giving convicted defendants only thirty days to petition for a new trial. The restriction, he wrote, did not violate "a principle of fundamental fairness 'rooted in the traditions and conscience of our people.'" Rehnquist assured Herrera, however, that he would still have a forum in which to raise his claim of actual innocence: he could simply petition the Texas governor for clemency.

In a biting dissent, Justice Blackmun scorned the hurdles the majority expected defendants to overcome before becoming eligible for a new hearing based on evidence of their innocence. For the justice, "nothing could be more contrary to contemporary standards of decency...or more shocking to the conscience...than to execute a person who is actually innocent." If a defendant could show that he was "probably actually innocent," he deserved a new trial.[59]

In his concluding paragraph, the only portion of his dissent Justices Stevens and Souter declined to join, the justice also revealed his mounting disenchantment not only with the Court's approach to capital cases, but with the validity of capital punishment itself. "I have voiced disappointment over the Court's obvious eagerness to do away with any restriction on the States' power to execute whomever and however they please," he observed. "I have also expressed doubts about whether, in the absence of such restrictions, capital punishment remains constitutional at all....Of one thing, however, I am certain. Just as an execution without adequate safeguards is unacceptable, so too is an execution when the condemned prisoner can prove that he is innocent. The execution of a person who can show that he is innocent comes perilously close to simple murder."[60]

Blackmun clerks had long been lobbying the justice to abandon his *Furman* stance and file a dissent declaring capital punishment unconstitutional. "I know [a draft opinion] was floating around before I got there [in 1985]," Pamela Karlan remembers. "We tried it with him my year, and people tried it with him a couple of years after that....People nearly every year would kind of float this up to him. 'Maybe you just want to step up to the plate and say, "Enough's enough."...Don't you want to do this?'" When *Herrera v. Collins* was before the Court, Geoffrey Klineberg, who was clerking that term, remembers, "It was clear really in all of our minds that he was struggling very hard with the whole process."[61]

Blackmun, who had always been considerably more deferential to government in criminal cases than in most other fields, resisted his clerks' entreaties for at least a decade. But advancing age and the election of Bill Clinton, a president committed to abortion rights, had convinced him that the 1993 term would be his last on the bench. If he was to take a stand on capital punishment, he had to act soon.

On February 22, 1994, the justice filed the opinion his clerks had long hoped for. Dissenting from a denial of certiorari in *Callins v. Collins*, a Texas murder case, he proclaimed:

From this day forward, I no longer shall tinker with the machinery of death. For more than 20 years I have endeavored—indeed, I have struggled—along with a majority of this Court, to develop procedural and substantive rules that would lend more than the mere appearance of fairness to the death penalty endeavor. Rather than continue to coddle the Court's delusion that the desired level of fairness has been achieved and the need for regulation eviscerated, I feel morally and intellectually obligated simply to concede that the death penalty experiment has failed. It is virtually self-evident to me now that no combination of procedural rules or substantive regulations ever can save the death penalty from its inherent constitutional deficiencies. The basic questions—does the system accurately and consistently determine which defendants "deserve" to die?—cannot be answered in the affirmative. It is not simply that this Court has allowed vague aggravating circumstances [justifying death sentences] to be employed,...relevant mitigating evidence to be disregarded,...and vital judicial review to be blocked....The problem is that the inevitability of factual, legal, and moral error gives us a system that we know must wrongly kill some defendants, a system that fails to deliver the fair, consistent, and reliable sentences of death required by the Constitution.[62]

In a brief concurrence, Justice Scalia was at his sarcastic best, or worst, depending on one's perspective. "Convictions in opposition to the death penalty are often passionate and deeply held," he declared, but "that would be no excuse for reading them into a Constitution that does not contain them, even if they represented the convictions of a majority of Americans. Much less is there any excuse for using that course to thrust a minority's views upon the people."

Scalia also took careful aim at the poignant description of the execution the petitioner faced, with which Blackmun had begun his dissent: "On February 23, 1994, at approximately 1:00 a.m.," the justice had solemnly observed, "Brian Edwin Callins will be executed by the State of Texas. Intravenous tubes attached to the arms will carry the instrument of death, a toxic fluid designed specifically for the purpose of killing human beings.

The witnesses, standing a few feet away, will behold Callins, no longer a defendant, an appellant, or a petitioner, but a man, strapped to a gurney, and seconds away from extinction." Blackmun's colleague was not moved. Blackmun had chosen to make his statement against capital punishment, noted Scalia, in a case involving "one of the less brutal of the murders that regularly come before us—the murder of a man ripped by a bullet suddenly and unexpectedly…and left to bleed to death on the floor of a tavern. The death-by-injection which Justice Blackmun describes looks pretty desirable next to that. It looks even better next to some of the other cases before us which Justice Blackmun did not select as the vehicle for his announcement that the death penalty is always unconstitutional—for example, the case of the 11-year-old girl raped by four men and then killed by stuffing her panties down her throat…, now pending before the Court. How enviable a quiet death by lethal injection compared with that!"[63]

Chapter 10

Citizen Blackmun

In a column entitled "Justice Blackmun's Outburst," the conservative commentator George Will complained that the justice, in his *Callins* dissent, was "again confusing autobiography with constitutional reasoning" when he announced that he was simply "too personally distressed ever again to sanction the death penalty." The justice had recently appeared on ABC's *Nightline* with Nina Totenberg. To Will, Blackmun had become "a moral exhibitionist, telling *Nightline* and law students and others about the agony of decision-making.... Surely it is time for him to take his anti-constitutional egotism into retirement."[1]

Soon Will was to get his wish. Asked about his retirement plans during his annual visit to the Aspen Institute in August 1992, Justice Blackmun replied, "I don't want to stay long enough to be asked by the chief justice to step aside. This happened to Oliver Wendell Holmes, you know. This is one reason why Dottie and I have annual checkups and find out whether we'll last till Thanksgiving. I have three or four good medical friends who have promised to let me know when my level of senility is unacceptable." Meaningfully, he then added, "At least, I'll stay there until the third day of November 1992."[2]

No one could have missed the import of that last remark. When Bill Clinton denied President Bush a second term on November 3, speculation spread that the justice's retirement was imminent. Several former Blackmun clerks dismissed such talk as premature. "He's a workaholic," David Van Zandt told one reporter, "works seven days a week during the term, and I just can't see him puttering around a golf course." "It's far more up in the air than the press thinks," another remarked. Randall Bezanson, who had become law dean at Washington and Lee University, thought that the justice would be reluctant to turn his position over to a freshman justice, even one chosen by President Clinton, during a period of growing conservatism at the Court. "He is a stabilizing force at a time of change," Bezanson said. "I'd be surprised if he considered retirement at this stage of the game."[3]

Blackmun, however, had his own schedule. Each New Year's since 1981, a host of notables from virtually all walks of life had gathered in Hilton Head, South Carolina, for Renaissance Weekend, a four-day series of seminars, speeches, and related events focusing on issues of public concern. Bill and Hillary Clinton were prominently associated with Renaissance Weekend, and during the New Year's 1993 session, the president-elect and Justice Blackmun were paired for a seminar on "The Changing of the Guard." The justice apparently did not broach the subject of his retirement directly with Clinton on that occasion. But in a private conversation with the president-elect, Blackmun later reported, he had urged Clinton to take the selection of federal judges "seriously." Presidents Reagan and Bush were frequently accused of applying an anti-*Roe* "litmus test" to prospective judicial nominees. "I asked [Clinton] not to use a litmus test," the justice later said, "but get just good judges, judges of experience, judgment, honor, and above all integrity of the highest order." Renaissance Weekend sessions were off the record, and participants declined to divulge details of the justice's remarks to the audience, noting only, according to a reporter, that "Blackmun captivated [them] with an emotional and inspirational speech directed in part to his wife, daughters, and grandchildren, who were in the room." When asked whether the justice offered any hints about retirement, one participant responded, "Let me put it this way. He did not seem or sound like a man who is packing his bags anytime soon."[4]

But Blackmun also made no secret of his elation at Clinton's election and thus, presumably, his willingness to put the naming of his successor in the new president's hands. At the end of January, during a speech to the Minnesota Bar Association in his hometown, he said that he had been "on an emotional roller coaster of late," saddened by the recent death of Justice Marshall yet optimistic about the new administration and its promise for the nation's future.[5]

In March he appeared to be moving closer to a decision, telling a law school audience, "I know how old I am and I don't intend to stay there much longer." But subsequent signals were mixed at best. Although Justice White reportedly wanted to retire, he was delaying an announcement because, as "someone close to White" put it, he did not "want to steal the spotlight from Harry" in the event his colleague retired. White's retirement at the end of the 1992–93 term fueled speculation that Blackmun had decided to remain on the bench. The justice had decided, the story ran, that President Clinton would replace the generally conservative White with a liberal, thereby increasing Blackmun's chances of being on the winning side of cases, with the corresponding control over opinion assignments the senior justice would enjoy whenever the chief justice was in dissent. Yet when asked in November whether the 1993–94 term then under way would be his last, he declined comment, repeated his statement that "I know how old I am," but added, enigmatically, "One is as old as one feels, and I feel pretty well." When confronted by a reporter with a chart indicating that he was the fourth-oldest justice to have served on the Court and would soon be the third-oldest (after only Oliver Wendell Holmes and Roger B. Taney), he jokingly exclaimed, "Holy smokes— I hadn't been aware of that. I may have to start packing!"[6]

By the next Renaissance Weekend, however, the justice had made his decision. In a conversation with President Clinton less than two months before the appearance of his *Callins* dissent, he shared his decision to renounce the death penalty, but also informed the president of his plans to retire. Especially after his *Callins* dissent appeared, Court watchers again began predicting that an announcement of his retirement was imminent. Almost invariably, such speculation was tied to his reversal of position on capital punishment, and was not always complimentary. In a March article, Carl Rowan, the African American columnist and biographer of

Justice Marshall, cited reports that *Callins* was enabling Blackmun to retire free of guilt for years of cases in which he had upheld death sentences. But the journalist was not so forgiving. "[Blackmun] has declared unconstitutional the imposition of the death penalty [only] after his votes helped to allow several states to have more than 15 years of electrocution, gassings and poisonings. The Blackmun mea culpa comes with more than 2,800 people now sitting on Death Row—more than enough for an execution a day right into the 21st century."[7]

On April 6 morning newspapers carried reports the justice was expected to announce his retirement later that day. Leaving a speaking engagement in Charlotte, the president had declined comment, but noted, "As I understand it, [the justice] has an announcement to make tomorrow, so I think we should let him make it." Asked whether he considered Blackmun a great justice, the president was no longer reticent. "Oh, absolutely. You know, I think he's a great man."[8]

At a White House press conference later, a smiling but at times emotional justice, with the president at his side, announced that his nearly quarter century tenure on the high bench was ending. Terming Blackmun a man for whom "justice" was not merely a title but "his guiding light," Clinton praised his focus on the law's "human dimension":

> Those of us who have studied the law can at times be lost in its abstractions. The habits, the procedures, the language of the law can separate lawyers from the people who look to the bar for justice. Justice Blackmun's identification was firmly and decisively with the ordinary people of this country, with their concerns, and his humanity was often given voice not only in majority opinions but in his dissents.... I can only say that every one of us who serves in any capacity in public life would do well by the people of the United States if we could bring to our work half the integrity, the passion and the love for this country that Justice Blackmun has given us on the United States Supreme Court for 24 years.[9]

With characteristic humility, Justice Blackmun thanked the president for his "far too generous ... remarks," then pointed out the obvious: "There

are those who don't agree with you, of course." In equally typical Blackmun fashion, he also emphasized that his tenure on the Court "hasn't
been much fun on most occasions," but he also pronounced it "a fantastic
experience," adding, "It's not easy to step aside, but I know what the num-
bers are, and it's time."[10]

Nor, of course, could the ceremony end without a reference to the
justice's signature opinion and the uproar it continued to provoke. One
reporter wondered whether, in retirement, the justice would be able to
"get along without a daily fix of hate mail." The justice did not hear the
question, but the controversial Clinton had a ready response: "He offered
to take some of mine."[11]

As the Court's term and Blackmun's tenure neared an end, the justice, citing his *Callins* dissent, repeatedly dissented from denials of review
in death penalty cases but made no further last-minute jurisprudential
shifts. The former Harvard Glee Club member also marked another anniversary of his most enduring contribution to the Court's cultural life. In
1983, Stephen Strickland, a prominent businessman and president of the
National Peace Foundation, whom Blackmun had met at Aspen, arranged
a concert at the Court in celebration of the justice's seventy-fifth birthday. The Court's piano at the time was an old upright donated by the
granddaughter of Chief Justice Hughes. When Blackmun suggested that
it would "be great to have a real piano" at the Court "so we could do this
more often," Strickland persuaded Baldwin Piano Co. to provide the Court
a grand piano at cost. Since 1988, the justice had hosted biennial musicales.
On May 25, he played host to a program that included a work commis-
sioned in his honor.[12]

On June 30, his last day on the bench, the justice filed two opinions.
Both, fittingly, were in death penalty cases. In *McFarland v. Scott* (1994),
he spoke for the Court in making it somewhat easier for state death row
inmates to seek stays of execution. But he registered a final dissent from the
Court's ruling in *Tuilaepa v. California* (1994), upholding that state's death
penalty statute. In addition to reiterating his *Callins* stance, he concluded
that three factors the challenged law required juries and judges to consider
in determining whether to impose a death sentence were unconstitutionally vague. "For two decades now," he declared, "the Court has professed a
commitment to guiding sentencers' discretion so as to 'minimize the risk

of wholly arbitrary and capricious action,'...and to achieve principled distinctions between those who receive the death penalty and those who do not....The Court's approval today of these California...factors calls into question the continued strength of that commitment." For his final day on the bench, the justice also had another opportunity to participate in an abortion-related decision, joining the majority, as he had in the past, in upholding certain restrictions on antiabortion protests while invalidating others as violations of free speech.[13]

After the day's decisions were announced, Chief Justice Rehnquist read the justice a letter of tribute from his colleagues. Although quite laudatory, certain language in the letter struck some in the courtroom as "double-edged," in the *New York Times*' words. "Your opinions have covered a wide range of the issues that come before the Court," observed Rehnquist. "You are undoubtedly best known for having authored the Court's opinion in Roe v. Wade in 1973, but that distinction should not obscure the many other important issues on which you have spoken for the Court." For his part, Blackmun resisted any temptation to lecture the other justices. Instead, emphasizing that "ours is a common, not an individual, task," he expressed hope that history would record "that we strove, in our small ways and with our limited capabilities, for the righting of injustices of both ancient and current origins."[14]

Many reacted sadly at the justice's departure and praised his record. "It may be difficult for Americans under 40 to imagine the days when abortion was illegal and unsafe," the *Washington Post* reminded readers, "but it is important to remember the conditions prevailing at that time in order to appreciate Justice Blackmun's courage and leadership." The pro-choice leader Kate Michelman lamented the "terrible void" Blackmun's retirement created. It was "imperative," she asserted, "that President Clinton balance the court by appointing a new justice with a vigorous, unswerving commitment" to abortion rights. Others stressed his resolute commitment to society's "little people."[15]

But such sentiments were hardly universal. "This is Justice Blackmun's deplorable legacy," one antiabortion leader declared: "children who had their lives violently cut short." The conservative columnist James J. Kilpatrick dismissed the justice's *Roe* opinion as "memorable chiefly as a terrible piece of constitutional law," adding, "Justice Byron White called the decision 'an exercise of raw judicial power,' and indeed it was." Kilpatrick asked, "How will Harry Blackmun rank in judicial history?" then answered his own question: "Not well. He was a sleeping volcano. Now and then he would erupt, but most of his opinions were as colorless as cold lava. A slow writer, he often took months to draft an opinion. In recent years he has drawn little but dog cases." Sherman Minton, a Truman appointee, is considered one of the most mediocre justices ever. When Minton retired in 1956, Kilpatrick observed, "he left a forlorn statement for the press: 'There will be more interest in who will succeed me than in my passing. I'm an echo.'" The journalist thought Minton's statement "would do as an epitaph for Harry Blackmun, a good man who has earned a peaceful retirement." Columnists closely associated with the conservative fringe were decidedly less restrained. Comparing *Roe* to the *Dred Scott* decision, the columnist Cal Thomas called Blackmun's signature ruling not a milestone, but a "millstone for America and American law." Blackmun had often said *Roe* would follow him to his grave. Thomas agreed. "Yes, and beyond. Justice Blackmun is not an evil man; he is part of an age in which a virus of immorality has touched us all. Still, he cannot wash his hands of personal responsibility for Roe, any more than Pontius Pilate could wash his hands of his decision 2,000 years ago."[16]

Nor were attacks on Blackmun limited to those with a political ax to grind. In a harsh but incisive analysis of the justice's "Sentimental Journey," Jeffrey Rosen, legal affairs editor of the *New Republic*, conceded that the justice "cared about the Court and the country with a sincerity that commands respect," but asserted, "Feeling deeply is no substitute for arguing rigorously." In Rosen's judgment, Blackmun's "jurisprudence of sentiment," his predilection for "reducing so many cases to their human dimensions and refusing to justify his impulses with principled legal arguments," had created the impression that liberal judicial constructions of the Constitution rested on little more than personal sympathy rather than legal methodology. This overriding element in the justice's thinking, Rosen contended, had been evident from the beginning of his Court tenure and "in both his conservative and his liberal incarnations." In *Wyman v. James* (1972), his very first opinion for the Court, he had drawn on his "impulsive sympathy" for an abused child in upholding warrantless welfare home visits—and narrowing the scope of the Fourth Amendment's guarantee against unreasonable searches and seizures. Similarly, his lament for "Poor Joshua! Victim of repeated attacks by an irresponsible, bullying, cowardly and intemperate father," made it "hard to avoid the impression that he was moved by sympathy alone" in finding constitutional violations in the tragic *DeShaney* case.[17]

Rosen did not doubt that Blackmun occasionally filed eloquent, legally convincing opinions. But he attributed those primarily to the varying quality of the justice's clerks, observing at one point, "A long-standing joke depicted Blackmun as the clerk and his clerks as the justice; he would fret about spelling errors and typos, and laboriously check all the case citations by hand, as they drafted opinions aspiring to the grand scale." Left on his own during oral argument and at conference, according to Rosen, the "legally unsophisticated" justice was typically unable to make a winning defense of his positions with his colleagues. "Blackmun shows, in the end," wrote Rosen, "that a big heart and the capacity to feel pain are not enough for success on the Supreme Court. Liberals need an intellectually sophisticated craftsman—not for aesthetic reasons, but because the alternative is a Court that governs by impulse rather than argument, by emotion rather than law." President Clinton had "promised to replace Blackmun with a justice in Blackmun's image." If the president "really cares about giving liberals an effective voice on the Court," Rosen recommended, "perhaps he should think again."[18]

While critics were questioning Blackmun's jurisprudence and qualities as a jurist, the justice's former clerks were offering up affectionate and admiring tributes. Edward Lazarus described "Breakfast with Harry Blackmun" for the *Washington Post*. Frank Holleman, in a piece entitled "The Humanity and Humility of 'Old No. 3,'" detailed his prodigious work ethic. Perhaps unwittingly supplying ammunition for Blackmun's critics, Bill McDaniel applauded, among other qualities, the justice's attention to detail. "We dreaded any spelling error, grammatical lapse, or mis-citation that crept into our submissions to him," wrote McDaniel. "He always corrected them, usually silently, sometimes not so silently. To this day, when I write him, I check and recheck my spelling and grammar, not out of fear anymore, but to show him that I try to honor the standards he exemplifies. (And maybe a little bit out of fear.)"[19]

The clerks also took aim at the justice's critics. "I'd rather have Blackmun, who uses the wrong reasoning in *Roe* to get to the right results, and let other people figure out the right reasoning," said Harold Koh. To those who complained about the justice's highly personalized approach to questions before the Court, Koh had a ready rejoinder: "He's being honest in a way that other people aren't. He sees something that really offends him, and if it offends him, he doesn't censor himself." During a roundtable with Koh and other former clerks, Pamela Karlan was more pointed: "The thing that makes you a good law professor is that you're clever and you can manipulate doctrine. The thing that makes you a good justice is that you're wise. Justice Blackmun is not a flashy, clever person. He is a wise, good person. And goodness and wisdom are not always the sorts of things that people who admire cleverness admire." In that and other settings, clerks invariably stressed the justice's humility as well. "I think one thing he found so frustrating," observed Karlan, "is that the humility quotient on the Court has gone down. I think he's always surprised at the number of cases other people find easy." His love of baseball, intense loyalty to his Minnesota Twins, obvious affection for his wife—his clerks catalogued all the justice's endearing and admirable qualities, while dismissing the contentions of detractors.[20]

As Court observers debated his judicial legacy, Justice Blackmun adjusted to life off the bench. Two of his daughters, Susie and Sally, were living in Florida, and it was initially assumed that the Blackmuns would move there. In fact, during the retirement ceremony at the end of the term, Chief Justice Rehnquist had noted, with a touch of irony, "We shall miss you—especially if you go through with your present plans to move to Florida." Ultimately, the couple decided to remain in their Normandy House apartment in Arlington. Soon after retiring, however, Blackmun's chambers were moved to the Thurgood Marshall Building near Union Station.

Technically, Blackmun did not vacate his position and acquire senior status until Stephen Breyer, his successor, took the oath of office on August 3, during the Court's summer recess. As the legal reporter Tony Mauro observed, that arrangement made it appear briefly on that day that the Court had ten rather than nine justices. Three Arkansas executions were scheduled for August 3. If the Court, Blackmun informed his colleagues, denied review before Breyer took the oath, he planned to "note a *Callins* dissent." If afterward,

Blackmun would not vote and Breyer could participate or not, as he chose. The following order was entered in one of the cases: "The application for stay of execution of sentence of death presented to Justice Blackmun and by him referred to the Court is denied. The petition to the Court is denied. The petition for a writ of certiorari…is denied. Justice Breyer took no part in the consideration or decision of this application and this petition."[21]

Not surprisingly, given his advanced age, the justice did not exercise the prerogative of retired justices to hear cases on lower federal courts. He did insist, however, on maintaining the same rigorous office schedule in retirement that he had observed on the Court. He also continued to receive speaking engagements and honors. At George Washington University's 1995 law school graduation, for example, he received an honorary doctorate and challenged graduates with a long litany of social ills confronting the nation.[22]

As the rigors of age became increasingly noticeable, Blackmun's family and staff resorted to various tactics in an effort to conserve his strength. Although an avid motion picture fan in his youth, the justice probably had not visited a movie theater in twenty years. One day Wanda Martinson convinced him to attend a matinee showing of *Toy Story*, a popular animated feature, at a nearby theater. "His concern the whole time we were gone," Martinson recalls, "was, 'what if someone sees us? This is going to be in the papers that we're shirking our responsibilities.' To take two hours off, in the middle of the day, to watch a movie! I think he was overwhelmed with guilt because he was not working." The justice's reaction was the same when, toward the end of his life, he was persuaded to work from home on Wednesdays. " 'All this staying home Wednesdays amounts to,' " Martinson recalls his grumbling, " 'is cheating the government out of a day's work.' He did not say that to be funny; that was the way he felt. He had a German mother and a German work ethic, and never gave it up."[23]

Movie Star

Whatever the justice's declining condition, however, his admirers had not forgotten him. In January 1997, the movie director Steven Spielberg's casting director Vicki Thomas telephoned Blackmun's chambers with a proposition. Spielberg wanted the justice for a cameo role in *Amistad*, chronicling the 1839 rebellion of fifty-three African slaves on a Spanish slave ship. When captured by a U.S. Navy ship off the coast of Long Island, the slaves were charged with the murder of the slave ship's captain and cook. The U.S. district court at Hartford, Connecticut, ruled that the slave traders were holding them illegally and that they were thus not liable for criminal acts committed in attempting to gain their freedom. In *United States v. Amistad* (1841), the U.S. Supreme Court, speaking through Justice Joseph Story, upheld the lower court's decision. Spielberg hoped that Blackmun would assay the Story role.[24]

The moviemakers' initial contact with the justice was hardly auspicious; they thought Chief Justice Roger B. Taney, not Story, had issued the Court's *Amistad* decision. But Blackmun's daughters, Wanda Martinson, his clerk Cecillia Wang, and aide Todd Gustin thought, as Martinson put it, that it would be "a wonderful thing for him to do. We just thought he should, you know, be a star." The casting director also assured Martinson that Spielberg "would love the fact that [the justice] served in the Story seat and that it was known [pre-Nixon] as the Jewish seat." "What do you think about this?" Martinson wrote the justice. "It would be awfully fun! I told Vicki Thomas about your nonjudicial/nonlegal experience doing readings of 'Peter and the Wolf' and the 'Lincoln Portrait.' We'll let you sleep on it some more."[25]

With former clerk Bill McDaniel acting as the justice's "agent," favorable terms were negotiated, including Spielberg's agreement to make a donation to the Harry A. Blackmun Scholarship Foundation, which McDaniel and other former clerks had established to fund scholarships for outstanding law students with the potential to make a contribution to society at large, as well as the legal profession. In typical Hollywood fashion, McDaniel insisted that the justice receive proper billing. In a summary of the contractual terms that she prepared for the justice, Cecillia Wang noted, "You will be given on-screen credit for your role, during the credits that roll at the *beginning* of the movie. (That way, you won't be hidden in the long list at the end.)" The producer also had to agree not to use the justice's "name, voice, likeness, or biography in advertising the film." But the role was not to be a money maker for the justice, who received the standard Screen Actors Guild rate for dayplayers.[26]

At Blackmun's request, Wanda Martinson enlisted Chief Justice Rehnquist's administrative assistant Jim Duff "to run the Amistad invitation by the Chief." Soon Martinson conveyed Rehnquist's reaction to the justice: "He said, 'He's retired. He can do whatever he wants to do.' The Chief seemed amused and said he was happy for you. He also said he appreciated being asked about this."[27]

On March 19 the Blackmuns and their "entourage," as his staff had jokingly begun referring to themselves, flew to Providence, Rhode Island, for filming on a sound stage in nearby Hartford. As Justice Story, Blackmun was to declare for the Court, "Therefore, it is our judgment—with one dissention—that the defendants are to be released from custody, at once, and, if they so choose, be returned to their homes in Africa." With Dottie watching anxiously on the sidelines, concerned that the experience would exhaust her husband, then eighty-nine and frail, the justice endured take after take, sitting in a wheelchair between takes, a blanket draped over his knees. Given Blackmun's own civil rights record, the scene was intensely moving to those present. "I stood on the side of the courtroom," Wanda Martinson wrote the justice during their flight back to Washington, "and watched you deliver your lines over and over and over, tears streaming from my cheeks, thankful for all that you stand for—you would have freed the slaves, just as you fought for the rights of all of life's underdogs. I was not alone. People were obviously moved by your words, not the least of whom was your Director, Steven Spielberg. It was after hearing you deliver your lines that he said: 'Now, this movie is real'—it was the magic moment for him (Asst Producer Bonnie Curtis told us) that made 'Amistad' come to life."[28]

Spielberg and his staff did their best to make the experience memorable for the justice and his family and staff. Blackmun was not the only "star" in his "entourage." His daughters Susie and Nancy, Nancy's son Nicholas Coniaris, and Blackmun's aide Todd Gustin were made Amistad extras. When Cecillia Wang was told she would have no part because there were no Chinese in New England in the 1830s, she jokingly told the justice that she "wanted him to represent me in a Title VII suit against Steven Spielberg, and he said he didn't know whether I had a cause of action." Star Anthony Hopkins gave a "completely smitten" Wanda Martinson a kiss on the check and an autographed photograph. When the justice, Martinson, and Todd Gustin missed their commercial flights back to Washington, Spielberg graciously had them flown home in his Lear jet.[29]

Blackmun's performance drew rave reviews from friends. After seeing *Amistad* at Christmas, Linda Greenhouse of the *New York Times* sent the justice a fan letter. "You were terrific. Even considering how much practice you had in the role, you outdid yourself." "Bravo! Bravissimo!" Justice Ginsburg exclaimed. Peter Dorsey of Blackmun's old firm was also impressed. "So now you're a movie star! I should have known. Congratulations!"[30]

Apparently the justice enjoyed his brief movie career. When a St. Paul friend wrote her "favorite Hollywood actor...[and] favorite Supreme Court Justice," praising his performance, Blackmun replied, "I am still not sure how this came about, but I have concluded it was a bit of fun."[31]

Time, however, was closing in on Justice Blackmun. He and Mrs. Blackmun were now living at The Jefferson, an assisted living high-rise in Arlington. In early December, DreamWorks, Spielberg's production company, hosted a Washington screening of *Amistad*, with President and Mrs. Clinton and a host of celebrities in attendance. But the justice was unable to attend. The next day the justice's grandson Nicholas, who had borrowed Blackmun's formal wear for the event, visited "Grandpa Judgie" and "Grandma Dot." When Nicholas leaned over his sleeping grandfather to say, "Good Morning, Grandpa," the justice awoke with a start. "Am I dying?" he asked. "Grandma Dot," Nicholas later wrote, "says that he worries about dying a great deal, but that he doesn't talk about it often."[32]

Closed Chambers

In fifteen months the justice would be dead, but not before being drawn indirectly into one final controversy involving the institution he had served for nearly a quarter century. In 1998, Random House published former clerk Edward Lazarus's *Closed Chambers: The First Eyewitness Account of the Epic Struggle Inside the Supreme Court*. Much of the five-hundred-plus-page book was a straightforward account of the Court's disposition of death penalty and privacy cases. But Lazarus also drew on e-mails and other private exchanges among the chambers to depict a Court wracked with internal intrigue, especially what the author saw as a campaign by conservative clerks during his term (1988–89) to undermine liberal precedents and thus exact revenge for the Senate's rejection of their hero, Robert Bork. Lazarus named names, identifying, for example, the O'Connor clerk who sent other conservative clerks the following e-mail: "Every time I draw blood I'll think of what they did to Robert H. Bork." He also described the growing tendency of justices to delegate opinion drafting to their clerks, becoming editors rather than authors of their opinions.[33]

Before the book appeared, the *Washington Post* reporter Joan Biskupic, then beginning research for a biography of Justice O'Connor, obtained a copy and wrote a *Post* article emphasizing the author's unflattering descriptions of the justices and their clerks and what she considered Lazarus's break with a long tradition of clerk confidentiality. "A new tell-all book by a former Supreme Court clerk," Biskupic began, "portrays the nation's high court justices as strongly influenced by politics and manipulated by ideological law clerks who not only play a dominant role in drafting opinions but sway how the justices vote on individual cases.... This is the first time that a former law clerk has provided a lens on the court by breaking with the tradition of remaining publicly silent on matters pertaining to the court's inner sanctum." Noting that Lazarus had clerked for Justice Blackmun during the 1988 term, she further reported, "Some people close to [the justice] said he was unaware until yesterday that his former clerk was publishing a book."[34]

Distressed at Biskupic's account, Lazarus quickly dashed off a plaintive letter to the justice. "That article, as I hope you know," he wrote, "was a gross caricature of the book. I didn't spend four years or more writing some petty screed about clerks and such. As I believe you will find when the book appears in a few weeks, it is the book I always said I was writing— an extremely serious, historically rooted analysis of the Court. That isn't to say it isn't critical. It is. But not in the way portrayed yesterday. You should also know that I make clear at the outset of the book that you had absolutely nothing to do with it....I fear yesterday was an agonizing one for you. For that I am very, very sorry."[35]

Publicly, Lazarus disputed Joan Biskupic's contention that Justice Blackmun had been "surprised" by news that the book was being published. Insisting that he and the justice had maintained "very close" contact in the years since his clerkship and that he had kept the justice regularly apprised of his progress with the book, Lazarus told a reporter, "I did not discuss it with [the justice] in detail, and he did not help me with the book. But he was certainly aware of it." Biskupic stood by her story, declaring, "That's what people close to Blackmun said when they were told about the book last month." The justice's chambers issued no comment. In the margin of a *Legal Times* piece quoting Biskupic's assertion, however, Wanda Martinson wrote, "This did not come from HAB chambers."[36]

Fallout from the Biskupic article and *Closed Chambers*'s appearance was often bitter. Other former Supreme Court clerks insisted that it was indeed the justices, not their clerks, who called the shots. Richard Painter, a former clerk to a federal appeals court judge and coauthor of a casebook on the professional responsibilities of lawyers, accused Lazarus of "sacrific[ing] the dignity of the Supreme Court and the privacy of the justices in order to write a sensationalistic book." Construing the clerks' code of conduct as requiring them to maintain the confidentiality of the Court's papers and inner workings even after their clerkships ended, Painter charged that Lazarus may have violated provisions of federal criminal law. Lyle Denniston of the Baltimore *Sun* concluded that the book was "based primarily upon a single, utterly preposterous premise: Faced with heavy legal controversy, no justice of the modern Supreme Court could or can be counted on to act out of principle or high-minded motive." "Perhaps Lazarus thinks of himself as courageous, bucking the potential wrath of the justices to shed 'light and clarity' on important truths," observed a former O'Connor clerk. "But it's a poor sort of courage to betray the trust of your colleagues for your own advancement." In various forums, David Garrow expressed concern that Lazarus's book might chill an important source of "significant and highly detailed contributions to Supreme Court historiography." In a telephone interview, Garrow told the *Legal Times* reporter Tony Mauro that "the most dangerous and regrettable part of the whole Lazarus thing is what it may do to that tradition. If clerks are made to think they can't say 'boo' about their work at the Court, what will that do to the quality of Court history?" Under pressure from alumni and others, Yale law dean Anthony Kronman, who had written a glowing blurb for the dust jacket of *Closed Chambers*'s hardback edition, declined to endorse the paperback version and in letters to the Yale community apologized for his "real lapse" of judgment in failing to consider the "ethical implications" of Lazarus's work. If he did not make the retraction, Kronman reportedly feared, Yale might be penalized by the Court in various ways, from its graduates not being hired as clerks to justices turning down speaking engagements and participation in moot court competitions there.[37]

Lazarus may have taken the outcry from critics (which obviously did not hurt book sales) in stride, but not the decision of the justice, or his staff and family, to cut off all contact with the former clerk. In September 1998, he wrote Justice Blackmun an anguished letter:

> I assume from the fact I no longer receive even routine mailings from the Chambers that I am now subject to some kind of excommunication. Of course, neither you nor Wanda nor anyone else has thought it appropriate to confront me directly with the reasons for such an action—which, I guess, reflects the depth of the betrayal you evidently feel. Of the many wounds that others have sought to inflict on me—from misstating my beliefs to assassinating my character, pressuring those who have endorsed my work, trying to get me fired, and seeking to have me investigated—the only one that has caused any real pain is the estrangement from you, Dottie, and Wanda.
>
> ... I do not believe that I have committed any disloyal or unethical act. And I am hurt that after so many years of deep affection you have seen fit to cut me off without a word. That hurt, however, does not diminish what has always been and will always remain my love for you and your family.[38]

The justice never replied to the letter.

By that point in his life, Justice Blackmun was beginning to suffer from serious memory lapses, and the extent to which he was aware of the controversy surrounding *Closed Chambers* is uncertain. "I was told," Edward Lazarus said several years later, that at that stage his Alzheimer's had proceeded to a point where it wasn't because he wouldn't respond, but that he wasn't independently answering his correspondence. I don't know whether that's true or not. I was never told that the justice himself was mad.... The justice knew about my book, had known about the book for years. He had always been very supportive of my writing. As a matter of fact, he gave me the Court's internal file.... When I started writing *Closed Chambers*, I told him I was writing. And he certainly knew I was talking to his clerks, other clerks, that I inquired [about] talking with some of the other justices. And we kind of did a little dance about whether he would ever talk to me. And I ultimately decided not to put him in that [position].... I had breakfast with him during that period, though, many, many times, because my family lived in Washington and I was back there [often]. He married [my wife and] me while I was writing *Closed Chambers*. There was a newspaper article saying he didn't know anything about it. That's absurd![39]

"Get Me Out of Here"

However aware or unaware of the *Closed Chambers* controversy Justice Blackmun might have been would soon be irrelevant. Bill McDaniel, a Baltimore attorney, had remained one of the most solicitous of the justice's former clerks. An inveterate baseball fan like the justice, McDaniel had persuaded Blackmun toward the end of his career on the bench to join him for an evening at the Baltimore Orioles Park. While watching the game, they observed a young boy try repeatedly to get one of the players to sign his baseball, but to no avail. Finally, McDaniel took the ball from the boy and said, "Here, let me get this man to sign it," and handed the ball to the justice. "The boy," McDaniel recalls, "reached over, grabbed the ball out of Harry's hand, and said, 'That ball is for Cal Ripkin!' And the justice just loved that."[40]

Like others close to the justice, however, McDaniel had watched helplessly as Blackmun's health deteriorated. "He had five years after he retired. I'd say the first two and a half were pretty good. He was in good shape mentally, and he received a lot of accolades and appreciation during that period, and that meant a great deal to him. But the last couple of years were not good. [During the filming of *Amistad*] he was physically frail...and so thin. But he was fine otherwise....After that he began to have difficulties: mentally, it was rough the last year and a half. It was hard to watch."[41]

On February 22, 1999, McDaniel was driving to Washington for breakfast at the Court when he received a telephone call. "I got a call from Wanda, saying, 'We're at the hospital; he's broken his hip.'...I went right over to the hospital and went in to see him. And there he was lying there; it was heart-breaking. He was so thin and frail. But he looked up at me and said, 'Bill, get me out of here!' And I said, 'I don't know how I could do that. What about a writ of habeas corpus?' And he said, 'You draft it, and I'll sign it.' "[42]

For a time after surgery, the justice seemed to rally. Clare Huntington, his clerk for the 1998–99 term, visited his hospital room every day, telling him what was going on at the Court. But the ordeal of the operation was simply too much for his already weakened and enlarged heart to bear. On Thursday, March 4, Wanda Martinson sent former clerks an e-mail informing them that the justice had died at one o'clock that morning. In a touching gesture, she lined through and corrected a grammatical error in her message.[43]

The justice's family was convinced, Sally Blackmun later wrote friends, "that Dad ordered the weather on Monday and Tuesday" following his death. "Both were typical Minnesota winter days." On Monday, "a very cold, but bright and sunny day," the justice paid a final visit to the institution he had served for twenty-four years. With most of his colleagues lining the front steps and his five grandchildren leading the processional, his casket was placed in the Supreme Court's Great Hall. Through the afternoon and early evening, Justice Blackmun's clerks and Court police stood vigil as mourners filed by his casket, which was draped with the forty-eight-star flag that had covered his father's coffin. That evening, clerks, colleagues, family, and friends shared their memories of the justice.[44]

Although Blackmun's weak heart had made him ineligible for military service, he and Dottie had often enjoyed walks over the beautiful hills of Arlington National Cemetery. With President Clinton's assistance, the family secured a burial plot there on a knoll overlooking the city. An overnight storm had blanketed Washington with a heavy snow, but on Tuesday morning, the justice's family and a few close friends drove with his remains from the Court to Arlington. Security precautions after the 1985 shooting incident had brought an end to Blackmun's driving days. But his family, thinking it only fitting that the justice, who had chosen to be cremated, make his final journey in his vehicle of choice since 1961, had rented a Volkswagen Beetle for the occasion. "The procession [that morning] from the Court down Constitution Avenue," Sally Blackmun later wrote President and Mrs. Clinton, "was quite a sight—the 'bug' followed by two stretch limos!" At one point, a DC policeman, mistaking the Volkswagen for an interloper, ordered the vehicle out of the procession![45]

That afternoon, following the private morning ceremony at Arlington, friends and family, including President and Mrs. Clinton, celebrated the justice's life and career in a service at Metropolitan Memorial Methodist Church, where Blackmun had served as a lay reader. Speaking for his colleagues, Justice Breyer recalled Blackmun's reply to one of the thousands of post-*Roe* letters demanding his resignation: "Dear Sir, No. Sincerely, Harry A. Blackmun." Representing the justice's ninety-three clerks, Pamela Karlan, Harold Koh, and Bill McDaniel stressed his humility and empathy for the underdog. "Harry Blackmun's great spirit," said McDaniel, "breathed life into the law—for the poor, for the dispossessed, for those living on what he called the 'raw edges of existence.'" Fellow Minnesotan Garrison Keillor also took part in the memorial to his friend; the Blackmuns were faithful listeners to Keillor's *A Prairie Home Companion* on public radio. Indeed, when other commitments prevented them from listening for three successive Saturday nights, the justice wrote the program's producer, "It amazes me how mildly resentful one can feel about this." At a Washington appearance that the Blackmuns attended, Keillor inscribed the justice's program, "To Mr. Justice Blackmun, the shy person's judge." Keillor serenaded the funeral congregation with Yale's "The Whiffenpoof Song," the Harvard graduate's favorite, and "Toura Loura Loura," the Irish melody the justice had sung to his daughters when they were children. Robert McDuffie, a violinist and close friend who had regularly performed at the concerts the justice arranged at the Court, played Fritz Kreisler's *Liebeslied*, another of the justice's favorites. The service concluded with Bach's triumphant *Toccata and Fugue in D Minor*, performed, a draft of the memorial program had instructed, on a "blasting organ."[46]

Newspaper editorialists and abortion rights activists, among others, praised the justice's record. Writer Bob Herbert even contrasted Blackmun's resolute commitment to abortion rights with presidential candidate George W. Bush's efforts to dodge a firm stand on the issue. "One made a stand on principle and will be remembered as a man of courage and integrity," wrote Herbert. "The other has carefully gauged the direction of the wind, and may well end up as President." Blackmun, the writer declared, "was both revered and vilified as a result [of *Roe*]. But no amount of obloquy could make him doubt the correctness or the value of the decision." Bush's "primary motivation," however, was "to get the White House. The last thing he wants to do is stumble upon a principle. If he were to favor a woman's right to choose, he would be ambushed from the right. And if he were to absolutely follow what he says is in his heart and in his mind—that we should amend the Constitution and ban abortion outright—the boulders would immediately begin falling on him from the left. Poor George. There is nothing left to do, but equivocate."[47]

Former clerks also offered their final tributes. Writing for a legal newspaper, Chai Feldbaum praised Blackmun's remarkable "understanding and empathy" for people who "lived a life completely foreign to [his own]." Feldbaum, a lesbian who had clerked for the justice the term after his *Bowers* dissent appeared, recalled his reaction to the volume of mail he received from gays, including the sons and daughters of close family friends. "He was amazed, and enormously gratified, at how the words of his dissent were making a difference in the lives of these people." To Feldbaum, the justice's "capacity to engage in such understanding and empathy was one of his most consistent, important and endearing qualities. Most lawyers I know focus on the law first; the people whose lives make up the stuff of law are typically an afterthought. For Justice Blackmun, it was the exact opposite. The people came first; the law could be applied only once there was an understanding of its real-life effects on individual people."[48]

But the justice's critics would not long remain silent. After Chief Justice Burger's death in 1995, a bust of Blackmun's estranged boyhood friend was placed outside the entrance to the Minnesota Supreme Court chamber. A state legislative proposal to place a bust of Blackmun there went down to defeat, however, in the face of opposition from antiabortion leaders. "Blackmun...has the blood of 39 million babies on his hands," said one. "I think this is the last place we should be erecting a memorial to him."[49]

Release of the Blackmun papers—a huge collection spanning 630 linear feet and 1,576 cartons—also proved controversial. Archivists at the Library of Congress, repository of the Blackmun archives, completed the formidable task of organizing and indexing the papers with dispatch. But Sally Blackmun, whose father had named her executrix of his estate, had hopes of writing her own memoir of her father and delayed general access to the papers until March 4, 2004, the fifth anniversary of the justice's death. After that date, according to his will, access could no longer be blocked. But much to the dismay of other reporters, not to mention academic researchers, the justice's family, through his former clerk Harold Koh, did approach Linda Greenhouse of the *New York Times*, offering her two months' advance access to the papers beginning January 1, 2004. Sometime later, NPR's Nina Totenberg, another reporter with long ties to the justice, was given the same opportunity as a representative of broadcast journalists. The *Washington Post*, among other media outlets, vehemently protested the favored treatment extended Greenhouse and repeatedly sought early access as well, even sending all nine sitting justices a copy of one letter to the justice's family. But to no avail. Chief Justice Rehnquist made clear to the *Post* that the Court had no role in determining access to a colleague's papers.

Greenhouse's critics had long complained of the "Greenhouse Effect," the alleged willingness of certain justices—most recently, Justice Kennedy in the abortion field, the charge ran—to shift their votes in liberal directions in order to win the influential reporter's favor. Such a theory is a stretch at best. But Greenhouse's early access to the Blackmun papers enabled her to scoop potential competitors with a series of newspaper articles that became the core of the first Blackmun biography, an admiring portrait of the justice's life and commitment to civil liberties that was based entirely on the papers and surely must have pleased his family.[50]

When the Library of Congress made Justice Marshall's papers fully available to researchers the day after his death in 1993, members of the

Court had threatened a lawsuit in a vain effort to rebuff what they considered a highly premature intrusion on the privacy of the decisional process. Release of Justice Blackmun's papers only five years after his death may have been equally disturbing to his former colleagues, especially since the Blackmun collection was much more extensive and revealing than the Marshall archives. But some Court observers speculated, as one reporter put it, that Justice Blackmun might actually "have relished the prospect of exposing at least some of his colleagues to unwanted publicity." As one unnamed historian remarked, according to a press report, "When [Blackmun] talked about these papers, he sometimes had an impish grin, as if he knew that they would cause dyspepsia for some of his fellow justices."[51]

Nor was Blackmun's penchant for self-revelation and uninhibited observations about his colleagues confined to his papers. Between July 6, 1994, and December 13, 1995, he conducted thirty-eight hours of videotaped interviews with his former clerk Harold Koh. Much of that oral history focused, of course, on the justice's own life and career. The sentimental, whimsical side of his personality came through as well. At the very end of his sessions with Koh, he gently scolded his former clerk for not asking him to wiggle his ears, a Blackmun trademark, then demonstrated his skill. "That has been a great attribute for little children," he explained, "because if they come to visit the chambers, and I wiggle my ears at them, they're much more fascinated with that than they are with what's hanging on the wall or the history of the Court or all those things. So I wiggle my ears in farewell."[52]

During the sessions, the justice also offered up his at times unflattering personal impressions of his colleagues. Koh asked Blackmun about *Madsen v. Women's Health Center* (1994), a decision announced on his last day on the bench, in which a majority, over Justice Scalia's vigorous dissent, upheld a number of restrictions on protests at abortion clinics. "I was a little in a state of wonderment," the justice replied, "about why Justice Scalia read his dissent [in the courtroom] to end that term, and it was my impression...that the chief justice was rather annoyed about it, because it was the last opinion announced....Justice Scalia went on at some length, and the term ended with his dissent, which maybe from his point of view is what he wanted, but...struck me as an unusual note [on which] to end the term."[53]

Harry A. Blackmun

342

Following release of the oral history and Blackmun papers, two of the justice's daughters also agreed to discuss life with their father. Several clerks interviewed for this book made vague references to Blackmun's at times strained relationship with his daughters. "You always knew," one remarked, "that the justice had some kind of difficulty with the daughters, but he never talked to us about it." Susie, the youngest, probably caused her father the greatest consternation—and ironically so, given the liberal record he ultimately forged on the bench. When Susie graduated from DePauw University in 1971, she recalled in 2004 for an *Orlando Sentinel* reporter, "I was opposing the war in Vietnam, hating Nixon, but I was supposed to go home and look and act like Julie and Tricia Nixon." For the self-styled "hippie" who had worn jeans, a crocheted vest, and love beads to her graduation, Nixon's appointment of her father to the Court was a major shock. "I was totally confused and conflicted when that happened." Only after a decades-long estrangement had she and the justice come to terms. "Dad and I reconciled over the years. We slowly came to accept each other. Now I see Dad was a great champion of free speech and privacy and individual rights, especially for minorities and women. He's the person I most admire and respect." Even so, the fact that her father spent more time with his clerks than his daughters, she conceded, continued to cause her pain.[54]

In contrast to her younger sister, Sally Blackmun, the middle daughter, shared not only her father's facial features and choice of a career in the law, but also his deep-seated sense of duty. "I'm the born rebel," Susie told the reporter. "Sally was born to please and do her duty. She probably would have made a good royal." Sally, who had worked at the Nixon White House early in her father's Supreme Court tenure, essentially agreed. "We all march to different drummers. Susie always knew how to push Dad's buttons. I'm more like him—less confrontational, more disciplined....Dad was a straight arrow, serious, critical....He was missing in action a lot of the time. But he worked extremely hard. I understood. I didn't resent it."

Sally also had a closer connection than her sisters with her father's signature judicial opinion. In 1966, while a sophomore at Skidmore College, she had become pregnant. "It was one of those things I was not at all proud of," she would later say. "It was a big disappointment to my parents. I did what so many young women of my era did. I quit college and married my

20-year-old college boyfriend. It was a decision that I might have made differently, had *Roe v. Wade* been around."[55]

Three weeks into that first marriage, which lasted six years, Sally suffered a miscarriage. For years, she said nothing publicly about what the justice's critics would later call his daughter's "shotgun wedding." Standing in for her father at an awards ceremony toward the end of his life, however, she told her story. After his death, she repeated it often as a leader in the activities of the Greater Orlando Planned Parenthood organization and even in the introduction to a book, *The War on Choice* (2004), by the national president of the Planned Parenthood Federation of America. "Sally," a friend explained, "sees [her pro-choice efforts] as a way to honor her father's legacy." For abortion opponents, though, Sally's pregnancy and inability to secure a legal abortion in those pre-*Roe* days meant only that her father should have disqualified himself from hearing abortion cases.[56]

Justice Blackmun always said that *Roe* would follow him to his grave and be inscribed on his tombstone. His family spared him that fate, placing on his monument four words that, in their judgment, best reflected the justice's life and career: "Compassion," "Humility," "Integrity," and "Courage." As the justice predicted, however, he will always be remembered primarily as the author of the Court's first decision recognizing abortion rights. When Dottie Blackmun died in 2006 at age ninety-five, she was living in a Florida nursing home near Sally and Susie. Like the wire service reports from which they were drawn, the lead sentence in every obituary announcing her death reminded readers that her husband wrote the Court's opinion in *Roe v. Wade*.[57]

Epilogue

"Poor Harry!"

Justice Blackmun was a member of one of the world's most powerful and elite institutions. Yet in her funeral eulogy to her father, his daughter Nancy described the "shadow of pessimism, of sadness, of intermittent depression about him," and the "series of losses and difficulties in his early life that set a stamp on him." The untimely and sudden death of his mother's favorite brother, for whom Harry would be named, had begun Theo Blackmun's descent into melancholia. The death of her infant son when Harry was only two left her "unavailable emotionally for months, for her toddler firstborn." For the justice's psychologist daughter, the impact on her father was obvious: "A stretch of time that involves months of having a mother who is there, but not there, is unbearable for a little person. It creates a sense of insecurity. It creates a pessimistic view of what is likely to happen. It creates a vulnerability to depression." The suicide of Justice Blackmun's uncle under a cloud of scandal; the imprisonment of another uncle, the husband of his favorite aunt, and their divorce; and the influenza death of Harry's favorite cousin had further contributed to his mother's tendencies toward depression—and her son's own dark outlook.[1]

The vulnerability of women in a harsh world, Nancy added, caused him particular anguish: his divorced aunt, left "alone in the world"; Warren

Burger's mother, widowed young, with many young children to support; Justice Blackmun's own mother, whose husband "had a hard time earning an adequate living"; even the maid in his living quarters at Harvard, "a young single mother, bright and dignified, but without the formal work skills to earn a better living." Her father's heart "ached over [that woman's] plight in having to work as a maid, and he kept in touch with her all her life."

It is not surprising, then, that throughout his life Justice Blackmun appeared to see himself as an outsider, as someone who did not belong. The angst of his childhood and years at Harvard is readily understandable. Family tragedies and growing up in humble surroundings with a loving but melancholy mother and a father who seemed doomed to failure would not have inspired confidence in the future justice whatever his academic successes. Nor would the intimidating atmosphere of Cambridge have been any comfort to a poor midwestern boy surrounded by children of privilege.

Blackmun's deep-seated feelings of insecurity and self-doubt would persist over time, through his accumulation of honors at Harvard, a senior partnership with a major Minnesota law firm, a decade as counsel for one of the nation's leading clinics, appointment to the Eighth Circuit, and even after nearly a quarter century of service on the nation's highest tribunal. Asked in later years about his feelings on assuming the robes of a Supreme Court justice, he described himself as being "almost desperate" rather than consumed with exhilaration, anticipation, or similar emotions one would expect of a new justice. When Justice Black, the member of the Court whom he perhaps most respected, complained during Blackmun's first term about his new colleague's failure to produce a promised opinion in a timely fashion, the justice was devastated and defensive, blaming his slow pace on his recent arrival at the Court. Soon, however, he had delegated virtually all opinion drafting to his clerks—confident, one suspects, that they would do a better job of the task than he could ever have hoped to do. From that point and throughout his career, he spent hundreds of hours each term cloistered in the justices' library, painstakingly checking his clerks' citations and closely monitoring their drafts, ever alert to their grammatical and spelling errors—while they largely sculpted the substantive elements of his jurisprudence.

Arguably, the justice's insistence that exchanges with his clerks, or for that matter with other justices, be handled almost entirely on paper may also have stemmed from Blackmun's continuing doubts about his capacities as a jurist. His personal case summaries and postconference descriptions of the justices' deliberations for his clerks make clear that he was familiar not only with the facts of cases, but also with prevailing precedent and legal doctrine. Even so, lacking confidence in his grasp of the doctrinal nuances of cases, he may have sought to avoid face-to-face interchanges that might expose what he feared were his jurisprudential deficiencies. Most interactions, in fact, may have been difficult for this man described so often at various stages of his life as remote and aloof.

Blackmun's clerks and other admirers have stressed his humility. The justice was indeed humble. But more was at work there than mere humility. Even friends describe a person who could be difficult, whose feelings were easily hurt, who took offense at even minor slights. Some have suggested that he peevishly declined to interview Ruth Bader Ginsburg's clerks for Supreme Court clerkships when she was a judge on the DC Circuit because, as a lawyer advocating women's rights, his future colleague had criticized the broad sweep and detail of his *Roe* opinion. Such traits were evidence of lifelong feelings of insecurity, not Blackmun's conceded and admirable humility.

Interestingly, though, the same self-doubts that helped to explain the more unappealing as well as desirable aspects of Blackmun's personality and his extensive reliance on his clerks—a delegation of authority his harshest critics scorned as a virtual abdication of his responsibilities—probably also contributed significantly to his well-deserved reputation as champion of life's underdogs. In many cases, childhood insecurities no doubt produce insensitive adults contemptuous of society's most vulnerable citizens. But Blackmun's own inner doubts and fears arguably helped to make him unusually conscious and solicitous of such people from the beginning of his years on the Court. Even in his confirmation hearing he spoke of his concern for society's "little people." And though his positions in two early cases, *Wyman v. James* and *United States v. Kras*, appeared to belie his assertion, ultimately they did not. For in upholding welfare home visits in *Wyman*, he simply considered the welfare of the child paramount over the Fourth Amendment claims of the child's mother, and he viewed *Kras* as a test challenge to bankruptcy filing fees rather than as a genuine effort to protect a truly impoverished person from his creditors. For the balance of his career, his focus remained on the human dimension of cases before the Court, whether they involved desperate women faced with an unwanted pregnancy, women confronting sexual stereotypes, homosexuals challenging another sort of sexual bias, or, ultimately, death row inmates subjected to inherently arbitrary capital punishment schemes.

By thus striking blows for society's relatively dispossessed, the justice was perhaps also able to do battle with his own demons. Publicly he often expressed frustration at the degree of attention focused on him as a result of *Roe*. After all, he said, he had been only one member of a seven-justice majority. But *Roe* and certain of Blackmun's other opinions undoubtedly gave him a kind of national stature he might never have otherwise acquired, even if he continued to be only a mediocre jurist in the eyes of most colleagues and legal scholars, and to some degree in his own mind as well. For a judge at least, the extent to which he made himself available to print and broadcast journalists probably did amount to exhibitionism, as George Will and other critics claimed. And although he was retired from the bench when *Amistad* was filmed, surely few other jurists, active or retired, would have consented to appear in a motion picture, even one with a serious historical theme. But the media attention the justice garnered, the acclaim he received from admiring audiences, even the truly unprecedented volume of hate mail he attracted probably did much to bolster his confidence, as well as his commitment to his judicial agenda. Indeed, each blow he struck for one of society's "Poor Joshua[s]!" was in a very real sense a blow for "Poor Harry!"

Suggesting that Justice Blackmun's judicial tenure constituted a sort of continuing psychological therapy in no way minimizes the tremendous courage and resolve he displayed on the high bench as the target of more sustained invective than any other justice in the Supreme Court's history. Throughout his life there was a decidedly stubborn streak in the slight, bespectacled boy who defiantly wrote his parents from Harvard, "We will show them," and the man who refused to be dominated by Warren Burger or intimidated by detractors. Abraham Lincoln was one of the justice's heroes. Hanging in a frame on the wall of his chambers was a Lincoln quote to which the justice frequently referred "when the criticism gets going rather heavily." It read: "I do the best I know how—the very best I can; and I mean to keep on doing so until the end. If the end brings me out all right, what is said against me won't amount to anything. If the end brings me out wrong, ten angels swearing I was right would make no difference." Lincoln's words are a fitting epitaph for Harry Andrew Blackmun.

Bibliographic Note

One of Justice Blackmun's daughters risked understatement when she described her father as a "world-class pack rat." The justice saved everything. Indeed, the archives of most other justices appear almost minuscule in comparison with the 1,576 cartons that comprise the Harry A. Blackmun Papers, on file in the Manuscript Division of the Library of Congress, the principal research source for this book. Of materials in the Blackmun Papers, the justice's letters to his parents and sister, and particularly the detailed diaries that he began in 1919, when he was eleven, and maintained for almost two decades, were especially critical to an understanding of the justice's early life, outlook, and career. Extremely helpful as a source of insight into the justice's thinking about the issues confronting the Supreme Court during his tenure were the personal analyses of cases that he dictated before oral argument, as well as his exchanges with clerks and other justices, all carefully preserved in his papers. The papers are truly a treasure trove, however, of revealing information about every aspect of Blackmun's life and career. The papers of his contemporaries, especially the William J. Brennan and Thurgood Marshall Papers at the Library of Congress and the Lewis F. Powell Jr., Papers at Washington and Lee University, were also very helpful, as was the justice's testimony before the Senate Judiciary Committee during his confirmation proceedings—testimony that offered distinct signals as to the sort of justice he would ultimately become.

In recorded telephone interviews, a number of Blackmun's clerks furnished interesting perspectives regarding, among other things, the justice's personality, recruitment of clerks, the processing of cases in his chambers, and his relations with Warren Burger and other justices. Interviewed for this book, with their terms of service, were the following Blackmun clerks: Robert Gooding (O.T. 1970), Randall Bezanson (O.T. 1972), William Block (O.T. 1975), William Alden McDaniel (O.T. 1978), Frank Holleman (O.T. 1981), David Van Zandt (O.T. 1982), Alan Madans (O.T. 1982), David Ogden (O.T. 1982), Pamela Karlan (O.T. 1985), Edward Lazarus (O.T. 1988), Geoffrey Klineberg (O.T. 1992), Cecillia Wang (O.T. 1996), and Clare Huntington (O.T. 1998). Equally helpful was his secretary Wanda Martinson, who served with Blackmun from 1974, when she was barely twenty, until his death and who has said that the justice "really became like a father to me." She knew Justice Blackmun as well as anyone, better than most, and her assistance was truly invaluable.

Complementing these sources was the voluminous newspaper and magazine coverage of the justice's life and career, as well as the work of legal scholars. The Blackmun Papers include a huge collection of materials from national, Minnesota, and other publications, but an independent survey of online and traditional indexes was also conducted.

Notes

Preface

1. *The Justice Harry A. Blackmun Oral History Project*, July 6, 1994–December 15, 1995 (hereinafter Oral History), p. 11.
2. See Robert C. Bradley's chapter in William D. Pederson and Norman W. Provizer, eds., *Leaders of the Pack: Polls and Case Studies of Great Supreme Court Justices* (New York: Peter Lang, 2003), pp. 1–22.
3. Oral History, p. 52.
4. Ibid.
5. DeShaney v. Winnebago County Department of Social Services, 489 U. S. 189, 213 (1989) (Blackmun, J., dissenting).
6. John C. Jeffries Jr., *Justice Lewis F. Powell, Jr.: A Biography* (New York: Scribner's, 1994), pp. 339–40.

Chapter I

1. Oral History, p. 48.
2. Oral History, pp. 3, 46–47. The Blackmun genealogy appeared in NEXUS 11 (1994): 94–95 (hereinafter Blackmun Genealogy), a publication of the New England Historic Genealogical Society.
3. Oral History, pp. 45–46; unidentified newspaper obituary of John Huegely Sr., Harry A. Blackmun Papers, Manuscript Division, Library of Congress, Box 13.
4. The unidentified article is in the Blackmun Papers, Box 13. The justice's daughter Nancy Blackmun mentioned the suicide and embezzlement charges in her funeral eulogy to her father, March 9, 1999, Blackmun Papers, Box 1326.

5. Oral History, pp. 4, 47.

6. Ibid., pp. 46–47; Blackmun Genealogy.

7. While a student at Harvard, Blackmun often wrote home on discarded stationery from his father's wholesale fruit and vegetable business. An announcement of Corwin Blackmun's association with the Mutual Insurance Company—a position Warren Burger, who also worked for Mutual while working his way through law school, may have helped his friend's father obtain—appears in an unidentified newspaper clipping, December 31, 1930. A brief newspaper article of the same date noted Corwin Blackmun's earlier connection with the Twin Cities Building and Loan Association. Blackmun Papers, Boxes 10, 13; Oral History, p. 52.

8. Blackmun Papers, Box 1.

9. Oral History, p. 49.

10. Ibid.; *St. Paul Pioneer Press* clipping, October 1956, in Blackmun Papers, Box 12. For a profile of Chief Justice Burger, see Tinsley E. Yarbrough, *The Burger Court: Justices, Rulings, and Legacy* (Santa Barbara: ABC-CLIO, 2000), pp. 78–83.

11. Oral History, pp. 49–50. The justice's diaries are in the Blackmun Papers, Boxes 11 and 12.

12. Oral History, p. 49.

13. Ibid., p. 55. The essay, entitled "The Constitution," is in the Blackmun Papers, Box 7.

14. Blackmun Diaries, November 12, September 24, November 21, 1924, June 18, 1925, Blackmun Papers, Box 11. The theme, entitled "My Auto-biography," is in the Blackmun Papers, Box 10.

15. Oral History, pp. 56–57.

16. Ibid.

17. Blackmun Diaries, July 24, 25, 1925; Oral History, p. 57.

18. E. B. Young to Henry Pennypacker, September 15, 1925, Blackmun Papers, Box 1.

19. R. W. Coues to Harry A. Blackmun, September 15, 1925, Blackmun Papers, Box 1; Committee on Admissions telegram to Edward B. Young, September 18, 1925, Blackmun Papers, Box 1; certificate of admission, Harvard University, September 18, 1925, Box 1.

20. Oral History, p. 56. A profile of Lange is available online as part of the Minnesota Historical Society's Minnesota Author Biographies Project, www.people.mnhs.org/authors/index.cfm.

21. Harry A. Blackmun to his family, September 24, 1925, Blackmun Papers, Box 10.

22. Ibid.

23. Ibid; Oral History, p. 62.

24. Harry A. Blackmun to his family, September 24, 1925, Blackmun Papers, Box 10.

25. Harry A. Blackmun to Betty Blackmun, October 20, 1925, Blackmun Papers, Box 10.

26. Harry A. Blackmun to his parents, October 10, 2, 6, 1925, Blackmun Papers, Box 10.
27. Harry A. Blackmun to his parents, September 28, 1925, Blackmun Papers, Box 10.
28. The theme, "My Impressions of Harvard College," and his other freshman themes are in Blackmun Papers, Box 10.
29. Ibid.
30. Harry A. Blackmun to his parents, October 10, 17, 1925, Blackmun Papers, Box 10; unidentified clipping, 1926, Blackmun Papers, Box 1.
31. Harry A. Blackmun to his parents, September 28, 1925, Blackmun Papers, Box 10.
32. Harry A. Blackmun to his parents, October 10, 27, 31, 1925, Blackmun Papers, Box 10.
33. Harry A. Blackmun to his parents, November 7, 1925, Blackmun Papers, Box 10.
34. Harry A. Blackmun to Sandra Day O'Connor, March 8, 1988, Blackmun Papers, Box 1406. Blackmun's description of "My Illness—Appendicitis," dated March 21, 1923, is in the Blackmun Papers, Box 11.
35. Harry A. Blackmun to his parents, October 31, 1925, Blackmun Papers, Box 10; Harry A. Blackmun to Betty Blackmun, November 28, 1925, Blackmun Papers, Box 10.
36. Harry A. Blackmun, October 10, November 3, 1925, Blackmun Papers, Box 10.
37. Harry A. Blackmun to Betty Blackmun, November 28, 1925, Blackmun Papers, Box 10.
38. Harry A. Blackmun to his family, December 25, 1925, Blackmun Papers, Box 10.
39. Ibid.
40. Ibid.
41. Harry A. Blackmun to his parents, October 13, 1925; Harry A. Blackmun to Betty Blackmun, November 28, 1925, Blackmun Papers, Box 10.
42. Dietrich Lange to Harry A. Blackmun, December 10, 1925, Blackmun Papers, Box 1; Edward B. Young to Harry A. Blackmun, December 4, 1925, Blackmun Papers, Box 1.
43. *The Cogwell*, March 5, 1926.
44. Harry A. Blackmun to Theo Blackmun, October 6, 1925, Blackmun Papers, Box 10; E. B. Young to Harry A. Blackmun, April 13, 1926, Blackmun Papers, Box 1; Oral History, pp. 63–64, 65.
45. Oral History, p. 65.
46. Ibid., p. 63. Correspondence regarding his fraternity and other extracurricular activities is in Blackmun Papers, Box 1.
47. Oral History, pp. 67, 5.
48. Ibid., pp. 48, 63.
49. R. E. Witthauer to Harry A. Blackmun, July 26, 1926; T. E. Reynolds to Harry A. Blackmun, May 5, 1926, Blackmun Papers, Box 1; Oral History, pp. 64–65.

50. R. F. Clayton to Harry A. Blackmun, August 17, October 18, 1926, April 26, 1927, Blackmun Papers, Box 11; Irvin Richter to Harry A. Blackmun, August 10, 1927, Blackmun Papers, Box 11; Frederic A. Washburn to "Dear Sir," undated, Blackmun Papers, Box 1.
51. *Boston Evening Globe*, June 20, 1929; Oral History, p. 64.
52. Oral History, p. 70.
53. Ibid., pp. 54, 60, 73; Harry A. Blackmun to School of Medicine, University of Minnesota, July 11, 1928, Blackmun Papers, Box 1.
54. Oral History, p. 54.
55. Unidentified clipping, November 30, 1924, Blackmun Papers, Box 12.
56. *Pioneer Press* (St. Paul), October 7, 1979.
57. Warren Burger to Harry A. Blackmun, May 19, 1929, Blackmun Papers, Box 12.
58. Oral History, p. 76.
59. Ibid., pp. 79, 78.
60. Ibid., p. 78; Felix Frankfurter to Harry A. Blackmun, October 18, 1932, January 11, 1933, Blackmun Papers, Box 11; Texas & Pacific Railway Co. v. Abilene Cotton Oil Co., 204 U.S. 426 (1907).
61. Oral History, pp. 77, 71.
62. His course notes are in Blackmun Papers, Boxes 2–6; a resolution accompanying presentation of the squash racket, signed by other players, is in Box 1.
63. Oral History, pp. 75–76.
64. Ibid., p. 79. Harvard mailed Blackmun a certified copy of his law school grades October 16, 1942, Blackmun Papers, Box 11.
65. Oral History, p. 4.

Chapter 2

1. Robert Driscoll to Harry A. Blackmun, February 3, 1932, Blackmun Papers, Box 11.
2. Bergmann Richards to John B. Sanborn, July 13, 1932; John B. Sanborn to Bergmann Richards, July 14, 1932, Blackmun Papers, Box 11.
3. Blackmun Diaries, August 1, 1932; *Nashville Journal*, September 8, 1932.
4. For an official history of the Eighth Circuit, see Theodore J. Fetter, *A History of the United States Court of Appeals for the Eighth Circuit* (Washington, DC: Judicial Conference of the United States, Bicentennial Committee, 1977).
5. Blackmun Diaries, August 1, September 19, 20, November 3, 4, 1932, July 10, 1933.
6. Oral History, p. 84; letter to Harry A. Blackmun, September 6, 1932, Blackmun Papers, Box 11.
7. Oral History, pp. 85–86.
8. Blackmun Diaries, November 28, 1933.
9. Blackmun Diaries, September 22, 23, 1932.
10. Blackmun Diaries, November 3, 1932.
11. Blackmun Diaries, November 5, 1932.

12. Blackmun Diaries, November 5, 7, 1932.

13. Blackmun Diaries, November 8, 1932.

14. Blackmun Diaries, March 4, 1933, September 11, 1935. A copy of the "1938 Psalm" is in the Blackmun Papers, Box 14.

15. Blackmun Diaries, September 27, 1933.

16. A typed summary of an entry on the case in the 1931–32 annual report of the U.S. attorney general is in the Blackmun Papers, Box 13.

17. Blackmun Diaries, February 20, 1933.

18. Ibid.

19. Blackmun Diaries, February 21, 1933.

20. Blackmun Diaries, July 24–28, 1932, August 18, April 15, 1933.

21. Blackmun Diaries, July 10, September 13, March 5, 1933.

22. Blackmun Diaries, July 17, September 7, 25, November 8, 1933; Oral History, p. 100.

23. Blackmun Diaries, January 23, February 23, November 20, September 19, 1933.

24. Blackmun Diaries, April 10, September 17, 1933.

25. Blackmun Diaries, May 1, 1933; Horton v. Reynolds, 65 F. 2d 430 (1933); Oral History, p. 91.

26. Oral History, p. 87.

27. Charles E. Wyzanski Jr., to Harry A. Blackmun, August 5, 1933, Blackmun Papers, Box 11.

28. Harry A. Blackmun to Charles E. Wyzanski Jr., April 17, May 2, 1935, Blackmun Papers, Box 11.

29. Oral History, p. 92; a file on the firm and its history is in the Blackmun Papers, Box 91.

30. Oral History, p. 92; Blackmun Diaries, September 12, December 28, 1933.

31. Blackmun Diaries, September 11, December 28, 29, 1933.

32. Blackmun Diaries, December 30, 1933.

33. Oral History, pp. 93, 94.

34. Ibid., p. 94.

35. Blackmun Diaries, February 11, March 2, 1935, January 30, March 4, August 12, November 13, 1935.

36. Blackmun Diaries, March 15, 17, 1935.

37. Blackmun Diaries, March 22, 24, 25, 26, 1935.

38. Douglas v. Willcuts, 296 U.S. 1 (1935); Oral History, p. 95.

39. Dobson v. Commissioner of Internal Revenue, 320 U.S. 489 (1943); William L. Prosser, *Handbook of the Law of Torts* (St. Paul, MN: West Publishing, 1941).

40. Blackmun Diaries, July 15, 1935.

41. Blackmun Diaries, May 24, June 11, October 31, 1935.

42. Blackmun Diaries, June 11, 1935.

43. Blackmun Diaries, November 6, 1932, January 21, May 8, September 13, September 21, November 11, 1933, July 2, 7, August 2, 1935, June 24, 1936.

44. Blackmun Diaries, October 10, 1935, February 4, 5, 1936.

45. Oral History, pp. 70–71; e-mail, Wanda Martinson to author, June 9, 2005, author's files.

46. Blackmun Diaries, September 23, 1932, September 15, 1933.

47. Blackmun Diaries, July 11, 17, 18, 1935.

48. Blackmun Diaries, August 15, 16, 17, 18, 1935.

49. Blackmun Diaries, August 19, 22, 23, 24, 1935.

50. Blackmun Diaries, August 23, 24, 25, 1935.

51. Blackmun Diaries, October 28, 1935, March 2, September 19, 27, 1936.

52. Oral History, p. 98.

53. Ibid., p. 99; undated, unidentified clippings announcing the Blackmuns' engagement, Blackmun Papers, Box 14. Articles and photographs regarding sports competitions are in Box 12.

54. Harry A. Blackmun to Frank H. Sloss, April 26, 1941; Frank H. Sloss to Harry A. Blackmun, April 30, 1941; Harry A. Blackmun to Frank H. Sloss, May 12, 1941, Blackmun Papers, Box 11.

55. *Minneapolis Star Journal*, July 27, 1941; *St. Paul Dispatch*, July 27, 1941.

56. Harry A. Blackmun to Kahler Hotel, June 9, 1941, Blackmun Papers, Box 11; Oral History, p. 100.

57. Oral History, p. 100; Harry A. Blackmun to Local Board No. 3, October 30, 1942, Blackmun Papers, Box 11.

58. Dave Raudenbush to Harry A. Blackmun, May 27, 1944, Blackmun Papers, Box 11.

59. Oral History, p. 103; Harry A. Blackmun to H. J. Harwick, January 17, 1950, Blackmun Papers, Box 13.

60. Maria Tymoczko and Nancy Blackmun, eds., *Born into a World at War* (Manchester, UK: St. Jerome Publishing, 2000), p. 60.

61. *Hennepin Lawyer*, July 23, 1939; Charles F. Noonan to Harry A. Blackmun, undated, Blackmun Papers, Box 11; *St. Paul Sunday Pioneer Press*, magazine supplement, February 2, 1947; Winfield S. Hayenk to the Blackmuns, November 6, 1947, Blackmun Papers, Box 11.

62. Harry A. Blackmun to Everett Fraser, April 25, May 15, 1946; Everett Fraser to Harry A. Blackmun, April 30, 1946, Blackmun Papers, Box 11.

63. "The Court of Last Resort," *Time*, October 23, 1964, p. 96; Alan Edward Nounse, *Inside the Mayo Clinic* (New York: McGraw-Hill, 1979).

64. Oral History, p. 107.

65. Ibid., pp. 107–8.

66. Ibid., pp. 108–9.

67. Harry A. Blackmun to Harry J. Harwick, January 17, 1950, Blackmun Papers, Box 13.

68. Harry A. Blackmun to Harry J. Harwick, also dated January 17, 1950, Blackmun Papers, Box 13.

69. Harry J. Harwick to Harry A. Blackmun, January 18, 1950, Blackmun Papers, Box 13.

70. Harry A. Blackmun to E. A. Wobschall, June 29, 1950; Harry A. Blackmun to Harry J. Harwick, April 26, 1950; David E. Bronson to R. A. Bezoier, April 17, 1950, Blackmun Papers, Box 13.

71. Harry A. Blackmun to David E. Bronson, November 17, 1950, Blackmun Papers, Box 13.

72. The anonymous composition is in the Blackmun Papers, Box 13.

73. *Rochester Post-Bulletin*, January 25, 1951, January 24, 1953; *Minneapolis Tribune*, September 29, 1952.

74. Harry A. Blackmun to G. S. Schuster, confidential memorandum, March 4, 1954; M. C. Roberts to Dr. Thompson, November 3, 1952; S. B. Hilliard to G. K. McCoun, August 1, 1953, Blackmun Papers, Box 13.

75. *Houston Chronicle*, January 21, 22, 1955.

76. Harry A. Blackmun, memorandum "Re. Houston Chronicle Controversy," February 5, 1955, Blackmun Papers, Box 13.

77. Harry A. Blackmun to Howard K. Gray, February 10, 1955; Blackmun memorandum to Howard K. Gray and Woltman Walters, February 7, 1955; Harry A. Blackmun to George W. Waldron, February 18, 1955; George W. Waldron to Harry A. Blackmun, February 28, 1955; George W. Waldron to Howard K. Gray, February 28, 1955, Blackmun Papers, Box 13.

78. Harry A. Blackmun to Dr. Buie, January 20, 1955; unidentified newspaper clipping, Blackmun Papers, Box 13.

79. James Eckman to Harry A. Blackmun, January 14, 1955, Blackmun Papers, Box 13. The "firm" letterhead and many other Eckman creations are in Box 13.

80. Discussion drawn from numerous clippings in the Blackmun Papers, Box 13; Oral History, p. 115.

81. Oral History, pp. 104, 117.

82. Ibid., pp. 109, 115.

Chapter 3

1. *Minneapolis Star*, January 5, 1953; Harry A. Blackmun to Warren Burger, January 6, 1953; Warren Burger to Harry A. Blackmun, January 8, 1953; Harry A. Blackmun to Warren Burger, January 29, 1953, Blackmun Papers, Box 12.

2. Blackmun to Burger, January 29, 1953; Warren Burger to Harry A. Blackmun, October 12, 1953; Harry A. Blackmun to Warren Burger, October 20, 1953, Blackmun Papers, Box 12.

3. Warren Burger to Harry A. Blackmun, November 17, 1953, Blackmun Papers, Box 12.

4. Ibid.

5. Peters v. Hobby, 349 U.S. 331 (1955); Yarbrough, *The Burger Court*, p. 80; Warren Burger to Harry A. Blackmun, undated, Blackmun Papers, Box 12.

6. Oral History, pp. 88–89, 105.

7. Warren Burger to Harry A. Blackmun, February 6, 1954, Blackmun Papers, Box 12. The case was Maple Island Farm v. Bitterling, 209 F. 2d 867 (1954).

8. Ibid.

9. Harry A. Blackmun to Warren Burger, February 9, 1954, Blackmun Papers, Box 12.
10. Warren Burger to Harry A. Blackmun, February 17, 1954, Blackmun Papers, Box 12.
11. Harry A. Blackmun to Warren Burger, August 31, 1954, Blackmun Papers, Box 12.
12. Richard Russell to Harry A. Blackmun, July 16, 1955; Harry A. Blackmun to Hubert H. Humphrey, July 13, 1955; Hubert H. Humphrey to Harry A. Blackmun, July 16, 1955; Harry A. Blackmun to Alexander Wiley, July 13, 1955; Warren Burger to Harry A. Blackmun, January, 1956, Blackmun Papers, Box 12.
13. Harry A. Blackmun to Warren Burger, October 26, February 20, 1957; Warren Burger to Harry A. Blackmun, February 17, 1957, Blackmun Papers, Box 12. Box 12 contains much additional correspondence regarding social and related contacts between Blackmun, Burger, and their families.
14. Warren Burger to Harry A. Blackmun, January 13, 1959, February 17, September 16, 1957, Blackmun Papers, Box 12.
15. Warren Burger to Harry A. Blackmun, July 19, 1959, Blackmun Papers, Box 12.
16. Some of this discussion of Blackmun's appointment to the court of appeals is based on a summary of events dated September 25, 1959, that he wrote, Blackmun Papers, Box 50.
17. Harry A. Blackmun to John B. Sanborn, November 8, 1958, Blackmun Papers, Box 49.
18. John B. Sanborn to Harry A. Blackmun, November 10, 1958, Blackmun Papers, Box 49.
19. Warren Burger to Harry A. Blackmun, two letters dated November 10, 1958, Blackmun Papers, Box 49.
20. Warren Burger to Harry A. Blackmun, November 28, 1958, Blackmun Papers, Box 49.
21. Theo Blackmun to Harry A. Blackmun, December 3, 1958, Blackmun Papers, Box 49.
22. John B. Sanborn to Harry A. Blackmun, February 14, 1959, Blackmun Papers, Box 49.
23. Morris B. Mitchell to Warren Burger, March 9, 1959, Blackmun Papers, Box 49.
24. John B. Sanborn to Harry A. Blackmun, March 21, 1959, Blackmun Papers, Box 49.
25. Warren Burger to Harry A. Blackmun, April 28, 1959, Blackmun Papers, Box 49.
26. John B. Sanborn to Harry A. Blackmun, April 30, 1959, Blackmun Papers, Box 49.
27. Harry A. Blackmun to John B. Sanborn, May 4, 1959, Blackmun Papers, Box 49.

28. Ibid.

29. Harry A. Blackmun to Roy E. Willy, May 14, 1959, Blackmun Papers, Box 49.

30. *St. Paul Pioneer Press*, May 22, 1959; *Rochester Post-Bulletin*, May 22, 1959; numerous unidentified clippings; Theo Blackmun to Harry A. Blackmun, May 22, 1959; Warren Burger to Harry A. Blackmun, May 20, 1959, Blackmun Papers, Box 49.

31. *Minneapolis Morning Tribune*, May 25, 1959.

32. Harry A. Blackmun to Warren Burger, May 25, 28, 1959; Warren Burger to Harry A. Blackmun, May 28, 1959, Blackmun Papers, Box 49.

33. Harry A. Blackmun to Warren Burger, June 11, 1959; Arnold Hatfield to Dwight D. Eisenhower, June 12, 1959; Leo F. Murphy to Eugene McCarthy, June 23, 1959, Blackmun Papers, Box 49.

34. Warren Burger to John B. Sanborn, undated but received by Sanborn on June 24, 1959, Blackmun Papers, Box 49.

35. Harry A. Blackmun to Warren Burger, July 9, 1959, Blackmun Papers, Box 49.

36. Warren Burger to Harry A. Blackmun, July 17, 1959, Blackmun Papers, Box 49.

37. *St. Paul Pioneer Press*, July 21, 1959; Harry A. Blackmun to John B. Sanborn, July 23, 1959; John B. Sanborn to Harry A. Blackmun, July 27, 1959; Harry A. Blackmun to John B. Sanborn, July 28, 1959, Blackmun Papers, Box 49.

38. Warren Burger to John B. Sanborn, September 1, 1959; Warren Burger to Harry A. Blackmun, undated; Harry A. Blackmun to Warren Burger, August 22, 1959; Warren Burger to Harry A. Blackmun, August 28, 1959, Blackmun Papers, Box 49.

39. *New York Times*, August 22, 1959; Warren Burger to John B. Sanborn, September 1, 1959, Blackmun Papers, Box 49.

40. A copy of the telegram is in the Blackmun Papers, Box 49; Morris Mitchell to Bernard G. Segal, September 9, 1959, Blackmun Papers, Box 49; *Minneapolis Star Tribune*, September 10, 1959.

41. *Rochester Post-Bulletin*, September 21, 15, 1959.

42. Betty Blackmun Gilchrist to Harry A. Blackmun, September 11 [*sic*], 1959; Theo Blackmun to Harry A. Blackmun, September 15, 1959, Blackmun Papers, Box 49.

43. John B. Sanborn to Harry A. Blackmun, September 16, 1959; Bernard G. Segal to Harry A. Blackmun, September 17, 1959; Hubert H. Humphrey to Susan Blackmun, September 18, 1959, Blackmun Papers, Box 49.

44. Harry A. Blackmun to Percy McDonald, September 12, 1959; Harry A. Blackmun to John B. Sanborn, September 12, 1959; Hubert H. Humphrey to Charles F. Ninin, September 23, 1959; Harry A. Blackmun to Charles F. Ninin, September 29, 1959, Blackmun Papers, Box 49.

45. *Minneapolis Sunday Tribune*, September 20, 1959.

46. Oral History, p. 120; Harry A. Blackmun to Warren Burger, September 24, 1959; Warren Burger to Harry A. Blackmun, September 29, 1959; Harry A.

Blackmun to John C. McDonald, September 30, 1959, Blackmun Papers, Boxes 12 and 49.

47. Harry A. Blackmun to Warren Burger, October 2, 1959, Blackmun Papers, Box 12; *Rochester Post-Bulletin*, October 30, 1959.

48. Warren Burger to Harry A. Blackmun, October 7, 1959, Blackmun Papers, Box 49.

49. Harry A. Blackmun to Warren Burger, October 14, 1959, Blackmun Papers, Box 12.

50. Ibid.; Warren Burger to Harry A. Blackmun, October 20, 1959; Theo Blackmun to Harry A. Blackmun, November 5, 1959, Blackmun Papers, Boxes 12 and 49; *St. Paul Dispatch*, November 4, 1959; *Rochester Post-Bulletin*, November 4, 1959.

51. Oral History, pp. 122, 121. The Judge's Bill was enacted on August 6, 1958, 72 Stat. 497.

52. Oral History, p. 124.

53. Ibid., pp. 122–23.

54. Ibid., p. 137.

55. Marion v. Gardner, 359 F. 2d 175, 182 (1966).

56. Howard Rome to Harry A. Blackmun, April 15, 1966, Blackmun Papers, Box 37.

57. Ibid.; Harry A. Blackmun to Howard P. Rome, April 15, 1966; Roy L. Stephenson to Harry A. Blackmun, April 25, 1966, Blackmun Papers, Box 37.

58. Briggs v. Elliott, 132 F. Supp. 776, 777 (E.D.S.C. 1955); Kemp v. Beasley, 352 F. 2d 14, 20 (1965); Yarbrough v. Hulbert-West Memphis School District, 380 F. 2d 962, 970 (1967); Harry A. Blackmun to Judges, July 8, 1967; Donald P. Lay to Harry A. Blackmun, July 11, 13, 1967; Harry A. Blackmun to Donald P. Lay, July 13, 14, 1967, Blackmun Papers, Box 39.

59. Walton v. Nashville, Arkansas Special School District, 401 F. 2d 137, 141–42, 144 (1968).

60. Maxwell v. Stephens, 348 F. 2d 325, 331 (1965); Pat Mehaffy to Harry A. Blackmun, June 14, 1965, Blackmun Papers, Box 34.

61. Harry A. Blackmun to Pat Mehaffy, June 22, 1965, Blackmun Papers, Box 34.

62. Jones v. Alfred H. Mayer Co., 379 F. 2d 33, 43 (1967), 392 U.S. 409 (1968); Leland W. Scott to Harry A. Blackmun, June 2, 1967; Harry A. Blackmun to Judges, June 7, 1967; Harry A. Blackmun to Donald P. Lay, December 13, 1967, Blackmun Papers, Box 38.

63. Erwin N. Griswold to Harry A. Blackmun, April 1, 1968; Harry A. Blackmun to Erwin N. Griswold, April 8, 1968; Harry A. Blackmun to Gerald W. Heaney, July 19, 1967, Blackmun Papers, Box 38.

64. Brown v. United States, 283 F. 2d 792 (1960); John B. Sanborn note to Harry A. Blackmun, undated, Blackmun Papers, Box 27.

65. Escobedo v. Illinois, 378 U.S. 478 (1964); Mitchell v. Stephens, 353 F. 2d 129 (1965); Harry A. Blackmun to Judges, October 22, 1965, Blackmun Papers, Box 36.

66. Minnesota *ex rel*. Holscher v. Tahash, 364 F. 2d 922 (1966); Miranda v. Arizona, 384 U.S. 436 (1966).
67. Miner v. Erickson, 428 F. 2d 623, 625, 631 (1970).
68. Kaufman v. United States, 350 F. 2d 408 (1965), 394 U.S. 217 (1969); Stone v. Powell, 428 U.S. 465 (1976); Warren v. United States, 311 F. 2d 673 (1963); Springer v. United States, 340 F. 2d 950 (1965); Peters v. United States, 312 F. 2d 481 (1963).
69. Ashe v. Swenson, 399 F. 2d 40 (1960); Harry A. Blackmun to Judges, July 23, 1968, Blackmun Papers, Box 41.
70. Ashe v. Swenson, 397 U.S. 436 (1970); Benton v. Maryland, 395 U.S. 784 (1969). The page from the slip opinion is in the Blackmun Papers, Box 41.
71. United States v. Kahriger, 345 U.S. 22 (1953); Deckard v. United States, 381 F. 2d 77 (1967); Marchetti v. United States, 390 U.S. 39 (1968); Haynes v. United States, 390 U.S. 85 (1968); Leary v. United States, 395 U.S. 6 (1969).
72. Durham v. United States, 214 F. 2d 862 (1954); M'Naghten's Case, 8 Eng. Rep. 718 (H.L. 1843); Davis v. United States, 160 U.S. 469 (1895); Blocker v. United States, 288 F. 2d 853, 872 (1961).
73. Dusky v. United States, 271 F. 2d 385, 401 (1959), 362 U.S. 402 (1960), 295 F. 2d 743, 759 (1961).
74. Warren Burger to Harry A. Blackmun, undated but received October 18, 1961; Harry A. Blackmun to Warren Burger, October 18, 1961, Blackmun Papers, Box 28. The undated note is in the file for Pope v. United States, 372 F. 2d 710 (1967), a death penalty case involving an insanity claim, Blackmun Papers, Box 38.
75. Feguer v. United States, 302 F. 2d 214, 217 (1962).
76. Pope v. United States, 372 F. 2d 710, 741 (1967); Harry A. Blackmun to Warren Burger, December 14, 1966; Harry A. Blackmun to Judges, January 4, 1967; Donald P. Lay to Harry A. Blackmun, January 10, 1967; Charles J. Vogel to Harry A. Blackmun, January 9, 1967; M. C. Matthes to Harry A. Blackmun, January 9, 1967, Blackmun Papers, Box 38.
77. Maxwell v. Bishop, 398 F. 2d 138, 148 (1968).
78. The summary is in the Maxwell v. Bishop file, Blackmun Papers, Box 40.
79. Ibid.
80. Harry A. Blackmun to Judges, June 21, 1968, Blackmun Papers, Box 40.
81. Ibid.
82. The draft opinion is in the Blackmun Papers, Box 40.
83. Donald P. Lay to Harry A. Blackmun, undated; M. C. Matthes to Harry A. Blackmun, June 25, 1968, Blackmun Papers, Box 40.
84. Maxwell v. Bishop, 398 U.S. 262 (1970); Witherspoon v. Illinois, 391 U.S. 510 (1960).
85. Jackson v. Bishop, 404 F. 2d 571 (1968); Holt v. Sarver, 300 F. Supp. 825 (E.D. Ark., 1969), 309 F. Supp. 362 (E.D. Ark., 1970), 442 F. 2d 304 (1971).
86. Jackson v. Bishop, 404 F. 2d at 570, 580.

87. Hans W. Mattick to Harry A. Blackmun, December 20, 1968; Gordon E. Young to Harry A. Blackmun, December 12, 1968; Oren Harris to Harry A. Blackmun, January 24, 1969; Edward L. Wright to Gordon E. Young, December 11, 1968; Edward L. Wright to Harry A. Blackmun, March 4, 1969, Blackmun Papers, Box 41.

88. Young to Blackmun; Harris to Blackmun: Harry A. Blackmun to Gordon E. Young, December 16, 1968; Harry A. Blackmun to Oren Harris, January 27, 1969, Blackmun Papers, Box 41.

89. Sharp v. Sigler, 408 F. 2d 966, 971, 972 (1969).

90. *In Re* Weitzman, 426 F. 2d 439 (1970).

91. Ibid., p. 460.

92. Ibid., pp. 444, 451, 454.

93. New York Times v. Sullivan, 376 U.S. 254 (1964); Pauling v. Globe-Democrat Publishing Co., 362 F. 2d 188 (1966).

94. *St. Louis Globe-Democrat*, October 10, 1960.

95. Pauling v. Globe-Democrat, 362 F. 2d at 191, 195, 198.

96. Harry A. Blackmun to Judges, June 8, 1966; Floyd R. Gibson to Harry A. Blackmun, June 13, 1966; Charles J. Vogel to Harry A. Blackmun, June 14, 1966; Warren Burger to Harry A. Blackmun, undated but received June 15, 1966, Blackmun Papers, Box 36.

97. Curtis Publishing Co. v. Butts, Associated Press v. Walker, 388 U.S. 130 (1967); Pauling v. Globe-Democrat Publishing Co., 388 U.S. 909 (1967); Walker v. Pulitzer Publishing Co., 394 F. 2d 800 (1968).

98. Janko v. United States, 281 F. 2d 156 (1960), 366 U.S. 716 (1961).

99. John B. Sanborn to Harry A. Blackmun, June 8, 1961; Harry A. Blackmun, August 23, 1962; Irvin v. Dowd, 366 U.S. 717, 730 (1961); Harry A. Blackmun to M. C. Matthes, June 8, 1961.

100. Oral History, p. 131. The summary is on file in the Blackmun Papers, Box 40.

101. Case summary; Burnside v. Byars, 363 F. 2d 744 (1966).

102. Tinker v. Des Moines Independent School District, 393 U.S. 503 (1969).

103. Esteban v. Central Missouri State College, 415 F. 2d 1077, 1085 (1969).

104. Ibid., pp. 1086, 1089.

105. Ibid., p. 1095.

106. Leland W. Scott to Harry A. Blackmun, August 31, 1969; Gwenyth Jones to Harry A. Blackmun, November 17, 1969, Blackmun Papers, Box 45.

107. Nancy Blackmun to Harry A. Blackmun, September 14, 1969, Blackmun Papers, Box 45.

Chapter 4

1. Oral History, p. 141.

2. *New York Times*, May 22, 1969; Frazier v. United States, 419 F. 2d 1161, 1176 (1969); "What to Do about Crime in U.S.: A Federal Judge Speaks," *U.S. News & World Report*, August 7, 1967, pp. 70, 72, 73; *New York Times*, October 5, 1969.

3. Oral History, pp. 28, 148–49. Some of this discussion is drawn from unidentified newspaper clippings in various boxes of the Blackmun Papers.
4. Oral History, p. 146.
5. *New York Times*, April 12, 15, 1970; *St. Louis Post Dispatch*, April 14, 1970; *Washington Evening Star*, April 15, 1970.
6. Oral History, p. 147.
7. Unidentified clippings, Blackmun Papers.
8. Ibid.; Oral History, p. 147.
9. Unidentified clippings, Blackmun Papers; *New York Times*, April 15, 1970; Oral History, pp. 147–48.
10. *Washington Evening Star*, April 15, 1970.
11. *New York Times*, April 15, 1970; *Minneapolis Star*, April 15, 1970.
12. *Rochester Post-Bulletin*, April 11, 1970; *New York Times*, April 17, 1970.
13. Kemp v. Beasley, 423 F. 2d 851, 857 (1970); United States v. Sheet Metal Workers, 416 F. 2d 123 (1969); Mitchell v. Donovan, 290 F. Supp. 642 (1968); Honsey v. Donovan, 236 F. Supp. 8 (1964).
14. *Washington Post*, April 18, 1970; *New York Times*, April 15, 1970; *Honolulu Star-Bulletin*, April 16, 1970; *Louisville Courier-Journal*, April 16, 1970; *Houston Chronicle*, April 15, 1970; *Wall Street Journal*, April 13, 1970.
15. *New York Times*, April 20, 1970; *Houston Chronicle*, April 20, 1970; unidentified clippings in Blackmun Papers.
16. *New York Times*, April 19, 1970.
17. Richard G. Kleindienst to James O. Eastland, April 15, 1970, reprinted in U.S. Congress, Senate, *Hearing on the Nomination of Harry A.Blackmun, of Minnesota, to Be Associate Justice of the Supreme Court of the United States*, 91st Cong., 2d Sess., pp. 18–26 [hereinafter Blackmun Senate Hearing]; *Washington Evening Star*, April 16, 1970; *St.Louis Post-Dispatch*, April 15, 1970; Hanson v. Ford Motor Company, 278 F. 2d 586 (1960); Kotula v. Ford Motor Company, 338 F. 2d 732 (1964); Bridgeman v. Gateway Ford Truck Sales, Docket No. 19,749, February 4, 1970; Mahoney v. Northwestern Bell Telephone Co., 377 F. 2d 549 (1967).
18. Blackmun Senate Hearing, pp. 18–26.
19. *New York Times*, April 18, 19, 1970. See Lawrence E. Walsh, "Selection of Supreme Court Justices," *American Bar Association Journal*, June 1970, pp. 555–60.
20. *Washington Post*, April 18, 1970.
21. Ibid.
22. *Houston Chronicle*, April 20, 1970; unidentified clippings in Blackmun Papers.
23. Blackmun Papers, Box 13.
24. Oral History, p. 151.
25. Ibid., pp. 151–52.
26. *St. Louis Globe Democrat*, April 14, 1970; Oral History, p. 146.

27. Cartoon reprinted from *St. Paul Dispatch* in the *Rochester Post-Bulletin*, April 18, 1970; cartoon from the *Philadelphia Inquirer*, reprinted in the *New York Times*, April 19, 1970; *New York Times*, April 22, 1970.
28. *New York Times*, April 25, 1970.
29. *Shelley's Case*, 1 Co. Rep. 93b (1581); Blackmun Papers, Box 1357; Oral History, p. 120.
30. Blackmun Senate Hearing, pp. 1–2.
31. Ibid., pp. 2–6.
32. Ibid., p. 31.
33. Ibid., pp. 9–12.
34. Ibid., pp. 12–26, 27–28, 30.
35. Ibid., p. 48; Judge Johnsen's letter was dated April 17, 1970.
36. Ibid., pp. 49, 51. The case in which Justice Black's remarks appeared was Commonwealth Coatings Corp. v. Continental Casualty Co., 393 U.S. 145, 150 (1968).
37. Blackmun Senate Hearing, pp. 32–33.
38. Ibid., pp. 33, 34–35.
39. Ibid., p. 37.
40. Ibid., pp. 37, 39.
41. Ibid., pp. 38, 39.
42. Ibid., pp. 39–41.
43. Ibid., pp. 41, 42, 59–60, 43.
44. "Will He (Yawn) Make It?" *National Review*, May 5, 1970, p. 446; *New York Times*, May 6, 9, 13, 1970.
45. *New York Times*, May 14, 17, 1970.
46. *New York Times*, June 10, 1970.
47. Ibid.; Oral History, p. 298.

Chapter 5

1. Oral History, p. 11.
2. Ibid., pp. 154–55.
3. Ibid.; Harry A. Blackmun to Warren Burger, July 16, 1970, Blackmun Papers, Box 1403.
4. Shirley J. Bartlett to Harry A. Blackmun, May 8, 28, 1970, Blackmun Papers, Box 1456.
5. Oral History, p. 176; telephone interview with Wanda Syverson Martinson, March 17, 2005.
6. Martinson interview; Harry A. Blackmun to Wanda Syverson, September 12, 1974, Blackmun Papers, Box 1457.
7. Martinson interview.
8. Ibid.
9. Ibid.; *Washington Post*, January 30, 1979.
10. Harry A. Blackmun to Warren Burger, June 28, 1979, Blackmun Papers, Box 1457.

11. Blackmun continued to promote his secretaries' advancement during Chief Justice Rehnquist's tenure; Harry A. Blackmun to William H. Rehnquist, March 10, 1987, Blackmun Papers, Box 1457.
12. The wedding program, a typescript of Blackmun's remarks, and the announcement of the party for Wannett are in the Blackmun Papers, Box 1457.
13. Martinson interview.
14. Basic information on clerks is available in the law clerk database maintained in the Supreme Court library.
15. Telephone interview with Geoffrey M. Klineberg, March 15, 2005.
16. Telephone interview with Edward Lazarus, March 14, 2005.
17. Martinson interview.
18. Martinson interview; telephone interview with William Alden McDaniel, April 6, 2005.
19. Lazarus interview; United States v. Sioux Nation, 448 U.S. 371 (1980).
20. Telephone interview with Cecillia Wang, April 15, 2005.
21. Lazarus interview; telephone interview with Pamela Karlan, March 23, 2005; telephone interview with David Ogden, March 17, 2005.
22. Telephone interview with Alan Madans, March 23, 2005.
23. McDaniel interview.
24. Karlan interview.
25. McDaniel interview.
26. Telephone interview with Robert Gooding, March 21, 2005; telephone interview with Randall Bezanson, March 16, 2005.
27. McDaniel interview.
28. Harry A. Blackmun to John Paul Stevens, June 22, 1982, Blackmun Papers, Box 358, regarding NAACP v. Claiborne Hardware Co., 458 U.S. 886 (1982); Edward Lazarus, "Breakfast with Harry," unidentified clipping, Blackmun Papers, Box 1561.
29. *Lakewood* [Connecticut] *Journal*, August 11, 1988; Ruth Wedgwood to Harry A. Blackmun, August 13, 1988, Blackmun Papers, Box 1567.
30. Karlan interview; Ogden interview.
31. Karlan interview.
32. Ibid.
33. Ibid.
34. Ibid.; Wang interview; McDaniel interview; telephone interview with William Block, March 16, 2005.
35. Telephone interview with David Van Zandt, March 16, 2005.
36. McDaniel interview; Lazarus interview.
37. Oral History, p. 176; McDaniel interview.
38. Martinson interview; telephone interview with Frank Holleman, March 15, 2005.
39. Holleman interview.
40. Gooding interview; Bezanson interview; Oral History, p. 188.

41. Karlan interview. Several clerks interviewed for this book indicated that they were expected to annotate pool memos from other chambers, and the justice's case files contain many such notations.
42. McDaniel interview. Other clerks who served at various stages of Justice Blackmun's career described essentially this same rotation arrangement.
43. Oral History, p. 33.
44. Ogden interview.
45. Karlan interview.
46. Gooding interview.
47. Baird v. State Bar of Arizona, 401 U.S. 1 (1971); *In Re* Stolar, 401 U.S. 23 (1971); Hugo L. Black to Harry A. Blackmun, January 11, 1971, Harry A. Blackmun to Hugo L. Black, January 12, 1971, Blackmun Papers, Box 1402.
48. Gooding interview.
49. Ibid.; Graham v. Richardson, 403 U.S. 365 (1971).
50. Madans interview; Martinson interview.
51. Madans interview; Karlan interview; Lazarus interview.
52. Ogden interview.
53. Flood v. Kuhn, 407 U.S. 258 (1972); Lewis Powell to Harry A. Blackmun, May 8, 1972; Warren Burger to Harry A. Blackmun, June 13, 1972, Blackmun Papers, Box 145.
54. Oral History, pp. 2, 185.
55. David J. Garrow, "The Brains behind Blackmun," *Legal Affairs*, May/June 2005, www.legalaffairs.org/issues/May-June-2005.msp.
56. Ibid.
57. Martinson interview.
58. Marsh v. Chambers, 463 U.S. 783 (1983); Ogden interview; Blackmun Papers, Box 682.
59. Karlan interview.

Chapter 6

1. Harry A. Blackmun to Warren Burger, June 2, 1969, Blackmun Papers, Box 50.
2. Bob Woodward and Scott Armstrong, *The Brethren: Inside the Supreme Court* (New York: Simon and Schuster, 1979).
3. Warren Burger to Harry A. Blackmun, October 12, 1970, Blackmun Papers, Box 1403.
4. Harry A. Blackmun to Warren Burger, January 18, 1957, Blackmun Papers, Box 12.
5. Harry A. Blackmun to Warren Burger, November 23, 1971; Harry A. Blackmun to J. W. Harwick, January 7, 1972, Blackmun Papers, Box 1403.
6. Wyman v. James, 400 U.S. 309 (1971).
7. Ibid., pp. 317–18.
8. Ibid., pp. 318, 319.
9. Ibid., pp. 319, 321–22, 323, 324.

10. Harry A. Blackmun to Thomas N. Wies, February 2, 1970, Blackmun Papers, Box 1537.
11. Wyman v. James, 400 U.S. at 338, 339, 342, 334.
12. John Marshall Harlan to Harry A. Blackmun, December 7, 1970; Potter Stewart to Harry A. Blackmun, December 7, 1970; Warren Burger to Harry A. Blackmun, December 7, 1970, Blackmun Papers, Box 133. The slip opinion with Burger's congratulatory note is in the same container.
13. Barbara Ann Fort to Harry A. Blackmun, January 12, 1971; Mrs. Joseph H. Harper to Harry A. Blackmun, January 13, 1971; Thomas O. Strutzel to Harry A. Blackmun, February 8, 1971; Dr. Charles A. Layton to Harry A. Blackmun, undated; Edith A. Berman to Harry A. Blackmun, January 18, 1971, Blackmun Papers, Box 122.
14. *Albuquerque Tribune*, January 16, 1971; *Chicago Tribune*, January 13, 1971; *St. Paul Dispatch*, undated; *New York Times*, January 25, 1971.
15. *Washington Post*, January 20, 1971.
16. Ibid.; Wyman v. James, 400 U.S. at 323–24, 331.
17. Martin Spiegel to Harry A. Blackmun, January 18, 1971, Blackmun Papers, Box 122; King v. Smith, 392 U.S. 309 (1968).
18. Unidentified clippings, Blackmun Papers, Box 175.
19. Hoyt v. Minnesota, 399 U.S. 524 (1970); Redrup v. New York, 386 U.S. 767 (1967); Roth v. United States, 354 U.S. 476, 496, 500–3 (1957) (Harlan, J., concurring and dissenting); Cain v. Kentucky, 397 U.S. 319 (1970) (Burger, C. J., dissenting); Walker v. Ohio, 398 U.S. 434 (1970) (Burger, C. J., dissenting).
20. Cohen v. California, 403 U.S. 15, 25–26 (1971).
21. Blackmun's summary and draft opinion are in Blackmun Papers, Box 127.
22. Dan Edelman to Harry A. Blackmun, May 3, 1971, Blackmun Papers, Box 127; United States v. O'Brien, 391 U.S. 367 (1968).
23. Edelman to Blackmun.
24. Ibid.; *In Re* Bushman, 463 P. 2d 727 (1970).
25. Hugo L. Black to Harry A. Blackmun, June 3, 1971, Blackmun Papers, Box 127; Tinsley E. Yarbrough, *Mr. Justice Black and His Critics* (Durham, NC: Duke University Press, 1988), chaps. 4–5.
26. Burger's draft is in Blackmun Papers, Box 127.
27. New York Times Co. v. United States, 403 U.S. 713 (1971).
28. The summary is in Blackmun Papers, Box 131.
29. New York Times v. United States, 403 U.S. at 759–61.
30. Ibid., p. 761.
31. Ibid., pp. 762–63.
32. Michael A. LaFond to Harry A. Blackmun, June 28, 30, 1971, Blackmun Papers, Box 131.
33. *Washington Star*, July 7, 1971.
34. Art Schlosser to Harry A. Blackmun, undated; Harvey A. Silverglate to Harry A. Blackmun, July 21, 1971; Robert L. Bernstein to Harry A. Blackmun, July 1, 1971, Blackmun Papers, Box 131.

35. Boddie v. Connecticut, 401 U.S. 371 (1971); United States v. Kras, 409 U.S. 434 (1973).

36. United States v. Kras, 409 U.S. at 452.

37. Ibid., 445, 449. The case summary is in Blackmun Papers, Box 156.

38. United States v. Kras, 409 U.S. at 452.

39. Ibid., pp. 455–56, 457.

40. Ibid., p. 460.

41. Bezanson interview.

42. Edward R. Korman to Harry A. Blackmun, June 17, 1974, Blackmun Papers, Box 156.

43. Harry A. Blackmun to Edward R. Korman, June 19, 1974; Harry A. Blackmun to William O. Douglas and Potter Stewart, June 20, 1974, Blackmun Papers, Box 156.

44. Oral History, p. 191.

45. Important Warren Court equal protection cases other than in the core area of racial discrimination include Harper v. Virginia Board of Elections, 383 U.S. 663 (1966); Levy v. Louisiana, 391 U.S. 68 (1968); Shapiro v. Thompson, 394 U.S. 618 (1969).

46. Swann v. Charlotte-Mecklenburg Board of Education, 402 U.S. 1 (1971); Keyes v. School District No. 1, Denver, 413 U.S. 189 (1973); Milliken v. Bradley, 418 U.S. 717 (1974); Harry A. Blackmun to William Brennan, January 9, 1973, Blackmun Papers, Box 154.

47. Tillman v. Wheaton-Haven Recreation Assn, 410 U.S. 431 (1973); Runyon v. McCrary, 427 U.S. 160 (1976); Moose Lodge v. Irvis, 407 U.S. 162 (1972). The summary is in Blackmun Papers, Box 227.

48. Palmer v. Thompson, 403 U.S. 217 (1971); Orleans Parish School Board v. Bush, 365 U.S. 569 (1961); Harry A. Blackmun to Hugo L. Black, February 12, 1971 (two letters), Blackmun Papers, Box 124. Blackmun's preargument analysis of *Palmer* is in Box 124.

49. Hugo L. Black to Harry A. Blackmun, February 16, 1971, Blackmun Papers, Box 124.

50. Warren Burger to Harry A. Blackmun, undated, Blackmun Papers, Box 124. The draft opinion, with Burger's marginal note, is in Blackmun Papers, Box 124.

51. Palmer v. Thompson, 403 U.S. at 229, 230.

52. Graham v. Richardson, Sailer v. Legere, 403 U.S. 365 (1971); Shapiro v. Thompson, 394 U.S. 618 (1969). The case summary is in Blackmun Papers, Box 129.

53. Sugarman v. Dougall, 413 U.S. 634, 643 (1973).

54. Ibid., pp. 647, 648.

55. *In Re* Griffiths, 413 U.S. 717, 721–22 (1973). Randall Bezanson memorandum to Harry A. Blackmun, April 14, 1973, Blackmun Papers, Box 160.

56. *In Re* Griffiths, 413 U.S. at 630, 649.

57. San Antonio Indep. School Dist. v. Rodriguez, 411 U.S. 1 (1973).

58. The summary is in Blackmun Papers, Box 161.

59. Ibid.; James W. Ziglar Jr., memorandum regarding *Rodriguez*, undated, Blackmun Papers, Box 161.
60. James v. Valtierra, 402 U.S. 137, 141, 145 (1971).
61. Reed v. Reed, 404 U.S. 71, 76 (1971).
62. Frontiero v. Richardson, 411 U.S. 677 (1973).
63. Ibid., pp. 691–92.
64. The summary is in Blackmun Papers, Box 135.
65. The memoranda are in Blackmun Papers, Box 163.
66. Harry A. Blackmun to William Brennan, March 5, 1973, Blackmun Papers, Box 163.
67. Stanton v. Stanton, 421 U.S. 7, 17 (1975).
68. Craig v. Boren, 429 U.S. 190, 197–98 (1976).
69. Ibid., p. 217.
70. Levy v. Louisiana, 391 U.S. 68 (1968); Labine v. Vincent, 401 U.S. 532, 557 (1971).
71. Daniel B. Edelman memorandum to Harry A. Blackmun, undated, Blackmun Papers, Box 131.
72. Weber v. Aetna Casualty & Surety Co., 406 U.S. 164, 172, 176–77 (1972).
73. Jimenez v. Weinberger, 417 U.S. 628 (1974); Trimble v. Gordon, 430 U.S. 762, 776–77 (1977). The summary is in the *Jimenez* file, Blackmun Papers, Box 184.
74. Sierra Club v. Morton, 405 U.S. 727, 755–56, 757 (1972).
75. United States v. Richardson, 418 U.S. 166 (1974); Younger v. Harris, 401 U.S. 37 (1971); United States v. Calandra, 414 U.S. 338 (1974); Harris v. New York, 401 U.S. 222 (1971); Furman v. Georgia, 408 U.S. 238 (1972); Sheldon Goldman, *Constitutional Law: Cases and Essays*, 2d ed. (New York: HarperCollins, 1991), chap. 5.
76. Ballew v. Georgia, 435 U.S. 223 (1977); Furman v. Georgia, 408 U.S. at 375.
77. Furman v. Georgia, 408 U.S. at 410, 405; McGautha v. California, 402 U.S. 183 (1971).
78. United States v. Nixon, 418 U.S. 683 (1974). For archival materials on the case, see, for example, the Brennan Papers, Box 423, and Lewis Powell Papers, School of Law, Washington and Lee University, Box 168, both in Library of Congress; also see Blackmun Papers, Box 190. The memo with the message from Blackmun's daughter is in Box 190.
79. Powell's conference notes are in Powell Papers, Box 168.
80. William Brennan to Warren Burger, July 12, 1974; Harry A. Blackmun to Warren Burger, July 12, 1974, Blackmun Papers, Box 190; Oral History, pp. 228, 230.
81. Bezanson interview.

Chapter 7

1. Griswold v. Connecticut, 381 U.S. 479 (1965).
2. *Washington Post*, February 4, 1973.
3. Eisenstadt v. Baird, 405 U.S. 438 (1972).

4. Ibid., p. 453.
5. United States v. Vuitch, 402 U.S. 62, 72 (1971).
6. Justice Brennan's *Vuitch* conference notes are in Brennan Papers, Box 419.
7. The summary is in Blackmun Papers, Box 123.
8. Mike LaFond memorandum to Harry A. Blackmun, February 10, March 16, 1971, Blackmun Papers, Box 123.
9. LaFond memo to Blackmun, March 21, 1971.
10. Roe v. Wade, 314 F. Supp. 1217 (1970); David Garrow's *Liberty and Sexuality: The Right to Privacy and the Making of* Roe v. Wade (Berkeley: University of California Press, 1988) is one of many major studies.
11. Doe v. Bolton, 319 F. Supp. 1048 (1970).
12. Blackmun's notes on the 1971 oral argument session are in Blackmun Papers, Box 151; Brennan's conference notes are in Brennan Papers, Box 420B.
13. Brennan Papers, Box 420B.
14. William O. Douglas to Warren Burger, December 18, 1971, Thurgood Marshall Papers, Library of Congress, Box 19.
15. Warren Burger to William O. Douglas, December 20, 1971, Marshall Papers, Box 99.
16. The draft opinion is in the Blackmun Papers, Box 151.
17. Harry A. Blackmun, memorandum to the conference, May 18, 1972, Marshall Papers, Box 99.
18. The *Doe* draft and cover memorandum are in Marshall Papers, Box 99.
19. William Brennan to Harry A. Blackmun, May 18, 1972, Marshall Papers, Box 99.
20. William O. Douglas to Harry A. Blackmun, May 19, 1972, Marshall Papers, Box 99.
21. William Brennan to Harry A. Blackmun, May 25, 1972; William O. Douglas to Harry A. Blackmun, May 25, 1972; Thurgood Marshall to Harry A. Blackmun, May 25, 1972; Potter Stewart to Harry A. Blackmun, May 30, 1972; William O. Douglas to Harry A. Blackmun, May 31, 1972, Marshall Papers, Box 99.
22. Warren Burger, memorandum to the conference, May 31, 1972, Marshall Papers, Box 99.
23. Harry A. Blackmun, memorandum to the conference, May 31, 1972, Marshall Papers, Box 99.
24. The justices' memoranda to the conference are in Marshall Papers, Box 99.
25. A copy of Douglas's draft dissent is in Marshall Papers, Box 99.
26. This discussion is based on the conference notes of Justice Blackmun, Blackmun Papers, in-house online *Roe* and *Doe* files, Manuscript Division, Library of Congress, and Justice Brennan, Brennan Papers, Box 420B.
27. Harry A. Blackmun to Thomas Keys, December 23, 1971, Blackmun Papers, in-house online *Roe* and *Doe* files.
28. Harry A. Blackmun to Thomas Keys, July 3, 1972; Thomas Keys to Harry A. Blackmun, July 6, 1972, Blackmun Papers, in-house online *Roe* and *Doe* files.

29. Lewis Powell to Harry A. Blackmun, November 29, 1972, Blackmun Papers, in-house online *Roe* and *Doe* files. Blackmun's draft opinions and cover letters are also in the files.
30. Harry A. Blackmun to Lewis Powell, December 4, 1972, Powell Papers, Box 150.
31. Harry A. Blackmun, memorandum to the conference, December 11, 1972, Powell Papers, Box 150.
32. Thurgood Marshall to Harry A. Blackmun, December 12, 1972, Powell Papers, Box 150; William Brennan to Harry A. Blackmun, December 13, 1972, Blackmun Papers, in-house online *Roe* and *Doe* files; William O. Douglas to Harry A. Blackmun, December 11, 1972; Larry Hammond to Lewis Powell, December 12, 1972; Potter Stewart to Harry A. Blackmun, December 14, 1972; Warren Burger to Harry A. Blackmun, December 13, 1972, Powell Papers, Box 150.
33. Randall Bezanson to Harry A. Blackmun, November 29, 1972, Blackmun Papers, in-house online *Roe* and *Doe* files.
34. Randall Bezanson to Harry A. Blackmun, December 13, 1972, Blackmun Papers, in-house online *Roe* and *Doe* files.
35. William Rehnquist to Harry A. Blackmun, November 24, 1972, Powell Papers, Box 150. Rehnquist referred specifically to Blackmun's dissent in Gooding v. Wilson, 405 U.S. 518, 534 (1972). When the Court narrowed the overbreadth doctrine in Broadrick v. Oklahoma, 413 U.S. 601 (1973), Blackmun joined the majority.
36. Harry A. Blackmun to William Rehnquist, November 27, 1972, Powell Papers, Box 150.
37. Randall Bezanson to Harry A. Blackmun, January 11, 1973, Blackmun Papers, in-house online *Roe* and *Doe* files.
38. Roe v. Wade, 410 U.S. 113, 117 (1973), quoting Lochner v. New York, 198 U.S. 45, 76 (1905).
39. Harry A. Blackmun to William Brennan, November 21, 1972; Harry A. Blackmun, memorandum to the conference, December 21, 1972, Blackmun Papers, in-house online *Roe* and *Doe* files.
40. The bench notes are in the Blackmun Papers, in-house online *Roe* and *Doe* files.
41. Ibid.; Warren Burger to Harry A. Blackmun, January 16, 1973, Marshall Papers, Box 98.
42. Harry A. Blackmun, memorandum to the conference, January 16, 1973, Marshall Papers, Box 98. The draft announcement is in the in-house online *Roe* and *Doe* files.
43. William Brennan to Harry A. Blackmun, January 17, 1973; Warren Burger to Harry A. Blackmun, January 17, 1973, Blackmun Papers, in-house online *Roe* and *Doe* files.
44. Lewis Powell to Dottie Blackmun, January 22, 1973, Blackmun Papers, in-house online *Roe* and *Doe* files.
45. Roe v. Wade, 410 U.S. 113, 116–17, 174 (1973).

46. Ibid., pp. 164–65.

47. Ibid., p. 173. For contrasts between the Warren and Burger Court approaches to the fundamental rights branch of equal protection doctrine, see Shapiro v. Thompson, 394 U.S. 618 (1969); San Antonio Indep. School Dist. v. Rodriguez, 411 U.S. 1 (1973).

48. Roe v. Wade, 410 U.S. at 171, 221–22.

49. Ibid., pp. 221–22.

50. See, for example, Linda Greenhouse, *Becoming Justice Blackmun: Harry Blackmun's Supreme Court Journey* (New York: Henry Holt, 2005), p. 207.

51. Bezanson interview.

52. Martinson interview.

53. Janet J. White to Harry A. Blackmun, July 20, 1972; Jeremy Jackson to Harry A. Blackmun, July 8, 1972, Blackmun Papers, in-house online *Roe* and *Doe* files.

54. *Washington Post*, January 26, 1973; *Minneapolis Tribune*, February 5, 1974.

55. Ibid.

56. *New York Times*, January 24, 1973; *Wall Street Journal*, January 26, 1973; *Washington Evening Star*, January 27, 1973; *Washington Post*, January 31, 1973; *St. Louis Post-Dispatch*, undated copy in Blackmun Papers, in-house online *Roe* and *Doe* files; Anthony Lewis, "Liberty, New and Old," *New York Times*, February 3, 1973.

57. *Washington Post*, January 24, 1973; *Catholic Standard*, January 25, 1973; *St. Paul Dispatch*, January 26, 1973; unidentified clipping in Blackmun Papers, in-house online *Roe* and *Doe* files.

58. *Rochester Post-Bulletin*, January 24, 1973; unidentified clippings in Blackmun Papers, in-house online *Roe* and *Doe* files.

59. *Minneapolis Star*, February 9, 1973.

60. John Hart Ely, "The Wages of Crying Wolf: A Comment on *Roe* v. *Wade*," *Yale Law Journal* 82 (1973): 935.

61. Ibid., pp. 935–36.

62. Ibid., pp. 946, 947, 949.

63. Jim Ziglar memorandum, undated, in-house online *Roe* and *Doe* files.

64. Oral History, p. 201; Laurence Tribe, "The Supreme Court, 1972 Term—Foreword: Toward a Model of Roles in the Due Process of Life and Law," *Harvard Law Review* 87 (1973): 7.

65. Roe v. Wade, 410 U.S. at 207–8; Planned Parenthood v. Casey, 505 U.S. 833 (1992).

66. Planned Parenthood v. Danforth, 428 U.S. 52, 93, 94 (1976).

67. Bellotti v. Baird, 443 U.S. 622 (1979).

68. H. L. v. Matheson, 450 U.S. 398, 438–41 (1981).

69. Maher v. Roe, 432 U.S. 464, 473–74 (1977).

70. Ibid., p. 479, quoting Lindsey v. Normet, 405 U.S. 56, 74 (1972).

71. Richard Willard to Harry A. Blackmun, January 22, 1977, Blackmun Papers, Box 246.

72. The Powell draft opinion in *Maher*, with Blackmun's notation, is in Blackmun Papers, Box 246.

73. Beal v. Doe, 432 U.S. 438, 462 (1977).

74. Ibid., p. 463.

75. Ibid.

76. Richard Willard to Harry A. Blackmun, May 31, 1977, Blackmun Papers, Box 246.

77. Harris v. McRae, 448 U.S. 297, 349 (1980).

78. Valentine v. Chrestensen, 316 U.S. 52 (1942); Pittsburgh Press Co. v. Pittsburgh Comm'n on Human Relations, 413 U.S. 376, 401, 400, 403–4 (1973).

79. Pittsburgh Press Co. v. Pittsburgh Comm'n on Human Relations, 413 U.S. at 402; Harry A. Blackmun to Potter Stewart, June 12, 1973, Blackmun Papers, Box 167. The Stewart draft with Blackmun's notation is also in Box 167.

80. New York Times v. Sullivan, 376 U.S. 254, 266 (1964).

81. Bigelow v. Virginia, 421 U.S. 809, 822 (1975).

82. Ibid., p. 826.

83. David Patterson memorandum to Harry A. Blackmun, undated, Blackmun Papers, Box 218; Virginia State Bd. of Pharmacy v. Consumer Council, 425 U.S. 748 (1976).

84. Lewis Powell to Harry A. Blackmun, March 29, 1976, Blackmun Papers, Box 218.

85. Ibid.

86. Harry A. Blackmun to Lewis Powell, April 1, 1976; William Brennan to Harry A. Blackmun, March 31, 1976; David Patterson memorandum to Harry A. Blackmun, undated, Blackmun Papers, Box 218.

87. Bates v. State Bar, 433 U.S. 350, 403–4 (1977).

88. Central Hudson Gas Corp. v. Public Service Comm'n, 447 U.S. 557 (1980).

89. Ibid., pp. 573–74, 575.

90. Ibid., p. 599, quoting Virginia State Bd. of Pharmacy v. Consumer Council, 425 U.S. at 770.

91. *New York Times*, May 28, 1976; Leslie Chrismer, letter to *New York Times*, undated, Blackmun Papers, Box 218.

92. Harry A. Blackmun to Leslie Chrismer, June 2, 1976; Leslie Chrismer to Harry A. Blackmun, June 21, 1976: Harry A. Blackmun to Leslie Chrismer, July 1, 1976, Blackmun Papers, Box 218.

93. Harry A. Blackmun to Warren Burger, April 28, 1977, Blackmun Papers, Box 218; Neal Robert Platt, "Commercial Speech and the First Amendment: An Emerging Doctrine," *Hofstra Law Review* 5 (1977): 666–67.

Chapter 8

1. This material is drawn from Sheldon Goldman, *Constitutional Law: Cases and Essays*, 2d ed. (New York: Harper & Row, 1991), p. 149.

2. Nebraska Press Assn v. Stuart, 427 U.S. 539 (1976).

3. *Washington Star*, November 26, 1975.
4. *Washington Post*, November 27, 1975; *Los Angeles Times*, November 26, 1975; *New York Times*, November 28, 1975; *Washington Evening Star*, December 4, 1975.
5. Harry W. Wellford to Tom Wicker, December 1, 1975; Harry A. Blackmun to Harry W. Wellford, December 4, 1975, Blackmun Papers, Boxes 233 and 234.
6. James B. Ginty to Harry A. Blackmun, December 3, 1975, Blackmun Papers, Boxes 233 and 234.
7. The summary and other notes are in Blackmun Papers, Boxes 233 and 234.
8. Nebraska Press Assn v. Stuart; Cox Broadcasting Corp. v. Cohn, 420 U.S. 469 (1975).
9. Gannett Co., Inc. v. DePasquale, 443 U.S. 368 (1979); Lewis Powell to Harry A. Blackmun, May 9, 1979, Blackmun Papers, Box 285.
10. Bill McDaniel to Harry A. Blackmun, May 21, 1979, Blackmun Papers, Box 285.
11. Bill McDaniel to Harry A. Blackmun, May 29, 1979, Blackmun Papers, Box 285.
12. Bill McDaniel to Harry A. Blackmun, May 30, 1979, Blackmun Papers, Box 285.
13. Lewis Powell to Harry A. Blackmun, May 31, 1979; Warren Burger, memorandum to the conference, June 1, 1979, Blackmun Papers, Box 285.
14. Bill McDaniel to Harry A. Blackmun, April 3, 1979, Blackmun Papers, Box 285.
15. Gannett Co., Inc. v. DePasquale, 443 U.S. at 436–37, 448.
16. "Open and Shut Cases," *Newsweek*, August 27, 1979, p. 69; *Washington Star*, August 29, 1979.
17. Wanda Martinson's notes on the exchange are in Blackmun Papers, Box 285.
18. E. Barrett Prettyman Jr., "Building Walls with Gannett," *District Lawyer* 4 (October/November 1979): 38.
19. Richmond Newspapers v. Virginia, 448 U.S. 555, 604 (1980).
20. Press-Enterprise Co. v. Superior Court, 464 U.S. 501 (1964); Chandler v. Florida, 449 U.S. 560 (1981); Estes v. Texas, 381 U.S. 532 (1965); Harry A. Blackmun to Warren Burger, January 19, 1981; Warren Burger to Harry A. Blackmun, January 19, 1981, Blackmun Papers, Box 326.
21. National League of Cities v. Usery, 426 U.S. 833 (1976).
22. United States v. Darby Lumber Co., 312 U.S. 100, 124 (1941); Gibbons v. Ogden, 9 Wheat. 1 (1824). Justice Stevens also filed a *Usery* dissent.
23. The summary is in Blackmun Papers, Box 217.
24. National League of Cities v. Usery, 426 U.S. at 856.
25. Ibid., p. 876.
26. Garcia v. San Antonio Metropolitan Transit Authority, 469 U.S. 528 (1985).

27. Transportation Union v. Long Island R. Co., 455 U.S. 678 (1982). The memorandum, dated May 8, 1984, is in Blackmun Papers, in-house online *Garcia* file.

28. The draft opinion and memorandum, dated May 13, 1984, are in the Blackmun Papers, in-house online *Garcia* file.

29. The memorandum is in the Blackmun Papers, in-house online *Garcia* file.

30. William Brennan to Harry A. Blackmun, June 11, 1984; Thurgood Marshall to Harry A. Blackmun, June 12, 1984; Sandra Day O'Connor to Harry A. Blackmun, June 11, 1984; Warren Burger to Harry A. Blackmun, June 11, 1984; William Rehnquist to Harry A. Blackmun, June 11, 1984, Blackmun Papers, in-house online *Garcia* file.

31. The clerk's memo is in the Blackmun Papers, in-house online *Garcia* file.

32. Harry A. Blackmun to Lewis Powell, July 3, 1984, Blackmun Papers, in-house online *Garcia* file.

33. Lewis Powell to Harry A. Blackmun, July 3, 1984, Blackmun Papers, in-house online *Garcia* file.

34. The memorandum, dated October 17, 1984, is in the Blackmun Papers, in-house online *Garcia* file.

35. Garcia v. San Antonio Metropolitan Transit Authority, 469 U.S. at 546, 556–57.

36. Ibid., pp. 558, 560, 567.

37. Ibid., pp. 588, 589, 580.

38. Laurence Tribe to Harry A. Blackmun, February 21, 1985, Blackmun Papers, in-house online *Garcia* file.

39. Erwin Griswold to Harry A. Blackmun, February 27, 1985, Blackmun Papers, in-house online *Garcia* file.

40. *Richmond Times-Dispatch*, February 20, 1985; *New York Times*, February 21, 1985; *Washington Post*, February 24, 1985.

41. United States v. Lopez, 514 U.S. 549 (1995); United States v. Morrison, 529 U.S. 598 (2000).

42. Regents of University of California v. Bakke, 438 U.S. 265 (1978).

43. The memo, dated August 24, 1977, is in Blackmun Papers, in-house online *Bakke* file.

44. The memorandum is in Blackmun Papers, in-house online *Bakke* file.

45. Ibid.

46. See Alexander Bickel, *The Morality of Consent* (New Haven: Yale University Press, 1975), pp. 132–33.

47. Regents of University of California v. Bakke, 438 U.S. at 407.

48. John M. Sperry to Harry A. Blackmun, July 3, 1978; Harvey Pearson to Harry A. Blackmun, July 4, 1978, Blackmun Papers, in-house online *Bakke* file.

49. Simmons Fentress to Harry A. Blackmun, June 30, 1978, Blackmun Papers, in-house online *Bakke* file.

50. Ibid.

51. City of Richmond v. Croson, 488 U.S. 469, 561–62 (1989).

52. William A. Holmes to Harry A. Blackmun, June 30, 1978, Blackmun Papers, in-house online *Bakke* file.

53. This discussion is based largely on Dennis J. Hutchinson, "Aspen and the Transformation of Harry Blackmun," in *Supreme Court Review*—2005 (Chicago: University of Chicago Press, 2006), pp. 307–31.

54. Karlan interview.

55. Lazarus interview.

56. Hutchinson, "Aspen and the Transformation of Harry Blackmun," p. 323.

57. Ibid., pp. 323–24; Karlan interview.

58. Hutchinson, "Aspen and the Transformation of Harry Blackmun," p. 324.

59. Quoted in *New York Times*, July 14, 1975.

60. Quoted in *Washington Post*, December 5, 1982.

61. Quoted in Ibid.

62. John A. Jenkins, "A Candid Talk with Justice Blackmun," *New York Times Magazine*, February 20, 1983, p. 20.

63. Ibid., pp. 22, 23, 28, 29.

64. Ibid., p. 28.

65. Ibid., p. 23.

66. Burt Neuborne, "Blackmun: Intellectual Openness Elicits Needed Respect for the Judicial Process," *National Law Journal*, February 18, 1980; Harry A. Blackmun to Burt Neuborne, February 12, 1980, Blackmun Papers, Box 1437.

67. Jenkins, "A Candid Talk," pp. 60–61.

68. Ibid., pp. 61–62, 24.

69. Ibid., p. 26.

70. Akron v. Akron Center for Reproductive Health, 462 U.S. 416 (1983); Ogden interview.

71. Wanda Martinson memo to Harry A. Blackmun, February 27, 1985, Blackmun Papers, Box 151. The letter, dated October 11, 1984, is in the Blackmun Papers, Box 151.

72. *New York Times*, October 11, 1984.

73. Harry A. Blackmun to Alfred Wong, October 10, 1984, Blackmun Papers, Box 151.

74. Warren Burger to Harry A. Blackmun, October 11, 1984, Blackmun Papers, Box 151.

75. Harry A. Blackmun to Warren Burger, October 11, 1984, Blackmun Papers, Box 151.

76. Ibid.

77. Harry A. Blackmun to Warren Burger, December 19, 1984, Blackmun Papers, Box 151.

78. Martinson interview; *Washington Post*, March 5, 1985.

79. *Washington Post*, March 5, 1985.

80. *Miami News*, March 6, 1985; Randall Bezanson to Harry A. Blackmun, March 8, 1985; Bob Packwood to Harry A. Blackmun, March 5, 1985; Cary

W. Akins to Harry A. Blackmun, March 14, 1985, Blackmun Papers, Box 151. The newspaper clipping with the Dorsey letter is unidentified.

81. Harry A. Blackmun to Cary Akins, March 20, 1985; Harry A. Blackmun to Mrs. John B. Hayford, March 13, 1985; Harry A. Blackmun to Burton Laub, March 12, 1985, Blackmun Papers, Box 151.

82. *Washington Post*, January 13, 1986.

83. *Miami News*, March 5, 1985; Wanda Martinson to James S. Zagami, January 25, 1985; Wanda Martinson to Harry A. Blackmun, February 7, 1985, Blackmun Papers, Box 151. The extortion note, dated March 8, 1985, is in Blackmun Papers, Box 1425.

84. *Washington Post*, March 5, 1985.

85. Bowers v. Hardwick, 478 U.S. 186 (1986); Stanley v. Georgia, 394 U.S. 557 (1969).

86. Bowers v. Hardwick, 478 U.S. at 194–95.

87. Ibid., pp. 197–98. The discussion of the *Bowers* conference is based on the notes of Justices Brennan, Brennan Papers, Box 696, and Powell, Powell Papers, Drawer 63.

88. Robinson v. California, 370 U.S. 660 (1962); John C. Jeffries Jr., *Justice Lewis F. Powell, Jr.: A Biography* (New York: Scribner's, 1994), p. 530; Warren Burger to Lewis Powell, April 3, 1986, Powell Papers, Drawer 63. The clerk's memo is in Powell Papers, Drawer 63.

89. Karlan interview; Bowers v. Hardwick, 478 U.S. at 196–97.

90. Karlan interview.

91. Bowers v. Hardwick, 478 U.S. at 199–200; Stanley v. Georgia, 394 U.S.; Katz v. United States, 389 U.S. 347 (1967).

92. Bowers v. Hardwick, 478 U.S. at 208.

93. Ibid., pp. 211–12, 213.

94. Ibid., p. 214; Minersville School District v. Gobitis, 310 U.S. 586 (1940); West Virginia Bd. of Education v. Barnette, 319 U.S. 624 (1943).

95. Karlan interview.

96. Ibid.

97. A typescript of the statement, dated June 25, 1995, is in the Blackmun Papers, Box 1404.

98. Harry A. Blackmun, "A Tribute to Warren E. Burger," *William Mitchell Law Review* 22 (1996): 16–17.

Chapter 9

1. Klineberg interview.

2. Lazarus interview.

3. Klineberg interview; Oral History, pp. 425–26.

4. Edward Lazarus, *Closed Chambers* (New York: Times Books, 1998).

5. For a fuller account of the Blackmun-Souter relationship, see Tinsley E. Yarbrough, *David Hackett Souter: Traditional Republican on the Rehnquist Court* (New York: Oxford University Press, 2005), pp. 190–95.

6. DeShaney v. Winnebago County Department of Social Services, 489 U.S. 189 (1989).
7. Ibid., p. 203.
8. Oral History, p. 397.
9. Cecillia Wang to Harry A. Blackmun, May 5, 1996, Blackmun Papers, Box 1567.
10. Lemon v. Kurtzman, 403 U.S. 602 (1971); Wolman v. Walter, 433 U.S. 229 (1977); Lee v. Weisman, 505 U.S. 577, 607 (1992).
11. Lynch v. Donnelly, 465 U.S. 668 (1984); County of Allegheny v. ACLU, 492 U.S. 573 (1989).
12. Sherbert v. Verner, 374 U.S. 398 (1963); Employment Division v. Smith, 494 U.S. 872 (1990).
13. Akron v. Akron Center for Reproductive Health, 462 U.S. 416, 458 (1983).
14. Webster v. Reproductive Health Services, 492 U.S. 490 (1989); Blackmun's *Webster* file is in the Blackmun Papers, Box 536. The note is dated April 23, 1989.
15. Justice Marshall's *Webster* notes are in the Marshall Papers, Box 554.
16. Webster v. Reproductive Health Services, 492 U.S. at 526, 534.
17. *Legal Times*, December 8, 1986.
18. *Washington Post*, July 28, 1987.
19. *Legal Times*, September 26, 1988; *New York Times*, September 14, 1988; *Washington Post*, September 14, 1988.
20. Lazarus interview. The memorandum, dated April 27, 1989, is in the Blackmun Papers, Box 536.
21. Edward Lazarus to Harry A. Blackmun, June 22, 1989, Blackmun Papers, Box 536.
22. Edward Lazarus to Harry A. Blackmun, June 6, 1989, Blackmun Papers, Box 536. Blackmun's passages, dated June 1989, are in the Blackmun Papers, Box 536.
23. Webster v. Reproductive Health Services, 492 U.S. at 538, 557.
24. Ibid., p. 548.
25. Ibid., pp. 537, 538, 560.
26. Edward Lazarus to Harry A. Blackmun, June 30, 1989, Blackmun Papers, Box 536.
27. *New York Times*, July 4, 1989; *Manhattan Lawyer*, July 11, 1989.
28. *New York Times*, July 4, 1989; *Washington Post*, July 8, 1989.
29. Hodgson v. Minnesota, 497 U.S. 417 (1990); Ohio v. Akron Center for Reproductive Health, 497 U.S. 502 (1990).
30. Anne Dupre to Harry A. Blackmun, November 29, 1989, Blackmun Papers, Box 545.
31. Anne Dupre to Harry A. Blackmun, December 18, 1989, Blackmun Papers, Box 545; Daniel A. Farber, "Abortion after *Webster*," *Constitutional Commentary* 6 (1989): 225.
32. Harry A. Blackmun to William Brennan, Thurgood Marshall, and John Paul Stevens, June 18, 1990; William Brennan to Harry A. Blackmun, June 18, 1990, Blackmun Papers, Box 545.

33. Rust v. Sullivan, 500 U.S. 175 (1991).
34. Yarbrough, *David Hackett Souter*, p. 155; David Souter to William Rehnquist, April 25, 1991; William Rehnquist to David Souter, April 29, 1991, Blackmun Papers, Box 568.
35. Rust v. Sullivan, 500 U.S. at 220.
36. John Paul Stevens to Harry A. Blackmun, February 7, 1991, Blackmun Papers, Box 568.
37. Ibid.
38. Harry A. Blackmun interview with James F. Simon, March 27, 1992, Blackmun Papers, Box 108; *Legal Times*, April 9, 1990.
39. Planned Parenthood v. Casey, 505 U.S. 833 (1992).
40. Clerks to Harry A. Blackmun, January 16, 1992, Blackmun Papers, Box 602.
41. A copy of the draft dissent is in the Blackmun Papers, Box 601.
42. *Boston Globe*, April 23, 1992.
43. Ibid.
44. Stephanie Dangel to Harry A. Blackmun, January 10, 1992, Blackmun Papers, Box 602.
45. Joan Biskupic, *Sandra Day O'Connor* (New York: HarperCollins, 2005), p. 269. The Casey conference notes are in the Blackmun Papers, Box 602.
46. Anthony Kennedy to Harry A. Blackmun, May 29, 1992, Blackmun Papers, Box 601.
47. Stephanie Dangel to Harry A. Blackmun, June 8, 11, 1992, Blackmun Papers, Box 602; Planned Parenthood v. Casey, 505 U.S. at 869.
48. Dangel to Blackmun, June 8, 1992.
49. Stephanie Dangel to Harry A. Blackmun, June 16, 1992, Blackmun Papers, Box 602.
50. Stephanie Dangel to Harry A. Blackmun, June 20, 26, 1992, Blackmun Papers, Box 602.
51. Dangel to Blackmun, June 20, 1992.
52. Planned Parenthood v. Casey, 505 U.S. at 943.
53. *USA Today*, June 30, 1992; Planned Parenthood v. Casey, 505 U.S. at 923.
54. Planned Parenthood v. Casey, 505 U.S. at 923.
55. Summaries of telephone messages from Karlan and others are in the Blackmun Papers, Box 601.
56. *Minneapolis Star Tribune*, July 25, 1992.
57. Furman v. Georgia, 408 U.S. 238 (1972); Gregg v. Georgia, 428 U.S. 153 (1976); Coker v. Georgia, 433 U.S. 584 (1977); Penry v. Lynaugh, 492 U.S. 304 (1989); Stanford v. Kentucky, 492 U.S. 361 (1989); Payne v. Tennessee, 501 U.S. 808 (1991); McCleskey v. Kemp, 481 U.S. 279 (1987).
58. Ogden interview; Barefoot v. Estelle, 463 U.S. 880, 928 (1983).
59. Herrera v. Collins, 506 U.S. 390, 430 (1993).
60. Ibid., p. 446.
61. Karlan interview; Klineberg interview.
62. Callins v. Collins, 510 U.S. 1141, 1145 (1999).
63. Ibid., pp. 1142–43.

Chapter 10

1. *Washington Post*, February 27, 1994.
2. *Texas Lawyer*, November 16, 1992.
3. *USA Today*, November 23, 1992; *Legal Times*, November 23, 1992.
4. *USA Today*, April 7, 1994; *Legal Times*, January 18, 1993.
5. *Minneapolis Star Tribune*, January 30, 1993.
6. *New York Times*, March 12, November 9, 1993; Gregory Cerio and Lucy Howard, "Who's Out First?" *Newsweek*, March 22, 1993, p. 4; *Cleveland Plain Dealer*, March 13, 1993.
7. *Chicago Sun-Times*, March 4, 1994.
8. *Washington Post*, April 6, 1994; *Arizona Republic*, April 6, 1994.
9. *New York Times*, April 7, 1994.
10. Ibid.
11. Ibid.
12. *Christian Science Monitor*, June 1, 1994.
13. McFarland v. Scott, 512 U.S. 849 (1994); Tuilaepa v. California, 512 U.S. 967, 995 (1994); Madsen v. Women's Health Center, 512 U.S. 735 (1994).
14. *New York Times*, July 1, 1994.
15. *Washington Post*, April 7, 1994; *USA Today*, April 7, 1994.
16. *Cleveland Plain Dealer*, April 9, 1994; *Denver Post*, April 10, 1994.
17. Jeffrey Rosen, "Sentimental Journey," *New Republic*, May 2, 1994, pp. 13, 14, 18.
18. Ibid., pp. 17, 18, 14.
19. *Washington Post*, April 7, 1994; *Legal Times*, April 11, 1994 (two articles).
20. Rosen, "Sentimental Journey," p. 18; "ABA Journal Roundtable," *ABA Journal* 80 (July 1994): 52–56.
21. Clines v. Norris, 512 U.S. 1272 (1994); Harry A. Blackmun, memorandum to the conference, August 3, 1994, Blackmun Papers, in-house online *Callins* file.
22. *New York Times*, May 30, 1995.
23. Martinson interview.
24. Wanda Martinson to Harry A. Blackmun, January 23, 1997, Blackmun Papers, Boxes 1479 and 1480.
25. Ibid.; Martinson interview.
26. Cecillia Wang to Harry A. Blackmun, March 5, 1997; Wanda Martinson to Angela Heald, May 8, 1997, Blackmun Papers, Boxes 1479 and 1480.
27. Wanda Martinson to Harry A. Blackmun, March 13, 1997, Blackmun Papers, Boxes 1479 and 1480.
28. Wanda Martinson to Harry A. Blackmun, March 21, 1997, Blackmun Papers, Boxes 1479 and 1480.
29. Wang interview; Martinson interview.
30. Linda Greenhouse to Harry A. Blackmun, November 10, 1997; Ruth Bader Ginsburg to Harry A. Blackmun, December 5, 1997; Peter Dorsey to Harry A. Blackmun, November 10, 1997, Blackmun Papers, Boxes 1479 and 1480.

31. Jane L. Boadwine to Harry A. Blackmun, January 14, 1988; Harry A. Blackmun to June L. Boadwine, January 30, 1998, Blackmun Papers, Boxes 1479 and 1480.

32. Nicholas Coniaris, "The Amistad Affair: An Epic of Epic Proportions," unpublished manuscript, Blackmun Papers, Boxes 1479 and 1480.

33. Lazarus, *Closed Chambers,* p. 265.

34. *Washington Post*, March 4, 1998.

35. Edward Lazarus to Harry A. Blackmun, March 6, 1998, Blackmun Papers, Box 1561.

36. *Legal Times*, April 13, 1998.

37. *Wall Street Journal*, April 13, 1998; *Baltimore Sun*, April 12, 1998; *Washington Post*, June 17, 1998; David Garrow, " 'The Lowest Form of Animal Life'? Supreme Court Clerks and Court History," *Cornell Law Review* 84 (1999): 855; *Legal Times*, May 10, 1999.

38. Edward Lazarus to Harry A. Blackmun, undated [but with "Sept 1998" penned in the margin], Blackmun Papers, Box 1561.

39. Lazarus interview.

40. McDaniel interview.

41. Ibid.

42. Ibid.

43. Telephone interview with Clare Huntington, March 15, 2005; *Washington Times*, March 5, 1999. The message is in the Blackmun Papers, Box 1376.

44. This discussion is largely drawn from materials in the Blackmun Papers, Box 1376.

45. Sally Blackmun to President and Mrs. William Jefferson Clinton, March 16, 1999, Blackmun Papers, Box 376.

46. *Washington Post*, March 10, 1999; *Minneapolis Star Tribune*, March 10, 1999. The Keillor program with the inscription to the justice is in the Blackmun Papers, Box 1431. Materials relating to the memorial service are in Box 1376.

47. Bob Herbert, "Bush v. Blackmun," *New York Times*, March 14, 1999.

48. *National Law Journal*, March 15, 1999.

49. *Minneapolis Star Tribune*, March 22, 2000.

50. Linda Greenhouse, *Becoming Justice Blackmun: Harry Blackmun's Supreme Court Journey* (New York: Henry Holt, 2005). For a summary of the dispute by Tony Mauro, another journalist who unsuccessfully sought early access to the papers, see *Legal Times*, January 26, 2004. On the "Greenhouse Effect," see Terry Eastland, "The Tempting of Justice Kennedy," *American Spectator*, February 1993, pp. 32–37. Greenhouse gave her account of gaining access to the Blackmun papers in "Writing Justice Blackmun," an address to a meeting of the American Association of Law Libraries, in St. Louis, July 9, 2006, available online, www.llrx.com/features/writingjusticeblackmun.htm.

51. *Legal Times*, January 26, 2004. For a summary of the dispute over release of the Marshall papers, see Tinsley E. Yarbrough, *The Rehnquist Court and the Constitution* (New York: Oxford University Press, 2000), pp. 64–66.
52. Oral History, p. 483.
53. Ibid.; Madsen v. Women's Health Center, 512 U.S. 735 (1994).
54. *Orlando Sentinel*, July 27, 2004.
55. *Women's News*, February 29, 2004.
56. Ibid.; Gloria Feldt, *The War on Choice: The Right-Wing Attack on Women's Rights and How to Fight Back* (New York: Bantam Books, 2004).
57. See, for example, *Washington Post*, July 18, 2006; *Los Angeles Times*, July 20, 2006; *Minneapolis Star-Tribune*, July 17, 2006; *St. Paul Pioneer Press*, July 18, 2006. Dottie Blackmun died July 13, 2006.

Epilogue

1. The eulogy, dated March 9, 1999, is in the Blackmun Papers, Box 1376.

Index

Specific cases are indexed under their individual titles; *Miranda v. Arizona*, for instance, will be found under M. Cases brought by the United States government, however, are reversed and alphabetized under the defendant's name (e.g., *Sioux Nation, United States v.*).

certoriari, writs of, 141–42, 157–58, 306–7
Chandler v. Florida, 257, 376n20
chaplains, legislative, 168
child abuse, 173–79, 180, 292–94, 327–28
Chrismer, Leslie, 248
Churchill, Winston, 281
circuit judge, Blackmun as. *See also* opinions
of Blackmun as circuit court judge:
Burger's appointment to D.C. appeals
circuit, 67–70; Burger's support for,
71–78, 81, 82, 83; chambers, location of,
81–82; clerks and staff, 84–85; installation
ceremony, 82–83; nomination and
confirmation, 77–81; relationship with
other judges on circuit, 83–84; Sanborn's
retirement and Blackmun's succession,
69, 70–83; unfinished assignments, 141–42;
U.S. Supreme Court decisions and, 89–90,
91–94, 95, 100, 104–8, 109, 121
citizen, conscientious objector,
naturalization as, 104–5
civil liberties. *See* liberal icon, Blackmun as,
and also specific civil liberties, e.g. free
speech cases
Civil Rights Act of 1964, 121, 266–68
civil rights issues, racial. *See* racial/civil rights
issues
Clark, Dorothy Eugenia (Dottie, later
Blackmun; wife), 50–54, 56, 61–62, 83,
117, 119, 120, 136, 138, 142, 152, 153–54, 156,
277, 279, 281, 316, 321, 332, 333, 338, 344,
384n57
clerk for Sanborn, Blackmun as, vii, viii, 26,
29–39, 41
clerks and staff of Blackmun as circuit judge,
84–85
clerks and staff of Blackmun as U.S.
Supreme Court judge. *See also* specific
clerks, secretaries, and messengers/aides:
agreements and disagreements of clerks
with Blackmun's opinions, 181–82, 184,
196–97, 199, 201–2, 239–41, 258–62, 272–
73, 293, 318; breakfast and other social
meetings with, 151–54; *Closed Chambers*
(Lazarus), 166, 290, 333–37; interviews
with, 352; messengers/aides, 146;
opinions, drafting, 160–63, 164–69, 328,
346–47; opinions of Blackmun expressed
following retirement/death, 328–29,
340; processing cases in chambers,
157–59; recruitment and hiring, 142–51;
reunions, 152–53; *Roe,* effects of, 273;
secretaries, 142–46, 147–48; spelling and

grammatical errors of, 143, 152, 338, 346;
women clerks, 146
Clines v. Norris, 382n21
Clinton, Bill, 292, 316, 318, 322–26, 328, 333,
339
Clinton, Hillary, 322, 333, 339
Closed Chambers (Lazarus), 166, 290, 333–37
cloture of criminal proceedings, 253–57
Coffee, Linda, 212
Cohen v. California, 180–82, 243, 369n20
Coker v. Georgia, 381n57
Commerce Clause, 260, 262, 263
commercial speech cases, 242–48
*Commonwealth Coatings Corp. v. Continental
Casualty Co.,* 366n36
Communism, 65, 66, 106, 121
compelling state interests, 196, 200, 203,
228, 295
conflict of interest issues in nomination of
Blackmun as U.S. Supreme Court Justice,
124–27, 133–34
Coniaris, Nancy Clark Blackmun (daughter),
xi, 53, 62, 82, 83, 111–12, 119, 120, 122, 136, 138,
331, 332, 343, 345–46, 353n4
Coniaris, Nicholas (grandson), 332, 333
Connally, Dan, and Ruth, 123
conscientious objector cases, 104–5
contraceptives, use of, 209–10
Cooley, Eliza Jane (paternal grandmother), 4
corporal punishment of prisoners, 100–103
counseling on abortion, public funding for,
304–5
County of Allegheny v. ACLU, 380n11
Cox Broadcasting Corp. v. Cohn, 253, 376n8
Craig v. Boren, 200–201, 371n68
criminal justice: Burger's record on,
114–15; eighth circuit cases of Blackmun
regarding, 90–94, 121–22; open criminal
proceedings, 253–57; press gag order to
ensure fair trial, 249–53; U.S. Supreme
Court cases of Blackmun regarding, 204,
249–57
Curtis, Bonnie, 332
Curtis, Charles, 32, 33
Curtis Publishing Co. v. Butts, 364n97
Cutler, William, 12

Dangel, Stephanie, 307–14
Darby Lumber Co., United States v., 376n22
Davies, Ronald, 69
Davis, University of California at, 265–70
Davis v. United States, 363n72
death penalty. *See* capital punishment cases

Fortas, Abe, x, 109, 113–14, 115, 118
Foshay, Wilbur B., 40
Fourteenth Amendment, 89–90, 93, 193, 195, 197, 213, 266–67, 312
Fourth Amendment, 174, 286
Frankfurter, Felix, 26, 115, 126, 176
Fraser, Everett, 54, 56
Frazier v. United States, 364n2
free press cases, 182–85, 242–48, 249–57, 250
free speech cases: as circuit judge, 103–12; commercial speech, 242–48; as U.S. Supreme Court justice, 179–85, 223, 242–48
Frontiero v. Richardson, 198–200, 371n62
fundamental rights cases, 195–97, 228
funding for abortion, public, 238–42, 296, 304–5
Funk, Richard, 119
Funk, Sally Ann Blackmun (daughter), 53, 62, 83, 119, 122, 136, 138, 177, 279, 329, 331, 338, 339, 341, 342–44, 351
Furman v. Georgia, 204–5, 316, 318, 371nn75–77, 381n57
future dangerousness predictions in capital punishment cases, 316–17

gambling cases, 93–94
Gannett Press v. DePasquale, 253–57, 275, 376n9, 376n15
Garcia v. San Antonio Metropolitan Transit Authority, 259–65, 376n26, 377n35
Gardner, Archibald K., 83
Garrow, David, 164–69, 273, 335
Gibbons v. Ogden, 376n22
Gibson, Floyd, 87
Gignoux, Edward T., 117
Gilchrist, Peter, 79
Gilchrist, Theo "Betty" Blackmun (sister), 5, 12, 34, 47, 49, 79–80, 138
Ginsburg, Ruth Bader, 158, 292, 333, 347
Glenn, Alton, 59–60
Goldberg, Arthur, 194
Gooding, Robert, 151, 160, 161, 190, 352
Goodwin, Alfred T., 117
Graham, Fred, 122, 123
Graham v. Richardson, 161, 192–93, 368n49, 370n52
Gray, Howard K., 60
Great Depression, 27, 188
Greene, Graham, 158
Greenhouse, Linda, 153, 165, 166, 333, 341
Gregg v. Georgia, 381n57
Griffiths, In re, 194–95, 270nn55–56
Grigson, John, 316
Grimm, Norman, and Trevor, 11, 18

Griswold, Erwin, 90, 264
Griswold v. Connecticut, 209, 210, 211, 214, 224, 225, 236, 371n1
Gustin, Todd, 146, 331, 333

H. L. v. Matheson, 374n68
habeas corpus review in capital punishment cases, 317–18
Hamm, William, 32
Hand, Learned, 64, 69
Hanson v. Ford Motor Company, 365n17
Hardwick, Michael, 283–87
Harlan, John Marshall, vii, 52, 109, 176, 180, 182, 183, 190, 213, 214
Harper v. Virginia Board of Elections, 370n45
Harris, Oren, 102, 103
Harris v. McRae, 375n77
Harris v. New York, 371n75
Hart, H. L. A., 285, 287
Hart, Philip A., 134–35
Harvard, Blackmun at, 8–27
Harwick, Harry J., 55–58
Harwick, J. W., 173
Haynes v. United States, 363n71
Haynsworth, Clement, x, 115, 123, 124, 125, 133, 137
Hazard, Geoffrey, 298
Heaney, Gerald W., 80, 90, 104
Heifetz, Beth, 271
Herbert, Bob, 340
Herrera v. Collins, 317–18, 381n59
the "hide," 100–103
Hilton Head, Renaissance Weekend at, 322, 323
"Hip Pocket Harry," xii, 205. *See also* "Minnesota Twins," Burger and Blackmun as
Hoag v. New Jersey, 92–93
Hodgson v. Minnesota, 303, 380n29
Holleman, Frank, 156, 328, 352
Holmes, Oliver Wendell, 25, 224, 226, 321, 323
Holmes, William A., 270–71
Holscher v. Tahash, 363n66
home visit regulation under AFDC, 173–79
homosexuality, 85–86, 283–87, 340
Honsey v. Donovan, 365n13
Hoover, Herbert, 21, 32–33, 35
Hopkins, Anthony, 332
housing, low-income, 197
Hoyt v. Minnesota, 180, 369n19
Hruska, Roman L., 115–16
Huegely, John (maternal great-grandfather), 4
Huegely, Mary (maternal grandmother), 4, 30
Hughes, Charles Evans, 44, 325

Humphrey, Hubert H., 68, 72, 78–81, 82, 126, 128–29, 267
Huntingdon, Clare, 338, 352
Hurley, Martin, 47
Hutchinson, Dennis, 272
Hyde Amendment, 242

illegitimacy cases, 189, 200, 201–3
Indians, American, cases involving, 148–49, 295
influenza epidemic of 1918, 4
insanity defense, 94–95
Irvin v. Dowd, 364n99

Jackson v. Bishop, 101–3, 363nn85–86
James, Barbara, 173–79
James v. Valtierra, 197, 371n60
Janko v. United States, 107–8, 364n98
Jenkins, John, 274–76
Jews and Judaism, 32, 126, 153, 268, 331
Jimenez v. Weinberger, 371n73
Johnsen, Harvey, 83–84, 87, 124, 133
Johnson, Lyndon B., 68, 79, 113
Jones, Annette Reuter (aunt), 4, 345
Jones, Gwenyth, 111
Jones, W. R. (uncle), 4, 345
Jones v. Alfred H. Mayer Co., 89–90, 121, 189–90, 362n62
Judd, Walter, 72
Junell, John, 40–41
Junell, Oakley, Driscoll and Fletcher/Junell, Driscoll, Fletch, Dorsey, and Barker (The Dorsey Firm), 29, 40–45, 54, 55, 57–58

Kahler Corporation, Blackmun's directorship with, 124, 127
Kahriger, United States v., 93–94, 363n71
Kamisar, Yale, 123, 275–76
Karlan, Pamela, 149, 150, 153, 154, 159, 271, 272, 285, 288, 315, 318, 329, 339, 352
Katz v. United States, 286, 379n91
Kaufman v. United States, 92, 363n68
Keillor, Garrison, 339
Kemp v. Beasley, 362n58, 365n13
Kennedy, Anthony, 290, 292, 294, 297–303, 305, 308, 311, 312, 314, 341
Kennedy, Edward M., 128, 135–37
Kennedy, John F., 87
Keyes v. School District No. 1, Denver, 370n46
Keys, Thomas, 219
Kilpatrick, James J., 251, 326–27
King v. Smith, 369n17
Kleindienst, Richard, 116, 124, 126, 127, 132
Klineberg, Geoffrey, 147, 289–90, 318, 352

Koh, Harold, x, 111, 147, 236, 329, 339, 341, 342
Kollner, Gretchen, 46
Korman, Edward R., 188
Kotula v. Ford Motor Company, 365n17
Kras, United States v., 185–88, 347–48, 370nn35–40
Kreisler, Fritz, 339
Kronman, Anthony, 336

Labine v. Vincent, 201–3, 371n70
Labor Department, possible job at, 39
LaFond, Michael, 147, 184, 212
laissez-faire Court, 223, 225, 234, 258
Landis, James M., 25
Lange, Dietrich, 10–11, 19, 36
Langer, William, 130
Larson, Ethel, 30, 38, 41
Lay, Donald, 87, 92, 97, 99, 104, 110, 111, 297
Lazarus, Edward, 147–49, 152, 155, 165–66, 271–72, 289, 298–99, 301, 328, 333–37, 352
Leach, Barton, 25, 52–53
Leary v. United States, 363n71
Lee v. Weisman, 294, 380n10
legislative chaplains, 168
legislative reapportionment, 122
Lemon v. Kurtzman, 294, 380n10
Levy v. Louisiana, 201–2, 370n45, 371n70
Lewis, Anthony, 232–33
libel cases, 105–7
liberal icon, Blackmun as, 249–88. *See also* specific civil liberties cases, e.g. free speech cases; Burger's discomfort with, 249, 252, 255–57, 259, 261, 263, 268, 273, 275, 277–80, 283–85, 287–88; possible influences on Blackmun's views, 270–77; *Roe*'s influence on, 249
liberty, negative *vs.* positive concepts of, 239–40
Lichtman, Judith, 302
Lincoln, Abraham, 348–49
"little people," Blackmun's empathy for, ix, xi, xii, 135–36, 175, 185–88, 277, 292–94, 345–49
Little Rock, AK school desegregation case, 69, 88–89
Lobb, A. J., 55
Lochner v. New York, 224, 226–27, 234, 235, 258, 373n38
Lopez, United States v., 377n41
Lord, Miles W., 131
low-income housing, 197
Lowell, A. Laurence, 23
Lynch v. Donnelly, 294–95, 380n11

MacGregor, Clark, 131
MacKinnon, George, 75, 76, 80
Madans, Alan, 149–50, 352
Madsen v. Women's Health Center, 342, 382n13, 384n53
Magruder, Calvert, 25
Maguire, Daniel, 278
Maher v. Roe, 374n69, 375n72
Mahoney, Maureen, 150, 151
Mahoney v. Northwestern Bell Telephone Co., 365n17
Marbury v. Madison, 263
Marchetti v. United States, 363n71
Marion v. Gardner, 85–86
marriage: contraceptive use and marital privacy, 209; spousal consent requirements for abortion, 237, 306, 309
Marsh v. Chambers, 168, 368n58
Marshall, Thurgood, xii; archives of, 341–42, 351; Blackmun's imitation of, 159; Blackmun's political assessment of, 273; civil liberties cases, 249, 252, 258, 261, 268, 276, 285, 288; clerical memos, 165; death of, 323; early cases in Blackmun's career as justice and, 174, 175–76, 186, 187, 188, 190, 192, 197, 201; liberal voting record of, 249; retirement of, 291; on *Roe v. Wade* and other abortion cases, 213, 216, 221, 222, 238, 297, 299, 304
Martinson, Ronald, 145
Martinson, Wanda Syverson, 47, 143–46, 148, 153, 156, 162, 167, 231, 256, 280–81, 315, 330–32, 334, 336, 338, 352
Matthes, Marion, 84, 97, 99, 100, 108
Mattick, Hans W., 102
Mauro, Tony, 329, 335, 383n50
Maxwell v. Bishop, 97–100, 363nn77–78, 363n84
Maxwell v. Stephens, 362n60
Mayo Clinic, viiii, 27, 55–62, 68, 127, 233–34, 266
Mayo, William J., 55, 127
McCarthy, Eugene, 72, 78–79, 80, 82, 129, 130–31
McCarthy, Joseph, 66
McCleskey v. Kemp, 381n57
McCorvey, Norma, 212. *See also Roe v. Wade* and *Doe v. Bolton*
McDaniel, William Alden, 150–55, 158, 166, 168, 254–55, 328, 331, 337–39, 352
McDonald, John C., 80
McDuffie, Robert, 339
McFarland v. Scott, 325, 382n13
McGautha v. California, 371n77

McIntosh, Scott, 258–62
McUsic, Molly, 294
media: archives of Blackmun and, 341–42, 351–52; Blackmun's suspicion of, 59–61; Blackmun's willingness to be questioned by, 273–77; free press cases, 182–85, 242–48, 249–57, 250; prejudicial publicity cases, 107–8
medical career, Blackmun's interest in, 22–23, 27, 230
medical rights of physicians, 230
Mehaffy, Pat, 87, 88
Merry, Robert Ethan, 16, 17, 20
Mill, John Stuart, 285, 287
Milliken v. Bradley, 370n46
Miner v. Erickson, 363n67
Minersville School District v. Gobitis, 379n94
Minnesota bar examination, 31
Minnesota ex rel. Holscher v. Tahash, 363n66
Minnesota Supreme Court chamber, busts outside, 340–41
"Minnesota Twins," Burger and Blackmun as, xii, 169, 171–207; breach in relationship, 205–7, 249, 275; Burger's personality, 171–73; early tendency to vote together, 204; environmental cases, disagreement on, 203–4; on filing fees and due process, 185–88; on First Amendment/free speech cases, 179–85; on fundamental rights cases, 195–97; on illegitimacy cases, 189, 200, 201–3; maiden opinion of Blackmun in *Wyman v. James* (welfare system home visit regulations), 173–79; as overstatement, 204–5; on racial/civil rights issues, 188–92; sex discrimination cases, 197–201
Minton, Sherman, 327
Miranda v. Arizona, 91, 114, 204, 235, 363n66
Mitchell, John, 116–17, 118, 126, 129
Mitchell, Morris B., 73, 80
Mitchell v. Donovan, 365n13
M'Naghten's Case, 94, 363n72
Mondale, Walter, 129, 131
Moose Lodge v. Irvis, 190, 370n47
"morality considerations," 179, 187
Morris, Norval, 271, 272
movies, Blackmun's fondness for, 36, 330–33

National Association for the Advancement of People of Color (NAACP) v. Claiborne Hardware Co., 357n28
National Family Planning and Reproductive Health Association (NFPRHA), 298
National League of Cities v. Usery, 257–65, 376n21, 376n24

National Right to Life, 298, 302
national security concerns, 65, 182–85, 250
Native Americans, cases involving, 148–49, 295
Nebraska Press Association v. Stuart, 249–53, 375n2, 376n8
negative *vs.* positive concepts of liberty, 239–40
Neuborne, Burt, 276
New York Times Co. v. United States (Pentagon Papers cases), 182–85, 243, 250, 251, 369n27, 369n29
New York Times v. Sullivan, 105–7, 243, 364n93, 375n80
NFPRHA (National Family Planning and Reproductive Health Association), 298
"nigger," Blackmun on use of, 87
Ninth Amendment, 209, 212, 214
Nixon, Julie, and Tricia, 343
Nixon, Richard, viii, x, 112, 113–18, 121–22, 123, 126, 129, 138, 151, 343
Nixon, United States v., 205–6, 371n78
Noonan, Charles F., 54

obscenity cases, 180, 211
Ochsner, Alton, 61
O'Connor, Sandra Day: appendectomy of, 16; Blackmun's imitation of, 159; dual federalism doctrine, 261–65; Rehnquist and, 277; on *Roe v. Wade* and other abortion cases, 290, 292, 296, 297, 299, 301–6, 308, 310, 312, 314, 315; in U.S. Supreme Court library, 155–56
Ogden, David, 146, 149, 153, 159, 163, 166, 168, 316–17, 352
Ogden, Wannett Smith, 145–46, 148, 153, 167
O'Hara, Joseph P., 77
Ohio v. Akron Center for Reproductive Health, 380n29
open criminal proceedings, 253–57
opinions of Blackmun as circuit court judge, 84–85; capital punishment cases, 96–100, 121–22; criminal justice cases, 90–94, 121–22; freedom of expression and religion cases, 103–12; fundamental rights cases, 195–97; insanity defense, 94–95; prejudicial publicity cases, 107–8; prison brutality and the "hide," 100–103; privacy cases, 85–86; racial/civil rights cases, 86–90, 121–22; student rights cases, 108–12, 138
opinions of Blackmun as U.S. Supreme Court justice: abortion cases (*see* abortion;

Roe v. Wade and *Doe v. Bolton*); alienage classifications, 192–95; Burger's influence on (*see* "Minnesota Twins," Burger and Blackmun as); capital punishment cases, 204–5, 315–20, 323–26, 329–30; child abuse, 292–94; controversy over clerks' involvement in composing, 164–69, 328, 346–47; criminal justice cases, 204, 253–57; drafting process, 160–63, 346–47; environmental cases, 203–4; federalism, 204; filing fees and due process, 185–88; free press cases, 182–85, 242–48, 249–57, 250; free speech cases, 179–85, 223, 242–48; illegitimacy cases, 189, 200, 201–3; maiden opinion on welfare system home visit regulations in *Wyman v. James,* 173–79; racial/civil rights issues, 188–92, 265–70; religious liberty/separation of church and state cases, 168, 294–95; *Roe v. Wade* and *Doe v. Bolton,* 226–30; sex discrimination cases, 197–201; strict constructionism, 114, 121, 129, 134–35, 185, 209, 235
Orleans Parish School Board v. Bush, 370n48
Ott, Mel, 163
outsider, Blackmun as, vii, ix–xi, 6, 12–13, 20, 38, 141, 149–50, 167–68, 273, 291, 324–25, 345–49
overbreadth doctrine, 223, 373n35

Packwood, Bob, 281
Painter, Richard, 335
Palmer v. Thompson, 190–92, 370n48, 370n51
paper shredders, 173
parental notification in abortion cases, 221, 237–38, 296, 302–4
paternal rights in abortion cases, 221, 224–25, 237
Patterson, David, 244, 246
Pauling, Linus, 105–6
Pauling v. Globe Democrat Publishing Co., 364n93, 364n95, 364n97
Payne v. Tennessee, 381n57
Pearl Harbor, 52
Pennypacker, Henry, 10
Penry v. Lynaugh, 381n57
Pentagon Papers cases (New York Times Co. v. United States), 182–85, 243, 250, 251, 369n27, 369n29
Peters, John P., 65
Peters v. Hobby, 359n5
Peters v. United States, 363n68
physicians, medical rights of, 230

Reuter, Theo Huegely (later Blackmun; mother), x, 3–6, 21, 30, 35, 36, 41, 50, 62, 72, 74–75, 79–80, 83, 138–39, 345, 346
Reuter, Theodore Louis (maternal grandfather), 4
Rich, John, 157
Richard, Bergmann, 29
Richardson, United States v., 371n75
Richmond, City of, v. Croson, 378n51
Richmond Newspapers v. Virginia, 256–57, 376n19
"right to be left alone," 286
Ripkin, Cal, 337
Roberds, Steve, 110
Robinson v. California, 379n88
Roe v. Wade and *Doe v. Bolton,* viii, xi–xii, 209–48, 372nn10–11; Aspen Institute sessions, 271; background to cases, 212–13; Blackmun, Sally, and, 343–44; Burger and, 206–7, 210, 213, 214, 216–19, 221, 224–26, 228, 236–38, 242, 247, 248, 275, 278–79; cases anticipating, 209–12; circuit court cases and, 85, 86; clerks' involvement in composing opinions for, 164, 167; clerks of Blackmun following, 273; *Dred Scott* decision compared to, viii, 327; fallout from national debate following, 230–36, 273–74, 277–82, 298, 326–29, 340–41, 344; fetal life thesis, 213, 218–19; first round of oral arguments and draft opinions, 213–18; historical section on abortion law, 227; liberal icon, view of Blackmun as, 249; as litmus test for justice candidates, 322; opinions, 164, 167, 226–30; parental notification, 221, 237–38, 296, 302–4; paternal rights, 221, 224–25; physicians, medical rights of, 230; post-*Roe* abortion issues, 236–48; potential clerks questioned regarding, 149; privacy rights and, 211, 212, 214, 227, 236; reaffirmations, 296; Reagan Administration and, 282; Rehnquist court and, 290, 296–315; second round of oral arguments and draft opinions, 218–26; stare decisis doctrine and, 298, 308, 309, 311; strict scrutiny approach of, 311, 315; substantive due process arguments, 209, 213, 223–25, 227, 228, 235, 299; trimester formula, 220–23, 227–29, 236, 296, 300, 305; viability argument, 220–22, 227, 296–97, 306; *Webster v. Reproductive Health Services* and, 296–302; women's rights and, 230
Rogers, William, 75, 77

Roman Catholicism, 46, 224, 232
Rome, Howard, 85–86, 95
Roosevelt administration, possible job for Blackmun at Department of Labor in, 39
Roosevelt, Franklin D., 22, 25, 33–34
Roosevelt, Theodore, 171
Rosen, Jeffrey, 327–28
Roth v. United States, 369n19
Rowan, Carl, 323–24
Rubin, Peter, 307–8
Runyon v. McCrary, 190, 370n47
Russell, Richard, 68
Rust v. Sullivan, 304–5, 307, 381n33, 381n35

Sailer v. Legere, 370n52
San Antonio Independent School District v. Rodriguez, 195–97, 370n57, 374n47
Sanborn, John Benjamin, vii, viii, 26, 29–39, 41, 69, 70–83, 90–91, 94–95, 107–8, 113, 131
Sanborn, Walter Henry, 30
Scalia, Antonin: Blackmun's view of, 342; on capital punishment, 315, 319, 320; on freedom of religion, 295; questions asked by, 158, 315; on *Roe v. Wade* and other abortion cases, 290, 291, 297–99, 303, 305, 307, 311, 314, 315, 342; sarcasm of, 292, 319
Schneider, Mark, 262
scholarship foundation in Blackmun's name, 331
Schoor, Daniel, 273
Scott, Leland, 42, 44, 55, 88, 111, 171
search and seizure cases, 173–79
Segal, Bernard, 80
sex discrimination cases, 197–201
Shapiro v. Thompson, 193, 370n45, 370n52, 374n47
Sharp v. Sigler, 103–4, 364n89
Shaw, Leslie M., 171
Sheet Metal Workers, United States v., 365n13
Shelley's Case, 130, 366n29
Sherbert v. Verner, 380n12
"Sherry," 47, 52
shredding paper, 173
Sierra Club v. Morton, 203–4, 371n74
Sioux Nation, United States v., 148–49
Sixth Amendment, 252, 253, 255, 256, 257
Sloss, Frank, 51
Smith, Sally, 144
Smith, Wannett (later Ogden), 145–46, 148, 153, 167
Sobeloff, Simon, 65
sodomy, homosexual, 283–87

clerks and staff (see clerks and staff of Blackmun as U.S. Supreme Court judge); conference discussions of pending cases, 159; conflict of interest issues, 124–27, 133–34; as liberal icon (see liberal icon, Blackmun as); nomination, 113, 115–22; opinions on service as, 326–29, 340–41; processing cases in chambers, 157–59; questions during oral argument, 158–59; retirement from bench, 321–30; Senate confirmation hearing and vote, 130–38; strict constructionism, 114, 121, 129, 134–35, 185, 209, 235; swearing-in ceremony, 138–39; tax cases, 163; vetting process, 123–30; work schedule of, x, 154–56

Usery doctrine, 257–65

vagueness, unconstitutional, 211, 214, 216, 236
Valentine v. Chrestensen, 242, 244, 375n78
Van Oosterhout, Martin D., 84, 118, 132–33
Van Zandt, David, 155, 322, 352
venereal disease of Blackmun's father, 35–36
viability of fetuses, 220–22, 227, 296–97, 306
Vietnam War, 108–12, 182–85, 250, 343
Virginia State Board of Pharmacy v. Virginia Consumer Council, 245–48, 375n90
Vogel, Charles J., 84, 97, 99, 100, 106, 131
Voting Rights Act, 135
Vuitch, United States v., 211–12, 236, 372n5

Waldron, George W., 59–60
Walker, Edwin A., 106–7
Walker v. Ohio, 369n19
Walker v. Pulitzer Publishing Co., 364n97
Walsh, Lawrence F., 72, 73, 75, 76, 125–26, 131–32
Walters, Johnnie, 116
Walton v. Nashville, 362n59
Wang, Cecillia, 149, 293–94, 331, 332, 352
warrantless home visit regulations under AFDC, 173–79
Warren, Earl, 64–65, 92, 108, 113–15, 135, 171–72, 188–89, 281
Warren v. United States, 363n68
Watergate, 151, 205–7
Waxman, Seth, 165, 166
Weber v. Aetna Casualty & Surety Co., 371n72
Webster v. Reproductive Health Services, 296–302, 307, 308, 311, 314, 380nn14–16, 380n23

Webster, William H., 153, 280
Weddington, Sarah, 212, 213
Wedgwood, Ruth Glushien, 152
Weitzman, Brenda Barbara, 104–5
Weitzman, In re, 364n90
welfare system: abortion, public funding for, 238–42, 296, 304–5; alienage/residency requirements, 193; home visit regulations under AFDC, 173–79
West Virginia Bd. of Education v. Barnette, 379n94
Whitaker, Charles Evans, 69
White, Byron: Blackmun's political assessment of, 273; civil liberties cases, 252, 262, 268, 283–85; early cases in Blackmun's career as justice and, 163–64, 190, 192, 201, 206; retirement of, 292, 323; on Roe v. Wade and other abortion cases, 210, 214, 217, 219, 223, 228, 229, 237, 296, 297, 302, 303, 305, 306, 326–27
Wicker, Tom, 250, 251
wigs, suggestion that counsel wear, 287–88
Wiley, Alexander, 68
Will, George, 265, 321
Willard, Richard, 239–41
Williams, Coleman, 144
Willy, Roy, 73, 74
Witherspoon v. Illinois, 100
Wolman v. Walter, 380n10
women. See also abortion; Roe v. Wade and Doe v. Bolton: Blackmun's empathy for, 345–46; as clerks to Blackmun, 146; contraceptives, use of, 209–10; ERA (Equal Rights Amendment), 200; rights of, and Roe, 230; sex discrimination cases, 197–201
Wong, Alfred, 278–80
Woodrough, Joe, 84
World War II, 51–53
Wright, Edward L., 102–3
writs of certiorari, 141–42, 157–58, 306–7
Wyman v. James, 173–79, 180, 327, 347
Wyzanski, Charles E., Jr., 39

Yarbrough v. Hulbert-West Memphis School District, 362n58
Yard, Molly, 301
Young, Edward B., 9, 10, 19
Young, Gordon E., 102, 103
Younger v. Harris, 371n75

Zeigler, Ronald, 117–18
Ziglar, James W., Jr., 196–97, 199, 235–36